MILITARY STRATEGY

MILITARY STRATEGY
A GLOBAL HISTORY

JEREMY BLACK

YALE UNIVERSITY PRESS
NEW HAVEN AND LONDON

For information about this and other Yale University Press publications, please contact:
U.S. Office: sales.press@yale.edu   yalebooks.com
Europe Office: sales@yaleup.co.uk   yalebooks.co.uk

Set in Adobe Garamond Pro by IDSUK (DataConnection) Ltd
Printed in Great Britain by TJ International Ltd, Padstow, Cornwall

Library of Congress Control Number: 2019948676

ISBN 978-0-300-21718-6

A catalogue record for this book is available from the British Library.

10 9 8 7 6 5 4 3 2 1

For Steve Bodger

CONTENTS

PREFACE

Strategy, an overarching vision of what an organisation or individual wants to achieve, coupled with a set of objectives designed to make that possible, is not the details of the plans by which goals are implemented by military means. Instead, strategy is the ways by which nations, states, rulers, élites and others seek to shape their situation, producing international and domestic systems and pursuing outcomes that provide security, and that safeguard and advance interests. The key element and the crucial context are the contest for power, and at every level. This is the case for strategy as both goals and means, and indeed for strategy in both goals and means. These are phenomena that in practice, despite efforts to dissect them for analytical purposes, are rarely as separate as envisaged. Moreover, power takes different forms, has varied uses, and is not understood in a uniform fashion. This is true of the character and use of military power as well as of other types of power.

In assessing strategy and strategic culture, it is necessary, if focusing solely on military strategy, to consider how states, or rather their élites and leaderships, seeking to maintain and increase power, pursue internal as well as external agendas, and do so knowing that it will make them better able to obtain goals and to wage war. The relationship between the two agendas, internal and external, is important and also affects both. They cannot be readily separated.

Linked to this were (and are) the perennial questions of who directed strategy (however defined), and to what ends. The latter question affects the evaluation of both competence and success. Indeed, any strategy is contingent on complex contexts, both international and domestic, short- and long-term, and has no optimum dimensions. Moreover, the people who direct strategy are not always the same as those who evaluate its success. One of the major problems in executing strategy is for decision-makers at that level to convince those who frame the criteria of success that they are doing the right thing, and doing it well.

Any focus on ruling individuals and groups helps explain why the later matrix frequently adopted for military strategy, that of the general staffs which developed from the late nineteenth century, a matrix that helped drive the process of defining strategy, is not, however, readily, or sensibly, applicable to much of history; and, as a separate issue, possibly not so today either. A focus not on general staffs but, instead, on the (royal) court context of the long earlier period of human history ironically also directs attention to reconsidering strategy during the last quarter-millennium, the period when the word has been used and the concept developed. In particular, leaders over the last quarter-millennium, including to the present, frequently operated in a fashion that would not have been out of character or, indeed, context for their predecessors who presided over these courts.

Thus, there are elements of decision-making under Napoleon, Hitler, Putin and Trump that would not have been totally out of place for Louis XIV of France (r. 1643–1715). In many cases, irrespective of whether the comparison across time was longer or shorter, it was deliberately sought, as with Benito Mussolini, Italy's Fascist dictator from 1922 to 1943, and his repeated attempt to strike a resonance using explicit reference to the founding Roman emperor, Augustus Caesar, who ruled nineteen centuries earlier. This continuity is more especially the case if the focus is on strategic culture or strategic process, rather than strategic content (especially in the case of specific military means) or the broader international context.

In particular, there is the question of how far *gloire*, the search for prestige, and the use of the resulting reputation to secure international and domestic goals, are, while important for all, especially attractive and important in monarchical or pseudo-monarchical systems, indeed providing them in many respects with their prime strategic purpose, tone and drive. This approach towards strategy understandably works in a diachronic fashion, in other words across time, however much the latter approach may appear surprising in a subject, military history, that focuses so much on technological change and thus the immediate context, with time as non-diachronic. An emphasis on the value of prestige and reputation adopts a cultural functionalism based on their value that is linked to a psychological approach to image and competition. In part, a competition for prestige can enhance all the powers involved. More commonly, however, the competition was necessarily at the expense of other powers, and was very much desired and affirmed in these terms. This situation has continued to the present.

The rhetorical character that is part of strategy's essentially political nature should also attract attention. Separately, so also should the frequent fluidity of strategy, or rather of the alliances involved, and, in contrast, the fixedness of particular plans. Focusing on the latter, and on their genesis, can lead to an underplaying of the former. Conversely, plans can change more rapidly. None of these characteristics, however, necessarily appeals to those seeking a science of strategy and/or a set of lessons that allegedly can be readily learned, and the teaching of which provides them with point, position and profit.

'Strategy' is a term much debated now and in recent years. Indeed, in the West, helping both to provoke and to focus or refocus this debate, there is a sense that strategy is in some way a lost art, and there is a much-repeated argument to that effect. This sense reflects a crisis of confidence, notably in Britain but also in the United States, as a result of repeated setbacks, or at least serious difficulties, for Western forces in Iraq and Afghanistan in the 2000s and 2010s, and the linked problems for Western goals. The rhetoric and associated disquiet about absent or flawed strategy, and about a confusion of policy and strategy, rose even more in the mid- and late 2010s. This was specifically in response to the general imbroglio concerning Western policy towards Syria and, indeed, the Middle East as a whole. The House of Commons Foreign Affairs Committee referred in 2016 to the 'failure to develop a coherent Libya strategy'.[1] In part, there is the loss of the ability to determine and maintain plausible goals, which then leads to an inability to formulate effective strategy, let alone the problems with individual strategies.

The rhetoric and disquiet about strategy also reflected a more general concern in the West in the 2000s and 2010s about drift. This was drift in the case of the conception and implementation of what was variously described as policy and strategy, and that referred, variously, to goals and implementation. The confused and largely unsuccessful response to Chinese and Russian assertion and expansionism was an aspect of this disquiet. Anxiety about President Donald Trump's attitudes and policies, notably his hostility to multilateralism and to many of the institutions involved, including NATO (the North Atlantic Treaty Organization) and the WTO (World Trade Organization), was a major issue in 2017–19. Earlier, there had been very different, but nevertheless also pressing and repeated anxieties about the strategic grasp of presidents Bill Clinton (1993–2001), George W. Bush (2001–9) and Barack Obama (2009–17), anxieties that tended to be forgotten when the focus was on President Trump.

In this context of concern, and of the response to concern, the term 'strategy' was much employed in the 2000s and 2010s, and not always in an illuminating fashion. That itself was an instructive comment on the vocabulary of strategy, and its role in politics, variously the politics of policy-making and the public politics of contestation. In both, the use of strategy served rhetorical and political purposes, and, although generally in different ways, these purposes also affected the use of the term within the military and among academic commentators.

The extent to which commentators focused on differences and tensions arising from contrasting goals between the powers, notably China and Russia on the one hand and the Western powers on the other, and indeed among the Western powers, was also an instructive comment on the vocabulary of strategy. These contrasts underlined the extent to which alliances and would-be alliances entailed commitments and possibilities in terms of goals and means that involved the pressures and problems of co-operation. To offer any account of strategy as a military activity that does not take adequate note of the international context, its role as an independent variable and its consequences is evidently flawed.

There is no reason why the same should not be the case for the past. Indeed, the use of the present to guide and equip questions and thoughts about the past is an integral aspect of assessing the historical dimension of strategy. Modern terms, such as strategy or geopolitics, are employed to provide a twenty-first-century appraisal of what happened. As long as ahistorical perspectives are avoided, this is a rewarding approach and, in practice, a necessary one.

Conversely, military history might be employed to ascertain and define lessons from the past for the present, and can be justified in these terms within the military.[2] However, the process of lesson-learning, notably the understanding of this history and the search for lessons, tends very much to be approached in current terms, and this can be misleading. This present-centred characteristic is reflected in different editions of particular studies.[3]

This book proceeds from an introduction, through a series of case-studies of states, periods and conflicts, to a conclusion. The case-studies are contextualised in terms of shifts across the last six centuries. Much of the book will be devoted to those case-studies. Linked to this, there will be a discussion of strategic culture and practice and, specifically, of the degree to which it is appropriate to use the terms of strategy. The case-studies are chosen to illustrate the range of strategy, and also to draw attention to key issues, notably the changing nature and importance of strategic culture.

This is a book about the reality of strategy and, in particular, strategic decision-making: its practice in the past, the present and, very likely, the future. Much of current writing on strategy, in contrast, deals with the strategic thought of leading thinkers, such as Sun Tzu, Clausewitz and Mahan. While engaging with aspects of this thought, I propose to focus on the strategic practice of leading military figures over the past four centuries, and particularly over the last two, with an emphasis on those who wielded power, and took and implemented decisions, for example Napoleon and Hitler.

Crucially, strategy is not a document but a practice. It can be understood in terms of what needs to be achieved (the 'ends'), how this will be done (the 'ways'), and which resources will be used to do it (the 'means'), each of which affects the others, both in terms of content and of how it is understood. At the same time, 'strategy' has become a synonym for 'something very important' or 'aspiration'. Military-focused definitions, as in the employment of battles to gain the end of war, or the art of distributing and applying military means to fulfil the ends of policy, do not address non-military usages of strategy, nor the conflation of policy and strategy that pertains in practice, both for the military and for others.

Much current writing, both historical and addressing the present, focuses on the West, and to such an extent that Western commentators and the Western public frequently fail to appreciate the strategic assumptions and values, and hence strategies, of non-Western opponents. That asymmetry has significant consequences in terms of a failure to understand the culturally varying equations of military success, such as the response to casualties. These consequences were visible recently during the conflicts in Iraq and Afghanistan. In contrast to the focus on the West, it is necessary also to engage with the Asian dimension, and to consider China, India and Japan not as passive spectators or victims, but either as major players in opposition to other strategic movers, or as aspects of the power of those movers. Thus, for example, India was a crucial constituent in Britain's Asian strategy from 1762 (successful expedition from Madras/Chennai to Spanish-ruled Manila) to 1947 (independence). In addition, Japan played a major role in America's East Asian strategy. This was the case not only as an enemy in 1941–5, but also at other times including, passively yet as a crucial base, during the Korean and Vietnam Wars, and also in the current rise of the Chinese peer competitor and the resulting territorial and resource tensions over the East and South China Seas.

At the same time as differences, there are important overlaps between Western and non-Western strategies. Thus, for both, divide and rule was the key imperial strategy, and notably in newly conquered territories, such as Egypt after Turkish conquest from the Mamluks in 1517. In 1522, the governor defeated a Mamluk insurgency having bought off the Mamluks' allies among the Arab sheiks.

The important areas for consideration, therefore, are war, the international system, domestic politics and their interrelated dynamism. The kind of victory that is sought is fundamental to the strategy pursued. Strategy is not viewed exclusively as the process of formulating military goals and the means, in every context, to implement them. Instead, a 'total' view of strategy, one that encompasses domestic and international strengths, interests and issues, and that matches much of the popular usage of the term,[4] makes best sense of the war-preparation and war-making that are the prime dimension of strategy and of the related discussion. Domestic policies and politics are an integral part of pragmatic strategy: assuaging domestic grievances, for example, makes it easier to ensure support for a foreign war. Thus, strategy is an important aspect of total history, both as component and as consequence.

In both international and domestic terms, strategies emerge in response to, and in order to forward, coalitions of interest; although the domestic dimension of these coalitions tends to be overlooked or, rather, underrated in much writing on military strategy. The terms by which these coalitions are formed and re-formed become relevant to the process by which strategies are advanced, debated and reformulated. Indeed, the ability to maintain such coalitions is a key element of strategic activity, and a central link between the domestic and international politics and war-making that this book takes as its theme. Arguing that 'strategic practice . . . is always the expression of an entire culture', a well-founded claim, Edward Luttwak, for example, concluded for the Byzantines that 'military strategy was subordinated to diplomacy' and that the latter focused on playing off enemies against each other,[5] a practice that is more general and that was both cause and consequence of the prioritisation central to strategy. More generally, military plans and preparations were/are frequently a form of insurance policy against the failure of diplomacy, and only become really significant in that context.[6] At the same time, such plans and preparations, on one or both sides, can help cause the failure of diplomacy.

The context and process of coalition formation, both domestic and international, and the related goal-setting, are not static. Thus, for example, war posed a particular challenge to the cohesion of multi-ethnic empires, and notably so in a context of rising nationalism or proto-nationalism.[7] The dynamic character of strategic evolution includes changes in the relationships between the constituent parts of the strategic equations of purpose, force, implementation and effectiveness. These changes illuminate the present day and offer suggestions for the future. Suggestions for the future are no more than that, although some facets are highly likely, notably strategy continuing at least in part to provide an element in the rhetorical politics of power.

The analytical approach outlined here is deployed in a consideration of the development of strategy over the last six centuries. I argue that the idea and practice of strategy predated the vocabulary, which is essentially nineteenth and twentieth century. Indeed, modern terminology is not a crucial precondition. It was possible, for example, to have a 'strategic hamlet' programme for civilian control well before the formal use of that term during America's Vietnam War.[8]

Irrespective of vocabulary, the idea and practice of strategy contributed to what would subsequently be described as 'strategic culture', a central concept for this book, albeit one that is not fixed in institutional forms. The idea of strategic culture, a term employed to discuss the context within which military tasks are 'shaped', is based on the idea that general beliefs, attitudes and patterns of behaviour were integral to the politics of power, rather than being dependent on the policy circumstances of a particular conjuncture. At the same time, the use of this, and other, concepts has to address specific historical contexts, and doing so underlines the important roles of politics and contingency.[9] Indeed, strategic culture is an aspect, both cause and consequence, of what has been presented as 'great strategic rivalries'.[10]

This book seeks to develop these ideas in a dynamic consideration of key conflicts in the past, major issues in the present, and the strategic development of several leading powers. Allowing for significant variations across the world, conflicts and states can be presented as typical of a particular period of conflict and international relations (the two treated as linked, but different); and yet also as being understood in terms of domestic realities, notably the particular identity and specific interests of dynasties, peoples, countries and states.

As such, this book will contribute to an understanding of international relations and of the extent to which neither these relations, nor the pursuit of military goals, were distinct from domestic policies. Moreover, attitudes towards conflict or the means for conflict, such as conscription and popular mobilisation, cannot be separated from the discussion of the domestic sphere.

I have benefited greatly from the opportunity to speak on this topic over many years, most recently at the National World War Two Museum in New Orleans, the *École Militaire* in Paris, the National Defence College in Copenhagen, the National Defense University in Washington, a RUSI meeting in the Diet building in Tokyo, a joint dinner-meeting of the House of Commons and House of Lords Select Committees on Defence, the Prince's Teaching Institute in London, the Naval War College in Newport, Rhode Island, the College for Defence Studies in London, the Malvern Military History Festival, Marlborough College, Radley College, Oundle School, Stowe School and Torquay Museum; and for the Foreign Policy Research Institute in New York and Philadelphia, the World Affairs Council in Wilmington, the New York Military Affairs Symposium and the D-Group. A more extensive treatment of the 'long eighteenth century' and of some of the historiography can be found in my *Plotting Power: Strategy in the Eighteenth Century* (2017).

For this book, I have benefited from advice on particular points from Rodney Atwood, Pete Brown, John Buchanan, Jonathan Fennell, Chris Gill, John Gill, John Haldon, J. E. Lendon, Graham Loud and John Peaty. I would like to thank Stan Carpenter, David Graf, Eric Grove, Richard Harding, Gaynor Johnson, Peter Luff, Kevin McCranie, Thomas Otte, Kaushik Roy, Alaric Searle, Doug Stokes, Ulf Sundberg, Ken Swope and two anonymous readers, for commenting on all or part of an earlier draft. They are not responsible for any errors that remain. Heather McCallum has proved a most supportive editor and I would also like to note the earlier support of her predecessor Robert Baldock. I am conscious of how long this book has taken and of their patience. I am also grateful for the help at Yale University Press of Rachael Lonsdale, Marika Lysandrou and Jonathan Wadman. It is a great pleasure to dedicate this book to Steve Bodger, whose friendship, launched on the battlefield of Waterloo, I much enjoy.

INTRODUCTION
THE STRUGGLE FOR POWER

DEFINITIONS

There are major and persistent problems with defining strategy. Historically, strategic decision-makers kept being influenced by (and kept taking into account) a vast range of developing factors, including the extent to which they were themselves groping towards an understanding of strategy as a concept. Undermining any precise definition, there was no coherent set of factors influencing these decision-makers. Instead, there was a varied inclusion of politics, domestic as well as international. Moreover, while the non-military tools of implementation, such as diplomacy and economic pressure, could be very important, they were not constant in their character and impact. Analysing how strategy was influenced and made helps to explain the difficulty of arriving at a consistently applied definition.

Definition is sometimes fast-forwarded by reference to Clausewitz, but, partly because the range of any discussion should be at least global in aspiration, it is probably best not to write in the shadow of Clausewitz. This is even more the case now than in the past because, notably in the light of developments since 1945, Western-centric approaches to military matters and history no longer appear so helpful on a global scale.[1] Clausewitz, furthermore, understood that war is dynamic and keeps changing its character over time, and that his work should not be taken as doctrine.

Indeed, the strategic assumptions of any theorist, however abstract, only hold good in specific contexts, and these contexts change, making the theory more or less relevant. Theorists try to generalise from specifics,

1

but their approach is inherently flawed unless their theory is so resistant to exception that it becomes a 'law', which is not likely in the field of strategy.

Issues over definition arise not solely because of, first, the problematic nature of the standard Western-centric approach to war and its analysis, and, second, the absence of the use of the term for most of history; although the latter is a potentially important issue. There is also the relationship with other possible classifications and/or typologies of strategy, most obviously grand strategy, a term favoured by some commentators from the 1920s but also applied to earlier periods.[2] The concept of grand strategy leads to a contrasting of policy/planning, in the shape of grand strategy, with implementation, in that of strategy. However, this is not a helpful contrasting of what in practice was and is generally a continuum or overlap. The two categories are easier to define as separate than to practise as separate, a situation that is more generally the case.

In addition, the application of the understanding of strategy in particular circumstances poses questions that underline the problem with the otherwise apparently attractive concept of the optimum strategy. Moreover, the challenge of the task, notably its immediacy, does not always lend itself to such an optimisation, as in the following exchange from the satirical James Bond film *Casino Royale* (1967): 'What's the strategy, Sir?' 'Get us out of here as soon as possible,' the latter from Bond. In such cases, the strategy, the operation and the tactics all run together very rapidly.

Wayne Lee pointed out that most readers and authors think they intuitively know the difference between strategy, operations and tactics, but that in practice there are many definitions. For Lee, 'strategy refers to the deployment of resources and forces on a national scale and the identification of key objectives (territorial or otherwise) that operations are then designed to achieve'. Operations are defined as 'campaigns'.[3] Adopting a frequently used approach, Thomas Kane and David Lonsdale described strategy as 'the process that converts military power into policy effect'.[4]

More generally, strategy is often employed to cover the use of conflict for the purpose of war or, more usually, a particular war. Strategy to a degree focuses on the ability to ensure and sustain a measure of political cohesion, and to translate this into military capacity, and not on the pursuit of a particular war-fighting style and its implications. The military essentially provide the force to give strategy effect, just as diplomacy is also important to its implementation. There are also understandings of strategy in terms of theories and practices of security, whether or not understood as national strategy. At the same time, this common approach, with its specific understanding, is not sufficient as an account of a more complex reality that entailed and entails both patterns and issues of history, geography and discourse in the response to conflict, and matters of procurement, prioritisation, planning and alliance systems in deciding how best to respond.

Yet, there is also the cynical argument, as offered by Dean Acheson, that 'every once in a while, you have to give a speech, so you take a look at what you've been doing in the past few months, you write it out, and that's your strategy'.[5] This remark can be reconceptualised to argue that strategy is essentially the rationalisation, at the time or subsequently, of an events-based practice. To a degree, this is certainly the case, one that draws on thought and argument often, indeed generally, being intuitive not deductive, and one that helps to explain why strategy, therefore, can be such a rationalisation. That approach looks towards an emphasis on strategy as inherently political in that this rationalisation can be seen as a political process. Separately, an events-based practice or 'emergent strategy' provides more flexible possibilities, and notably in the face of the discovery of a disruptive enemy strategy.

The approach offered by Lee, Kane, Lonsdale and many others downplays any alternative to a distinctive military character to strategy, and this is an approach which needs to be addressed explicitly. Indeed, the function of strategy, if understood as the relationships between ends, ways and means in power politics, is not necessarily military. Separately, even in the case of conflict, the prioritisation in goals and means at the international level is a matter of the foreign policy establishment, and not just the military. This establishment is an amorphous body that includes formal institutions and intelligence services, notably foreign ministries, as well as decision-makers at the centre of government. At the same time, it is unclear why the national scale should always be the key one in studying strategy, as opposed sometimes to an inclusion of the sub-national or, indeed, the supra-national. Furthermore, the impact of each of the latter can compromise the autonomy of decision-making at the national scale.

3

Even during the two centuries, or just over, when the term 'strategy' has been employed in English, French, German, Italian and other languages, and the concept applied, there is much difference, not to say controversy, over its definition, employment, application and value. 'Strategy' has been taken to refer to the full range of human activity, as in 'strategic merit' and 'strategic facet'.[6] Thus, in 1991, Patricia Crimmin referred to 'the [English] Channel's strategic significance' and, in doing so, drew attention to the multiple character of such significance: 'invasion threat, line of defence, prison wall, escape route'. In this context, 'strategic geography' is another pertinent term.[7] At the same time as the vocabulary around strategy, especially the ubiquitous use of the adjective 'strategic', began to expand in an inflationary manner in the late twentieth century, the number of traps around terminology began to increase.

Goals, methods and outcomes all play a role in definitions of strategy, and in the application of these definitions, but so also do habit, inclination, institutional practice and personal preference. This leads to a very varied situation, Indeed, readers of journals might be forgiven for confusion when the same issue can contain pieces on 'Grand Strategy' and 'Military Strategy', as well as reference to strategic engagement.[8] Moreover, alongside different usages come their ready juxtaposition, as in an editorial in *The Times* of 5 December 2018 on the European Union: 'As a rules-based institution with complex decision-making processes, it lacks the capacity to act strategically. In any case, strategic action requires a capacity to deliver compromises. That may be easier for strong governments than weak governments.' In this case, the context is presented as inherent to the process of strategy-making.

In addition, strategy can be seen, for example, as a path, rather than a plan for implementation.[9] Indeed, alongside those who seek precision in the analysis, there is, in practice, a level of activity and energy that is far less focused. This includes the idea of a grand strategic impulse, rather than simply a plan, with any plan sometimes being a matter of sticking a series of operational possibilities, or even tactics, together.

Much of the current discussion pays no attention to military issues. Thus, in 2016, there were over 56,000 entries on Amazon.com for strategy under 'Business and Money'. Indeed, strategy is a 'buzzword' in the field of management and economics, one frequently employed alongside terms such as 'managing' and 'directing'. Business strategy ranges from which products to sell on which markets, to more complex and varied topics including quality and environmentalism.

There is also 'strategic communications' as a term for information operations, propaganda and public relations. In 2016, Conservative Eurosceptic MP Steve Baker boasted of having used Robert Greene's book *The 33 Strategies of War* (2006) to help win the referendum on leaving the European Union.[10] This book set out to provide a guide to everyday life 'informed by the . . . military principles in war'. The banal and facile, but best-selling, book provided what it termed offensive and defensive strategies. It followed Greene's *The 48 Laws of Power* (1998) and his *The Art of Seduction* (2001).

As instances of the widespread use of military imagery, and of strategy in that context, in 2018, Facebook created a 'war room' in its Silicon Valley headquarters, in order to fight misinformation ahead of the US mid-term elections. That December, in Britain, the director of the Police Foundation complained that, because of the system of local police forces rather than a national force, 'fraud is a third of all crime but there is no national strategy for dealing with it'.[11]

The tendency to treat strategy as akin to an adjective, describing a process to confront a dangerous issue, a process involving serious consideration and difficult planning, is readily apparent, as in Prime Minister David Cameron's account in 2015 of his drawing up a strategy for tackling hate language. Separately, Alan Downie has profitably used the concept of 'polemical strategy'.[12] Thus, on 11 October 2018, President Trump, very much employing military terminology, warned of an 'onslaught' of migrants reaching the Mexican border with the United States and threatened to send the army 'to defend' the border,[13] subsequently doing so. There was no onslaught and no need to employ the army. Polemical strategy overlaps with rhetorical strategy.

Linked to this, but also separate, there is the concept of 'strategic narratives', both positive and critical, and covering areas both military and non-military. Thus, in the case of Anglo-American intervention in Afghanistan and Iraq in the 2000s, there were narratives advanced to explain policy, including opposition to terrorism and, in contrast, stabilisation.

Strategy, understandably, is usually discussed by military historians in terms of war-winning. That, however, is to operationalise it in terms of military activity. In practice, strategy, whether military or non-military, and, in the former case, whether or not focused on war, is both a process of defining interests, understanding problems and determining goals, and a product of this process. A ready separation of the two may be attractive in conceptual terms, but does not match the interactions that occur. Moreover, the salience of politics in the process helps make the concept of an apolitical national strategy implausible, as well as encouraging an emphasis on outcomes rather than inputs. Strategy, however, is not the details of the plans by which goals are implemented by military means. These are the operational components of strategy, to employ another, later, term in the shape of 'operational'.

There is an important element of variety in the understanding of strategy, including national difference and, separately, change through time. Mackubin Owens, an American commentator, observed in 2014: 'Strategy is designed to secure national interests and to attain the objectives of national policy by the application of force or threat of force. Strategy is dynamic, changing as the factors that influence it change.'[14] This dynamism clearly extends to the definition and use of strategy.

STRATEGIC CULTURE

Differences over definition, application and impact extend to related concepts, notably that of strategic culture.[15] Although controversial, the latter concept provides a context within which strategy and statecraft, which in some respects is the same, can be approached.[16] This is noticeably so for cases where there was no relevant vocabulary of strategy or institutional culture and practice. Strategic culture is employed to discuss the context within which military tasks were, and are, 'shaped'. This concept owes much to a 1977 report on Soviet strategic ideas by Jack Snyder for the American RAND Corporation.[17] Written for a specific audience, the concept of strategic culture drew on George Kennan's influential analysis in his 'long telegram' from Moscow of 22 February 1946,[18] and on his Mr 'X' article in the American periodical *Foreign Affairs* in April 1947, which made the strategy of containment more public. The concept provided a way to help explain the Soviet Union, a government system and political culture for which sources were manipulated for propaganda reasons and accurate reports were few and problematic. This response to the Soviet Union prefigured that to Communist China.

States aside, the notion of strategic culture is also very valuable for leaders who did not commit much to paper. This was not only the case for figures in the distant past, but also for many more recent counterparts, such as President Franklin Delano Roosevelt, who did not like to commit to paper, in part due to his personality but also for reasons of accountability, as with his verbal approval to implement unrestricted submarine warfare against Japan after its attack on Pearl Harbor.

The idea of explaining and discussing a system, in whole and parts, in terms of a culture captured not only the social and cultural construction and contextualisation of power politics,[19] but also the role of established patterns of thought.[20] Moreover, the concept drew on the notion of bounded rationality, a term coined by Herbert Simon, an American economist and decision theorist who sought to emphasise the limitations to rational decision-making. The assumption of classical economists, which was also in line with contemporary beliefs about people and leaders, was that they pursued rational goals and means. In contrast, in the aftermath of the horrors of the first half of the century, Simon posed the idea that people's rationality is bounded by what they know, and how they perceive ideological attachments and psychological factors.[21] What the bounds are, and how they are influenced or changed, are matters of debate and research to this day. While there is a great deal of disagreement on this, the high tide of unquestioning belief in rational humanity has passed. The classical paradigm remains attractive to some theorists for modelling purposes, but has generally been discarded in favour of some kind of bounded-rationality idea.

There is an obvious relevance for contemporary strategy and its discussion. The classic model of rational strategy-making outlined in the nineteenth century no longer exists in the same way, although the idea of an optimal solution seeks to provide a different route. In addition, as another constraint on rationality, at the same time as increasingly sophisticated quantitative methods are producing more reliable data for decision-making – coming from many more different perspectives and sources – there is an inability to sift, process and codify data in time. That provides different boundaries for decision-makers.

The shifting nature of contexts operates in a number of respects. For example, the notion of distinctive generational experiences[22] is valuable not only with reference to contrasting understandings of the possibilities and practice of strategy, but also in terms of the changing character of strategic culture. These experiences could readily become politically charged, both at the time and in subsequent discussion, as with the link between the idea of a nation in arms and republicanism in France from the 1790s.[23]

Separately, both for religious and for secular societies, there were differing accounts of providential systems of behaviour and should-be predictable outcomes. The implication was that a correct understanding would lead to an assured outcome. This approach was to be all too common in the discussion that followed the introduction of a formal language of strategy from the late eighteenth century. The implication was at once reassuring and misleading, and contributes to the current idea of the 'lost art of strategy', a notion that in part rests on a supposed prelapsarian past linked to a theory of decline.

The delay in the development of the term 'strategy' reflects for some commentators conceptual and institutional limitations affecting the prior understanding of strategy. However, in his study of strategy before the term in the case of Russia, an empire whose extensive territories from the seventeenth century, from the Pacific to the Baltic, entailed a range of commitments and opportunities, John P. LeDonne addressed the possible criticism that he presented 'nothing but "virtual strategy", in which the author attributes to the Russian political élite a vision they never had' and in language they would not have used.[24] LeDonne added a helpful defini-tion of what he termed 'grand strategy', namely 'an integrated military, geopolitical, economic, and cultural vision'.[25] That, indeed, is a worth-while definition, but without any need to add the word 'grand' to 'strategy'. Ironically, this term looks back to the late eighteenth-century use in France of the term 'grand tactics', which was a term usually employed to discuss what would today be referred to as the operational level.

Focusing on the significance of élite views in the past entails a welcome grounding in particular historical contexts, and thus a rejection of any ahistorical, non-cultural, non-realist framework for analysing strategic choices. Instead, how an élite saw and presented both itself and its iden-tity and interests comprised (and continues to comprise) the most important component of strategic choice,[26] and, thereby, of resulting outcomes. Indeed, strategic consequences were central to an important feedback mechanism in which élites either came to reconceptualise their assumptions, those constituting their strategic culture, or did not do so. This process is important to the contemporary and later evaluation of strategic assumptions. This focus on élites has been broadened in order to discuss how nations see their roles and objectives.[27] That presentation of strategic culture is also an approach which covers the inherent political character of strategy and strategic choice, because these choices were contested as they were shaped and reshaped.

INSTITUTIONS AND THINKERS

Compared to the formal, institutional, processes of strategic discussion and planning in recent decades, notably its military context as a supposedly distinct activity, strategy prior to the nineteenth century appears, in at least that context, as at best limited and *ad hoc*, and as lacking both well-developed structure and doctrine to match an empirical process of learning and ideas. Thus, in the War of American Independence (1775–83), British strategy in North America was essentially created by the field commanders rather than by the Cabinet or by the Secretary of State for America, Lord George Germain. This was the case even though setting the strategy was in his domain and he was a former general and had had experience of counter-insurgency warfare.

That situation, however, does not mean that strategy was unfit for purpose. Moreover, in the case of Christian Europe (then the 'West'), it has been claimed by Peter Wilson, a specialist in German forces, that general staffs of a type emerged during the Thirty Years' War (1618–48), with the staff designed to assist the commander and maintain communications with the political centre. Such staffs evolved from the personal assistants initially paid by the general himself,[28] but they generally remained very limited in numbers and method. Indeed, applied then, the term 'general staff' may well be highly misleading, not least as it looks towards the nineteenth century.

In addition to the Thirty Years' War, other episodes have attracted attention. For example, it has been argued that, under the direction of Field Marshal Count Franz Moritz Lacy, Austria, at war with Prussia during the Seven Years' War (1756–63), established what became an effective proto-general staff.[29] Such an argument necessarily puts earlier developments in the Thirty Years' War in the shade and/or implies a process of episodic development. Logistics, a key element in the planning of campaigns in both centuries, certainly involved staff work.

In his *History of the Late War in Germany* (1766), Henry Lloyd (c.1729–83), who had served in the Seven Years' War, claimed: 'It is universally agreed upon, that no art or science is more difficult, than that of war; yet, by an unaccountable contradiction of the human mind, those who embrace this profession take little or no pains to study it. They seem to think that the knowledge of a few insignificant and useless trifles, constitute a great officer. This opinion is so general, that little or nothing else is taught at present in any army whatever.'[30] That account was substantially correct as far as formal education was concerned. However, Lloyd underrated the very important method of learning on the job, notably by example, experience and discussion. This was seen not only with training but also in the public sphere, for example with pamphlet and newspaper debates during and after particular operations discussing their wisdom, in conception and execution.

The limited institutional character to military education and command practice for most of history can be presented as having lessened the possibility of moving on from strategic culture to strategy or at least strategic planning. Conversely, the absence of a mechanism for the creation and dissemination of institutional wisdom on strategy may well have ensured that the body of assumptions and norms referred to as strategic culture was, instead, more effective, indeed more normative. This body of assumptions and norms affected both strategic thinkers and strategic actors; and, in turn, they each sustained assumptions. Differentiating strategic culture from strategy in terms of firm distinctions is not in practice overly helpful, but the attempt can capture the extent to which there are contrasts in emphasis.

The arguments and role of strategic thinkers (generally presented as military theorists), whether they, like Lloyd, Clausewitz, Jomini, Mahan, Douhet, Fuller and Liddell Hart, served in the military, or whether they did not, attract the attention of intellectuals, both military and non-military. This is particularly so in the case of academics who write on the military and who tend to seek intellectual assessments of war. Notably this is so for a focus on Clausewitz, as he was, and is, taken by some to help in some way explain and characterise subsequent Prussian, and then German, military success, as well as, in his writings, to provide a benchmark for the effectiveness of past states and of other thinkers and, indeed, to capture essential characteristics of warfare.[31] In practice, such thinkers might have been largely irrelevant, or relevant only in so far as they captured, and focused, general nostrums and current orthodoxies, and therefore served in some way to validate them.

It is instructive to note that in the case of China, the state for much of history prior to the nineteenth century with the most developed literary treatment of war, there is scant evidence of the use of texts for guidance. Indeed, the Kangxi Emperor (r. 1662–1723), a ruler far more successful as a military leader than his contemporary, Louis XIV of France, let alone Napoleon, allegedly declared the military classics, such as the works of Sun Tzu, worthless; and references to these classics in Chinese military documents were rare.[32] That emperor faced a variety of serious military challenges, foreign and domestic, and surmounted all of them. Strategic practice was longstanding in the Chinese case.[33] The marginality of explicitly military thinkers can also be considered for other states, including even Clausewitz's Prussia.

Alternatively, these thinkers can, in part, be profitably presented as an instance of the rhetoric of power, an aspect of power that was as significant to contemporaries as its analysis, indeed far more so. As a result of this formulation of strategy, domestic attitudes, policies and politicians can be as significant in the understanding of interests, and in the formulation and execution of strategy, as their military counterparts, again indeed generally far more so. Thus, in the 'War on Terror', in the 2000s and 2010s, measures taken to try to secure the support of the bulk of the Muslim population of countries threatened by terrorism, such as Britain, are as germane as the use of force against new or suspected terrorists. Deterrence is an aspect of both.

Conversely, an ISIS manual, apparently written in 2014, that set out plans for a centralised, self-sufficient state included the establishment of an army but also of military schools to create further generations of fighters, as well as bureaucratic planning, covering health, education, industry, propaganda and resource management. With its broad approach, this was another iteration of the revolutionary strategies outlined in the twentieth century, notably in 'national liberation struggles'.

A key point throughout the history of strategy is that it is the activity, not the word nor the text, that is the basis of examination and analysis;

and an emphasis on activity makes it easier to make comparisons across time, space and cultures. Treating the existence of strategy as highly problematic for a period when the term is absent mistakes the absence of an articulated school of strategic thinking for the lack of strategic awareness. At the same time, there is the issue of shaping into a false coherence the often disparate discussion, limited planning and isolated and frequently indirect pointers of evidence that exist. This problem underlines the additional difficulties of aligning the situation in one state in one period with that in other states in the same or other periods. This is always a task for which historians lack the enthusiasm of social scientists, and one that, separately, brings to the fore the problems entailed in the search for what might be termed a 'unified theory of strategy'. A key element in encouraging caution in the pursuit of a narrow definition was the lack of any unpacking of strategy and policy, a lack which reflected the absence of any institutional body specifically for strategic planning and execution, and also the repeated tendency, in politics, government and political discussion, to see what could subsequently be differentiated as strategy and policy as, in fact, one, and necessarily so.

THE CHRONOLOGICAL BACKGROUND

Even though the terms of strategy have not been in use for most of history, the concepts of strategic thinking have been around since humans engaged in organised conflict, while the 'institutional body' for strategic planning and execution was the ruler, with the generals part of this body as they carried out the ruler's orders. This situation became more apparent when it was a question of large-scale organised conflict.

The first states that have been widely discussed as having a strategy are those of Classical Greece. The discussion of strategy in the Classical period is longstanding. If it conventionally began with Thucydides writing on the strategy of the Peloponnesian War between Athens and Sparta (431–404 BCE) in which he participated, it has continued, as with Hans Delbrück's *Die Strategie des Perikles, erläutert durch die Strategie Friedrichs des Grossen* ('The Strategy of Pericles Clarified by the Strategy of Frederick the Great') (1890). Thucydides began an approach to strategy that became dominant in the modern world.

However, a broader and far older approach can be found in Homer's *Iliad*, with its gripping account of the central roles of honour and revenge in the causes, pursuit and course of the Trojan War. Moreover, this approach linked the world of men to that of the gods in a fashion that made sense to the Greeks: each was seen as a warring world.

Modern work has offered much insight into this period. Paul Rahe's *The Grand Strategy of Classical Sparta: The Persian Challenge* (2015) related military activity, notably in the fifth century BCE, to what Rahe presented as a strategy of life and living, notably the customs and laws that constituted the background of politics both domestic and foreign. The retention of troops at home to deal with any revolt by helots or slaves was seen as a key element. Victor Davis Hanson directed attention to Athens.[34] Notions of honour and status, and therefore revenge, were significant in the rivalry between the two powers in the Peloponnesian War.[35]

The claim that because there was no term for strategy Rome lacked strategic thinking fails to give sufficient weight to the lasting need to prioritise possibilities and threats, and, in response, to allocate resources and to decide how to use them.[36] This is a need at all levels, but one that is particularly apparent for far-flung states such as the Roman Empire. The earlier three Punic Wars between Carthage and Republican Rome (264–241, 218–201, 149–146 BCE) have been profitably discussed in terms of what are presented as contemporary views of strategy, with the latter seen to depend on long-term planning and a good perception of geographical relationships.[37] The location of fortifications is another instance of the latter, and not only by the Romans.[38] Alfred Thayer Mahan (1840–1914), the American theorist of command of the sea, was influenced by the German historian Theodor Mommsen (1817–1903), who, in his *Römische Geschichte* ('History of Rome') (3 vols, 1854–6), presented Roman naval power as playing a crucial strategical role against Carthage in the Second Punic War, which was a valuable counter to the operational-level analysis of concentrating on Hannibal's campaigning in Italy. Mommsen also treated Julius Caesar as the epitome of a strategist-statesman. An application of modern international relations theory was a significant element in Arthur Eckstein's *Mediterranean Anarchy, Interstate War, and the Rise of Rome* (2006). Eckstein explained Rome's success in the multipolar anarchy of the Mediterranean in part in terms of its ability to understand and manage the resulting web of relationships.[39] Thus, strategy entailed adroit prioritisation.

Conversely, alongside a presentation of Roman strategy in terms of modern concepts of defence has come, as with Greece, a stress on factors such as honour and revenge.[40] That emphasis, however, does not negate the existence of strategy. Instead, it underlines its complexity, a point also seen with China, for example in the relationship between fortifications, borders and the perception of the structure of the universe.[41]

Strategy has also been discerned in the case of other pre-modern civilisations. Byzantium, the Eastern Roman Empire, which lasted until 1453, is a clear example. It has been suggested that, under incessant pressure from other powers, Byzantium could not afford to wage wars of attrition nor to seek decisive battles. Instead, it is argued that Byzantium sought to ally with the tribal enemies of its current opponent, and that the tendency was to avoid battle. Fortifications for Byzantium were part of a larger strategy in which tribute payment played a role.[42] There was also a relevant contemporary literature from Byzantium, some of which excited interest from the eighteenth century.

As far as medieval western Europe is concerned, sources are few, and there is little or no theoretical literature on strategy, which, indeed, did not exist as an explicit concept. The standard chronicle narratives of war are of scant help because the contemporary chroniclers were clerical outsiders and simply gave narratives of campaigns or accounts of hand-to-hand encounters, as with treatments of the Norman conquest of England in 1066. They generally had little grasp of the thinking and planning behind activities.

Medieval Western (European) strategy existed, but has to be worked out from what commanders did, and not, on the whole, from documents in which it was discussed, although there are valuable records, for example from Peter IV of Aragon (r. 1336–87). Medieval leaders knew what they wanted to do, but there was no school or forum to produce a dialectic; and each leader chose his methods. Despite a contrasting language, this is essentially the case today, and is so whatever the theory of strategy. Features of medieval strategy, in Christendom, the Islamic world, India, China and Japan, included logistics, concentric advances, and defensive strategy in the shape of the location of fortifications.

Modern writers have gone to much effort to discuss medieval strategy in western Europe and have done so with profit, not least when assessing the wider context of the choices between battle, siegecraft and raiding, choices indeed that were relevant across the world and for much of military history. Indeed, they reach to the present.[43] This discussion has helped illuminate particular conflicts and individual rulers. The choices made in targets and methods have been tackled, for example why the Second Crusade attacked Damascus and not Aleppo in 1148, an analysis that presciently warns about being misled 'by modern-day calculations of strategic interest that cannot be reconciled with twelfth-century realities'.[44] In invading France in the 1340s and 1350s, during the Hundred Years' War (1337–1453), Edward III of England sought to wear down his enemy by ravaging the countryside. This was an instance of strategy as, at least in part, the extension of tactical thinking, but also of using war to pay for itself, as well as of demonstrating to subjects of the enemy that their overlord could not protect them, so they had better change sides.[45] The same goals and processes were seen in other areas, for example India, including in the eighteenth century as new polities were formed alongside the decline of the Mughal Empire.[46]

Repeatedly, the political context was crucial, including during the Anglo-French wars. When, in the mid-1430s, the English lost the support of Duke Philip of Burgundy, their defeat in France became inevitable as, hitherto, the fundamentals of their strategy in the fifteenth century had rested on exploiting divisions within France, and notably poor relations between the Crown and Burgundy. There was a similar pattern in India, with the pursuit of conciliation in order to incorporate new territories, as well as a struggle over resources, not least by blockading forts so as to drive them to surrender. An impression of control was crucial in India and elsewhere. Conflict could reflect a failure of strategy in the shape of an inability, on one or both parts, to manage the impression of power adequately. This was made more significant by the lack of cohesion in many political groups, however defined. This lack of cohesion could be found in ruling groups (including royal lineages), tribal networks and whatever might be defined as a state.[47]

The practicalities of warfare, of feeding armies and making sure they could move, were dominant requirements. Thus, scorched-earth was a method, at once tactical, operational and strategic, that hindered advances by others and that acted as a deterrent. Scorched-earth was employed for example by the Safavids against the Ottoman (Turkish) invasion of Iraq and Iran in 1514, and its success helps explain why the

Safavids were mistaken when they exposed themselves at Chaldiran to a battle in which they were to be defeated by Selim I. However, he was unable to exploit the victory. Scorched-earth also worked for the Crimean Tatars in thwarting Russian invasions in the 1680s.

In the case of Crusading warfare, Saladin in 1187 lured the poorly commanded army of the kingdom of Jerusalem into a waterless area where he could fight on his terms and destroyed his opponents at Hattin. Moreover, in part due to the supply issue, Richard I of England, a key figure in the Third Crusade, soon after advised a strategy of attacking Egypt (which ruled Palestine and Jerusalem), rather than going for Jerusalem itself. This was a strategy followed in the thirteenth century, notably by Louis IX of France: Egypt was seen as the key component of the Ayyubid Empire and two major expeditions were mounted, in 1218–21 and 1248–50, both of which were initially successful only to fail catastrophically, especially the latter. Subsequently, after the loss of the Holy Land in 1291, some proposals for its recovery, involving economic blockades of Egypt as a first step, were quite sophisticated, although European rulers were not able to co-operate sufficiently in order to implement the strategy. More generally, modern ideas of what was strategically sensible should only be applied with care in judging Crusading strategy. Political and, particularly, religious factors came into play.

A longstanding form of strategy, one readily understandable today and seen in the Middle Ages, for example, with the Christian *Reconquista* in Spain and Portugal, was to anchor conquest by means of new settlement. This was also a persistent aspect of Chinese strategy when operating in the steppe.[48] It was seen, moreover, with the Russian advances into Siberia, Ukraine and central Asia, and with American operations in the interior.

For outside Europe, there has been particular scholarly interest in Mongol strategy in the thirteenth century.[49] Force conservation was a major goal for the Mongols. The Mongol tsunami method of conquest involved invading and devastating a large region, but then withdrawing and holding only a small section of territory. As a result, troops were not tied down in garrison duty while the creation, by devastation, of a buffer zone made it impossible to attack them and also weakened the enemy's resources. Then there was another surging forward, again like a wave. As a consequence, the Mongols were able to fight on multiple fronts without overextending themselves.

At the same time, Mongol strategic culture developed, notably making a transition, in the thirteenth century, to city-taking conflict, especially in China. This transition was linked to administrative reforms that permitted a different level of organisation and sustaining forces. In part, this process entailed drawing on conquered regions, particularly China. As a result, a hybridised form of warfare developed, with hybridity seen in strategic, operational and tactical terms.

A different aspect of Mongol effectiveness invites consideration when assessing how best to discuss strategy. If opponents refused to accept terms, the Mongols employed terror, slaughtering many, in order to intimidate others. This policy may have increased resistance, but also encouraged surrender. More generally, success won support and maintained cohesion, both important strategic outcomes.

Mongol methods were revived by Timur the Lame (1336–1405; later called Tamerlane). A key element of his strategy was that of inheriting the mantle of Chinggis Khan, the most famous Mongol leader: Timur claimed descent from Chinggis, a significant source of legitimacy, although, in fact, he was not a Chinggisid. Timur married Chinggisid princesses so that he could have the title of *Güregen* or son-in-law. Sequential campaigning against a range of targets was crucial to Timur's successful career.[50] In turn, the fall of Timur's and other nomadic empires reflected not so much military limitations as the difficulties of maintaining cohesion. This was not least in the face of frequent succession struggles.

In total contrast to the strategic logic of Timur's goals, the Chinese presented their strategy as sustaining a world order of peace that held 'barbarism' at bay. Thus, Zheng He, who led naval expeditions into the Indian Ocean in the early fifteenth century, erected an explanatory statement: 'Upon arriving at foreign countries, capture those barbarian kings who resist civilisation and are disrespectful, and exterminate those bandit soldiers that indulge in violence and plunder. The ocean route will be safe thanks to this.'[51]

Western commentary on war, then and subsequently, was an aspect of thought that focused on choices as well as context.[52] In the case of Philip II of Spain (r. 1556–98), who repeatedly faced major pressures across his far-flung empire,[53] there is disagreement over the quality of his strategic practice. There was certainly tension between the goal of control and the more successful practice of soft power, a practice that included the threat of violence alongside propaganda, patronage, diplomatic initiatives and economic pressure.[54] The judgements bound up in various uses of the term 'strategy', including long-term strategy, grand strategy, strategic schizophrenia, and clear and coherent strategic vision, are apparent.[55]

Such a discussion, indeed debate, could be held about many other states and episodes. It has been argued, nevertheless, more specifically for the Thirty Years' War (1618–48) in Europe, but also for the subsequent European *ancien régime* of 1648–1789, that the logistical problems posed by supporting armies made it difficult to pursue a strategy reflecting political war aims, and thus hard to act in accordance with any overall strategy.[56] In practice, there were always political war aims directing the armies, although armies had to move according to logistical constraints. More broadly, choices in force structures and command methods in the early modern period, that of the sixteenth and seventeenth centuries, repeatedly reflected the fusion of strategy and policy, as they often arose from fundamental assumptions about the methods best placed to preserve social norms as well as state integrity. This was the key nexus of politics. Similar points can be made for other periods.

Fitness for purpose in terms of capabilities and choices could be affected by institutional as well as technological changes. Thus, in the 1850s, the coastal offensive dynamic in British planning emphasised the role of the Hydrographic Office in the development of theatre strategy, and, in turn, contributed to that dynamic. In marked contrast to the unsuccessful overland French attack on Russia in 1812, the Crimean War (1854–6) focused on Anglo-French naval and amphibious action against Russia, a process greatly aided by the recent development of steam-powered warships.[57] This situation has been seen more recently with the development of institutions for joint warfare and combined operations, institutions that sought to exploit in a systematic fashion the opportunities created by powered landing craft and helicopter-borne troops.

As another aspect of fitness for purpose, there was always, once states had developed, a functional strategy, even if it did not have a linguistic or institutional formulation. Since strategy is contextual, highly so, so are its definitions; or non-definitions. The 1976 *Encyclopaedia Britannica* noted that 'the demarcation between strategy as a purely military phenomenon and national strategy of the broader variety became blurred' in the nineteenth century and even less clear in the twentieth.[58] That did not affect the fitness-for-purpose of the military aspect of strategy.

THE OWNERSHIP OF STRATEGY

A particular and currently pressing difficulty arises because of the issue of 'ownership', which is a leading feature in the context of strategic analysis. The wide variation in the use of the term 'strategy', and of the concept, in part arises from this very issue, alongside the more commonplace problems stemming from the definition and usage of conceptual terms, and notably of ones that have differing resonances in specific cultural and national contexts. In large part, but far from exclusively, this issue of 'ownership' comes from the determination by, and on behalf of, militaries to define a sphere of activity and planning that is under their understanding and control, a process that is endorsed by their civilian supporters among commentators. Much of the writing about strategy, indeed, has been driven by, or for, military thinkers.

This context remains relevant today with strategy, and notably because modern militaries in many countries continue to seek a professionalism that both limits the intervention of other branches of government and accordingly enables them to define their role. The Powell Doctrine in the case of the American military in the 1990s (Colin Powell was chairman of the Joint Chiefs of Staff from 1989 to 1993) exemplified this point,[59] as did arguments over Anglo-American interventions in Afghanistan and Iraq in the 2000s and 2010s. Alongside areas generally left to the competence of military leaders, especially training, tactics and doctrine, came the determination by these leaders, a determination very publicly asserted, to maintain a key role in procurement, operations and policy. Annexing the last in terms of what is defined as strategy, and limiting government to a more anodyne and general field termed 'policy', serves this goal.

More positively, military leaders who insist upon clarity of roles, terms, missions and responsibilities are in part motivated by a suspicion that the political leaders do not truly understand what they themselves want or what they want done. As a result, this insistence is an effort to force the political leaders to articulate their goals. Sometimes this process is motivated by a sense of professional duty and sometimes it arises because the political leaders are, appear or can be presented as incompetent in devising policy and considering strategy. In practice, basing themselves on international and domestic circumstances and criteria, political leaders have frequently already made the decision before they consult the military experts, and consultation is often intended to help justify the decision or simply serves as an aspect of implementation.[60] This is a standard aspect of institutional politics.

Similarly, the criticism of civilian leaders can be an attempt to contest blame as well as assert control, one in which politicians in uniform are determined to have their say. The argument on behalf of military independence can certainly be queried, both in specifics and in general. The discussion of strategy is as worthy of attention in terms of this subject as it is with regard to the commonplace division between policy and strategy, although much depends upon an understanding of particular contexts and of institutional cultures.

As another instance of accountability, there is the question whether reliance on the argument of military independence is an aspect – very much a self-serving aspect – of what, in 2015, General Nicholas Houghton, the chief of the (British) General Staff, referred to as 'military conservatism'.[61] This conservatism includes historic funding trends for specific institutions, practices and weapon systems. Strategic reviews in Britain, with their focus on expenditure on specific military means, build into this approach. The attempt to separate out strategy from policy is, in some respects, not only a question of apparent terminological precision, but also an aspect of this conservatism, as well as being an effort to provide a distinctive military voice in the decision-making process and to try to ensure that this voice has coherence and weight. An instance of a comparable (although different) qualification to the distinction between strategy and policy is that between public and private in the organisation of war. The two in practice overlap considerably.[62]

CONTEXTS FOR STRATEGY

Clearly, even if a means-versus-ends distinction is to be advanced when discussing strategy and policy, and the relations between them, ends are in large part set in relation with, and to, means; while means are conceived of, and planned, in terms of ends. In addition, from another perspective, strategy was, and is, conceptualised in terms of strategic culture in the sense of long-term views on both world affairs and domestic political culture, with these views proving a key feature of the belief systems of policy-makers, as well as of their psychological drives. To separate out these factors is not only unhelpful as an account of the past, but also puts an emphasis on a precision that is ahistorical as an approach to the past, as well as being only an aspiration for present and future, and a misleading one at that.

The argument that American and British policy in the Muslim world in the 2000s was mistaken in its understanding of strategy served apparently to discredit imprecision, which was directly linked to failure in Iraq in the mid-2000s.[63] That failure, however, was not due to imprecision, but instead to a total misreading of the situation there, both political and military, one that exemplifies the point that understanding the nature of a particular conflict, rather than theorising about war in general, is crucially necessary.

Separately, aside from the argument that a lack of coherence in strategy was in fact an appropriate response to complexity, including changing circumstances,[64] the apparent imprecision in the understanding and practice of strategy is, in part, a reflection of the variety of environments in which policy is pursued. Thus, the real character of war varies in detail.[65] It is incumbent upon the strategic planner and operator to understand as fully as possible the nature of the particular war upon which they are embarking. Otherwise, the chances for crafting a successful and appropriate strategy are limited.

Separately, the valuable argument that 'strategy is designed to make war useable by the state, so that it can, if need be, use force to fulfil its political objectives'[66] also raises a number of issues, not only the distinction, or at least tension, between the use of force and political objectives, but also the role of non-state actors and the very diversity of state forms and cultures. There is no 'ur' (original and essential) form and dynamic of the state,[67] just as there is none for war. The real interests of a state – whether, for example, they are 'an increase of dominion'[68] – can vary across time, as can the form these interests take and the emphasis on the kinetic use of force.

Far from there being any fixed relationship between war and politics, it is the varied and often flexible nature of the links that helps explain the importance of each to the other. For example, military activity has greatly altered the contours and parameters of the politics that helped cause it, and sometimes of the states and others involved in conflict. In some cases, military activity has also had a comparable impact on social structures, as with the American Civil War (1861–5) in ending slavery and the transformative impact of communism in Russia, China and Indo-China. The centrality of war, and of preparation for war, as bases and processes of change, however, does not mean that there has been a consistent pattern of cause and effect. Moreover, cultural, political and social norms, as well as contingencies, have affected the willingness to pursue such strategies as supporting anti-governmental opposition within opposing states.

In another light, strategy was in part set by the results of international alignments, with these same alignments in turn affected by contingent circumstances, diplomatic, political and military, all of which were discussed in terms of the politics of power, and therefore of strategic rhetoric. So also today, and notably in terms of relations between China, Russia and the United States.

At the same time as the discussion of major states, which are the general units when considering strategy, most participants in conflict are not at the level of such states, and notably so if civil warfare is considered. That does not mean that these participants lack strategic awareness, strategic capability, a strategy, or whatever terms are to be deployed. Far from it, for it may be the case that strategic issues are more urgent in these cases because the participants are far more vulnerable than major states. Linked to that, these issues may be less detachable for the attention of a particular group of policy-makers than in the instance of major powers.

An anthropological level may be added by pointing to the significance across time of nomadic and semi-nomadic peoples.[69] Raiding was a key strategy, one that in practice collapsed into the more common distinctions of strategic, operational and tactical moves. Raiding is also an aspect of what has been referred to as 'little war', a form of conflict that lacks systematic study, and especially so at the strategic level. So also, somewhat differently, for what has been termed 'small war' in the case of the regular forces of settled societies. The latter could undermine or undo the consequences of victory in battle, the form of conflict that very much tends to dominate attention.[70] Raiding war cannot be dismissed as less significant simply because it was different to big-unit regular warfare, and this argument extends to the issue of strategy. Moreover, the entire situation was dynamic at all levels. The tasks and possibilities confronting fighters were subject to perception, contingency and testing. All of these remain valid.

It is most pertinent to consider parallels across time without assuming any automatic process of improvement thanks to modernisation, and without assuming that appropriate behaviour, let alone improvement, required the formal language and process of strategy. Indeed, to assume that the formal language of strategy is necessary or helpful is, itself, a 'strategy' of academic exposition and military presentation that is coherent and much repeated, but also unfounded. Instead, modernisation theory has created many analytical illusions for historians and military commentators, both seeking a theoretical underpinning and pursuing and finding coherence in a developmental fashion, a fashion that apparently links past to present. It is time that strategy as a practice was freed from these illusions.

DEVISING THE TERM

To focus on the eighteenth century, when the term 'strategy' was developed in western Europe, it is possible to point to a range of new circumstances and requirements, and to suggest that these made practical, indeed necessary, a new terminology. Such an approach might well centre on the new languages of classification and analysis associated with the Enlightenment, the leading European élite intellectual movement of the period, or on the greater global range of power projection of the leading European powers, particularly Britain and France, or on the need in Europe to adapt to the dynamic new geopolitics created by the rise of Russia and Prussia. Alternatively, the focus could be narrower, notably on the combination of the crisis in French power and self-confidence following the repeated defeats in the Seven Years' War (1756–63), with the attempts of French commentators to offer solutions. These attempts included looking back to Classical comparisons as part of an effort to derive a general typology of war. The modern use of the term 'strategy' originated with these commentators. These are overlapping explanations, not least as France was the centre of the Enlightenment.

This account can be taken forward to find this Enlightenment ferment helping shape the novelties of French Revolutionary warfare that began in 1792, and then its Napoleonic development. In turn, the assessment of the latter, and the need to respond to it, both at the time and subsequently, are given explanatory power when both nineteenth-century strategy and Clausewitz are rolled forward for consideration.

In 1771, a translation of the Byzantine Emperor Leo VI's *Tactica* appeared in French, published in Paris, as the *Institutions militaires de l'Empereur Léon le Philosophe*. This translation was the work of Lieutenant-Colonel Paul-Gédéon Joly de Maïzeroy, who used the term '*la stratégique*' to describe the art of the commander. He defined '*la stratégique*' as the art of command in employing all means to move all elements under control in order to achieve success. This replaced Maïzeroy's earlier use of the term 'dialectic' in his *Traité de tactique*, published in his *Essais militaires* in 1762. In this, he had referred to '*la dialectique militaire*', which he described as forming plans of campaign and directing operations.

In 1777, Maïzeroy pressed on to publish *Théorie de la guerre, où l'on expose la constitution et formations de l'Infanterie et de la Cavaleries, leurs manoeuvres élémentaires, avec l'application des principes à la grande tactique, suivie de demonstrations sur la stratégique*. The influential *Journal de Sçavans*, in its review that November, saw the book as scientific in intention and mathematical in approach. The book dealt in part with '*stratégie*', defined as the art of conducting war and directing all the operations. The review commented that Maïzeroy sought to offer a mathematical approach, but noted the dependence in practice on conjunctures, notably the political views of princes, and those that led generals to prefer one operation to another. In his introduction, Maïzeroy referred to the requirement to establish a theory which could serve as a guide.

The term 'strategy', however, did not gain a meaning or usage at the time that led to what it described being seen as a solution to the pressing needs of war. Moreover, there is scant sign that the word altered conduct or thought in this period, let alone that this prospect was considered. Yet, as already argued, that did not mean that there was no strategic dimension to military activity.[71]

24

1

STRATEGIC CONTEXTS IN THE EIGHTEENTH CENTURY

To consider the eighteenth century is to start with the period in which the formal language of strategy began in the West. As a result, it is possible to consider the historical background to the change of practice with the French Revolution and to the analyses offered in the nineteenth century by Jomini and Clausewitz. However, the relevance of these from the perspective of Beijing, Delhi or other non-Western centres, is unclear, while, as argued in the Introduction, the formal language of strategy was not the key element.

Instead, as in other periods, cultural values were highly significant in the conception and implementation of strategy. In the broadest sense, this is true of a world of competing religions in which toleration was generally regarded as weakness and religious warfare or at least conflict as necessary. Animosity was an ingrained background. More specifically, dynastic rivalry, whether of Habsburgs and Bourbons or of Ottomans and Safavids, should be approached in cultural terms, because of the wide-ranging dynamics of prestige and territorial control involved in dynastic considerations.[1]

To adopt a modern functional approach, it can be argued that dynasticism operated as a moderating norm by limiting claims, containing stakes and requiring the regulation of shifts in sovereignty.[2] As a result, dynasticism was an aspect of a rules-based system, one that can be described in terms of 'the law of nations and the usages commonly acknowledged and practised among all nations in Europe'.[3] Moreover, far from being incapable of new concepts, the international system was capable of development and expansion. This was particularly so in Europe where a number of independent states from a similar cultural background were close together. This led to innovations in international relations as in the peace settlement of the Treaty of Westphalia (1648) and, in the late eighteenth century, to the idea for maritime leagues to protect neutral trade from blockades. The strategy was designed to counter Britain's dominant position at sea or, at least, save trade from the more troublesome aspects of Britain's dominant position at sea.[4]

Alongside its practical strengths, however, a dynastically based or linked international system did not always cope well with relations between different cultures, and also, if war avoidance is seen as the goal, did not usually work well within an individual culture. Indeed, the dynastic drive was generally competitive and also, as with Austria in the 1690s–1730s, could readily take precedence over other elements. Wars of succession of one sort or another were the outcome of strategic marriage alliances, but with a greater element of chance involved than for many nineteenth-century expansionist schemes.

Dynastic politics were also specific and contingent and, as such, set very difficult tasks for the strategy of individual monarchs and ruling families. The protection of Hanover for Britain after the accession of the Hanoverian dynasty in 1714 was one of the striking examples, but even more so was the Austrian attempt during the War of the Spanish Succession (1701–14) to incorporate the Spanish Empire.

In addition to competition between the dynasties of different states, the search for status within dynasties, as rulers confronted the reputation of their predecessors, and also between successive dynasties ruling the same state, was in part an aspect of a necessary drive for *gloire*. This search was very much set by the justification for kingship in terms of success in battle, by the general emphasis on the value of reputation, and by the focus on the glory of predecessors.[5] Visual images of past success were to the fore. Philip V of Spain (r. 1700–46) spent time in his palace in Seville where tapestries that are still in place depict the success of the expeditions against North Africa of Charles V, Holy Roman Emperor (Charles I of Spain), in the early sixteenth century. Philip himself was with the army that unsuccessfully invaded Portugal in 1704. Louis XV of France, who did campaign, and Louis XVI, who did not, struggled with the need to match up to the image created by Louis XIV. France helped the thirteen British colonies that became the core of the United States win independence from Britain in 1783, but this brought no benefit to Louis XVI in terms of personal prestige as he never campaigned. The strong association between monarchical prestige and military success was demonstrated by the Qianlong Emperor in his treatise *Yuzhi shiquan ji* ('In Commemoration of the Ten Complete Military Victories'), composed in 1792, a treatise that claimed the Chinese failures against Burma (Myanmar) and Vietnam as successes.

That rulers tended, when they could, to command forces in battle, an integration of political and military leadership that itself could help ensure decisiveness, as with Frederick II 'the Great' (r. 1740–86), contributed greatly to this competition with each other and with the past. The direct interest and personal commitment of rulers were highly significant to the strategic culture, as was the idea of trial by battle in a form of almost ritualised conflict.[6] Royal splendour served, moreover, as the basis of noble splendour. The cult of valorous conflict helped define honour and fame, whether individual, family or collective. In 1734, Philip V claimed that war was necessary for the political stability of the French monarchy, which was a critical comment on Cardinal Fleury,[7] France's leading minister from 1726 to 1743, an elderly cleric who lacked commitment to war, although during his ministry France went to war in 1733 and 1741.

Personal honour and reputation were crucial for commanders,[8] and the related cultural conditioning that made the cult of honour dynamic was central to civil–military relations, limiting bureaucratic processes. Martial values for the élite could be advocated even in states such as Britain that had a more commercial ethos,[9] a process that was to recur in nineteenth-century America. As an aspect of *gloire*, the notion of a place in history is still very much seen today, which, again, serves as a reminder of continuities in strategy and of its historicised character. Many states pride themselves on their military power and on success, past and present.

Another element of continuity was provided by the holding up of the past, in the form of what are treated as discrete episodes with clear lessons, as warnings and also as strategic building blocks. Today, this is the case most notably with 'Munich', 'Suez', 'Vietnam', and now, also, 'Iraq', 'Afghanistan', 'Libya' and 'Syria'. There were obviously equivalents for earlier periods, and they helped guide strategic thought and discussion. For Britain in the eighteenth century, there were many references to earlier eras, notably Elizabeth I's struggle with Spain, while the legacy of the events of the period 1688–1714 proved significant in subsequent decades. In the House of Lords in November 1739, John, Lord Carteret, a talented former diplomat and Secretary of State, then in opposition, both pressed for a strategic focus on gains in the West Indies from Spain and argued that William III (r. 1689–1702), the monarch who was the lodestar of Whig virtue, had understood the logic of this policy.[10] In 1758, the term 'doctrine' was employed in discussing whether Britain was maintaining William's emphasis on keeping the Low Countries (modern Belgium and the Netherlands) out of French control.[11]

This process is readily easy to follow for Britain as there was an extensive debate in print and public about foreign policy, one that reflected the relatively liberal nature of British public culture and the role of Parliament. The situation was similar in the United Provinces (the Netherlands, Dutch Republic), but very different in most states. The particular character of the Maritime Powers (Britain and the United Provinces), however, did not mean that there was not in all states both a governmental and a public process of learning from the past, or, at least, of employing a reading of the past in the discussion of policy. The weight of the past could be highly selective, even if it focused on battles and challenges. The past also proved a moveable lesson. For the Dutch, the formative struggle for independence against Spain from the 1560s was succeeded as a strategic point of reference by the survival from a major and initially successful French assault in 1672. Such episodes proved important in narratives and analyses about domestic and international politics and concerning political and military strategies.

Governmental and public processes of discussion and response were, to a degree, related to the subsequent distinction between strategic thinkers and actors, although, as all actors are thinkers, this is better phrased as strategic writers and actors. Thought cannot be measured by writing, an unhelpful approach that reflects positivist approaches to evidence, as well as intellectual and academic bias. Indeed, during the eighteenth century, a strategic landscape, such as that presented in the iconography of a royal palace and garden,[12] or, differently, conversations during a hunt, shoot or other élite gatherings, represented thought and expression that were more central to the policy-makers than the strategic treatises that tend to attract modern attention and for which there is a search in a quest for Clausewitz's antecedents. By its nature, that remark about centrality is a claim that is impossible to prove, but that does not make it any less significant. It is particularly important not to abstract royal views from the court ideologies and cultures that influenced them and that set the context for their life. Strategy was seen in the enactment of power for identified ends, a process also displayed in royal patronage of art and literature.

For the past, as for today, it is important not to assume monocausal explanations for strategic goals and means. For example, in 1719, when Britain was at war with Spain, albeit allied with France, Charles Delafaye, the perceptive under-secretary in the Northern Department, commented on the plan for an attack on St Augustine, the most important Spanish base in Florida, that it would 'do real service' but also 'perhaps allay' the 'clamour' in Britain over colonial vulnerability.[13]

In terms of the practice of strategy, there were fundamental continuities in military affairs arising from the reliance on men alone as soldiers, the impact in the military of social hierarchies and practices, and, until the nineteenth century, the largely constant nature of economic and environmental contexts, and their consequences for military activity and planning. In particular, the limited productivity of economic activities was a key element. This helps explain the transformative context of large-scale industrialisation.

In addition, the role of climate, weather and seasons was central in tactical, operational and strategic terms. It affected, for example, both the safety of voyages and the availability of fodder. Fodder was necessary both for cavalry and for the draught animals that were crucial for artillery and logistics. Indeed, grass growing at the side of roads was a vital resource and a comment on the logistical capability. This factor did not prevent winter campaigns, but it made these operations more difficult, and thus lessened the chance of a strategy of constant pressure. This was especially so if the winter was combined with bad weather, and the latter was held as an indicator that there would be no campaigning. The springtime start of most campaigns was due not only to grass growing but also both to river levels falling as snowmelt ceased and to the ground no longer being frozen, although, conversely, freezing could make otherwise impassable ground passable. Road surfaces were greatly affected by the weather. In the summer and autumn, the need for action before the winter was a frequent theme. In late 1939, the Germans fixed the timing of their attack on France for the following spring.

Seasonality was a factor that varied across the world, creating constraints that were especially important for foreign forces that were unfamiliar with them, as with the difficulties the Germans encountered in the Soviet Union in late 1941. Monsoon conditions were a major issue, particularly in India where they encouraged winter campaigning and determined maritime power projection. Thus, in 1760, after the Marathas drove the Afghan garrison from Delhi in July, campaigning stopped in the monsoon season while inconclusive negotiations took place, only for the Marathas to advance anew in October. The storming of the Siamese capital, Ayuthia, by Burmese (Myanmar) forces in 1767 was possible only because the lengthy campaign against the city had persisted through two rainy seasons, the soldiers growing their own rice so that the army did not fade away in the meanwhile. This was very much an instance of logistics requiring a particular type of military economy.

The dependence of sailing ships on the winds and the vulnerability of wooden ships, whether wind-powered or rowed, to storms were also key factors linked to the weather. They rendered modern strategic concepts such as control of the sea flawed, if not inappropriate, during this period, and later discussion of the strategic options of any period has to take full heed of technological opportunities and constraints alongside cultural norms. It was certainly possible to evade blockades. Victory at sea required fixing opponents, which was not easy given the dependence of ships on the wind and the fact that it blew in the same direction for all combatants, although the better sailing ships should have been able to catch up with an enemy. Battle avoidance was important. In the early eighteenth century, Spain sought to avoid naval battles and to ensure the flow of the treasure fleets. Moreover, the viability of all naval moves was considered in light of the weather and, therefore, the advancing season. The weather was still a major constraint for the invasion of Normandy in 1944 and for the British reconquest of the Falklands in 1982.

Like conflict on land, an understanding of victory at sea, both in the present and in the past, requires an appreciation that success and strategic effectiveness are not necessarily measured in terms of the ratio of casualties. Indeed, given the difficulties of sinking wooden ships, unless they caught fire after gunpowder was ignited, battles sometimes did not result in any ships being sunk, for example the battle off Ushant between the British and French in 1778. Ships were taken, not sunk.

Like some of the convoy battles with submarines during the battle of the Atlantic in 1940–3, battles that might appear as draws were not necessarily indecisive. Indeed, victory can best be understood in terms of the strategic goals at stake, especially when fleets were being employed for specific missions rather than searching for triumph in battle. Thus, the French navy made one major attempt to challenge English naval predominance in the western Mediterranean during the War of the Spanish Succession, only to be checked at the battle of Malaga in 1704. Although no ships were sunk in the battle, which is therefore considered tactically and operationally indecisive, Malaga was strategically decisive because it helped limit the French fleet from having any significant role in the region.

Goals, both at sea and on land, varied by state and conflict, and are underplayed when the literature's emphasis is on uniformity and focuses either on change for all, notably in the shape of technological development, or on continuity for all, such as the nature of conflict. Thus, the understanding and application of the concept of decisiveness require an appreciation of strategic and operational goals and capabilities. For example, victory could be so hard won that the strategic goals of the defeated side were obtained, as with the French victory over William III at Steenkirk in 1692: William withdrew from the field, but the French abandoned plans for attacking the major fortress of Liège.[14]

Very differently, a successful defensive victory, such as that of Peter the Great of Russia over Charles XII of Sweden at Poltava in 1709, could be followed by a strategic offensive: Frederick the Great was wont to cite Charles's strategy of invading Russia as an instance of the danger of strategic overextension, and Clausewitz also repeatedly emphasised him as an example of overstretch. Charles definitely had insufficient resources. His defeat was followed by Peter's conquest of Estonia, Livonia and Finland, and the overthrow of Charles's protégé in Poland. Linked to goals, strategy was readily apparent in terms of ranking challenges and prioritising commitments. This process could require the military operationalisation of diplomatic objectives, with both elements affected by a high degree of volatility.

Despite the many limitations, there were marked improvements in pre-industrial military capabilities that could enhance strategic and operational opportunities. In particular, new and more effective administrative structures were important. Allowing for their many deficiencies in practice, administrative form and bureaucratic regularity were important to the ability to organise and sustain both mass and activity. Without this form and regularity, standing forces were difficult to maintain other than by adopting *ad hoc* remedies to ensure support. Larger and better supported armies and navies created a capacity to act effectively in more than one sphere simultaneously. At the same time, that itself posed problems. Thus, for the British navy, as in 1778 when France entered the American War of Independence, there was the question of how many warships to keep in home waters and how many to send further away. That is a lasting problem for naval strategy, the issue of concentration of power. It is also one affected by geopolitical and technological contexts. In 1778, the frictions of distance and communications ensured an *ad hoc* decentralised system of decision-making as well as implementation.

The increase in army size was the product of the Crown–aristocracy realignment of the late seventeenth century in Europe, an aspect of a stabilisation after mid-century civil wars also seen in China, India and Turkey. This factor demonstrated the significance of social underpinning and of the politics bound up in that. This realignment was, simultaneously, the foundation of the *ancien régime* (1648–1789) European military, the factor that kept it working,[15] and the demonstration of the significance of domestic strategies for their international counterparts. So also with other states on a comparable trajectory.

There was no necessary strategic outcome to enhanced capability. Instead, the varied political contexts for individual states and their interaction, for example the geopolitical dimension, were crucial. Maria Theresa enunciated a clear and consistent strategy with her focus, as in May 1756, on the defence of the *Erblande*, the Habsburg hereditary lands, notably Austria, and not on what she termed the 'remote parts of her dominions', such as the Austrian Netherlands (Belgium).[16]

The prospects for, and of, alliances encouraged strategic speculation as an aspect of alliance-building. This process can be seen, for example, with the pamphleteers and advice-writers setting out plans for large-scale and wide-ranging action against the Ottoman (Turkish) Empire, for instance, in the sixteenth century. There was no special conceptual vocabulary involved, but this in no way lessened the impact of such suggestions.[17]

In addition to such speculation, there was the continual flow of news, report and rumour,[18] much of it inaccurate. Indeed, the degree of unpredictability in international relations and in strategy led to insistent questions about how best to prepare for conflict and to manage risk. What might be called 'anti-strategy', or preventative strategy, was important, as the easiest forms of prevention were military strength and deterrent alliances. A basic theme was that of preparations for conflict, and, given that a key role of strategy was defence and deterrence, these reports led to pressure for verification by diplomats, military observers and spies. Scenario-planning in this context was a crucial aspect of strategy, as it remains.

Alongside the strategies, capability and dynamics of the state military systems came those of opponents within states. Indeed, the extent to which insurgencies were characterised by distinctive and appropriate strategies is a topic that does not have to wait for discussion of the American War of Independence that broke out in 1775. There is generally only limited material available for considering insurgent strategies, and much of that material comes from the governments being opposed. A key divide was between insurgent groups that essentially wished to keep the central government and its forces away, for example the Jinchuan of western Sichuan, who resisted the Chinese in 1747–9 and 1770–6 and proved very difficult to overcome; and, on the other hand, insurgent groups that sought to operate more widely, including overthrowing the government itself. The latter generally required the seizure of the capital and the defeat of government forces, whereas the first type of insurgency essentially rested on repelling, deterring or avoiding attack. In the case of seeking to seize power, there was also the hope, often justified, that the government would be affected by other commitments, as in China in 1644.[19]

Most states operated in an acutely threatening international order. This was not the case for isolationist Japan, which did not take part in any foreign war during the seventeenth or eighteenth centuries, but it was for established political systems and also for new regimes and for would-be states. Defining interests in this context was inherently dynamic, and changing strategies were an index of this dynamism.

For states as well as non-state actors, strategic elements focused on power politics, but there were also important ideological dimensions. For example, demonstrating the salience of domestic, as well as international, political elements, and the extent to which strategic culture could change, the 'Glorious Revolution' of 1688–9 ensured that Catholic France was regarded in England/Britain as the key strategic and ideological opponent, the two being closely linked. Moreover, this was to a degree that France had not been seen earlier in the century, when the focus had been on Spain until French expansionism changed the situation and perception in the mid-1660s.

The pursuit of security was not simply an external process. Security and strategy were very much domestic as well as international, and both have to be considered as well as their interaction. There was also the question of how best to control military forces. This question involved both the specific issue of loyalty, with the political consequences that might arise, and the more general one of the long-term political and social impact of these forces.

Throughout, a key element for strategy was set by the willingness of rulers, commanders and combatants not only to kill large numbers, but also to accept heavy casualties. Preserving the army was a central strategic priority, an end as well as a means, but there was a greater willingness to take casualties than with some, although by no means all, modern warfare. Moreover, there is a marked contrast between modern individualism and hedonism in at least some cultures, and, on the other hand, earlier concepts of duty and fatalism in a much harsher working environment. The acceptance of casualties was crucial to the bellicosity of the past and to the means of furthering aims, in other words strategy. This was more significant than any response to tactical and technological issues, constraints and opportunities. Furthermore, wars were believed to be not only necessary but also, in at least some respects, desirable. This was a key element in strategic culture and one that impacts war and strategy within total history.

General reflections on the nature of war were relatively uncommon unless expressed in terms of morality. However, including going back to ancient times, more practical remarks preceded the first use of the term 'strategy'. For example, it is instructive to consider the ideas of Henry Lloyd, who developed a critical approach to military thinking, and whose publications indicate enough public interest in the topic to sustain the appearance of a number of books. Lloyd served under Marshal Saxe in the Low Countries in the 1740s, thus providing a personal link between that key French general and thinker of the first half of the century and developing work on war in the second half. Having gone on to serve in the armies of Austria (1758–61) and Brunswick, Lloyd became a Russian major-general (1772) who helped plan the key campaign into the Balkans in 1774, an offensive that led both to the victorious end to the war with the Turks and to the subsequent Russian ability to concentrate forces against the Pugachev rebellion within Russia, an ability that led to its overthrow. Prefiguring Clausewitz, Lloyd emphasised the political context of warfare, as well as the role of 'passion' in the shape of psychological and moral factors.[20] Clausewitz, indeed, in part presented anew themes that had recently been advanced by Lloyd and others. That is a habitual issue with intellectual advances, one that cannot be countered by referring to particular individuals as seminal thinkers.

2

THE STRATEGIES OF CONTINENTAL EMPIRES
1400–1850

As in the modern age with China and Russia, the strength and intentions of continental empires were a matter of great concern not only to
each other but also to the maritime powers. Indeed, despite trium-
phalism at particular moments, there was scant sense other than for a
while in the nineteenth century that geopolitical destiny inevitably lay
with the latter. This perception rested on an assessment of the contemporary situation at the time any assessment was made, but also looked
back to the collective experience of Eurasia, as with Halford Mackinder's
geopolitical reflections in 1904.

That experience was a matter in part of tribal confederations, most
prominently the Huns and the Mongols, moving forward from what
might be termed 'Inner Asia' and attacking the more settled empires in
the prosperous, more geographically peripheral, regions of Eurasia. In
Eurasia and North Africa, the operational and tactical value of cavalry
gave rise to strategic ambition.[1]

At the same time, the more settled empires in Eurasia, empires in the
more prosperous periphery and not in the core areas of steppe and
mountainous 'Inner Asia', competed with each other. Moreover, far
from any clear greater significance for the latter struggles as opposed to
the attacks from the cavalry empires of the Eurasian interior, there were
interrelationships between struggles. These created not so much a
Eurasian strategic space as the need to prioritise across a broad span and
in a situation of some complexity. In particular, in the sixteenth and
seventeenth centuries, the Habsburgs, Ottomans, Safavids and Uzbeks
were involved in interrelated struggles, and these spread to include a

wide range of other forces. Combatants involved ranged from Ireland to Sumatra. Support for the opponents of opponents led England, for example, to back Morocco against Spain during the Anglo-Spanish War in 1585–1604. In turn, Portugal's total defeat in Morocco in 1578, and Spain's commitment to conflict with England and in France and the Low Countries, enabled Morocco to send a force across the Sahara into the Niger Valley in 1590–1. Decisions to fight were understood to have a wide-reaching impact, one that could be followed by Europeans on the newly more accurate world maps they used.

CHINA

Prefiguring aspects of the present situation, China, the leading land power in the world up to the development of their interiors by Russia and the United States in the nineteenth century, was both a 'satisfied' state, in that it had a clear world vision that it appeared able to sustain, and also pursued an expansionist policy designed to leave no doubt about the applicability of this vision. Each element can be seen in the history of Chinese strategy. Moreover, the Chinese had a sense that they dominated, and should dominate, the world. This was inaccurate, but, more generally, their concept of world power was not as a modern commentator would view it. However, there was no need on the part of China under the rule of dynastic empires for a comparable explicit geopolitical theory of land hegemony, a situation that is somewhat different in the case of what to others may appear its present imperialism.

At the same time, there were significant variations between individual Chinese dynasties, and indeed rulers, as well as the impact of other contingent aspects.[2] However, the play of contingency and conjuncture in Chinese power politics is generally underrated due to the tendency to focus on a structural account of Chinese policy, or, at least, on a structural exposition and explanation. Such an account certainly matched Chinese ideology, but it was a less than complete presentation of the situation. There were significant variations within, as well as between, dynasties, variations that need to be incorporated into the discussion of strategic culture. As a more specific instance of differing opinions, the conquest of the Ordos region as a pre-emptive defence was debated in 1547–8. In the event, it was decided not to advance, and the proponent of the policy was executed after a factional struggle.[3] The choice between defensive and offensive responses, at this and other junctures, was at once operational and strategic; the latter not least in so far as failure against the Mongols could have strategic consequences, as it did in the 1440s. These consequences might be short-term, but strategy very much is for the short term as well as the long term.

The Ming dynasty (r. 1368–1644) owed their position to driving out the Mongols, who had conquered China in the thirteenth century, and the Ming were the last Han Chinese dynasty. That background helped explain the strategic significance of the northern frontier and the concern about Mongol revival in the mid-fifteenth century and again in the sixteenth. In each case, the concern was more than justified. A threat-based account of Ming strategy is valid. This can be charted, as also for other periods in Chinese history, in the construction of fortifications. At the same time, this threat alone did not determine the choice between defensive and offensive responses. The destruction of the army at Tumu on 1 September 1449 and the capture of the Yingzong Emperor, after a foolish advance into the steppe, for a while brought to an end a period in which the Ming had launched numerous offensives beyond the Great Wall and taken the war to the Mongols.[4] However, this was dependent upon imperial personality. The Zhengde Emperor (r. 1506–21) was quite aggressive and personally took the field against the Mongols several times. Moreover, the reign of the Wanli Emperor (1573–1620), especially its first three decades, witnessed a significant revival of Ming military power, directed by the emperor's Grand Secretary, Zhang Juzheng.[5] An emphasis on walls, first to protect strategic passes, and then a reconstruction of the Great Wall of the first Qin emperor, was not simply defensive as they were used as a staging area to launch destabilising attacks. The defensive strategy that in part reflected the widespread agrarian rebellions of the 1440s, and was also seen in the acceptance of a loss of control over Dai Viet (northern Vietnam), did not last.

Another key element of strategy was the provision of a defensive buffer by means of maintaining influence through a tributary system. To the Chinese, tributes were designed to ensure stability in a peaceful system of nominal dependence on the emperor. Confirming the succession of foreign rulers ensured, in Chinese eyes, their legitimation as well as their vassalage, and this was an aspect of the Chinese attempt to exploit divisions among their neighbours. Trade was related to tribute in the complex relations with neighbours or near neighbours. The offer of goods by envoys, and the receipt in return of Chinese goods, however, was unstable as it depended on the meaning conveyed by these acts, and, more specifically, relied on each side finding the same value in the goods exchanged.[6]

War avoidance became the central Chinese strategy from the mid-fifteenth century. In theory, China maintained its moral and practical superiority, but in practice the tribute system alleviated tension as with the 1571 treaty with Altan, khan of the Mongols.[7] War avoidance was linked to a failure to give sufficient weight to the military, or at least what turned out to be a failure in the long term.

One major long-term consequence of the revival of the Mongol challenge was that it played a role, possibly the major one, in the failure to sustain the long-range naval operations into the Indian Ocean seen between 1405 and 1433. This is one of the leading counterfactuals – what-ifs and might-have-beens – of history, in that China's lack of the maritime initiative greatly affected the prospects for Portugal's maritime advance from the 1490s. Whereas Arab and Turkish fleets came to the assistance of Indian rulers contesting Portuguese power, albeit unsuccessfully so, there was no such intervention by China. Indeed, Malacca, a key entrepôt for Chinese trade, fell to the Portuguese in 1511 after a bitter struggle without such intervention. The Portuguese did not encounter Chinese warships until near Macao.

In the last iteration of dynastic change, the rise of the Manchu (or Qing) dynasty and its replacement of the Ming in 1644–52, a process in which campaigning, winning allies and legitimation were interlinked strategies of the takeover,[8] encouraged interest in further Chinese expansionism and helped make it possible. The resulting conflicts both countered possible external threats and made it easier to sustain the Manchu presence within China, which was a classic instance of the congruence of international with domestic themes. The awareness of challenge and threat was a key element in Manchu strategy. More generally, there is a balance between positive and defensive reasons for a strategy of expansionism, with the two frequently part of the same equation.

Creating an important link between the seventeenth and eighteenth centuries, the Manchu established a dynamic system willing and capable of subjugating at least some of China's neighbours, and repeatedly fought to expand. In 1680–1760, indeed, China conquered more territory than any other power in the world, principally Taiwan, Mongolia, Tibet and Xinjiang. This expansionism was imperialistic, and for glory and possessions, rather than for resources and trade. Indeed, a cost–benefit analysis would have focused on the costs of conquest and occupation, and the limited economic benefit from the areas conquered. At the same time, such a benefit could have been readily discerned in the shape of protecting core Chinese areas from attack.

Traditionally, the chief characteristic of the Chinese military was a certain remorseless persistence, but the Manchu brought a new dynamic and a greater ability to campaign successfully in the steppe. Thus, they took forward the traditional Chinese strategy of playing off steppe forces in order to win allies and weaken opponents, a strategy that was a way to cope with the scale of the steppe and its seeming intractability.

The Manchu, indeed, created a military system that was in effect a Manchu–Chinese hybrid, as well as having distinctive goals. Impressive in its operational extent, the army was able to act in very different terrains, producing strategic capacity as a result.[9] The ability to deliver power at a great range into Inner Asia matched the situation within the European world: organisational developments, range and capability were more important than military technology itself. These are points that, to a degree, challenge the standard interpretation of military development, especially that of technology-based revolutions.

This ability was at the service of a set of cultural and geographical assumptions, and of the need to revise constantly the empire-building strategy. In a mechanistic interpretation, this was a case of adjusting the strategy to changed realities.[10] However, there is always the risk that such an interpretation ignores the role of cultural assumptions in both the perception of realities and the adjustment, and thus of what is referred to as strategic culture. In particular, on a longstanding pattern, the Chinese were more ambitious and more successful in central Asia than on their southern frontiers. As with the Roman and Russian empires, for which the subject has been studied, the location of garrisons was a reflection of strategic, political and cultural factors, although these cannot be readily distinguished from each other. The major work on Russian strategy, that by John P. LeDonne,[11] focuses heavily and valuably on the location of troops in terms of opportunities and threats, which can be seen in terms of functional and instrumental or ideological factors. As the former were perceived in terms of assumptions, different ideological factors can also be seen in play.

Under the Manchu rulers, the bannermen – Manchu and Mongols who were regarded as more reliable troops – were stationed in northern China, around the centre of authority, Beijing, and down to the Yangtze River, and the garrisons lived in segregated walled compounds. In contrast, the more numerous Han Chinese Green Standard troops, who focused on dealing with rebellions, were stationed all over the country, but with many in the south, where the first permanent garrison of bannermen was not established until 1718. In addition, the generals sent to the southern frontiers were less competent.

In its most significant conflict to the south during the eighteenth century, China was defeated in Burma (Myanmar) in the late 1760s. War with Burma in 1765 broke out over what had hitherto been the buffer zone of the Shan states, but this was less important to China's rulers than eastern Mongolia, which had been contested with the Zunghars in the 1690s, a struggle followed by one with the Zunghars over western Mongolia. The Manchu, indeed, were much more comfortable with the people and cultures of central Asia than with the south. Similarly, Russia, and then the Soviet Union, were to be much more concerned with Europe than the Far East. There was a crucial geographical element in strategic culture.

At the same time, irrespective of Manchu rule, there was no Chinese tradition of sustained attempts at conquest in south Asia. Chinese activity was most apparent in Vietnam, where a revolt in 1429 overthrew only recently established Chinese control. China was to fail anew when it attacked Vietnam in 1788–9[12] and 1979. Whether such disparate campaigns amounted to a continual theme in a strategic culture is open to discussion. The area was certainly not of crucial strategic interest. This remains the case. China today is far more interested in the South China Sea than in Southeast Asia. The maritime routes through the South China Sea have a strategic weight lacking in the land frontiers there. It is also easier to project power by sea.

Strategic prioritisation, itself a product of a number of attitudes and factors, was not the sole issue in respective Chinese failure or success in different areas across history. In addition, there were important environmental and political factors. They presumably were fed back into assumptions and prioritisation, but it is unclear how and how far: the very process of framing tasks is a matter of uncertainty. For reasons of terrain and climate, cavalry, the key Manchu element, could not function adequately on the southern borders, while the heavily forested environment there was very difficult for large-scale military operations and certainly caused delays that exacerbated logistical issues. Disease also proved a crippling problem in operations in Myanmar.

In addition, the military organisation and achievement of Myanmar was greatly improved in the 1750s and 1760s by its dynamic new ruler, Alaung-hpaya. He focused on campaigning against Siam (Thailand), a pattern that was to be repeated in the 1780s, while, in the early nineteenth century, the borders towards British India were more significant for Myanmar than those with China. Plans by the Qianlong Emperor (r. 1736–95), who strongly felt the humiliation of failure in Myanmar, to try to reverse the defeat were abandoned. This was in part because the southern frontiers were not of central strategic interest to China.

The alternative opportunities that were not pursued are always striking when considering strategy. The Mongols, as a result of major and sustained efforts, after they had conquered China in the thirteenth century, had (unsuccessfully) pursued maritime expansion against Japan (twice) and Java. In contrast, Manchu goals by sea were restricted to nearby Taiwan, gained in 1683. There was no attempt to invade Japan as a counter to earlier, eventually unsuccessful, Japanese expansionism into Korea in the 1590s, nor, on land, any wish to repeat the brief frontier war with Russia in 1683–9 and to drive the Russians back beyond Lake Baikal, thus repeating the success and range shown against the Zunghars. As a result, the Manchu heartland was not to be protected and expanded to the north and north-west, as it had been to the south by the conquest of Ming China, although expansion to the north and north-west was less attractive as it would have been across barren terrain. The Mongols had not sought to conquer Siberia.

Like the later Ming, and the Mughals in India, the Manchu maintained coastal navies and were not interested in oceanic power projection. Their strategies were continental in nature. Indeed, to a considerable degree, Manchu expansion in central Asia in the eighteenth century and

Mughal operations in Afghanistan in the seventeenth both arose from attempts to stabilise key frontiers including integrating their enemies within the imperial framework. Similarly, in India, after the marked decline of Mughal power, the Marathas in the mid-eighteenth century sought to secure the Indus frontier against invasion via or from Afghanistan, being badly defeated at the battle of Third Panipat in 1761 as a consequence.

In the process of framing tasks, the role of determined and successful leadership is readily apparent. The personal determination of the Kangxi (r. 1662–1723) and Qianlong emperors was crucial to the defeat of the Zunghars. Both made it a personal crusade and pushed hard those generals who were more hesitant about campaigning on the steppe. The latter, indeed, was a risky proposition, in part for military reasons, including logistics, but also for political ones focused on the unrelia-bility of local support. The Kangxi Emperor wanted victory, and he appreciated the transient nature of the possession of territory, as opposed to the destruction of the opposing army. In turn, the Qianlong Emperor, who was well versed in dynastic history, wished to surpass the achieve-ments of his grandfather, the Kangxi Emperor, by putting an end to the frontier problem. He essentially did so, notably on the steppe.

The importance of personality is illustrated by the Qianlong Emperor's predecessor and successor, as neither was so ambitious nor successful. The Yongzheng Emperor (r. 1723–35) launched only one expedition against the Zunghars and did not persist after its defeat at Hoton Nor in 1731, which suggests that, had he ruled for long, the Zunghars might have revived and expanded. Neither was this reign characterised by major military initiatives. This point, however, raises the questions of assessment and of how best to characterise strategy. The Yongzheng Emperor's financial reforms laid the basis for the Qianlong Emperor's military successes; each was a strategy towards a policy of triumph. The Yongzheng Emperor established a Grand Council to facil-itate the conduct of the conflict with the Zunghars, and its remit was expanded under his successor in order to receive and analyse monthly reports of grain prices across China, and thus guide the use of stockpiled grain.[13] This is similar to earlier developments in logistical capability, for example the Grand Canal from the Yangtze River to Beijing, so as better to mobilise and support large forces.[14]

Until the mid-1750s, the Zunghars were a significant challenge to the Chinese position in Mongolia and Tibet, as well as to the Chinese and, more particularly, ruling Manchu sense of success and destiny. There was also an important religious dimension in the shape of competing authority over Buddhism between China and the Zunghars, a dimension that echoed that of rivalries between Shi'a and Sunni and between Protestant and Catholic powers in the worlds of Islam and Christianity respectively. To Chinese commentators, China's eventual success made it the proven recipient of heavenly grace.[15]

The Chinese appear to have been most concerned to avoid Russian support for the Zunghars, which would have been destabilising for China's position in the steppes by making it overextended. This point underlines the degree to which context is dependent on contingency, in this case the context, of overextension or not, on the consequences of contingent international relations.

In the event, both Russia and China sought stability, rather than the more unpredictable strategy of using the Zunghars to pursue gains at the expense of the other. This stance was linked, on the part of each empire, to a politics of prudence and, on that of China, to a strong desire for a stable and protective world order. With the centres of power of the two empires, St Petersburg and Beijing, far removed, and neither challenging the ideological role of the other, as rival Muslim and Christian empires did, it was possible, as well as desirable, for China and Russia both to co-exist and to pursue other goals, including those on other frontiers.

For China, under the Manchu and more generally, as also for other states, the extent to which strategic consistency is problematic challenges attempts to suggest a single strategic culture or, a very different point, to point to geopolitical determinism. So also if the nineteenth century is considered, when coastal threats from the Europeans and Japan can be juxtaposed with instability on landward frontiers, and both were overshadowed by rebellion within China. In practice, the situation repeatedly returns us to the realm of history, in the shape of considering the role of choice in developments, the impact of the past, its remaking under the stress of circumstances, ideas and personalities, and their repeated and inconstant interplay. Both contextual and contingent factors play a major role.

TURKEY

Whereas the Chinese Empire, alongside its changing borders and periods of division, notably in the twelfth and thirteenth centuries, had a core cohesion and continuity, this was not the case in India, where the Mughals in the seventeenth century created a wide-ranging state very different to the situation in the recent centuries. So also in the Middle East. There had been no empire ruling Anatolia, Syria, Egypt and the Balkans since Byzantium at its height in the seventh century. Thus, alongside elements of continuity also seen in comparable cases, the Ottoman Empire (Turkey for short) was a new empire. For its strategy, functional and ideological factors again played a role, as did the need to reconcile priorities on different frontiers and the interests of specific groups within the empire. Linked to an active process of information-gathering that was readily apparent from the sixteenth century, Turkish forces could be deployed in accordance with a strategy based on a considered analysis of intelligence and policy options. The period has been seen as witnessing the formation of Ottoman grand strategy. 'This involved the formulation of an imperial ideology and a universalist vision of empire; the collection of information both within and outside the borders of the Empire . . . the elaboration of a foreign policy and propaganda . . . and the mobilisation of . . . resources and military power in the service of imperial policy.'[16]

The product of largely continuous warfare and expansion, the extensive Turkish Empire from its outset lacked obvious boundaries on most of its frontiers and had a range of opponents, issues, opportunities and problems to address. There was scant clarity over how to determine choices. The example of previous generations was important, as with that of Mehmed II, the conqueror of Constantinople in 1453 who had pressed on to focus on the Balkans.

There were also army-based strategies, in the sense of campaigning in order to satisfy the desire of the army for activity and benefits. This had a social component in providing land for those who served as cavalry. Disappointed fief-holders were a major cause of rebellion in the 1600s. There was no naval equivalent, despite the extent to which the empire surrounded the eastern Mediterranean. Troops could refuse to campaign, as in 1518 against the Safavids of Persia.

In cultural terms, religion was significant in Turkish strategy. On a pattern already seen in the fifteenth century, there appears to have been more enthusiasm for campaigning against Christendom in the 1520s than against the (fellow) Sunni Mamluks of Egypt and Syria in 1516–17. However, total victory over the latter led to Selim, having gained control over Mecca and Medina in 1517, assuming the title of Servant of the Two Noble Sanctuaries. Making such choices and winning success were important to internal stability. In the latter case, Selim I (r. 1512–20) seized power as a result of his father's military failure and then won a number of major victories, while Suleiman the Magnificent (r. 1520–66), who led his army on thirteen campaigns, did not have to face coups because of his train of success. Turning against Hungary in 1526 offered his forces loot: he moved north in response to army complaints in 1525 about a lack of campaigning, and thus of plunder.

Anxiety played a key role in Turkish strategy. This element tends to be overlooked in a subsequent account that presents what was indeed a long period of expansion, but that is a misleading approach to Turkish strategy. For example, the successful invasion of Serbia in 1458 by the grand vizier, Mahmud Pasha Angevolić, arose in part due to the success of the Hungarian protégés among the Serbian regents. Similarly, the concerted attacks of Hungary and Venice on the Turks in 1463 led to rapid responses by the Turks. So also with the response to the Safavids and their Shi'a millenarianism of the early sixteenth century, a response that challenged Turkish control over eastern Anatolia. Thus, rebellion in this area in 1511–12, led by Shah Kulu, a Safavid proselytiser, was followed by the Turkish attack on the Safavids in 1514. Selim I's invasion of Syria in 1516 was a consequence of its Mamluk ruler aligning with the Safavids.

Religious factors could make it harder, but by no means impossible, to consolidate success through alliance. Such consolidation was a vital aspect of strategy in which military achievements were used to win support which, in turn, consolidated this success. This process for example was used in eastern Anatolia in 1515–16, with Selim I winning over the Kurdish chiefs who had been alienated by the Safavid preference for direct control. This political success was related to victories, with a two-way dependency.[17] So also in the struggle between Russia and the Crimean Tatars over the independent Muslim khanate of Kazan from the late fifteenth century until final Russian success in the 1550s.

Geography was certainly an element in prioritisation and in the response to it. In particular, there were major problems in campaigning against Persia, as there also were for its other neighbours or near neighbours: the Uzbeks, the Mughals and Russia. As far as bases were concerned, Baghdad was 1,334 miles from Constantinople, compared with Belgrade's 597. Moreover, there was no sea and river route to Iraq comparable to the Black Sea and the Danube and Dniester rivers to ease campaigning and logistics. Moreover, distance, exacerbated by logistical problems, made unworkable Turkish plans to advance to Astrakhan, conquered by Ivan the Terrible in 1556, both to drive back Russia and to act thence against Persia.[18] More generally, distances, as well as logistical issues, meant that the Turks preferred battle. Triumph in one would lessen the need to face lengthy sieges in order to capture fortresses. However, as the Turks found against Persia in 1514 after Chaldiran and against Austria in 1532, this gave much of the initiative to opponents who in both cases avoided battle. A military context of strategy emerges in this instance, with goals having to take note of practicalities.

Conversely, it was easier for Persian rulers to campaign against the Turks in modern-day Iraq than in central Asia, Afghanistan or even India. This strategic asymmetry served as a key element in helping frame the conflict between Turks and Persians, but did not dictate its course. Such strategic asymmetries are more generally important. In turn, in part under the pressure of Persian expansionism or, at least, issues, the Turks focused on war with Persia in 1578–90, 1603–18, 1623–39, 1730–6 and 1743–6, in each case turning down opportunities to campaign against Christian European powers by, for example, intervening in the Thirty Years' War (1618–48), the War of the Polish Succession (1733–5) and the War of the Austrian Succession (1740–8).

While frequently ambitious in their goals, the Turks showed a realism in the assessment of what was achievable, such that real limits were understood.[19] Yet this assessment was mediated through personal and factional rivalries, as with the assassination in 1579 of Mehmed Pasha Sokollu, the grand vizier, who was not enthusiastic about war with Persia. Instead, a war party came to the fore. Similarly, the interests and ambition of the Köprülü dynasty of grand viziers were important to Turkish expansionism from the early 1660s to the total failure of the advance on Vienna in 1683.

The situation in Turkey became more volatile due to the repeated experience of serious failure from 1683 onwards, notably at the hands of Austria in 1686–9, 1695–7 and 1716–18, failure leading to the overthrow of sultans in 1703 and 1730. The eighteenth and, even more, the nineteenth centuries were to be seen as ones of Ottoman decline, with strategy increasingly 'done to' the empire, rather than being done by it; an aspect of strategy as relative. However, the reactive strategy of the weak is also strategy. In particular, Turkey had to confront a resurgent Austria and a much stronger Russia. Each had faced serious domestic commitments in the early seventeenth century and then more pressing external commitments, but, having overcome these, focused increasing attention on Turkey from the late seventeenth century.

An absence of new conquests and success in battle acted as a powerful constraint for the Turks, causing a loss of prestige as well as a lack of pillage and fresh land to distribute. Alongside political tensions, the inability to pay the army reduced the sultan's control and led to rebellions. In a significant shift in the capacity for implementation, there was an increased need to turn to provincial militias as well as to forces raised by local strongmen, who were important to a more general crisis in command practices.[20] As a related point, but at a different level and tempo, one that created a dynamic that contrasted with that in the past, the Turks were now a settled society and developed state, and no longer the apparently inexorable people that had terrified Westerners in the fifteenth and early sixteenth centuries.

Whether on the offensive or on the defensive, it was necessary for the Turks to consider their range of possible commitments. For example, in 1715, the Turks were encouraged to turn against Venice by the absence of problems elsewhere: Russia had been beaten and there was peace with Persia, which was under grave pressure from Afghan rebellions that led in 1722 to the overthrow of the Safavid dynasty. Looking forward to the opportunity to regain the Morea, only recently lost to Venice and thus more prominent in strategic terms, the Turks were also angered by the refuge granted by Venice to Montenegrins who had unsuccessfully rebelled in 1711 against Turkish control.

In turn, the Austrian ruler, Charles VI, allied with Venice in 1716 because he was no longer anxious about a weakened France, Austria's recent opponent. France then was affected not only by defeat in the War of the Spanish Succession (1701–14) but also by the political instability that followed the accession of the infant Louis XV in 1715. Then and on other occasions, Turkish ministers and foreign envoys, each group seeking a Turkish focus on one opponent, tried to ensure peace for Turkey elsewhere.[21] Alongside the tendency to write the Turks off, it is appropriate to note not only considerable resilience, notably defeating Austria in 1737–9, but also a willingness to launch conflict, as when Russia was attacked in 1787. The last, however, proved a flawed strategy as Russia was able to repel the attack and, instead, to turn to what became a potent offensive. As in the 1768–74 war, the Turks were not able to hold the Danube and its fortresses against Russian attack. This might suggest some sort of parallel with the eventual failure of the Roman Empire to hold its Danube frontier, but there is no significant one: drawing strategic lessons across time can be highly misleading.

The conceptualisation of strategy took time. In the 1850s, the Turks began to use the term *sevkülceys*, the dictionary meaning of which is 'strategy' in the sense of managing the troops. The Turks had employed more general terms, such as 'art of war' or 'business of war', for strategy earlier.

RUSSIA

As with China, Russian strategy was characterised by 'the application of overwhelming force' to specific objectives, creating a perception of strength and invincibility'[22] and aiding the success both of military operations and of their fulfilment in a new political order. Adam Smith observed:

> Whoever examines, with attention, the improvements which Peter the Great [r. 1689–1725] introduced into the Russian empire, will find that they almost all resolve themselves into the establishment of a well-regulated standing army. It is the instrument which executes and maintains all his other regulations. That degree of order and internal peace, which that empire has ever since enjoyed, is altogether owing to the influence of that army.[23]

However, in focusing on military force, that approach underplays a key element of Russian strategy, one of seeking to keep challenges separate.

This strategy, which was very much the case with the sequential campaigning against Germany and Japan seen in the Second World War, reflected an awareness of the strategic landscape. In this, the legacy of the past was crucial, just as it was for Stalin looking back to the Russian Civil War of 1918–21. The Romanovs, like the Manchu and, later, like the Communists in both Russia and China, gained power as a result of a fundamental crisis, one that had linked insurrections to attacks from abroad. That this process occurred in the seventeenth century, albeit in the 1610s, and not further back in time, helped ensure the prominence of the memory, notably in the determination to defeat Poland and Sweden, both of which had intervened then in the Russian 'Time of Troubles'. The same was true for the Bourbons, albeit in the 1590s for France and the 1700s–1710s for Spain, and for the Hanoverians in Britain in the 1710s.

In Russia, the Romanovs had been the key beneficiaries of over-coming this threat of invasion and insurrection, whereas, in China, it was first the Ming who overthrew the invader, the Mongol, and later the Manchu, the invader, who rose to power through the combination of invasion and insurrection. In each case there was an awareness of the past. Indeed, such a 'deep history' was more generally true for dynastic systems and for ones that grounded their legitimacy upon the reality and presentation of continuity.

The challenge of the 1600s–1610s might have appeared very distant after the consolidation of Romanov power under Michael (r. 1613–45) and the large-scale military activity, especially against Poland and Sweden, under Alexis (r. 1645–76), activity that had brought the gain of Smolensk, Kiev and eastern Ukraine. Ended by the 1667 Truce of Andrusovo, which brought to an end a war begun (or rather resumed) in 1654, this indicated the ability of *ancien régime* warfare to deliver decisive results.

However, this challenge recurred in the 1700s. Heavy defeat in 1700 at Narva at the hands of Charles XII of Sweden was followed by his overthrow of Peter the Great's alliance system with Charles's conquest of Poland and his replacement as king there in 1704 of Peter's ally, Elector Augustus II of Saxony, by his own protégé, Stanislaus Leszczyński. Repeated victories by Swedish forces over Polish-Saxon armies, however, demonstrated the difficulties of translating victory into political outcomes and the consequent need to win in order to maintain control of the situation. The intractable Swedish intervention in Polish politics underlined both the role of choice in strategy and its unpredictable consequences. Then, in 1708, Charles invaded Russia in combination with Ivan Mazepa, the rebellious *hetman* of the Cossacks, thus reopening an issue of major concern in the 1640s–1660s and the 1680s.

Charles's disastrous invasion, which culminated in a heavy defeat by Peter at Poltava in 1709, a defeat that led to the destruction of the army with him, can be differently interpreted, and this throws light on some of the issues involved in strategy, and, therefore, the problems that are inherent aspects of its assessment. In the case of Sweden, the most popular explanation of Charles's defeat has been that of a lack of resources, both with regard to Russia and more generally in the face, during the Great Northern War (1700–21), of a coalition of hostile forces, albeit with differing members apart from the lodestar of Russian animosity. Yet, this account can be qualified by drawing attention to strategic choices, an approach that is also relevant when considering other discussions of strategic capability and asymmetry in terms of resources. In the case of Sweden, the use of a long-running defensive strategy to protect the Baltic provinces failed as it led to a reduction in the resource base. In contrast, an offensive strategy to protect those provinces, rather than campaigning into Poland, would have offered differing outcomes for Swedish and Russian resources.

Separately, Charles XII won or lost his battles when the major part of the Swedish armed forces was elsewhere. While understandable in terms of imperial extent, this hardly represented an efficient concentration of power. Charles certainly dissipated his resources. Whether these were sufficient for the task at hand is more unclear. The case that they actually were insufficient in the long run is quite strong, but that is less clear specifically in 1709. Concentration of power was an issue also in other Swedish wars, for example that of Gustav III with Russia in 1788–90. It related to central questions of prioritisation for all major powers, including Russia repeatedly, Britain, China, France under Napoleon, and Germany during the world wars.

Even after Poltava, Charles continued to pose a threat to Russia, for he fled to Turkey and played a role in court politics there. He helped direct Turkey against Peter, who was defeated in the subsequent Russo-Turkish

War at the river Pruth in 1711. Peter's invasion of the Turkish Empire was another instance of a lack of concentration of power, as Russia was still involved in the Great Northern War. The outcome, however, was crucial, as Peter was able to negotiate a settlement with the Turks and thus refocus on Sweden.

Peter's defeat, like Turkish success against Venice in 1715, rapidly conquering Venice's territories in Greece, indicated the difficulty with reading strategic options in terms of the run of recent military success, which had been very much against the Turks during the war of 1683–97. So also in 1737–9, when the Turks did much better against Austria than they had done in 1716–18. Turkish success against Russia in 1711 did not serve as a predictor of the situation over the following wars between the two powers.

The crises for Russia in 1708–11 might seem an irrelevant memory as a result of Peter's overrunning of much of the Swedish overseas empire, such that, when the Great Northern War came to an end in 1721 with the Treaty of Nystad, Russia very much appeared the rising power: under the treaty, Russia annexed Estonia and Livonia and returned the major part of Finland. The development of a navy, more-over, made Peter's gains and reputed schemes appear more threatening.

Nevertheless, Russian anxieties about the present and future continued from the 1730s to draw on concerns about the past. In 1733, Russian military intervention in Poland was primarily in order to prevent the election as king of Stanislaus, who had been driven out by Peter the Great after Poltava. The strategic threat to Russia was clear at the inter-national level, where it was alliance politics that provided the crucial equations of strength and the sphere for competition. In the late 1730s, bold Russian schemes at the expense of the Turks collapsed, not so much due to military difficulties, for Russia was increasingly successful, more so than in the 1711 conflict, but because of the breakdown of the supporting diplomatic coalition as, encouraged by France, Austria made peace with the Turks in 1739.

Russian policy-makers were concerned that a hostile Poland might seek to revise territorial losses to Russia in the seventeenth century, losses that included Kiev, eastern Ukraine and Smolensk, and might co-operate with Sweden and Turkey in opposing Russia. These concerns remained, with France trying to operate such an alliance in the 1730s and early

1740s. Louis XV was son-in-law to Stanislaus. This effort was revived with the French *secret du roi* policy of the 1750s–1770s and, subsequently, with French, and then British, opposition to Russian expansionism in the 1780s, the early 1790s and in the nineteenth century.

Looking towards the often paranoid anxieties of Soviet communism, Russian concerns thus rested on a basis of real plans and hopes on the part of others. Thus, George I of Britain had tried in 1719–21 to put together a European league to drive Russia from its Baltic gains, and had endeavoured in 1716–17 to get Russian troops out of Germany and Denmark. In 1790–1, the British government sought to organise another league, again in an unsuccessful attempt to make Russia return wartime territorial gains. However, these concerns were extrapolated by the Russians into a more fixed pattern of threat. Moreover, this was one that was located not only in terms of Russian anxieties but also with reference to a strong and growing feeling of entitlement to dominate eastern Europe. In opposition to defeated Sweden, weak Poland, Muslim Turkey and distant France, Russia, at least in the person of Alexis and even more clearly under his son Peter the Great, felt that it had a destiny and a right to be the dominant power. This attitude continues to the present, as in Vladimir Putin's strategy towards Ukraine, the Caucasus and the Baltic republics.

In contrast, following a short and episodic conflict in which the Chinese had driven the Russians from the Amur Valley in the 1680s, a verdict the Russians accepted with the Treaty of Nerchinsk in 1689, the two empires did not clash at all in the eighteenth or early nineteenth centuries. Indeed, Russian expansionism against China was not resumed until the late 1850s. Following the conquest of Kazan in 1552, Russia itself had made formidable gains in Siberia during the late sixteenth and seventeenth centuries, and there were to be Russian acquisitions in the mid- and late nineteenth century, at the expense of China, and, far more, in central Asia. In addition, the ability of Russia, despite its lack of a good Pacific port, to project power across the north Pacific to Alaska in the eighteenth century throws further light on Russian capability.[24]

Looked at differently, this capability appears irrelevant given Chinese strength in the period. In Russian operations in the Aleutian Islands, their relative numerical strength and the benefit of warships were aided by the contribution of firearms and the savage impact of smallpox on the local population, factors that had already been the case with Russian expansion in Siberia from the 1580s. These operations provided no indication of what would have happened against more populous and powerful China, but the situation might have been different had Russia intervened in the islands to the north of Honshu, the main island of Japan, as the Japanese government indeed feared with regard to the island of Hokkaido, where Japanese colonialism was at the expense of the indigenous Ainu population.

Alongside strong feelings of hostility to Turkey and Islam, the Russian élite, however, lacked any sense of Russia as an Asian power involved in a struggle for dominance with China, while the hostility towards Japan shown from the late nineteenth century was totally absent earlier. The spatial preponderance of dominions east of the Urals did not match Russian assumptions for there was a focus on Russia's part on Europe. For a long time, for example, no effort was made to repeat the intervention in Persia in 1722–3 by Peter the Great. In 1761, a British diplomat noted that 'the Russian sovereigns, instead of taking the fairest opportunity, during the troubles of Persia, to erect a mighty, Asiatic empire, have turned their views wholly upon Europe'.[25] Moreover, the means of strategy was deliberative and accretionary, rather than the bold advances seen with Peter. Thus, new lines of Russian forts were added as both ambitions and the settlements to substantiate them advanced southward in central Asia from Russia's existing possessions. Rather than extensive conquests in central Asia or the Far East in the eighteenth century, it was more plausible to think that Russia could have played its relationship differently with the other key player in the region, the Zunghar confederation of Xinjiang. Instead, Russia provided the Zunghars with no help against China.

For Russia strategy, or what would later be termed *strategiia*, was largely political, a matter of keeping potential opponents separate and of exploiting the ability to focus on individual ones, a policy seen in the Second World War with no attack on Japan until war with Germany had ended in 1945. Under Peter the Great, the invasion of the Turkish Empire in 1711 followed the crushing defeat of Charles XII at Poltava in 1709, while the successful end of the Great Northern War with Sweden in 1721 was to be succeeded in 1722–3 by successful Russian campaigning in the eastern Caucasus and northern Persia. In turn, Persian revival under Nadir Shah led Russia to return gains in 1735 in order to try to ensure that Nadir did not settle with the Turks. He, however, did so in 1736, which put Russia, then beginning a conflict with the Turks, in a far more difficult strategic situation than would otherwise have been the case. Fortunately for Russia, it succeeded in bringing Austria into the war in 1737 and the Turks concentrated on that enemy.

So also with Frederick the Great's need in the 1740s for Austria to focus on Bavaria, France and Spain, rather than Prussia, and his wish during the Seven Years' War to force opponents to separate peace agreements. This wish encouraged him to focus on the most vulnerable, Austria,[26] with strategy thus arising from the international context. In the event, far from Austria being forced to a separate peace, as it had been twice in the 1740s, it continued fighting Prussia, and it was the most potent opponent, Russia, that changed policy after the accession of Peter III in 1762.

Strategic success did not always require formal hostilities. Instead, intimidation and influence could work for Russia with both Poland and Sweden, although different methods were used and at times these techniques very much failed. Against Sweden, Russian strategic capability was very different to that in the conflicts between the two powers in the sixteenth and seventeenth centuries. The deployment, once a base was established in St Petersburg in 1703, of galley-borne Russian troops in the eighteenth century was a challenge to Swedish security, including that of the capital, Stockholm, a challenge that became an important aspect of Baltic power politics. This was very different to the earlier capacity to attack only Sweden's Baltic provinces. Aside from wars between the two powers, there were also frequent threats of Russian attack, for example in 1749 and 1772, as Russia sought to affect or direct Swedish policy. The ability to affect, or seek to affect, policy by means of intimidation linked strategy and the flow of international relations, giving a point to military preparedness, and ensuring that war was not the only measure of strategy.

Russian policy was rather like Chinese in that the pace of expansionism varied by individual ruler. In the case of Russia, it is easier than with China to note the role of court factionalism, in large part because there were foreign envoys able, and eager, to report on the matter and keen to negotiate, sustain or overthrow alliances. This process was not matched with China, which did not operate within a pattern of international alliances. Thus, under Peter II (r. 1727–30), alliance with Austria and Prussia was supported by a ministry that was hostile to much of the legacy of both Peter the Great and Catherine I (r. 1725–7). In turn, British links, both commercial and political, became more prominent in Russia from the mid-1730s, only to end for a while with the Seven Years' War.

Foreign envoys were linked to prominent Russian figures, each seeking to influence the other. A somewhat overly factionalised account of Russian policy was presented as a result, but this account indicated the extent to which rivalries between ministers and other figures did indeed largely play out in terms of diplomatic alignments and the related strategies. Military events proved a major part of this politics. Foreign commentators also speculated on which frontier was regarded as more sensitive, and thus on Russia's likely strategy.[27]

AUSTRIA

As with other far-flung empires, individual Austrian lobbies and minis-ters were associated with an emphasis on specific geographical areas and, as a result, with particular approaches towards their interdependence. At the same time, more was involved. The peace treaties of 1713–14 reflected the significant downplaying of past imperial and Spanish dynastic policies and the emergence of a geopolitical approach to war and diplomacy that centred on regional challenges.[28] Thus, in 1718, the Austrians abandoned their successful war with the Turks in order to cope with the crisis created in Italy by Spanish expansionism. Sequential conflict, a form of staggering threats or geopolitics in a time sequence, was important to their strategy, as it had earlier been for other empires such as that of Rome. So also was an adroit combination of hard and soft power.[29] At the same time, the role of the dynastic theme in Austrian strategic goals and methods was particularly distinct.

As with many other empires then, before and since, the military was integral to the process of focusing on specific areas, and not separate from it, or charged only with implementation. Thus, Prince Eugene, the president of the Council of War, was identified in the 1720s and 1730s with attempts to protect recent gains from the Turks by strengthening fortress-cities and building up local militias, and with a diplomatic strategy. The latter focused on developing good relations with Britain,

Prussia and Russia. Moreover, Eugene sought to further this goal by means of having protégés, several from a military background, appointed as diplomats, and also by pursuing a personal correspondence with diplomats. This process extended to military figures who served other rulers and were judged appropriate as a means to influence policies and thus give effect to strategy.[30] More generally, the use of military figures as diplomats serves as a reminder of the mistake of thinking of the military as necessarily a distinctly occupational group and lobby.

In turn, in the 1720s and 1730s, there were alternative prescriptions for Austrian power, as there had long been for the Habsburg rulers. A strategy of co-operation with France was pushed particularly hard by the Chancellor, Count Sinzendorf, one of co-operation with Spain by the Marquis of Rialp, and a Catholic, authoritarian stance hostile to German Protestant princes by Count Schönborn, each also major office-holders.[31] These were strategies designed to serve the policy of dynastic interests, notably aggrandisement but, at the very least, security. These strategies had implications that were defined, or at least affected, by the probabilities of particular enemies and allies. Geographical priorities were in part a matter of responses to an assessment of the threat environment. Strategy had to adapt to the dynamic character of this assessment, with offensive and defensive priorities changing accordingly, but also being adopted in an attempt to shape this very dynamism and to reflect political exigencies. Generals were participants in the continued struggle of military politics and pursued approaches to campaigning based on whose interest their ambition allied them with.[32]

Austria had to face attempts at co-operation by its opponents as well as the consequences for such co-operation arising from its size and location. Thus, in the Thirty Years' War (1618–48), as in 1703–4 during the War of the Spanish Succession, there was attempted co-operation against Austria with hostile advancing Hungarians, in the first case by Bohemian rebels and in the second by Bavaria;[33] and similar efforts were made on other occasions. Linked to this, France's concept of an Eastern alliance system proved highly adaptable. Developed against the Habsburgs in the early sixteenth century, with the Turks and the German Protestants playing the key alliance roles, leading to a crisis for Emperor Charles V in 1552, this concept subsequently also encompassed, or sought to include, Denmark, Sweden, Poland, Russia and Hungarian rebels.

In the eighteenth century, this strategy changed as France's international position altered, but the strategy also explained military moves. The dispatch of a French squadron to the Baltic in 1739 was designed to encourage a Swedish attack on Russia, which was then allied to Austria, and that of French forces to attack the Habsburg heartland in 1741 was seen as a way to keep Prussia and Saxony in the French alliance system. As a consequence, a key element for Austria was that of thwarting these moves and possible moves. In this strategy, at once reactive and proactive, there was no separation between military and political dimensions. Campaigning was primarily intended to strengthen or weaken alliances.[34]

Aside from resulting attempts at knock-out blows, diversionary attacks were a prime strategic resource. Thus, in November 1746, during the War of the Austrian Succession, Austrian forces invaded Provence in southern France from northern Italy. Encouraged by the British, and supported by their navy, the invasion was in part mounted to divert French efforts from the Low Countries.

The principal change in Austrian strategy, as in that of China, was one that arose from alterations in rulers. As a legacy of his struggle, as a second son, to take over the Spanish Habsburg inheritance which he claimed as Charles III during the War of the Spanish Succession, Charles VI (r. 1711–40) focused on the Mediterranean and, in particular, proved willing to go on listening to advisers, such as Rialp, who had served him before he succeeded his elder brother, Joseph I (r. 1705–11). This concern with Spain, more longstandingly with Italy, and with the significance of both when Austria was involved in alliances,[35] was not to characterise Charles's daughter and successor, Maria Theresa (r. 1740–80), and, even more, her son, Joseph II (r. 1780–90). Instead, Joseph in particular responded to the opportunities created by Polish and Turkish weakness as well as to the need to adapt to the strength and ambitions of Prussia and Russia.

This refocusing on eastern Europe was aided by the willingness of the Italian powers and Spain to accept a territorial settlement with Austria, notably with the Treaty of Aranjuez, in 1752, one that ensured that there was no conflict in Italy between 1748 and 1792. Thus, strategic parameters were again set by international needs and opportunities, each of which had a highly contingent character.

Defeat at the hands of Prussia in the early 1740s led to a major attempt to revive and strengthen the Austrian state and military, and thus to be prepared for whatever challenge occurred; an attempt that was to be more successful and urgent than that following defeat by Prussia in 1866, although in both cases new alliance partners proved important. This was an aspect of strategy that was on a continuum including the more specifically military policy of preparing and maintaining fortifications, but also fiscal reform, institutional reorganisation and the gathering of information. The strengthening of the military involved a structural process of reform designed to raise, support and use greater numbers. These changes made it possible to envisage more wide-ranging commitments, for example the planning for war with both the Turks and Prussia in 1790, as well as to deploy larger field forces, such as those that thwarted the Prussian invasions of Bohemia in 1778 and 1779.

There had been an earlier attempt, under Charles VI, at strengthening the state after the War of the Spanish Succession, one in particular using protectionism to develop trade and industry. This strategy clashed with the British governmental attempt to develop trade with the *Erblande* in order to make it part of an informal empire of British trade, a strategy, pursued without success by Britain in the late 1730s, that was designed to have direct consequences for power politics.

The need to reconcile a large range of far-flung commitments was more pressing for Austria than for states of a smaller scale, which raises the repeated issue of the relationship between greater state size and more acute problems of strategy. Moreover, the degree to which that problem encouraged the exercise of strategy provided another instance of the process by which the issues and problems of imperial governance more generally encouraged a search for new governmental solutions and political languages. This was definitely seen with the British Empire.

Charles Ingrao's thoughtful analysis of Austrian policy is based on the thesis that the government sought to create and maintain secure and stable buffer zones rather than pursuing extensive conquests in any specific direction, and that immediate needs dominated the situation.[36] This account finds strategy in geopolitical needs. However, strategic cultures entailed, and entail, a more active contribution from the assumptions and views of contemporaries, and these cannot be traced solely to geopolitics unless due weight is placed on the factors that moulded the perception of geopolitical elements.

FRANCE

The established political context for strategy in the reign of Louis XIV (r. 1643–1715), the leading monarch in *ancien régime* Europe, is primarily domestic: that of dynastic dynamics, ministerial factions mediated by a powerful and assertive monarch, and a concern, which became more significant for Louis from the 1680s, with how best to appeal to Catholic interests. This context was, in turn, affected after Louis's reign ended by a range of domestic, international and diplomatic factors. Covering the period to the outbreak of the French Revolution in 1789, these included a multifaceted and repeated domestic reaction against what was seen as Crown autocracy; the rise of trans-oceanic empire as an issue, at once opportunity and challenge for France; and the new ideals and idioms linked to values that can be defined as Enlightenment; as well as the pervasive pressure of events, notably international events, but also those within France. These factors and their contexts varied across time. A particular contrast arose from the differences between the essentially quiescent domestic response to Louis XIV's policies and the protracted controversy over the alignment with Austria following the Diplomatic Revolution of 1756. This alignment was widely seen, and presented, as both unpopular and unsuccessful. It was sustained by Louis XVI's marriage to Marie-Antoinette of Austria, and the two played a major role in criticism of the monarchy at the time of the French Revolution.

Throughout the seventeenth and eighteenth centuries, strategic choices owed much to tensions within France's government, with the overlapping categories of courtiers and ministers playing key roles, as was also the case in other states. This took forward medieval patterns when those categories were part of a world of competing members of the royal family and aristocrats. Put differently, in both war and peace, French politics had for long been related to major differences over strategy. A goal of national strength under royal leadership, the goal that followed the acute divisions and repeated failures of the first third of the fifteenth century, could include many possible strategies. This situation was much accentuated by the major divisions in France over policy stemming from the Protestant Reformation of the sixteenth century. The strategic inheritance, and, at times, incubus, from the past shaped much of the discussion during the eighteenth century, and especially during the first half; because different priorities came to the fore in, and after, the 1750s.

Taking forward the bitter civil conflict of the French Wars of Religion in the late sixteenth century (1562–98), the leading differences in France in the seventeenth century had been over religious, dynastic and geopolitical alignments. This was notably so between *dévot* support for a confessional (pro-Catholic) policy and, in particular, alliance with Spain, a pattern seen from the 1560s, and, in contrast, a *raison d'état* willingness to seek Protestant (and Muslim) allies against the Habsburgs (the rulers of Austria and Spain). The latter strategy was especially associated with Henry IV (r. 1594–1610) and, from 1624 to 1661, with the first ministers, successively cardinals Richelieu and Mazarin. This division continued after 1713, with tensions between co-operation with Catholic powers on the one hand, especially Spain and/or Austria, and with Protestant ones on the other, notably Britain, the Dutch, and/or Prussia, the latter the preference from 1716 to 1731 and 1741 to 1756.

Shaping the strategic analysis faces difficulties, not least in deciding the 'players' that should be considered and how best to consider them. It is possible, with France, to discern aristocrats keen on military glory, and to contrast them with ministers, many of a legal background, and to do so from the 1740s to the 1780s. At the same time, individuals could have contrasting priorities at particular stages of their career. Moreover, the contrast was frequently as much institutional as social in its dynamic, with the bellicose aristocrats counterpointed to ministers focused on finances.

Separately, as with so many strategic cultures, what might appear, and with reason, as aggression frequently had a defensive genesis as well, and one in which the legacy of the past played a major role. Habsburg expansion (both Austrian and Spanish) had posed problems for France from the early sixteenth century, and this was the case with respect not only to progressively more serious intervention in French domestic politics, but also to opposition to France in its borderlands. Ultimately, French hegemony over the lands between the rivers Saône/Marne and Rhine depended, as it had done from the fifteenth century, on military strength and success. The pursuit of this hegemony was the strategy, one seen as providing necessary strength, both international and domestic.

How the hegemony was to be pursued was significant, but secondary. In part, indeed, the particular strategy depended on the opponents in individual wars and the order in which they entered the war, whether because attacking or attacked. This can be seen as opportunism, which it was, but also as prudence. The situation was certainly both contextual and contingent. Thus, Louis XIV attacked Spain in 1667 in the War of Devolution, and not the Dutch, but he attacked the Dutch in 1672, while Spain only entered the latter conflict in 1673. This contrast determined the implementation of strategy, but the latter was essentially set by the longer-term goals of security and aggrandisement. They played out by means of, and through, the consequences of alliance agglomeration and disintegration, which were, in turn, related to the success of the campaigning, but were not dependent on it.

Under Louis XIV, a key element of the pursuit of hegemony was a large-scale programme of fortification, which was a major aspect of strategy, albeit one that tends to be underplayed. Fortifications demonstrated control, offered protection and provided bases for further expansion. Under Louis XIII (r. 1610–43), there were major fortifications, for example at Pinerolo on the Alpine frontier, but nothing that compared with the systematic attempt to defend vulnerable frontier regions seen under Louis XIV. A double line of fortresses was created to defend the vulnerable north-eastern frontier. Vauban also played a role in the fortification of naval bases. The ambiguous character of strategy – both defensive and offensive – was seen with Strasbourg, which was captured in 1681. This crossing point over the river Rhine served as a protection for the acquisition of Alsace in and after 1648 and also as a means to advance east into southern Germany.

So also for other states. Thus, Chinese fortifications were defensive against attack from the steppe, but also bases for power projection into it. Novara, Alessandria, Tortona and Valenza were links in a chain intended to defend Spanish-ruled Lombardy (the Milanese) from attack from the west by Savoy-Piedmont. Russia advanced south in Ukraine and central Asia by means of lines of outposts. Spain established fortified bases to guard the northern frontier of what became Mexico. At the same time, many fortifications were essentially designed against rebellion and, as such, protected centres of government and overawed cities.

Aside from fortification, military force was frequently employed short of war. Thus, after the Dutch War ended in 1678–9, France, using force, advanced and pursued a series of territorial claims in a unilateral fashion in the policy of the *réunions*, a practice already seen earlier in French intimidation of neighbours. Moreover, in 1688, in pursuit of his expansionist views in Rhineland disputes, Louis decided that a military demonstration was necessary. The army was not prepared for a major war, but a large army besieged the major fortress of Philippsburg. The strategy, that of diplomacy by means of force, was scarcely unique to Louis. It failed, however, in 1688, because the wider international context could not be determined consistently by intimidation. There was resistance, and a major war broke out, that of the League of Augsburg, otherwise known as the Nine Years' War. So also in 1701–2 as the crisis over the Spanish succession led to a large-scale war no one sought.

In this and other respects, there are many equivalents to modern 'hybrid warfare' in the strategic repertoire of the *ancien régime*. War, however defined and practised, was only part of the use of force, while the latter sat alongside intimidation, conspiracy, bribery, propaganda, the sponsoring of publications, and other means of weakening, or affecting, potential opponents. Too much of the discussion of strategy, however, focuses only on war, in the sense of large-scale operations by conventional forces seeking victory in battle.

So also with a different approach to the nature and range of strategy. In practice, prewar and wartime negotiations and agreements between powers, whether allies, opponents or neutrals, helped set strategy, as with the Franco-Spanish agreements against Britain in 1761 and 1779.[37] Moreover, this process could be linked to the half-way stages of conflict short of full-scale war, a situation that was commonplace around the world, for example in India. Britain and France fought from 1743 and 1754 respectively, but did not declare war until 1744 and 1756; and so on.

In addition, the extent to which diplomacy continued during most wars, both between allies and with neutrals and opponents, added a level of complexity to strategy, directing attention to the rulers, ministers and generals who had to handle such relations. In the absence of unconditional surrenders, wartime campaigning was generally intended to affect negotiations, and was frequently specifically to that end, as with French campaigning in Germany in the last stages of the Thirty Years'

War (1618–48): Austria was driven to abandon Spain, on which France could therefore focus. Similarly, in 1696, France focused on buying off Victor Amadeus II of Savoy-Piedmont in order to split the opposing coalition, a strategy which proved successful, while defeats in 1708–9 led France to negotiate. In 1719, France successfully mounted a limited invasion of Spain in order to get Philip V to change his policy and his ministry.

In 1733–5, during the War of the Polish Succession, France attacked Austria, but not the Austrian Netherlands (Belgium). The latter decision led to and reflected a Franco-Dutch neutrality convention of 1733, and France's determination to keep the Dutch, and their ally Britain, neutral. The contrast with the German invasion of Belgium in 1914 is readily apparent. Strategy in this case was as much about peace as war, as each played a role in forwarding France's interests in a complex international situation. The French did not take the opportunity to campaign to the east of the Rhine in 1733–5, attacking Saxony and encouraging Bavaria into the war.

In this and other wars, there was also (justified) distrust of allies and fear of the possibility of their *rapprochement* with opponents. Underlying the tension over strategy in 1734–5, with France opposed to Spain's plan to conquer Naples and Sicily and leave the defence of northern Italy to the French, was an unsuccessful Spanish determination to hold the diplomatic initiative. Fearing a unilateral Austro-Spanish settlement, France, instead, successfully pursued one itself through unilateral nego-tiations with Austria in 1735. This thwarted ideas of an Austro-Spanish settlement. Thus, a key element of the strategy was that of the exit from the war, a factor that remains pertinent today and for all states.

Like other states, France as an abstraction needs to be broken down. The first minister from 1726 to 1743, Cardinal André-Hercule de Fleury, twice presided (1733, 1741) over France going into a major conflict, but was also criticised as being overly cautious and unwilling to fight. The ministry was divided, which further complicated strategy, not least the perception by other powers that played a major role in responding to French moves. In 1741, those who pressed for war, led by Marshal Belle-Isle, increasingly took charge. His was a strategy of full-scale commitment, both in terms of French forces advancing far across the Rhine, and also in encouraging an alliance system predicated on major territorial changes. However, disunity in the French alliance system, notably in relations with Frederick the Great, contributed in 1741–2 to a failure to concentrate military resources and international alignments on achieving decisive victory by means of, or at least in the sense of, continuing to dictate the pace of events. This was a strategic failure, both of France and of its alliance system, which was weakened in part due to a more assertive anti-French ministry in Britain following the fall of Sir Robert Walpole in February 1742.

Unable to dominate Europe militarily, France required allies, but, in a classic strategic quandary, the very resort to war made it difficult to retain their support, a situation also seen in the Dutch War of 1672–8. Aside from allies retiring because exhausted, politically and/or militarily, as Charles II of England did from war with the Dutch in 1674, powers willing to accept peacetime subsidies proved unreliable, in part because, in wartime, other states increased their bids for support. Such bids proved more effective as alliances tended to lack any ideological, religious, sentimental, popular or economic bonds, a situation that looks towards most modern alliances. The assumption that war would be but short[38] further increased this tendency to sell support once the conflict continued for any time. Modern alliances have also proved disappointing when the transition was made from peace to war, as the United States discovered with France, Germany and Turkey, let alone Egypt and Pakistan, when attacking Iraq in 2003. Current plans to develop a European Union military face this issue.

Failure is the established theme if considering *ancien régime* (pre-revolutionary) France and its strategy. A standard approach today would be to focus on France's inability to defeat Britain in the struggle for transoceanic and naval primacy. Even when Britain also faced revolution in North America, and France was allied with Spain and the Dutch, a combination in 1780–3, the British Empire proved more resilient than anticipated. From that perspective, France's strategy more generally can readily be found wanting, both in conception and in implementation.

Moreover, this failure can be held to reflect the tendency of the past and to prefigure the fate of other continental powers opposed to oceanic rivals, notably Persia in the fifth century BCE, Spain in the late sixteenth century CE, Napoleon in the early nineteenth century, and Germany and the Soviet Union in the twentieth century.[39] Chinese policy-makers are interested in this trend and, therefore, keen to position China as a major oceanic power in addition to its strength on land. As with other states in this position, this aspiration is bifurcated, and possibly confused, by having a naval dimension but also one of offsetting and countering the naval strength of its rival, in this case the United States.

There are several problems, however, with this approach to France. First, it is by no means clear how accurate it is as a judgement. France had clearly failed by 1815 when it was occupied after Napoleon's total defeat at Waterloo. However, if the endpoint is 1783, then the situation was more complex. Thanks to the entry of France (1778) and Spain (1779) into the War of American Independence (1775–83), the British had been put under pressure, and from the Americas to the Indian Ocean, losing both territory and the sense of confidence enjoyed after repeated victories in the Seven Years' War (1756–63). France after that war had turned away from a policy focused on continental power and had built up its navy. Indeed, despite British resilience from 1776, when the Americans were driven from Canada, to 1783, it was widely feared in Britain in 1784–6 that France would press on to undermine the British Empire in Canada, Ireland and India.

More pertinently, French strategy was less focused on struggle with Britain than might appear subsequently, a situation indeed that anticipated the later policies of Napoleon and of Germany under Wilhelm II and Hitler. The last was more concerned about another Continental power, the Soviet Union. In particular, while maritime power, trade and colonies played an important role, as they do even more in present-day accounts of the past,[40] they did not dominate French policy and there was no persistent naval strategy. French strategy as a whole should not be assessed in terms of the struggle with Britain. Indeed, in 1812–14, it was an accelerating total failure at the hands of the other Continental powers that was more apparent.

Strategic culture is a relevant consideration, for the spatial composition of French power was that of inland France, a position that anticipated that of Prussia and then Germany. The landed nobility was crucial, and the role of land in élite identity was underlined under Napoleon by his reliance on a new service aristocracy who were provided with estates. The nobility were far more interested in the army than the navy, and in land rather than trade or colonies; and these values affected French society as a whole, which is why the earlier focus on maritime power was unsustainable. The loss of Canada in 1760 and Louisiana in 1763 was criticised in mercantile circles in the Atlantic ports, such as La Rochelle, but had only limited impact elsewhere. So also with Germany, notably the focus on Prussian interest in landownership, rather than on mercantile values. This continued under Hitler, with generals, such as Erich von Manstein awarded estates in eastern Europe as well as lots of money.

Strategic choices were made within this and other contexts, although the direct influence of contextual factors varied. For example, France did not introduce conscription under the *ancien régime* and, as a result, had a smaller army than Austria, Prussia and Russia in the 1760s, 1770s and 1780s. Instead, the introduction of conscription followed the early difficult stages of the French Revolutionary War and the radicalisation of the French Revolution, which indicated the dependence of war-making on the combination of domestic and international politics. Nevertheless, the size of the French army did not dictate strategy.

Looked at differently, strategy, inherently, was an integrated, or at least interacting, process, one with a wide range of factors at play. The central theme for France is that of the interplay of strategic culture and strategy, an interplay which captures the extent to which, alongside long-term interests and structural factors in policy-making and debate, there was no deterministic causation of strategic choice. Instead, alliance dynamics were crucial to strategic possibilities. The failure of France, from the second half of the seventeenth century, to produce lasting effective relationships with Britain, the Dutch, Spain, Austria, Prussia and Russia greatly affected its maritime and colonial position and options, as well as its hopes and strategies for European power politics.

The failure of strategic-level alliance approaches helped ensure that France did not realise the potential it appeared to have in both Europe and the world, not least as the most populous state in western Europe and a major colonial and naval power. This issue remains a challenge for powers today, and notably so for China and the United States. Their attempts to define the norms of the world order are linked to these alliance approaches.

French strategy in the War of the Spanish Succession (1701–14) is instructive. France was exposed from the outset by failing to prevent the creation in 1701–3 and operation of a potent hostile coalition, and strategy had to be calibrated accordingly. It was dependent on events in the field and yet also on diplomacy. For example, a decisive Anglo-Austrian victory over a French–Bavarian army at Blenheim in 1704 was followed by the overrunning of Bavaria. This was a campaign verdict that was not to be militarily challenged during the war. Instead, other than in Spain, where France and its ally won repeated success, French strategy became mostly a matter of frontier defence. This was to happen again in 1743–4, after defeat by the British at Dettingen, and in 1813–14, after defeat by an Austro-Prusso-Russo-Swedish army at Leipzig; in each case, therefore, after major French defeats to the east in Germany.

Frontier defence had major strategic implications for France as for other powers. It was a course of action that made it difficult to retain and gain allies, that posed a serious logistical strain in the shape of supporting French armies without 'contributions' from occupied areas, therefore increasing the domestic strain of war, and which made victory impossible. This looked towards the (different) quandaries facing Germany in late 1918 and late 1944, and, in very different contexts, Charles XII of Sweden during the Great Northern War, and the Confederacy during the American Civil War.

Louis XIV believed that his honour was involved in supporting Elector Max Emanuel of Bavaria; a key consideration. Backing allies was also necessary in order to prevent a general rallying to Louis's opponents, a theme that encouraged British intervention in favour of Greece in 1941. Indeed, in November 1704, a Franco-Bavarian treaty committed Louis to continue the war until Bavaria was retaken and enlarged.

The pattern of warfare was not that of the extirpation of enemies, as in the case of the Chinese treatment of the Zunghars in the 1750s. Instead, diplomacy continued in wartime. Thus, in 1706, a heavy defeat of the French army by an Anglo-Dutch army under John, Duke of Marlborough at Ramillies, and the subsequent expulsion of the French forces from the Spanish Netherlands (Belgium), led Louis to try peace proposals. Again, Marlborough's impressive victory over the French at Oudenaarde in 1708, and his capture of the major French fortress of Lille later that year, made Louis more eager to settle. In turn, Marlborough's pyrrhic victory at Malplaquet in 1709, followed by only slow progress in capturing French frontier fortresses, helped move the political dynamic more towards a position that was conducive for the French.

In part, this move was due to the course of the campaigning, but those of politics and diplomacy were also important, in fact more so, and provided a radically changing context for strategy, both British and, as a consequence, French. The Whig ministry committed to war was overthrown in Britain. In turn, the new Tory one was ready to negotiate a peace with France, the Peace of Utrecht (1713), that involved abandoning some of Britain's allies, notably Austria. In Germany, the Imperial Diet at Regensburg declared in July 1713 that the French proposals would 'tarnish the glory of the German nation'. However, defeat affected the room available for manoeuvre. Outnumbered and pushed back by the French, who captured the major fortresses of Freiburg, Kehl and Landau in 1713, Emperor Charles VI was forced to negotiate.

The War of the Polish Succession (1733–5) revealed anew the extent of strategic complexity. France entered the war in response to Russian pressure in Poland to prevent the election as king of Stanislaus Leszczyński, the Polish father-in-law of Louis XV, pressure that culminated in a successful invasion. In alliance with Sardinia (Savoy-Piedmont) and Spain, France attacked Russia's ally, Austria. The moves of French units were dependent on political goals, as well as on the economy of wartime gains: the need to make territorial acquisitions in order to compensate for Russian success in Poland. Such an economy was important in looking towards both a peace settlement and postwar politics. This pattern of conduct was one in which strategy was clearly under political direction. The absence of a relevant word was not of particular consequence.

French strategy was very much set by the need to keep its alliance together and to ensure that that of its opponents did not expand. This helped lead to a focus on operations in Italy, where Charles VI ruled Lombardy (the Milanese), Naples and Sicily, although that focus was also encouraged by the gains that could be made there. Military factors played a role. For example, a conflict that began late in the year, as this war did, was easier to conduct in a warmer environment.

Foreign policy became far more publicly politicised in France in the eighteenth century than had been the case in the late seventeenth, and with much of this politics played out in public. French ministries divided, for example over war with Britain in 1770 and 1778: deciding not to back Spain in 1770 in the Falkland Islands Crisis, but to support the Americans in 1778. The net effect was important to the response to particular military campaigns. Indeed, this process was taken further because of the pronounced overlap of military command with court politics and policy differences, a process also seen in other states. Diplomatic correspondence frequently focused on the intrigues and politics surrounding the choice of generals and their generalship.[41] As a result, French generals, such as Belle-Isle, Noailles, Broglie and Saxe in the 1740s, and Richelieu in the 1750s, and the moves they made, were very much located in a world of appealing to both monarch and a public of sorts, and without any dominant command system to gainsay them.

This situation looked towards that during the French Revolution, when some generals, notably Napoleon, pursued political advantage in their campaigning and did so as an aspect of a personal and political opportunism. In contrast, at the time of France's intervention of 1778–83 in the War of American Independence, the theme of politicised command was less prominently to the fore, in part due to the distance of operations and in part due to the focus on the navy.

The politics of command were linked to the struggles for resources and reputation that were so important to the nature of military operations, and that remain highly significant. In place of 'politics' and 'struggles', the word 'strategies' may be inserted; and this possibility highlights the problems involved both in establishing what the latter means and, also, how the term should be employed. If, indeed, too narrow a definition and application are offered, then the politics of command are misunderstood or neglected. 'Politics', like 'strategy', is a word capable of many definitions, and necessarily so.

In light of the politics of command, it is useful to reconsider the discussion of pre-1800 strategy offered by scholars who have argued that intelligence-gathering and communication systems were slow and unreliable, such that generals had to be on, or close to, the front line, while they dared not develop plans of any complexity. As a consequence, it is suggested, strategy was perforce primitive.[42] This minimalist view, however, does not capture the often complex nature of eighteenth-century strategy and, by extension, that in earlier periods. Closeness to the 'front line' may have little place in formulating 'grand strategy', certainly today, but that does not necessarily mean that theatre strategy was itself limited. Moreover, as far as 'grand strategy' was concerned, closeness to the 'front line' in practice described the situation in which rulers, including Frederick the Great and Napoleon, directed not only campaigns in person, as many did, but also the entire war effort.[43]

Separately, an overall presentation of strategy as primitive or limited is somewhat difficult to reconcile with the published correspondence of Frederick the Great or with the efforts of Marshal Belle-Isle in the early 1740s to direct French diplomatic and military policy in order to overthrow the Habsburg position and rearrange European politics. The same had been true of the plans of the French Secretary of State for Foreign Affairs, Germain-Louis Chauvelin, at the time of the War of the Polish Succession.

Alongside the more mundane, but pressing, concerns about where armies operated, with the consequences for the economies of particular rulers, armies were regarded as the enablers of international transformations, transformations that might reset strategic parameters. The contrast between conflicts indicates the extent to which strategic options, both within these parameters and those able to affect them, were in large part set by the possibilities of alliance support and the extent of political support from within the ministry.[44] In turn, such possibilities rested in large part on a reading of the military situation.

This situation very much reflected the impact of diplomacy. Thus, Austria and (neutral) Britain supported the westward move of Russian troops into Germany in 1735, a move designed to counteract France's position and prospects there. This move demonstrated the way in which the deployment of force (rather than its use in battle) offered a key strategic element, that of deterrence. This strategy was to be repeated in 1748 when Britain subsidised the westward movement of Russian troops in order to affect the outcome of the War of the Austrian Succession. France came to terms, returning gains in the Low Countries greater than those achieved by Louis XIV. However, as a reminder of the multiplicity of contexts that require consideration, France was under serious economic pressure as a result of British naval strength, notably as seen in two victories off Cape Finisterre in 1747. In addition, harvest difficulties were serious.

As a result of the successful efforts to win over Russia made from the mid-1730s, British strategy was at a very high level in 1735 and 1748: an alignment of the profits of an oceanic commercial system with the manpower and industrial resources of a land power. The British were to support such a Russian movement repeatedly during the French Revolutionary and Napoleonic Wars, notably during the wars of the Second and Third Coalitions, and ultimately it was the guarantee of Allied success in 1815, whatever happened at Waterloo. The world wars saw this alignment, most successfully so during the Second World War.

In turn, prefiguring the arguments of German navalists in the early twentieth century, a number of French ministers and commentators urged the need to weaken Britain in its colonies and to build up the French navy and colonial presence. These views were most strongly held in the Ministry of the Marine, notably by Jean-Frédéric, Count of Maurepas, minister from 1723 to 1749, but were also seen in mercantile circles.[45] Indeed, in the case of Maurepas, a naval strategy can be easily discerned, although insufficient resources were provided to bring it to successful fruition.[46] These strategic ideas continued to gain traction. In 1755, the need to build up the navy in order to prevent Britain from dominating trade and thus subsidising its allies was pressed.[47] Plans in the early 1760s for concerted Franco-Spanish action on land against Portugal, as a way to hit British trade as well as to make gains for both powers, reflected an ability to think in broad strategic terms, albeit one greatly hampered by British naval power. In the event, such action failed in 1762, but briefly succeeded in 1807. However, the difficulty of making the objective attainable underlined the risks of this expensive strategy, which in the specific case of Portugal served twice to take a neutral power into the British camp, unlike in the War of the Austrian Succession when Portugal had remained neutral. Wellington's armies in the Peninsular War of 1808–14 against Napoleon had a large Portuguese contingent, and Portugal provided an important base.

Alliances posed problems. Indeed, Clausewitz pointed out in *On War* that allies did not provide a commitment to match that which they expended on their own interests. He wrote: 'A moderately sized force will be sent to its help; but if things go wrong the operation is pretty well written off, and one tries to withdraw at the smallest possible cost.'[48] The absence of effective coalition integration during the Seven Years' War (1756–63), not least distrust of Russia by its allies, especially France but also Austria, was the fundamental aspect of the war, both strategically and operationally, that provided Frederick the Great with the opportunities for focusing on his opponents separately and sequentially even while at war with all of them. France was hit particularly hard by this absence, not least because it was also at war with Britain, whereas Austria and Russia were not; but they also suffered from a lack of co-ordination. Yet, alliances could provide crucial elements of force multiplication.

In 1763, France ended a conflict in which it had made a formidable effort, with humiliating defeats in Europe, especially Rossbach (1757) at the hands of Prussia, and Minden (1759) at those of Britain and allied forces, as well as the wartime loss to Britain of most of its trans-oceanic empire, notably Canada, Guadeloupe, Martinique and its bases in India. This was not an equivalent to the German defeats in 1918 and, even less so, 1945, but failure abroad and the wartime alliance with Austria increased problems within France, not least factional strife. Moreover, the war, and the alliance with Austria that continued postwar, conspicuously leached political support from the Crown and ministry, a loss of support that looked towards the French Revolution. This process underlined yet again the domestic context and consequences of strategy.

The outcome of the Seven Years' War provided the opportunity and need for rethinking France's position and policies. Doing so would have been much less pressing had France been militarily successful in the war. However, failure threw attention on the Austrian alliance, on the state of the French army, and on France's capacity to realise its goals, international, military and domestic. These factors encouraged the ferment of ideas, political and military,[49] that was a background to the advancing in France of a formal term for strategy over the following years.

More significantly, France was to launch two new strategies over the following half-century. The first, that of intervening in the American Revolution, was a new iteration of the long-established means of helping rebels against your opponent. This had been seen, for example, in 1640, when France acted to back Catalan rebels against Spain. However, as this was a new trans-oceanic format, France proved heavily dependent on naval strength, as also when seeking to help Irish or Scottish opponents of Britain in 1689–91, 1697, 1708, 1744–6, 1759 and 1795–8. The second new strategy was a different one of people's warfare, seen when France itself adopted this form in the French Revolutionary Wars of the 1790s.

COMPARISONS

Public politics were far less clearly to the fore in the powers discussed in this chapter than in the case of Britain considered in the next, although, to a degree, France offered an in-between stage. Nevertheless, work on later authoritarian, and even totalitarian, political systems has indicated that they also had and have public politics; and this, moreover, was the case earlier. In part, the symbolism of success staged by states represented an attempt to get to grips with their public politics. Indeed, the achievement of success was crucial and a central aspect of strategy, which was frequently not a matter of achieving specific goals, but rather of obtaining success itself. Means and ends thereby were closely linked, with the goal of war being victory itself or, at least, victory in a conflict that enabled victory to be claimed. Rather than seeing this factor as in some way a primitive aspect of strategy, and one that has subsequently been superseded, it can be found across history and is part of the psychology as well as the content of war and rule.

Alongside common tones, however, there were differences in strategic assumptions, both by state and through time. In particular, the extent varied to which élites saw themselves as facing a number of separate, localised challenges or a single crisis involving the state as a whole.[50] There was a contrast between a wide-ranging struggle for alliances on the part of many states fearful of such a crisis, and the extent to which no such challenge was seen in the case of China and Japan, and notably for the former after the Zunghars were crushed in 1757.

The variety of circumstances seen in the late eighteenth century is more generally apparent, and on regional scales as well as the global one. This makes it very difficult to offer a typology of military history or to see any common strand in strategic development. A key contrast is that between the trans-oceanic maritime power capacity of Atlantic European powers and the related state support for trade, and, on the other hand, the lack of similar capability and support for non-Western (and Eastern European) powers.[51] This contrast reflected geography, capability, opportunity and strategic vision, and was one that continued until the development of the Japanese navy in the late nineteenth century. The long-range plans of Atlantic European naval forces were not always successful, but no non-Western state could pursue a strategy at this range. Tipu Sultan of Mysore dispatched four warships to Basra in Iraq in 1786 in an attempt to seek Turkish support, but the failure of the mission was matched by the disastrous fate of most of the squadron. Indian rulers very much tended to focus on continental goals and on their armies.[52]

Whereas the Turks had sent significant naval forces into the Indian Ocean in the sixteenth century (although not on the scale of those deployed in the Mediterranean), they did not do so subsequently. This was a significant change in strategic capability, and, therefore, in the context for European activity, one that matched the end, in the fifteenth century, of Chinese operations into the Indian Ocean. Such changes were important to the 'deep history' that established the context for strategic choices. Moreover, in the seventeenth century, the Turks resumed deploying a large fleet in support of maritime power projection in the 1640s, and made no comparable move in the Indian Ocean.

Westernisation is a valid charge against much of the discussion of warfare in the period 1400–1850 because what is decried as a Western-centric view can lead to a failure to appreciate the extent to which other cultures were also well capable of strategic analysis and practice. This is the case whether these are conceived in the shape of narrow, more operational, military criteria or with reference to the broader approach offered in this book. Caveats can be readily offered in the shape of a lack of activity by Japan and of external warfare by China for most of the period 1770–1835.[53] However, there are many signs of strategic flexibility by non-Western states in response to the challenges of the period, although that explanation presents a somewhat mechanistic action–reaction explanation. This is less than a complete account of change. For example, the rapid and substantial developments in Maratha war-making in India late in the eighteenth century were only in part in response to British military capability and activity.[54]

When conflict between Western and non-Western states is considered, it is clear that strategy embraced a range of factors, and for both. For example, in India, Britain's ability to benefit from divisions between and within regional powers involved military, political and financial factors. Key structural advantages for British strategy included the institutional continuity of the East India Company, the world's leading corporation, and the ability of the most profitable global trading system, that of maritime Britain, to generate profits and provide credit that would enable both company and state to wage sustained, large-scale conflict. Funds helped ensure success in the crucial military labour market.[55] Operational factors, notably the improved logistics (in part a product of available funds) that underwrote mobility, were important, as were command skills and political factors. To abstract one of these factors and label it decisive is, at best, unhelpful. So also when considering non-Western powers, most obviously the most successful, China.

3

THE REACH FOR WORLD EMPIRE
BRITAIN, 1689–1815

The great global power of the nineteenth century, Britain established this position in the 'long eighteenth century', the period from the 'Glorious Revolution' of 1688–9, in which James II was overthrown, to 1815, when Napoleon was finally defeated. That period was crucial to later primacy, not least to the strategic experience of competition and conflict that was carried forward. Strategic culture, in the shape of the accumulated experience of the past, was particularly important in Britain due to a recent past in which Stuart kings had twice been over-thrown (1649, 1688), while a legacy of distrust of the autocratic conse-quences of a powerful army had been left from the 1650s and the 1680s. The combination of the two obliged defence against a Stuart riposte, but also accentuated distrust of the army. Indeed, the expulsion of James II in the 'Glorious Revolution' demonstrated the role of discontinuities, at once international and domestic, in shaping strategic culture.

With Britain having an especially active public politics, centred on Parliament and the press, and an accompanying strategic dialogue, a consideration of the nature of strategy there becomes a way to assess the importance of that context and also to look ahead to the later situation including that over the last century. The growth of public politics in Britain, notably from the 1690s, played a major role in the evolving discussion of strategy, as a sphere for, and means of, public debate. This situation has existed more generally, even if such debate was usually constrained by ideas and habits of secrecy, but the debate was more significant where there were ideas and practices of public accountability and where these took constitutional and political form. This prefigures the situation with the modern United States.

77

The development of strategy in states with public politics had two very different courses. On the one hand, there was the process by which the government and the military discussed and planned, and on the other, discussion in and by the public. The pivot, again looking to the present, was the government, more particularly in the case of Britain after the 'Glorious Revolution', the ministers who explained strategy in Parliament and who played a central role in formulating and implementing it. These two groups were not necessarily coterminous. However, in the persons of the secretaries of state, notably for the Northern and Southern departments, there was an overlap, with these individuals always responsible for such a defence, although, when they both sat in the House of Lords, as in 1721–54, 1761–2, 1762–5 and 1766–82, the defence of policy in the House of Commons rested on colleagues who held other posts. The secretaries of state shared the responsibility for foreign policy, ensuring that this aspect of strategy was the leading factor in political discussion. There was no comparable role for leading military figures.

In some respects, strategy in a broad sense was the key element of political debate until the twentieth century, in part because this was a period when government did not deal to the degree seen today with economic and social policy, or identity politics. That senior ministers in eighteenth-century Britain also electioneered and otherwise sought to bolster political support was part of the political equation involved in strategy, both in so far as foreign policy was concerned and with regard to warfare.[1] The need to sell strategy was linked by ministers and others to the value of receiving parliamentary support.[2]

In part, strategy was a matter of stating the blandest of nostrums about national security and the safety of trade and the constitution. Again, this was nothing new and has continued to the present. Indeed, the rhetorical character of strategy is an aspect of its political character. Linked to this, strategy involved an established litany of priorities and slogans, each of which was encoded in the partisan history of the period, as in other periods. 'Blue-water' and Continental strategies were the basic building blocks in both litany and partisanship in the eighteenth century, although, as with other strategic concepts across time, for example 'containment' during the Cold War, each in practice had a variety of meanings and associations, including for example confessionalism or alliance with Catholic powers. Thus, there was an inherent imprecision that reflected, and drew on, this variety of meanings in a potent feedback mechanism. Again, this description is still pertinent.

Both context and content changed in accordance with international and domestic political developments. For example, then at war with France, the British had to respond at once to the Austro-French alliance of 1756. This alliance posed a fundamental challenge to British assumptions about the international system as it brought Britain's hitherto leading ally to a pact with the French. These assumptions should not be separated from whatever is understood by the term 'strategy'. Indeed, the assumptions were crucial to strategic culture. As with the United States today, the public and governmental debates over strategy in Britain were followed abroad, not least due to the extent to which reports of parliamentary debates and newspapers were collected by foreign governments.

THE CHARACTER OF STRATEGY

As the leading naval power from the 1690s to the 1940s, Britain had particular strategic requirements, issues and opportunities. Prioritisation was a recurrent theme, as again today. For example, the need for planning, and the experience of it, can be seen with the detachment of naval squadrons from home waters, notably for the Mediterranean but also for the Baltic, the West Indies and North American waters. The viability of such a detachment remained a recurrent feature in naval planning as it underlined concerns about the deterrent situation in home waters. Moreover, sending out a naval force served to counter the charge that nothing was being done. Such a criticism, and such a response, were recurrent elements of the polemics and politics of strategy. That point might serve as the basis for a diatribe against politicians and politics, but aside from the degree to which 'the military' themselves entailed politicians and politics as well as overlapping with those of the 'non-military', it was, and is, unclear how best to prioritise. Looked at differently, a safe margin for particular choices was only established through the test of action, as Britain discovered when failing to deter the French attack on Minorca in 1756, and when being unable to relieve the British garrison on the island. Conversely, the total defeat of the French invasion attempt against Britain in 1759 overlaid the element of risk in detaching forces for trans-oceanic operations.

The pursuit of battle was not the major goal, but, generally a tangential product of strategic rivalries. Instead, a strategy of naval commercial interdiction played a role in operations against the Dutch in the late seventeenth century and, including a powerful trans-oceanic dimension, in conflict or confrontation with France and Spain. Thus, it was seen in the Anglo-Spanish crisis of 1725–7, in war with Spain in 1739–48 and 1762–3, and in wars against France, and successfully so, including in 1747–8. In operations, whether combined or single-service, the calibration of force, on land and sea, and of goals was necessary. However, this calibration was exposed to the friction of the events of the forthcoming campaigning season, a friction that, because of its impact, had tactical, operational and strategic aspects and consequences.[3]

Drawing on long-established views about blockade, views that can be seen for example in the Peloponnesian War, a linkage of war, trade and affecting the morale of opponents was commonplace among diplomats. Thus, in 1758, George, 2nd Earl of Bristol, British envoy in Turin, reported of France: 'Their commerce is entirely ruined in the Mediterranean, their manufactures are at a stand, and no money circulates in the southern provinces. The general cry is for peace.'[4] His successor, James Mackenzie, proposed to increase the pressure by using British warships to intercept grain shipments from Italy to France.[5] Looking towards the role of blockade during the Napoleonic Wars, and the two world wars, commercial warfare as a component of British strategy had many facets. Grain shipments were of particular significance as shortages and price rises in urban centres could cause disorder. The position of the British government on grain shipments to France was controversial both in wartime in 1748 and in peacetime in 1789, when the high price was linked to the outbreak of the Revolution.

More generally, the planned use of naval power by Britain in international crises, as in 1723, 1729, 1730, 1731, 1735, 1770, 1787, 1790 and 1791, was wide-ranging and reasonably sophisticated given serious contemporary limitations with communications and institutional support, as indeed was the actual use as crises moved towards conflict, as in 1726. The extent and range of discussion about the use of naval power are such that it is seriously mistaken to claim that 'political-strategic dimensions' were absent and that only tactical issues were covered.[6] In practice, the political ends of naval warfare were much considered, and notably so in public discussion and by government. So also with the strategic potential caused by naval bases and planned bases, for example Brest and Dunkirk for France, and the consequent discussion of securing them or inhibiting their use. The dismantling of Dunkirk under the terms of the Peace of Utrecht of 1713 was important to naval strategy and to the public discussion of strategy. Indeed, French repairs there caused a political storm in Britain during the 1730 parliamentary session and threatened the continuance of the British ministry.

Others, notably allies, also took a role in the discussion of bases and geopolitics, as in 1748 when the Austrian envoy in Turin, the envoy of one British ally to another ally, pressed the need for Britain to prevent France establishing itself in Corsica, and argued that this possibility had strategic implications both for Italy and for the Mediterranean.[7] Broader contextual issues played a role. Thus, in 1768, when France bought Corsica from Genoa, Austria was allied with France.

Planned operations on land were also varied, with options such as interventionism, in turn involving further choices over where to send troops and what to do with them. This prefigured the situation in the world wars. For example, in 1742, Britain, then not at war, intervened on the Continent in favour of Austria, albeit that year only by deploying troops in the Austrian Netherlands (Belgium), as it had not done in 1714, 1733–5 or 1741.[8] On land, there was a degree of greater complexity than at sea, because such operations more frequently involved coalition warfare and all the strains to which this gave rise. Prefiguring the situation for the United States from the 1940s, there was an intertwining of military planning and diplomatic exigencies; and whatever is meant by strategy cannot be separated from coalition diplomacy. Each, indeed, was an aspect of the other, a situation that is more generally true.

This intertwining can be seen with the Third Anglo-Dutch War of 1672–4, the Nine Years' War and the War of the Spanish Succession, in which Britain was involved from 1689 to 1697 and 1702 to 1713 respectively, and again in the War of the Austrian Succession, in which Britain was involved as a combatant from 1743 to 1748, although war with France was not declared until 1744. In 1755, George II argued that Robert, 4th Earl of Holdernesse, one of the two secretaries of state and a former diplomat, should meet a Dutch general in Brussels 'in order to settle some sketch of a plan in case of any immediate attack upon the

Low Countries'.[9] This was a reference to the risk of French attack that indicated the linkage of alliance politics and military planning, each a key factor in strategy, and, to a degree, bound in an interacting equation.

If that is one context for the subject, a second is provided by an understanding of strategy in its widest sense, namely in relation to the health and strength of the country and people as a whole. In military terms, this understanding engages with ideas of total war. Moreover, views on the strength, stability and future of states and peoples thus overlapped with the range of government and other activity and actions. These elements, in turn, affected or could help direct the politics of preparedness for war and of conflict.

The relationship between the theorisation and apparent rules of behaviour in international relations, on the one hand, and decision-making processes, on the other, varied by ruler and minister, but such discussion set and/or reflected normative standards that could help shape, or at least affect, strategies and responses.[10] Strategy as concept and practice, in short, drew on and was influenced by widely diffused concepts of how power could, should, indeed must, operate; concepts that, in part, reflected the perception of what occurred. The latter involved political placing and cultural conditioning. Thus, *The Craftsman*, an opposition London newspaper, in its issue of 15 September 1739, drew on the well-established opposition and popular hostility to a large army, arguing that 'whilst there is an equal division of power among the Princes of Europe, there will be no occasion for a numerous standing [permanent] army'. A very different view from that autumn emerged from the diary of Dudley Ryder, a government minister, which showed the highly experienced prime minister, Sir Robert Walpole, employing the idea of an attacking military strategy to plan domestic politics: 'He told me the true way in Parliament to oppose these people's violent measures was not to act on the defensive so much as to carry the war among the enemy and attack them.'[11]

States were regarded in the West as sovereign, but as linked, as if within a machine. This system was based on the model of the machine, which, in turn, was treated as well ordered and as enabling its parts to conduct activities only in accordance with its own construction. The mechanistic concept of the system of states was well suited to the wider currents of thought, specifically Cartesian rationalism and mathematics, as well as their successors. Similarly, modern ideas of strategy draw heavily on theories about the operations of systems.

Organic assumptions were important not so much at the level of the international system (until the nineteenth century), but at that of individual states. These assumptions, which were vitalist, helped provide a dynamic component that is generally lacking with the more structural nature of the mechanistic themes. Organic metaphors bled into international relations, notably with the fear of decay and decadence. There was a sense of a state as the expression of a nation, of the latter as linked in a national character, and of this character as capable of change and as prone to decay and collapse. This supposed trajectory looked in large part to longstanding cyclical accounts of the rise and fall of empires. This approach drew much of its authority from the commanding role of Classical Rome in the historicised political thought of the period in the West. There was comparable interest in the rise and fall of empires in China, India and the Islamic world.

A sense of the nation as akin to a family or a person remained important and affected notions of development and attitudes towards internal divisions. As also more recently, this sense greatly influenced the metaphors of politics and the consideration of strategy. This idea also translated into the international sphere with a view of nations as competitive, and as under threat from challenges that were foreign as well as domestic in their causation and mechanism. These were all notions that preceded what would later be termed social Darwinism.

Into the twentieth century, states sought simultaneously to consolidate authority and to gain territory. Each was a goal that involved normative and prudential valuations. To opt out would not have seemed sensible or even practical. With its stress on honour and dynastic responsibility, and its concern with *gloire* and the normative values of combat, the dominant political culture was scarcely cautious or pacific. This was the case irrespective of the more general commitment to territorial expansion, although much of that was presented in terms of advancing dynastic claims.

To respond to rivals by trying to avoid conflict and, instead, following a strategy defining mutually acceptable spheres of influence was a difficult, if not impracticable, diplomatic strategy, and, again, the parallel with the modern United States may be considered. Such a policy would have been politically and ideologically problematic. It would also have been a serious signalling of weakness. Moreover, in many cases, there seems little reason to believe that compromise could have been reached and sustained short of large-scale conflict. A similar point can be made at the military level when discussing the practicalities of solely adopting defensive operations.

Contingency played a major role, not least in the extent to which states could be confronted by significant discontent, and, more pointedly, rebellions. Britain (prior to 1707 England) repeatedly faced the prospect of rebellions supported by foreign invasion or assistance: by France from 1216 on, for example successfully so in 1470 and 1485 as Henry VI (temporarily) and Henry VII gained power. Nothing comparable could be launched by Britain against France after the Hundred Years' War (1337–1453), which, in part, was a fundamental strategic asymmetry reflecting the size of the respective armies. The frequency of the French attempts, and the even more insistent level of threat, brought forward the question of appropriate strategy, both for the British state and for the dynasty. Differentiating between the two became a major element in public debate, a debate that had to be taken into account when considering strategy.

The Jacobite challenge, French and/or Spanish backing for the cause of the exiled Stuarts, was very much an eighteenth-century version of total war and regime change. Indeed, the challenge posed by foreign support for the exiled Stuarts was such that an important strategic element became that of displaying the domestic stability of Britain. Arthur Villettes, the British envoy in Turin, suggested in 1739 to a fellow envoy that 'a quiet [parliamentary] session with the appearance of a little more unanimity, would be of more effect towards disappointing the schemes of our enemies and bringing the Spaniards to terms, than all our fleets and our armies'.[12]

The process of past debate and the contents of particular debates underline the highly problematic nature of the thesis that interests are clear, although that does not imply that national interests can only serve for rhetoric and politics. However, the very discussion about strategy itself inevitably is in part a matter of the debate over interests and their definition: national, state, dynastic, class and so on.

The nature of the available military capability was an important part of this debate and therefore of the strategic context. Britain had the world's largest navy from the early 1690s, but, to prevent invasion and protect trade, the British navy focused on tasks that forced it into a reactive operational stance. Yet, as a reminder of the multi-purpose character of military activity, this stance also formed the basis of effective sea projection as it caused attrition and deterrence to enemies and provided Britain with strategic flexibility in the middle and long term. In contrast, the French Atlantic fleet was largely cooped up in Brest. Many battles arose as a result of British blockades, as in 1759 and 1778, and thus were indicative of the essentially reactive strategy central to the use of British naval power.

The contemporary British conception of British naval power, in contrast, was proactive, not reactive. That assumption posed a different form of challenge, one, moreover, that was accentuated by the nature of British public politics. The call to action was frequent, both in peacetime and during war, and there was scant sense of any limits on what the navy could achieve. In 1739, for example, the government was urged not to attack the Spanish coast or bombard Cadiz, which were presented as useless, but, instead, to follow a strategy of amphibious operations, seizing Sicily and Spanish America, neither of which were viable options.[13] Failure repeatedly led to savage criticism, with the press very ready to condemn naval strategy and operations, as in 1744, 1756 and 1778.

Ultimately, it was possible to absorb specific defeats, notably the loss of Minorca in 1756, as long as capability was maintained in the English Channel, a situation that looked forward to twentieth-century strategy towards Germany. Moreover, British naval victories in 1692, 1718, 1747 and 1759, over France, Spain, France and France respectively, were strategically decisive as far as the naval aspect of the wars was concerned. Yet, that approach makes the mistake of leaving out politics. Failure at Minorca in 1756 led to the fall of the ministry, despite its strong position in the House of Commons, while total success in 1718 in the battle of Cape Passaro did not lead the Spaniards to abandon Sicily, which they had recently invaded, and the resulting war put serious pressure on Britain including a Spanish-backed Jacobite invasion attempt in 1719 that, in the event, was thwarted by the weather.

There has been a preference for focusing upon strategy in operational terms, especially the location of fleets, as in the discussion of the strategic grasp of John, 4th Earl of Sandwich, the First Lord of the Admiralty during war with France in 1778–83.[14] This issue is important but it does not exhaust the issue of strategy, and not least that of the wider politics of naval tasking and the rating of naval requirements within British public culture and government.

For Britain, not losing and staying in the war itself constituted a strategic success, as Britain thereby was able to benefit from long-haul financial attrition and to secure a major say in the peace negotiations. This was the 'long-war' strategy that was to be adopted against Germany in 1939–41, albeit unsuccessfully as German links with the Soviet Union meant that the British blockade was not a threat.[15]

THE TONE AND LANGUAGE OF STRATEGY

The concept of the tone of strategy is a way to consider or apply strategic culture, and, notably, without the somewhat determinist character the latter concept may seem to offer. Tone was a matter of form as well as content, but was primarily a question of how strategy was explained. Thus, with a parliamentary democracy of sorts in Britain and certainly so in contemporary terms, there was a need to explain strategy to the king and Parliament (and in the press) in a manner that was more politically relevant than in France. There was also a degree of accountability and exposure to popularity in Britain not seen in France.[16]

Religious factors could be apparent as elements in the tone of strategy. British anti-Catholicism was not only a matter of anger with, and suspicion towards, France,[17] but was also important in affecting British attitudes,[18] and thus making strategic choices more acceptable, notably encouraging a belief that the struggle must be persisted in even in the face of news that was very negative. Anti-Catholicism, indeed, led to a sense of existentialist and metahistorical struggle, and of a struggle that could be traced back to the Reformation. Thus, strategy rested on a clear ideological commitment, and one in which international and domestic goals and means were both important and overlapped. Similarly, Catholic powers referred to the need to stand firm against 'heretics'.[19]

A clear ideological commitment was particularly important due to the development in Britain, as a consequence of the overthrow of the autocratic James II of England (James VII of Scotland) in the 'Glorious

Revolution' of 1688–9, of a new 'domestic space' for strategy. This process was brought to fruition with the Seven Years' War. The constitutional, ideological, political, social and economic changes bound up in the 'Glorious Revolution' and its consequences, the so-called Revolution Settlement, ensured the rise of public discussion and of a political accountability through Parliament that, to a degree, resonated with public themes. A repeated consideration of strategy in parliamentary debates, pamphlets and newspapers was an especially noteworthy feature.

For Britain, by early 1791, the alliance with Prussia negotiated in 1788 had become focused on eastern Europe and, in particular, on limiting Russian gains at the expense of the Turks, with whom war had begun in 1787. This conflict had broadened out into a wider international crisis, one that divided both ministry and public opinion in Britain. As so often with strategy, international and domestic factors interacted without any clarity or consistency. Moreover, there was no segregation, neat or otherwise, of whatever is differentiated as policy and strategy, while issues of operational and political expediency affected goals and tasking. Whereas Prussia could strike at Russia by land across Poland, with which a treaty was signed in 1790, Britain could only act against Russia by the use of naval force. Though the dispatch of a squadron to the Black Sea, where Russian and Turkish fleets had been in conflict for several years, was discussed, this posed formidable logistical problems; also the Black Sea was unknown to the British navy. The contrast with the dispatch of a large British fleet to the Black Sea in 1854 during the Crimean War with Russia indicated the impact of technological and organisational developments, as well as a very different political context.

Looking also towards later wars with Germany, the burgeoning economy of Britain and of the oceanic trading system, and the strength of its public finances, were crucial to the British war effort against France, and thus helped set the parameters of strategy as well as providing facets that opponents could hope to turn into vulnerabilities, as with Napoleon's 'Continental System' of economic blockade.

Similar points can be made for other states. Strategy as politics does not exhaust the subject, but it makes sense of a context in which ministerial contention, and even public debate, were more potent than institutional continuity. In Britain, the presence of a developed public sphere resulted in a strategic debate that was readily open to political cross-currents, with 'a complex fusion of sentiment and realism' at play in strategic views.[20] Linked to this, strategy was not dominated by the military or the court, but emerged from real capabilities in the maritime economy.

4

THE RISE OF REPUBLICAN STRATEGIES
1775–1800

In the late eighteenth century, the United States and republican France, states born in violence and through war, each had to produce a new strategic logic. This was both for public consumption and to help define goals and means in a highly competitive and dangerous environment. Each also probed optimistic, even utopian, conceptions of strategy, for ends as well as means, before finding that the situation they faced was more difficult, as well as more divisive, than had been envisaged. Moreover, the legacies they variously adopted, adapted and reacted against (and with significant domestic differences for all three) were very different.

In France, as later with the Soviet Union, the transition was clear, as France was already a nation and a state. The Revolution both inherited institutions, military practices, political strategies and geopolitical issues from the pre-Revolutionary *ancien régime* and released, energised, organised and directed French resources. Yet, strategy was highly contextual as well as contingent, as both the American Patriots and the French Republicans were affected in their strategy by those followed by their powerful opponents as well as by domestic political developments.

UNITED STATES

In North America, the transition to a new strategic actor in a totally different context, that of the American Revolution and of American independence, was more abrupt because the American Revolution constituted foremost the creation of a new state, although a British organisational structure, albeit a colonial one, was already present in a relatively advanced fashion and could be used by the new government. As a result of the creation of a new state, there was the need to conceptualise, as well as implement, a new strategy and a new geopolitics.

There was a need for the Patriots (revolutionaries; their opponents also saw themselves as patriots) to create a strategy from the outset of the struggle, a strategy focused on changing British policy. The conspectus might appear clear, but, as also in the case of republican France (and, less radically, Britain after the 'Glorious Revolution' of 1688–9), a political struggle over the identity of the new state encompassed constitutional formulation, political practice, force structure, ideology and geopolitical alignment. For example, the powerful American ideological-political preference for militia was highly significant. It both looked back to political debates in Britain and responded to the particular ideas and requirements of America.

To abstract strategy from this political context is not only unhelpful but misleading. In the case of America, the Continental Army, created in 1775, explicitly represented a new notion of nationhood, political identity and social practice. This, indeed, helped to sustain the cohesion of the army and even the continuation of the Revolutionary cause when, having lost Philadelphia, the war went badly, as in the winter of 1777–8 when the army camped in rural Valley Forge, Pennsylvania.

In theory, creating the Continental Army made the planning of strategy easier. However, in practice, the creation of the army did not free military operations from the view of state governments (the source of resources), nor from the political disputes within the Continental Congress. The relationship between Congress and its commander, George Washington, was defined: Congress was to determine policy and the commander-in-chief to follow its orders. Yet, Washington's correspondence was replete with references to insufficient manpower and supplies, and to a lack of coherence in the war effort. Nathanael Greene, the commander in the south from December 1780, wrote to Governor Lee of Maryland:

> It is unfortunate for the public that the two great departments in which they are so deeply interested, Legislation and the Army, cannot be made to coincide better, but the pressing wants of the Army

cannot admit of the slow deliberation of Legislation, without being subject to many inconveniences nor can a Legislature with the best intentions always keep pace with the emergencies of war.[1]

More than organisation was at stake and in dispute. Appointed a general by Congress in 1775, Charles Lee, a veteran of the Seven Years' War, in which he had served as a British officer in North America and Portugal, and a major-general in the Polish army when it resisted Russian invasion, advocated radical solutions amounting to a militarisation of society and the creation of a national army under central control:

> 1st. A solemn league and covenant defensive and offensive to be taken by every man in America, particularly by those in or near the seaport towns; all those who refuse, to have their estates confiscated for the public use, and their persons removed to the interior part of the country with a small pension reserved for their subsistence.
>
> 2dly. New York to be well fortified and garrisoned or totally destroyed.
>
> 3dly. No regiments to be raised for any particular local purposes, but one general great Continental Army adequate to every purpose. South Carolina may be excepted from its distance . . .
>
> 4thly. The regiments to be exchanged. Those who are raised in one province to serve in another rather than in their own, viz. the New Englanders in New York, the New Yorkers in New England, and so on. This system will undoubtedly make them better soldiers.
>
> 5thly. A general militia to be established and the regular regiments to be formed by drafts from the militia or their substitutes.
>
> 6thly. A certain portion of lands to be assigned to every soldier who serves one campaign, a double portion who serves two, and so on.[2]

These notions conflicted with the profoundly local nature of American political culture, a product of the separate and different governmental, political, social, religious and demographic development of the individual colonies. Lee's proposals also clashed with the respect for the law and for individuals and property rights that, with the obvious exceptions of Native and African Americans, was central to this culture and that compromised any idea of a total mobilisation of national resources. Such a mobilisation was not to be achieved by legislation through the developing new political system. In effect, the individual colonies were to win independence first, and then to co-operate on their own terms through a federal structure. This genesis and situation greatly complicated the pursuit of an effective national strategy, as was to be amply seen in the War of 1812.

The overthrow of royal authority in 1775 in the thirteen colonies saw large-scale activity by those not yet in the politico-military system, activity that constituted a key element of the strategic context. A mixture of popular zeal, the determination of the Revolutionaries and the weakness of their opponents decided the fate of most of the colonies in late 1775. Intimidation by mob action proved an effective means, and the result gave the Patriots political strength and strategic depth in subsequent operations. The disorientating experience of the agencies of law and authority being taken over by those who were willing to connive at, or support, violence affected many who were unhappy about developments. To resist this situation, there was scant internal support to which the royal governors could turn and, other than in Massachusetts, few royal troops were available.

In July 1776, over a year after the initial outbreak of hostilities, the declaration of independence reflected the stiffening of Patriot resolve, prefiguring, in a different context, the change in Union strategy during the Civil War towards a harsher conduct of the war and the new goal of slave emancipation. In 1776, Loyalists were harried. Meanwhile, the new American government slowly became better prepared to wage war. A sense of reaction was important to the politics of strategic preparation. Thus, on 30 December 1776, John Hancock, the president of Congress, announced in a circular that 'the strength and progress of the enemy . . . have rendered it not only necessary that the American force should be augmented beyond what Congress had heretofore designed, but that it should be brought into the field with all possible expedition'.[3] Political determination and military preparedness, however, were not well synchronised.

Ironically, and underlining the problems of judging strategic capability and achievement, the Patriots in the long run probably profited from being driven out of Canada in 1776. Such extended lines of communication and supply, and the commitment of manpower required, would have bled the Continental Army dry and might have led to mutinies. More generally, the overall situation deteriorated when a British amphibious force took New York in 1776. As a consequence of British amphibious effectiveness, a repeatable capability, the Patriots had to follow a reactive strategy. Following the loss of New York and the long retreat through New Jersey, Washington's strategy was apparently to keep the army intact, and give up the cities, but, with the army and militia, control the countryside and harass the British forces. The *Annual Register* of 1777 called him 'the American Fabius'.

Yet that account was flawed. Washington abandoned that strategy in his decision to defend Philadelphia and lost at Brandywine. He again dared battle at Germantown (1777) and Monmouth Court House (1778); the former a defeat, the latter a drawn battle. After Monmouth Court House, there were no major battles in the north, but, once a French fleet was off the coast in 1781, there was no thought of a Fabian strategy.

The role of public opinion, however, gave the Patriots a key advantage. Britain needed a decisive victory to convince opinion, at home, in America and on the Continent, that it was winning and would triumph. In its absence, the Patriots could keep going. This situation, however, did not preclude choices for both sides that can be seen as strategic. For example, Valley Forge was selected as the Patriot wintering position for 1777–8 in order to be able to mount an attack on nearby British-held Philadelphia as well as to shadow any British moves from there. Moreover, Washington hoped that the rich Pennsylvania countryside would provide his men with food and forage, since what passed as Continental army logistics were weak at best, and New Jersey was bare. The decisions taken by the Council of War of the Continental Army provide opportunities for seeing how strategy was discussed. For example, in April 1778, Washington asked his leading officers whether they advised an attack on Philadelphia, an attack on New York, or remaining in camp while the army was prepared for a later confrontation. The response was divided. Concerned about morale and the more general state of the army, Anthony Wayne argued that any attack was better than remaining on the defensive and allowing the British to implement their plans, but Washington decided to remain at Valley

Forge and to await developments.[4] These materialised in the shape of the British withdrawal from Philadelphia in June and Washington was then able to advance to attack the British at Monmouth Court House.

It proved hard to repeat Washington's partial success in, at least, stabilising the situation in the Middle Colonies in the south. There, the political context was one in which Loyalism was more prominent. Opinion in the shape of local support became the key element in the war in the south after Patriot defeats there in 1779–80 left Major-General Nathanael Greene, the commander of the Southern Department of the Continental Army from October 1780, able to carry on only partisan warfare. The use of partisans was an obvious strategy in response to the Patriot defeats at Charleston and Camden, the uncontrollable vastness of the south, and the need to counter Loyalist activity. In contrast, British strategic planning for the Southern Campaign of 1778 was based on the strategic assumption of Loyalist support and the goal of re-establishing royal allegiance and rule over each colony in turn from Georgia up. The consequence was a vicious local war. Greene waged a successful war of posts in combined operations of regulars and partisan militia, while at the same time challenging the British army, so damaging the British forces that they gradually withdrew from the back country to within their lines at Charleston and thereafter conducted raids. Greene also pressed the partisan commanders to join him in a general plan of operations instead of carrying on with their freebooting raids. Eventually that occurred.

The war in the south was to play a major role in the subsequent American understanding and presentation of their success. However, in 1780 and 1781, Washington was far more hopeful of using French forces, land and sea. His initial target was New York. Its fall would be a fateful blow to the British military position in North America and might well lead to the effective end of the war. This was an outcome the Patriots desperately required in order to counter the domestic pressures arising from the strains of war that, in the shape of supply problems and desertion, greatly affected the army. Nevertheless, Washington was sufficiently flexible to appreciate that co-operation with the French came first and that, in response to their needs and wishes, it would be possible to focus on a different target, which, in 1781, turned out to be the British position in the Chesapeake at Yorktown.

Considering Patriot strategic options requires an assessment of those of their opponents. In turn, British options invite attention to how far other strategy choices would certainly have led to very different situations, affecting the possibility of rebellion, the likelihood of support within the areas that rebelled, and the prospect for a reconciliation short of conflict, let alone revolution. It is the very drive of the system that is at question when policies and the pressures for obedience and order are considered. Partly for this reason, domestic moves were a key aspect of strategy. As in other revolutionary struggles, strategy emerges as primarily political in background, goal and indeed means, with the use of force simply an aspect of the means, and frequently one that is only to be employed as a substitute for political failure.

The political context, both domestic and international, was very different, both in North America and for Britain, to that in the Seven Years' War, which underlines the extent to which, while any focus on war-winning involves understanding strategy, or, rather, operationalising it, in terms of military activity, the key to strategy is the political purposes that are pursued. There was a need on the part of Britain to respond to American strategy, but the prime requirement was an attempt to impose on it such that there was no basis for an American strategy. To employ modern terms, counter-insurgency was designed to ensure that there was no prospect for insurgency.

In the Seven Years' War, the British focus had been on conquest in North America from France, and not on pacification there. The latter was clearly subservient to the former, although different policies were pursued for the purpose of pacification, including an equivalent of ethnic cleansing in the expulsion of the Acadians from Nova Scotia, as well as the very different post-conquest accommodation of the Catholics of Quebec, which looked towards the Quebec Act of 1774. This accommodation proved highly successful, unlike the policies followed in the case of the British colonies further south. Indeed, the difficulties the government encountered in the latter made it more necessary to press for the accommodation of Quebec.

In the War of Independence, pacification was the British objective, and the question was how best to secure it, and thus ensure an avoidance of fresh rebellion and, in particular, one that might coincide with international war. To that extent, pacification was also the strategy. The purpose of the war was clear, the return of the Americans to their loyalty, and the method chosen was significantly different to that taken in response to the Jacobite rebellions in Scotland and northern England in 1715–16 and 1745–6. In the latter cases, as later in the face of the Irish rebellion in 1798, the remedy had been more clearly military, although there were postwar policies for stability through reorganisation in the introduction of radically new governmental and political systems for the Scottish Highlands and Ireland.

For America, there was not on the part of Britain this sequencing but, instead, a willingness to consider not only pacification alongside conflict, but also new political systems as an aspect of this pacification. Indeed, in one sense, pacification began at the outset in 1775, with the misconceived and mishandled British attempt to seize arms in New England, which led to the clashes at Concord and Lexington. Attempted pacification continued with the unsuccessful attempt to overawe resistance at Bunker Hill, for the display of British forces there in preparation for their attack had an intimidating character. The most prominent instances of pacification were the instructions to the Howe brothers, the commanders appointed in 1776, to negotiate as well as fight, and, even more clearly, the dispatch of the Carlisle Commission in 1778, again with instructions to negotiate, each of which were approaches rejected by the Americans. Moreover, the restoration of colonial government in the south was a concrete step indicating, during the war, what the British were seeking to achieve.

Alongside that, and more insistently, were the practices of British commanders. Although the Americans were traitors, they were treated with great leniency, and suggestions of harsher treatment were generally ignored. This point underlines the extent to which conduct in the field reflects both strategy and the realities of the campaigning and also affects the strategic context, as with the Germans on the Eastern Front in the Second World War. In most cases across the world during the eighteenth century, rebels were treated far more harshly, for example the Jacobites by the British army in 1745–6. So also, eventually, with the treatment of Confederate citizens and Southern society in the American Civil War of 1861–5. Despite suggestions, there was no comparable move in the War of Independence, at least in so far as British regular forces were concerned, towards the 'hard' approach eventually seen in Union conduct in the American Civil War. The Americans after 1777 had a large number of British prisoners, which was an important part of the equation.

This focus on pacification provides an essential continuity to British strategy during the War of American Independence, but there were differences in emphasis. Two key discontinuities changed the parameters for contemporaries: the declaration of American independence in 1776 and the internationalisation of the war with France's formal entry in 1778 on the American side. Alongside these discontinuities came military unpredictabilities, such as the initially successful, but eventually totally unsuccessful, American invasion of Canada in 1775–6, and the British failures at Saratoga (1777) and Yorktown (1781), each of which helped direct strategy.

The southern strategy, both military and political, the focus on regaining the Southern Colonies that dominated British policy from late 1778 when a British amphibious force swiftly captured Savannah, arose in large part from the impact of formal French entry into the war earlier in the year. That meant that British troops would have to protect other colonies, notably in the West Indies, against French attack, and thus encouraged a strategy focused on winning and using the support of southern Loyalists as a key source of manpower.

French entry ended the unusual situation in which Britain was at war solely in North America, and therefore able to concentrate attention and resources on it. In 1754–5, Britain had been at war with France in North America, and the conflict did not extend to Europe until 1756, but that extension had been widely anticipated. From French entry into the War of Independence in 1778, Britain was essentially pushed into a bifurcated struggle involving separate strategies. A struggle for pacification continued in the Thirteen Colonies (albeit greatly complicated by the French military presence there on land and at sea and by the prospect of a larger presence), while a straightforward military struggle with France began elsewhere, especially in the West Indies, India and west Africa. Again, this apparently clear distinction can be qualified by noting that Britain had political, as well as military, options to consider in both cases, as well as offensive and defensive aspects to strategy. France used its reinvigorated navy both to threaten the British Isles, notably in 1779, and to challenge Britain in the New World from

1778. The timing was right in that the American victory at the battle of Saratoga in 1777 indicated that the rebellion in the American colonies had the possibility of success. Otherwise, it was likely that France would only have continued to smuggle in military supplies.

The international dimension was made more complex by the need to consider the goals and moves of various powers. Aside from Britain's relations with the states with which it eventually came to war – France in 1778, Spain in 1779 and the Dutch in 1780 – there were relations with neutral powers, both friendly and unfriendly, Russia, the organiser of the League of Armed Neutrality, being prominent among the latter. These relations were, in part, linked to the military operationalisation of strategy, notably with the British commitment to commercial blockade as a means to employ, retain and enhance naval strength, and with the possibility that alliances and agreements in Europe would yield troops for North America. This was an important goal as, lacking conscription, Britain was very short of troops.

Furthermore, the European crisis of 1778, which led to the War of the Bavarian Succession of 1778–9 between Prussia and France's ally Austria, created diplomatic opportunities for Britain and, indeed, was seen in this light. There has since been discussion on the lines that a more interventionist European policy would have distracted France from taking part in the American war, with major consequences for British options there. However, a fundamental aspect of British strategy in the 1770s was that Britain was acting as a satisfied or status quo power, keen obviously to retain and safeguard its position, but not interested in gaining fresh territory. Representing a satisfied power, British ministers were also wary of becoming involved in Continental European power politics. Here, the American war fitted into a pattern that had begun with George III's rejection of the Prussian alliance in 1761–2. This wariness had continued with a subsequent refusal to accept Russian requirements for an alliance, as well as with the rebuff of French approaches for joint action against, and in response to, the First Partition of Poland by Austria, Prussia and Russia in 1772.

Thus, there was to be no recurrence, during the War of Independence, of the situation in the Seven Years' War, namely war in alliance with a Continental power. The situation then had proved particularly potent, both in terms of domestic politics and in terms of international relations,

or had been shaped as effective by William Pitt the Elder with his presentation of British policy in terms of conquering Canada in Europe. In
the War of American Independence, there would be no alliance with
Prussia (nor anywhere else) to distract France, and, thus, in military
terms, no commitment of the British army to the Continent, as had
occurred in 1758. Even more, subsidised German troops, such as those
deployed in 1757, in an unsuccessful attempt to defend the Electorate of
Hanover, would not be used for 'German' or European power-political
purposes. Instead, while some troops would be retained in Europe,
Hanoverians being dispatched to serve in Gibraltar, others, most notably
Hessians, but also regiments from other German states, were sent to
America where, at peak strength, they comprised nearly 40 per cent of
the British army. Britain's fundamental strategy thus rested on a coherence that had military consequences: passivity in Europe combined with
the preservation of status in America.

What this strategy appeared to entail in North America varied greatly
during the conflict. The initial British perception was of opposition
being largely only in Massachusetts, and this inaccurate assessment
suggested that a vigorous defence of imperial interests there would save
the situation. This view led to British legislation in 1774 specific to this
colony, and to a concentration of Britain's forces in North America
there. The initial military operationalisation of strategy continued after
the clashes at Concord and Lexington in 1775, both because the stress
on Massachusetts appeared vindicated and because there were not
enough troops for action elsewhere. This situation, specifically its force
profile, represented a key failure in British preparedness, but was also a
product of the small size of the British army, which was only about
45,000 men.

In the event, this policy failed, both in Massachusetts and elsewhere.
In the former, the military presence was unable to prevent rebellion or
to contain it, and, in March 1776, the British had to evacuate Boston
when the harbour was threatened by American cannon as they did not
know that the Americans had no gunpowder for them. Indeed,
gunpowder supplies were to be an important aspect of French help.
Elsewhere in North America, the lack of troops stemming from the
concentration on Boston ensured that British authority was overthrown
in the other twelve colonies involved in the revolution. Moreover, in

1775, the Americans were able to mount an invasion of Canada that achieved initial success, capturing Montreal and bottling up the British in Quebec.

As a result of the events of 1775–6, the second stage of the war, a stage expected and planned neither by most of the Patriots nor by the British government, led to a major British effort to regain control. This policy entailed both a formidable military effort and peace-making proposals. Here, as for the Patriots, it is necessary to look at the British military options in terms of the political situation and vice versa. The end of the rebellion/revolution could not be achieved by reconquering all of the Thirteen Colonies (and driving the Americans from Canada). Prefiguring in a way the Union's position during the American Civil War (1861–5), the task was simply too great, leaving aside the issue of maintaining any such verdict. Instead, it was necessary to secure military results that achieved the political outcome of an end to rebellion in the shape of surrender. Such an outcome was likely to require both a negotiated settlement and acquiescence in the return to loyalty, and in subsequently maintaining obedience. This outcome rested on a totally different politics to that of the conquest of New France (Canada) during the Seven Years' War.

What was unclear was which military results would best secure this outcome. Was the priority the defeat, indeed destruction, of the Continental Army, as it represented the Revolution, not least its unity, a point grasped by Washington;[5] or was it the capture of key American centres, notably New York in 1776 and Philadelphia in 1777? Each goal appeared possible, and in practice there was a mutual dependence between them. The British would not be able to defeat the Americans unless they could land and support troops, and, for this capability to be maintained, it was necessary to secure port cities. Conversely, these port cities could best be held if American forces were defeated.

The equations of troop numbers made this clear, not least the problems posed for finite British military resources by maintaining large garrison forces. Indeed, the latter point lent further military purpose to the political strategy of pacification, as such a strategy would reduce the need for garrisons and produce local Loyalist forces, as well as cutting the number of Patriots.

In an instance of a longstanding issue in both strategy and operational planning, notably, but not only, in counter-insurgency struggles, the British emphasis possibly should have been on destroying the Continental Army, which was definitely a prospect in 1776–7 in the New York and Philadelphia campaigns. Instead, although the pursuit of cities did lead to battle because of Washington's strategy of protecting them, the stress was on regaining major centres. This was in part as a way of demonstrating the return of royal authority, particularly by ensuring that large numbers of Americans again came under the Crown. Indeed, from the period when the Empire struck back, the summer of 1776, the British gained control of most of the leading cities, either for much of the war (New York from 1776, Savannah from 1778, Charleston from 1780) or, as it turned out, temporarily (Newport from 1776 to 1778, and Philadelphia from 1777 to 1778).

Yet this policy still left important centres, most obviously Boston from March 1776, that were not under British control, which under-lined the fundamental political problem facing the British, and one that is more generally true in strategic planning: whatever they won in the field, it would still be necessary to achieve a political settlement. While political efforts were needed to secure the persistence and coherence of the war effort, the British, in turn, could try, by political approaches and military efforts, to alter these political equations within the Thirteen Colonies. At times, they succeeded in doing so, as in the new political prospectus offered in South Carolina after the successful British siege of Charleston in 1780. Indeed, in tidewater South Carolina, the part of the colony most exposed to British amphibious power and most dependent on trade, and the part that was most significant in both political and economic terms, British authority was swiftly recognised. This success appeared to be a vindication of the British strategy of combining mili-tary force with a conciliatory political stance, one offering a new impe-rial relationship that granted most of the American demands made at the outbreak of the war.

Political goals affected not only the moves of armies, but even the nature of the forces deployed by both sides; and the latter, in turn, influ-enced the politics of the struggle. The British use of German 'mercenaries' and, far more, of Native Americans and African Americans provided opportunities for political mobilisation on the part of the Patriots hostile to this use, even though, in practice, there was little use of African Americans, again largely for political reasons. The American reliance on

France, correspondingly, increased domestic support for war in Britain and greatly hit sympathy there for the Patriots. They could now be presented as hypocrites, willing to ally with a Catholic autocracy (two, when Spain joined in in 1779), and with Britain's national enemy as well.

These alliances brought the war to a new stage, since there was no inherent clarity as to the allocation of British resources between the conflict with the Bourbons (France and Spain) and that with the Americans. The parliamentary opposition repeatedly pressed for a focus on the Bourbons, not the Americans, but the ministry was unwilling to follow suit to the same extent because it neither wished, nor thought it appropriate, to abandon hopes of regaining America. This debate was not settled until Yorktown, not so much, crucially, the surrender of the besieged and defeated British force on 19 October 1781 as, rather, the political consequences in Britain. In particular, the fall of the Lord North ministry on 20 March 1782 was followed not by a similar one heeding royal views, but, rather, the opposition, under Charles, 2nd Marquess of Rockingham came to power. A county in North Carolina was renamed after him as was a town.

As a consequence of the change in ministry, the strategy for fighting on in North America outlined after Yorktown by Lord George Germain, the Secretary of State for the American Department, was redundant. He had already left office in February. It is instructive, however, to note his plan for mounting amphibious expeditions along the coast, regaining Rhode Island if possible. Germain argued that, by retaining New York, Charleston and Savannah, British trade would be secured and bases maintained from which counter-operations directed against France and Spain could be mounted in the Caribbean.[6]

As a result of the central role of politics in strategy, 1782, therefore, was a key year of the war. It was a year, ironically, in which the Patriots achieved singularly little military success, Washington, in particular, getting nowhere with his plan to capture New York. Moreover, this failure was more generally significant as it marked the decline in the Franco-American alliance. This reflected the problems of pursuing very different military priorities, with the French focused on the West Indies, and, far more significantly, a war-weariness on the part of the French government that in part arose from the priorities of European power politics, notably French concern about Russian expansionism at the expense of the Turks. This point illustrates the complex and interlinked character of international relations and helps explain the resulting context for strategy.[7]

Furthermore, in 1782, the French fleet in the West Indies was heavily defeated by Admiral Rodney at the battle of the Saintes on 9–12 April, providing a major instance of the role of battle in determining strategic options. Militarily, the war was going Britain's way. New warships were being launched, public finances were robust, fears of rebellion in Ireland and of disaffection in Britain were largely assuaged, the Bourbons were increasingly unable to attempt another invasion of Britain, Gibraltar had been held against siege and large-scale attack, and the British position in both India and Canada was more resilient than had been feared. The equations of colonial gains and the likely offsetting in any eventual peace treaty thus altered. Yet the politics for Britain was now of peace and of a settlement that was not focused on a return of America to its loyalty; and strategy was framed accordingly. Instead, the priority was the disruption, if not destruction, of the coalition of powers fighting Britain and, hopefully, better relations with an independent United States (as it later became). Paradoxically, this strategy was to be successful, and in both the short and the long term, as Britain won the battle of the peace by dividing the opposing coalition and offering peace terms separately.[8] Moreover, peace created opportunities for new alignments. In June 1786, William Eden, an MP and the British envoy in Paris for negotiating a trade treaty, reported: 'There are strong appearances here of a disposition to believe that Great Britain and France ought to unite in some solid plan of permanent peace: and many of the most considerable people talk with little reserve of the dangers to be apprehended from the revolted colonies, if they should be encouraged to gain commercial strength and consistency of government.'[9]

In 1787 and 1790, when Britain and France came close to conflict, there was scant prospect of America wishing to help, or being able to help, the French.[10] Although there were many differences between the War of Independence (a rebellion within an imperial state, as well as a civil war) and the Vietnam War, the strategic dimension offers certain parallels, not least in the breakdown of the coalition that had opposed the United States. By the end of the 1970s, China was aligned with the United States and at war with Vietnam.

The roles of contextual factors and contingency in Patriot strategy therefore emerge clearly both in general terms and in specifics, and not least with reference to British options. Following the disasters of 1776, Washington recognised that for many the Continental Army was the Revolution. Thereafter, he did not take significant risks unless success was all but guaranteed. Had the British been more successful, the Patriots might well have resorted to more revolutionary military methods, such as guerrilla warfare and the strategy advocated by Lee. Indeed, Greene succeeded in the south in combining partisan bands with the manoeuvres of a field army.

Alternatively, and pursuing a very different strategy, the Patriots might have continued to rely on field armies, as the French Revolutionaries were to do in the 1790s, but, again as the French Revolutionaries did and the Union side in the Civil War was to do, those who took power in America could have taken a harsher attitude towards states' rights and private property. The consequence might have been a very different American public culture, one that stressed the national state more than the individual citizen or the individual state, and obligations more than rights.

STRATEGY FOR THE NEW STATE

The dissolution of the wartime coalition in 1783 made Britain more menacing and raised the threat that it might find European allies. For the United States, Canada in British hands underlined past failure and present threat. Thomas Jefferson, president from 1801 to 1809, backed the exploration of, and beyond, the lands acquired by the Louisiana Purchase of 1803, notably in supporting the Lewis and Clark transcontinental expedition to the Pacific.[11]

As another aspect of strategic culture, the very American conception of appropriate governance encouraged expansion. In response to their perception of mistreatment as part of the British Empire, Americans, both before and after independence, pressed for an eventual equality, but within a federalism that was seen as the means and ideology necessary to combine liberty with strength, and locality with extent. The ideological dimension of government and spatiality was crucial to this strategy of governance and expansionism. The federal approach in practical terms was a way to tackle the bold territorial claims of the pre-existing seven colonies that had extensive western lands. In terms of the ideology of the strategy involved, this approach made expansion appear normative without threatening the imperial excess allegedly associated with Classical Rome and modern Britain. Instead, Americans came to believe not only that their territory must expand, but also that the Union had to be dynamic. The new states were to be equal and uniform, as far as their government and the federal government were concerned. This solution was regarded as a way to ensure republican ideals.

Washington and Jefferson provided iconic comments for those subsequently seeking to discuss American strategy, comments that reflected an attempt to define a moral space for the new republic, and a strategy accordingly. The moral and prudential reasons offered for staying out of the maelstrom of great-power politics were clearly linked to an exceptionalist vision of America as better than, and also separate from, Europe.[12] So also with the determination to dispense with any idea that the universality of a supposed right to happiness proclaimed in the Declaration of Independence of 1776 carried with it a need to spread this right in foreign countries. In this respect, there was a difference to the situation with Revolutionary France from 1792 and, later, the communist Soviet Union. Aside from moral goals, such a spread appeared to the French Revolutionaries to be the best way to protect their achievement. A tension that was to be seen repeatedly in the geopolitics of strategy, one between realist and idealist conceptions, came to the fore with the United States and was settled then, in the face of British power, in favour of the former.

At the same time, strategy was capability-based, as well as task-orientated, and was also affected by the public narratives about goals and means. The new American state was very weak militarily. After independence, its navy was dismantled and its army savagely cut back in response to political views and fiscal needs.[13] Political factors were crucial, including the strong anti-army ideology derived from the British background and the colonial experience, the linked support for the militia, and the extent to which the unsettled governmental situation left any basis for military arrangements unclear, irrespective of the serious political differences and controversies bound up in issues of army purpose, size and command.

Subsequently, but also related to these tensions, the crisis caused in American politics by the growing radicalism of the French Revolution from 1793 ensured that strategy was reconceptualised and contested anew in a melange that comprised foreign policy, domestic politics and the nature of the American polity. To many American politicians, the response to the French Revolution had to be a strategy of vigilance against domestic radicals who might support France and be inspired by it, and against French power projection. Linked to this point, American foreign policy was republican, but not radical. Alexander Hamilton's sense of a menacing international system, and his more specific concerns about France, gave reason to his drive to develop America's public finances and national economy, and to his Anglophilia, which resulted in improved relations with Britain. In an approach that presented prudence in ideological terms and ideology as prudential, Hamilton, Secretary of the Treasury from 1789 to 1795 and commanding general of the army (senior officer) from 1799 to 1800, saw Britain as an essentially liberal state and therefore as less of a threat to America and, indeed, other states than, he argued, France was. Hamilton was determined to provide a national bank and a professional army able to unite America against internal subversion and foreign threat. The passage of the Alien and Sedition Acts was regarded as a means to strengthen the government against internal opposition.

To the Jeffersonians, in contrast, the struggle that had given rise to the American Revolution was being repeated, but with the threat now based in America. Indeed, in Jeffersonian eyes, Hamilton was another version of George III. This was a classic instance of strategy on the international–domestic continuum, and not only in revolutionary circumstances. The Jeffersonians were anxious about the problems for American public life that would come from the military, irrespective of the intentions of its commanders. These divisions were to be sustained in the shape of the Second Party System, operating from about 1828 to 1854, with the Whigs opposed by the Jacksonian Democrats. The United States thus represented an accentuation of a commonplace British reluctance to see large regular forces as anything other than supporters of centralisation and arbitrary government. Strategy was in part a product of the context established by domestic anxieties about force structures and international alignments.[14] In part, there was a clear tension between southern landowners who thought in Continental terms (forts and gunboats) and the New England merchants whose worldview was maritime and whose strategy focused on the establishment of an ocean-going navy.

Differences within America reflected a lack of unity over political identity and, even more, strategic culture. Aside from a major disagreement over the size and organisation of the military, a disagreement that arose from contrasting assumptions about the nature of America as a state and about American society, clashing conceptions of the international system were also important. Hamilton advanced a pessimistic interpretation of competing states, and of the need, in response, for strategies of governmental and military preparedness on the part of America, whereas Jefferson felt that a benign system was possible and/or that America could distance itself from the European powers.[15]

While American strategy was circumscribed by resources, debates about strategy were subordinate to political tensions and could not be separated from them. Moreover, these debates drew on a politicised historical account, one in which strategies appeared directly relevant, particularly in terms of how best to define the necessary national strategic culture as well as the relevant institutions. Jefferson preferred to rely not on a European-style military, but on national unity. This was an example of the comforting illusion, also seen with Revolutionary France, that virtue would necessarily prevail, and led him, in his Inaugural Address in 1801, to claim that America was the strongest country in the world.

THE FRENCH REVOLUTIONARY WAR

In April 1792, France declared war with Austria, beginning a period of conflict that, with brief interruptions (although long ones for many powers), continued until 1815. The contrast with recent French policy very much indicated the impact of ideology on strategy. Unlike during the Seven Years' War and the War of American Independence, France was alone in 1792, bar the backing of foreign radicals, the extent and effectiveness of which was greatly exaggerated in Paris. Even the republic it had helped from 1778, the United States, remained neutral, as did the other European republics. Moreover, France was not drawn into war as a result of alliance systems and of the action or problems of an ally, as had been the case in going to war in support of Austria against Prussia in 1756. As a consequence, French strategy in 1792 arose largely from domestic circumstances, although these were in part activated by the international situation. The domestic perceptions of this situation were crucial as instances of a markedly changing strategic culture.

France was not the sole player. Indeed, from July 1791, when Emperor Leopold II issued the Padua Circular, an appeal to Europe's rulers for concerted action to restore the liberty of the French royal family, a dynamic had been provided by counter-revolutionary steps. On 27 August 1791, the rulers of Austria and Prussia issued the Declaration of Pillnitz, which sought to give added force to the principles set forth in the Padua Circular.

As so often with strategy, a changing tone, as well as content and context, was important. In France, among the radicals the determination to secure a transformation contributed to aggressive goals and methods, with compromise not acceptable as a public aim. So also with the response. In 1792, the advancing Prussian commander, Charles, Duke of Brunswick, himself a sovereign ruler, issued a declaration setting out the aims of Francis II of Austria and Frederick William II of Prussia. They claimed to seek the re-establishment of Louis XVI's legislative authority and, to that end, Brunswick warned that Paris would be subject to exemplary vengeance if Louis was harmed, a deterrent threat that totally failed. In this crisis, appeals in France for revolutionary zeal against the invaders were matched by paranoia about betrayal.

In response, the strategy proposed for abroad was one of seeking popular support, notably, on 19 November 1792, with the National Convention, the successor to the National Assembly, declaring that the French people would extend fraternity and assistance to all peoples seeking to regain their liberty. As a general principle, this was subversive of all international order, as well as unrealistic, but it also appeared to offer hope and means. On 15 December, a decree to ensure that the *ancien régime* would be swept away in territories occupied by French forces was promulgated. On 1 February 1793, the National Convention decided unanimously to declare war on Britain and the Dutch, making novel use of the established notion that war was declared on sovereigns, and thus arguing that aggression was not being committed against other peoples. More generally, there was a wider struggle between radical and moderate views on the international order which helped to locate both the prospect of peace and the means of waging war.[16]

The mobilisation of French society was to be the key strategy adopted at home. Defeat at the hands of Austria in 1793 (but not total defeat) led to the army being given new scale and force by the *levée en masse* (conscription), able new commanders and more effective organisation. The armies enabled France to operate effectively on several fronts at once, to sustain casualties, and to match the opposing forces of much of Europe. Moreover, initially at least, Revolutionary enthusiasm was an important element in French capability, one that was helpful in providing the morale required for effective shock action, and, in particular, for crossing the killing ground produced by opposing firepower. In short, strategic culture and military tactics were closely linked. This has parallels elsewhere, for example in the American emphasis on air power after the Second World War. French success by 1797, and, again, by 1801, contrasted with a lack of similar Prussian decisive victory, when also up against a powerful coalition, during the Seven Years' War. The contrast reflected resource equations, notably of manpower, as well as strategic, geopolitical, organisational and operational factors.

In the French Revolutionary War, strategy was set by ideology and by the very military that had been created. Just as ideology, and the mechanism of terror, discouraged compromise, so the government, more particularly the military, and the generals, required continued warfare, notably operating abroad, in order to fund their activities. By keeping the generals busy, war served to contain their ambitions within France. For the generals, opportunism and the ability to make a new world created a strategic culture focused on aggressive action and on continual activity. Napoleon's seizure of power in 1799 brought elements of the new strategy to fruition.

The ability of popular movements to resist and, at times, even see off regular forces in the American and French Revolutions prefigured the situation with the Spanish rebellion/revolution against Napoleon in 1808; a rebellion/revolution staged in the absence of the imprisoned monarch, Charles IV. Clausewitz was influenced by this revolution, seeing it as an example that the Prussians should have followed after their devastating defeat by France in 1806, a defeat of a system.[17] This

Spanish resistance offered the possibility of thwarting the victors' ability to translate the output of victory in battle into the outcome of a successful war. Napoleon's successful advance on Madrid did not end a resistance, which instead repeated, as a military means and a moral step, the earlier persistence of both the Americans and the French in the face of defeats.

If, however, the Prussians failed to suppress the French Revolution in 1792, they overthrew the Dutch Patriots in 1787. If the French failed in Spain in 1808–13, their subsequent invasion was crucial to the overthrow of the liberals there in 1823. Contextual and contingent circumstances were crucial. In contrasting American and French strategic contexts, it is necessary to consider ideological drives, governmental capabilities, geopolitical circumstances, and the contingent requirements set by the actions of other states. These elements were independent variables but also interdependent. The United States had, like France, an ideology and practice of expansion, but its geopolitical circumstances were very different. The opposition posed by the British, French and Spanish in North America and by Native Americans did not pose a transforming threat comparable to that confronted by the Revolutionaries. Moreover, once France had succumbed to a military dictatorship in the person of Napoleon, then the needs of that dictatorship, as perceived by the dictator, set the strategy.

Other states responded. In 1796, Major-General David Dundas outlined the means that he felt should be pursued if the French invaded Britain:

> When an enemy lands, all the difficulties of civil government and the restraint of forms cease; everything must give way to the supplying and strengthening the army, repelling the enemy . . . The strongest and most effectual measures are necessary . . . every inch of ground, every field may to a degree be disputed, even by inferior numbers . . . The country must be driven, and everything useful within his reach destroyed without mercy.[18]

Confronting domestic challenges, real and alleged, was also a key aspect of the strategy of response to the threat posed by the French Revolution; and a similar dynamic could be seen in America's divided politics in response to the examples of Britain and France. The nexus of strategy was seen to lie in the reply to this linked threat.

CONCLUSIONS

The strategic elements faced by the new republican regimes were not themselves new. Nor were the responses to them. Indeed, the temptation to begin a trajectory of modern strategy in this period can be readily undercut by examples going back to antiquity and, more particularly, looking at the wars of religion of the sixteenth century, whether in the Middle East, between Sunni Ottomans and Shi'ite Safavids, or in Christendom between Catholics and Protestants. Ironically, the most significant element of modernity in 1775–1815 occurred in the shape of the response, notably the global oceanic capability of Britain, the world's leading naval power, one whose strategic assumptions rested on the consequences of commercial strength and requirements. Britain did not necessarily win, in that the United States gained and maintained independence while Russia played the key role in overthrowing Napoleon, as opposed to merely thwarting him. However, Britain's part was increasingly significant not only to the strategic context for other Western powers but also, increasingly, to non-Western powers.

5

NAPOLEON AND OTHERS
1790-1914

The pursuit of power in this 'long century' helped ensure that, as will be discussed in Chapter 7, control over most of the world's population was contested, while large amounts of territory changed hands. International competition was a key element, but so, also, were domestic anxieties, drives, interests and policies. The 'long century' also saw the establishment of general staffs and the impact on military planning of the development of the formal language of strategy. As a consequence, scholarly attention focuses on the development of strategic thought by Carl Maria von Clausewitz, a Prussian, and on Prussia, which, thanks to the German Wars of Unification of 1864–71, became the major power in the centre of Europe, and where the general staff became a model for developments elsewhere. This, however, is an approach that has only limited value.

IDEAS OF STRATEGY

Strategy was a fully fledged process and habit of thought prior to the increasingly widespread use of the concept with that term in the nineteenth century. The emphasis in international relations and conflict on both land and sea was placed on the skills and character of rulers and commanders, but, more broadly, strategy was employed to assess state interest, to further it and to expound it. This understanding and practice of strategy was both a traditional usage, but also, in part, one related, at least in its presentation, to the development, certainly in Europe from the sixteenth century, of the idea of the state and, thus, to political modernisation. Thus, strategy rested, at least in part, not only on an awareness of the situation that to a certain extent depended on a reading of both opportunities and the intentions of opponents, but also on a capacity for abstraction and on the conviction that planning was necessary.

The pressure of the moment, however, inevitably tended to be to the fore, and notably so in wartime. In 1758, Robert, 4th Earl of Holdernesse, one of the two British Secretaries of State, responded to a point made by Frederick the Great, then an ally, to the British envoys:

> The remark that was made to you, that our enemies acted upon a systematical plan, and guided their operations to the execution of it, is certainly a very true one, and if there is no fixed system, or particular plan of operations, settled between His Majesty and the King of Prussia, it has not arisen either from neglect, or want of good-will, on this side, but, from the nature and circumstances of the war . . . all that could be thought of was how to make head against so many enemies.[1]

Similarly, William Pitt the Elder, the other Secretary of State, pointed out the need in Germany to base strategy on the moves of opponents.[2]

Alongside the pressure of the moment, strategy to a degree drew from the eighteenth century on the measurement of factors and calibration of concerns linked to the mathematisation related to the Scientific Revolution, a process of intellectual change not seen across most of the world. More generally, concepts and their expression were linked to the categorisation of knowledge, to the means available for expressing opinion, and to their limitations. From that perspective, a degree of what can be seen as imprecision reflected the issues posed by the available vocabulary, the difficulties of definitions and, separately, the range of political cultures and their disparate views. That approach, however, underplays the inherent imprecision of strategy as a concept and practice. Rather than reacting to a well-established literature on war and on the practice of strategy, Clausewitz, a military practitioner first and foremost, was responding to an international situation that appeared singularly unfixed. In political and military terms, there was much that Prussian generals had not had to consider, notably in the example of popular resistance to Napoleon offered by Spain.[3] Instability, threat and the need for analysis were all linked.

Moreover, the situation would have appeared even more unfixed had Clausewitz been aware of the position around the world. From that perspective, Clausewitz's background was unfortunate as he had no direct experience of conflict with non-Western forces and/or in non-Western environments. In that, Clausewitz was very different not only to much of the British military but also to many of their Russian and Austrian counterparts, as well as a few of the French ones, notably Napoleon as a consequence of his campaigning in the Middle East in 1798–9. The standard focus on Clausewitz is an instance of the dominance of the study of war not only by Western commentators, but also by commentators whose willingness to engage with other traditions and with their implications can be limited, a point which underlines the issues, indeed problems, posed by his recent and current influence.[4] To work today, military analysis has to apply to Madagascar and Paraguay, as well as to Western powers, and the challenge looking forward is to produce a global account of strategy. The same was true of the past, just as Enlightenment historians were trying to produce a non-Christian understanding of world history. Given the variety of circumstances and developments that commentators could (and can) draw on, it is difficult to generalise or, indeed, discern a crucial identity to war and an inherent set of practices.

The capacity for reflecting on strategic cultures and parameters in the wider global sense was more present for a Wellington than for a Clausewitz; although the latter was interested in the dynamic of insurgency and counter-insurgency warfare. Wellington himself was extremely well read in military matters, but, more significantly, had held senior command positions in India as well as in Europe.[5] Any emphasis on Wellington underlines the point that it was Britain (and Russia), and not France, that was victorious in the long eighteenth century, and, therefore, that any concentration on the latter is misplaced.

This is even more the case if due weight is devoted to the significance of strategy for naval power, and vice versa. The political and organisational revolutions that underlay the development and sustaining of British naval power were more significant for the pursuit of strategy on a global scale than the French Revolution. So also with the geopolitical and strategic thinking that led Charles, 3rd Duke of Richmond, the Master-General of the Ordnance, to comment on France in 1785: 'Instead of drawing her off from the continent [Europe] to the ocean, we [Britain] want some power to draw her attention from the ocean to the continent.'[6] A strategy applied for centuries, it was to be followed anew in the French Revolutionary and Napoleonic Wars, with Russia, in particular, being the prime power in question in 1799, 1805–7 and 1812–14.

1790–1815

The standard focus for the 1790s is the outbreak in 1792 of the French Revolutionary Wars and the rise from 1795 of Napoleon to be France's leading general and, from 1799, the liquidator of the French Revolution. However, the important conflicts at the same time in southern and northern India and in Persia (Iran) indicated the range of the volatility in power politics, and the according need to approach strategy in a number of very different contexts and in light of the pressure of specific contingencies. For example, the activities of Agha Muhammad of Persia (r. 1779–97) and of Zaman Shah of Afghanistan (r. 1793–1800) deserve attention because they demonstrate the extent to which the personal and family strategies they pursued, and the tribal contexts in which they operated, were not residual features. In Persia, the late 1780s and early 1790s saw the Qajar tribe under Agha Muhammad take over, destroying the previously dominant Zand dynasty. This process was helped by Zand disunity, which, in turn, was accentuated by failure. Agha Muhammad also sought to reconquer former Persian territories and to assert sovereignty, which he did in Georgia in 1795 and Khurusan (in north-east Persia) in 1796.

His threat to Afghanistan in 1799, including backing Zaman's rebellious brothers, a threat encouraged by Britain but not dependent on it, ended the possibility that Zaman Shah would advance across northern India, defeating Britain's protégés.[7] Thus, Persia became part of the world of British power politics and strategy. This was not in order to look west and affect Turkey, as in past Western strategic speculation and even planning, for example that of Venice in the late fifteenth and early sixteenth centuries. Instead, the issue was whether Persia would look east and as part of a geopolitical concern focused on Britain's wider Indian policy. This concern interested Britain's rivals, France and Russia, and looked towards their greater engagement with Persia from the 1800s.

Napoleon seized power in late 1799, and 1800, his first year of campaigning in his new role, was chosen by Antoine-Henri de Jomini as the year in which 'the system of modern strategy was fully developed'.[8] This description of the Marengo campaign was ironic in light of the more recent stress on improvisation in explaining Napoleon's success, both that year against the Austrians and more generally, and, linked to this, on him as an opportunist.[9] Indeed, repeatedly he was tactically and operationally adroit, even brilliant, but an indifferent, increasingly poor, strategist, who, ultimately, failed completely, and did so twice, in 1814 and 1815. There are instructive parallels with German strategy in 1914–45.

Napoleon's opening campaign as first consul was an invasion of northern Italy boldly begun with a crossing of the Great St Bernard Pass so that he arrived in the Austrian rear and threatened their line of supply, undercutting the Austrian advance on Lyons. At the subsequent battle of Marengo, however, on 14 June 1800, Napoleon found the Austrians to be a formidable rival, as they had earlier often been to French Revolutionary forces, and Napoleon's enforced retreat for much of the battle was only reversed because of a successful counter-attack mounted by French re-inforcements. Napoleon had been driven by the desire to engage and win. By placing his army in a position where it had an opportunity to engage, and thus forcing a battle whose shape would be unclear, he, like the British admiral Horatio Nelson, most obviously at Trafalgar in 1805, placed great reliance on the subsequent mêlée, which rewarded the fighting qualities of individual units, the initiative and skill of subordinates and, in Napoleon's case, the ability to retain reserves until the crucial moment.

At Marengo, as elsewhere, Napoleon also was able to dominate the news agenda and present a positive spin on his generalship.[10] This was an important aspect of his *modus operandi* and his reputation as a strategist, one who led from the front.

It was ironic that Napoleon himself did not employ the term 'strategy' until after he was exiled by the British to St Helena in 1815 and then very infrequently.[11] Nevertheless, in addition to the usual term of the period, 'art of war', 'strategy' has been a term often applied to his actions, and that remains the case. It could have been applied to Nguyen Anh or Chakri, the successful contemporary counterparts in Vietnam and Thailand who established dynasties that lasted for a long while, but Jomini knew and cared little of their activities.

An emphasis on, and discussion of, Marengo and the Italian campaign in 1800 raises the question of the strategic purpose of Napoleon's invasion of Egypt in 1798, which was one of the most dramatic episodes in his career. This question emphasises the issue of 'whose strategy?', one that is always worth addressing when strategy is being considered. For Napoleon, like Julius Caesar when invading Britain in 55 and 54 BCE, concerned to keep his army together as a means of personal power, seeking the opportunity to win more fame and wishing to expand French imperial power eastward, the expedition fulfilled key purposes while also enabling him to lessen the unwelcome control of the Directory government in Paris. At the same time, the last came to support the invasion because it wished to hit Britain's routes to India.[12] This expedition was the first successful amphibious invasion of Egypt since those of the Romans; the Crusaders' attempt under Louis IX of France had totally failed.

Napoleon's victories in Egypt and his capture of Alexandria and Cairo, all in 1798, underlined the vulnerability of powerful centres of the Islamic world. Whether this vulnerability, and France's amphibious capability, contributed to a coherent French strategy is far less clear. However, the expedition revealed to those who knew of it a volatility in power politics that suggested new opportunities and needs for strategic insight and planning. That the expedition in practice exposed a portion of the French military to the strength of the British navy, and such that the army, with the attending fleet totally defeated at the battle of the Nile in 1798, was left vulnerable, was disastrous both militarily and politically, and notably so as France was under increasing pressure in the War of the Second Coalition. The risk of exposing strength to isolation and defeat is a crucial psychological as well as practical restraint for states that cannot dominate the maritime environment or control the consequences of this power projection. This risk looks back to the Greeks' near failure at Troy and to Athens's total failure at Syracuse.

Napoleon himself evaded responsibility for the debacle, which underlines the point about relevant strategic perspective as well as his skills as a propagandist. Leading from the front and following a diplomacy of bullying, Napoleon did not generally encumber himself by recognising alternatives, either in war or in international relations, or by devoting attention to those he did not see as readily advantageous. By thus restricting his strategic options, Napoleon weakened his position.

Separately, it is striking that much of the literature of the period discusses what can be seen as strategies although without necessarily using the term.[13] The focus on Napoleon is ironic as the more impressive strategic achievement in the Western world, instead, was that in countering him. This was a matter not only of the British naval movements in 1798 and the resistance to Napoleon's siege of Acre in 1799, but also of the concentration of British strength in 1801 to support an attack on the French forces in Egypt. This involved operations in the Mediterranean and in the Red Sea, each of which had multiple permutations or knock-on consequences depending on the process one envisages. The combination of deploying naval forces in 'home waters' and the Mediterranean was long established for Britain, but that with the Indian Ocean was not, and Britain had never before sought the degree of co-ordination and planning attempted in 1798–1801.

The successful attack on Mysore in southern India in 1799 was an aspect of the British strategy, as Tipu Sultan, its ruler, sought to be an ally of France. Plans for an expedition from India to Batavia (Djakarta), which was ruled by France's Dutch ally, were abandoned. It was not attacked (successfully) until 1812. Instead, Britain moved first ships, and then troops, to the Red Sea in order to support the main attack on Egypt from the Mediterranean. Already, in 1795, the British had carried out a reconnaissance of the Red Sea in order to gain necessary information. The British plans included seeking to extend influence into the Hijaz (in modern Saudi Arabia) in order to thwart any French use of the Red Sea to advance into the Indian Ocean. This prospectus echoed the (unsuccessful) Portuguese response to Mamluk (Egyptian) and Ottoman moves in the 1510s and subsequently, and serves to demonstrate continuing features of the geopolitical context of strategy. In the event, British troops, some from India and some from Cape Town, marched in 1801 from the Red Sea to the Nile, although the total defeat of the French forces in Egypt was essentially due to the force from the Mediterranean.[14]

British planning and execution rested on an increasingly sophisticated appreciation of the geopolitical and strategic linkages between different parts of the world, some of them far apart.[15] The British were far more used than Napoleon was to thinking of strategy as the mobilisation of global resources (including allies). They understood that such resources could be deployed to try to shift the balance in Europe and European waters. Repeatedly, the British emerged as more strategically astute than their opponents. In contrast, in the early 1800s, Napoleon sought to pursue a 'Western Design', seeking to create a major empire that would include Louisiana, Florida, Cayenne, Martinique, Guadeloupe and Saint-Domingue (Haiti). The plan focused on the dispatch of 20,000 troops to the last in 1802 in order to re-establish control in the former French colony. This expedition, however, fell victim to opposition, disease and the resumption of conflict with Britain in 1803. This failure does not encourage confidence in Napoleon's strategic trajectory.

JOMINI AND CLAUSEWITZ

Napoleon provided Western commentators with the ambition and apparent need to explain success in war. This task encouraged a bold attempt to write about a science of command, which has long proved a major route into discussing strategy. Jomini and Clausewitz were to be the major figures.[16] The key rule-master for long proved to be the Swiss-born Antoine-Henri de Jomini (1779–1869). He served in the French army as chief of staff to Marshal Ney, before switching, in 1813, to the Russian army, being made a lieutenant-general by Alexander I, the central figure in Napoleon's overthrow. Jomini's influential works, which included the *Traité des grands operations militaires* (1805–9) and the *Précis de l'art de la guerre* (which appeared first in 1810 as the conclusion to the *Traité*), aimed to find logical principles at work in warfare, which was seen, by Jomini, as having timeless essential characteristics. In particular, Jomini sought to explain the success of Frederick the Great and then of Napoleon in *Vie politique et militaire de Napoléon* (1827).

Jomini, like Clausewitz, wrote in the shadow of Napoleon, and self-consciously so. Jomini had to address the topics of Napoleon's sweeping success and of his subsequent complete failure. In doing so, Jomini's focus was operational and not strategic. To him, the crucial military point was the choice of a line of operations that would permit a successful attack. Napoleonic operational art was discussed in terms of envelopment – the use of 'exterior lines', and, alternatively, the selection of a central position that would permit the defeat in detail (separately) of opposing forces – a position which was described in terms of interior lines. The corps gave Napoleon, Jomini argued with reason, a 'force-multiplier' that greatly increased operational effectiveness. By focusing on decisive battles, Jomini emphasised battle-winning as decisive, rather than the wider consequences of social, economic and technological change.[17] He was, for example, critical of the Spanish guerrilla warfare against French occupation which he himself had witnessed.[18]

Jomini's emphasis continues to be widespread in the discussion of Napoleonic generalship. It can be seen, for example, in the focus on the battle of Waterloo (18 June), or on the operations of 15–18 June, when considering the events of 1815; and not, as it should also be, on Napoleon's diplomatic isolation, which helped force him onto the attack, nor on his failure to inspire widespread support within France after the battle. Each of the latter was highly significant in strategic terms. Jomini's influence remained strong into the 1860s, as in *The Operations of War Explained and Illustrated* (1866) by Edward Hamley, the professor of military history at the new British Staff College at Sandhurst.

Jomini was interested in practical lessons. His was really a 'how-to' approach, one of lessons to be learned from the past. Clausewitz (1780–1831), in contrast, sought to train the minds of commanders and statesmen and emphasised a broad approach, most notably the inherent political nature of war and, therefore, the balance of political determination. In 1804, he drafted a short work entitled *Strategie* which covered a range of topics. Unpublished, this study emphasised the importance of securing the object of the war, and, to that end, the value of battle.[19] In his posthumously published, but important, account of Napoleon's Russian campaign, Clausewitz presented the French strategy in 1812 as one of victory in campaign enabling the dictation of a peace that was to be aided by creating dissension between a weak government and the nobility.[20] The campaigns he took part in influenced his views.[21] In about 1827, Clausewitz also wrote *Feldzug von 1815: Strategische Übersicht des Feldzugs von 1815* ('The Campaign of 1815: Strategic Overview of the Campaign').[22]

The nature of Clausewitz's approach, based as the assessment is largely on *Vom Kriege* ('On War'), an unfinished work, although also usefully drawing on his other writings, has been subject to a variety of interpretations. This process has been encouraged by the somewhat opaque nature of much of the text, by his plentiful use of passive tenses and subordinate clauses, and by issues concerning the meanings of particular phrases and words. Clausewitz's early education in philosophy was reflected in his work, but, affected by the tension between Enlightenment-era thought and that of the period of Romanticism, he was not always systematic in his argumentation.[23] Approached differently, the interplay of passion, reason and possibility (all, very differently, elements in motivation profitably analysed by Thucydides), found in his thought scarcely allowed Clausewitz to be systematic. Indeed, it is possible to 're-read Clausewitz in . . . climatic terms of Romantic self-conception', in which atmospheric terms best capture the psychological transformation caused by war.[24]

In another context, Clausewitz embraced complexity because, as a pessimist, he was wary of the idea of simple answers, while, linked to the latter, he described 'a spectrum of war' rather than an inflexible model.[25] He also presented in his book what essentially was a debate about power; a debate, in accordance with the German hermeneutic tradition, in which the dialectical method of thesis and counter-thesis played a central role. Alongside this dialectic, there was that between theory and reality, a dialectic in which Clausewitz was well aware of exceptions to the universal experience of war he propounded. In addition, the very educational possibilities of *On War* for the modern audience can be complemented by the stress on the deliberately pedagogic nature of Clausewitz's work as a means to develop the sound intuition necessary for command.[26]

Clausewitz had read extensively in military history, and believed in its significance, and produced historical studies from his years at the Institute in the Military Sciences for Young Infantry and Cavalry Officers onwards.[27] He drew on Machiavelli,[28] but was not really interested in citing earlier writers, and notably so if they were French. In *On War*, he did not cite Saxe, Maïzeroy or Guibert, each a serious omission, while the two references to Lloyd are superficial, again a serious omission. A cadet at twelve, Clausewitz had no formal schooling after that, did not know Latin or Greek and was essentially an autodidact. This education encouraged his focus on modern military history.

Clausewitz wrote at a time of changes in the terminology used to comment on war. He addressed the issue of the nature of war in history, focusing on the problem of the significance of change during his military career and on the question of whether there was going to be more change. The validity of both offence and defence was one dichotomy altering in time that concerned him. His use of strategy was primarily in terms of how battle was employed for the purpose of war, a question that was at once operational and political. At the same time, the context and content of strategy greatly depended on the nature of the opponent.

Aside from the contradictions in the revised as well as unrevised parts of his work, Clausewitz did not really deal with the questions of the mechanisms for elucidating strategy as a concept and practice, or how militaries explained their strategic relevance to policy-makers. That is not a criticism, because these were not his intentions, but it is pertinent to note the significant consequences of the disjunctions, because Clausewitz's understanding of his subject, as well as the misreading of Clausewitz, have guided modern consideration of strategy to a dispro-portionate extent, and continue to do so.

Any translation of Clausewitz represents an interpretation, and not least because it is not always clear what the subject is in particular sentences. Differing emphases have been favoured in response to current intellectual trends and military exigencies.[29] For example, the intellectu-ally and commercially highly successful 1976 translation into English, an edition by Michael Howard and Peter Paret,[30] the third in English, one that was also published in Everyman's Library in 1993, was initially produced in the context of the Cold War and was republished in its aftermath. This context affected the use, and understanding, of partic-ular phrases. Thus, the 1970s' use of 'total war' had connotations which gave the text meaning, but, in the nineteenth century, there was not a comparable concept of total war.[31] So also with the term 'operations'. More generally, the nature of pedagogy was (and is) culturally constructed, which is a factor that helps make it highly problematic to read between periods or to establish supposedly universal laws.

The discussion of the political aspects of war was longstanding. For example, the medieval use of Flavius Vegetius's *Epitoma Rei Militaris*, a Latin work subsequently translated into French, English, Italian, German and Castilian, rested not on his adages about the practical nature of war, but, instead, on his argument that the army was for the public service, and thus that its moral value explained the need for state-controlled forces.[32] Machiavelli emphasised the inherent value of militia over mercenaries. In a very different context, the moral character of military forces was also important for the eighteenth-century commen-tators, and not only those of the American and French Revolution with their stress on citizen virtues. Clausewitz can be located in this tradition of assessing the moral character of military activity as an aspect of understanding and placing how war works, so that commanders would best be able to evaluate and respond to situations.

Clausewitz and Jomini addressed the changes stemming from the mobilisation of society seen with the French Revolution and, in opposition to Napoleon, with the German War of Liberation, and also the changes from the high-tempo offensive war-making developed by Napoleon. Neither commentator, however, devoted equivalent attention to the technological changes and, in part, industrialisation of warfare that became more insistent and incessant during the nineteenth century and, in particular, in its second half, from the battlefield to the shipyard.

This point may appear irrelevant if the emphasis is on lasting characteristics of strategy, an emphasis that downplays the fascination with changing weaponry in itself, although without excluding the significance of past, present and future changes in weaponry and related systems. Moreover, the developments in the nature of society and politics that were linked to the transformation of the late nineteenth century, notably in key areas of the West but also in Japan, had major consequences for strategy. Industrialisation and urbanisation were linked to significant developments in political understanding and behaviour. These had consequences for notions of the will of a society. So also with the idea of a centre of gravity. In the different contexts of the crucial role of industry and the existence of conscription, this was as much the 'home front' as the army in the field. Given the importance of the 'home front' in the previous revolutionary era, not least with reference to concerns over subversion, there was a transformation in the understanding of the domestic situation, and not a new determination to focus on it.

THE LANGUAGE AND PRACTICE OF STRATEGY

The works of Jomini and, later, Clausewitz, each of which was translated into other languages, were to affect the developing use of the term and concept of strategy. The use of both term and concept spread in the early nineteenth century. The Grimm brothers' *Wörterbuch* gives '*Strategie*' as first used in German in 1813, although it was written about by

Clausewitz in 1804 and employed in the title of a 1805 book by Adam Heinrich Dietrich von Bülow. There was no mention of the word in Johann Christoph Adelung's *Wörterbuch Hochdeutschen Mundart* (1793). In Danish, '*strategi*', meaning the preparation and planning for the operations of an army, first appeared (and with a Greek origin mentioned) in a dictionary which was published in Copenhagen in 1810, namely Hans Christian Amberg's *Dansk og Tydsk Ordbog* ('Danish and German Dictionary'). In Italy, the word '*strategia*' seems to have been used for the first time by Giuseppe Grassi in his *Dizionario militare italiano*, the first edition of which appeared, in 1817, in Turin, the capital of Piedmont, Italy's leading military power. Grassi inserted the entry on *strategia* followed by the French word '*stratégique*'. Strategy as a term was employed in Britain in a military context from the 1810s and was employed in a broader political context by the 1840s. In Spain, the first definition of the term 'strategy' was recorded in 1822 in the sixth edition of the *Diccionario de la Lengua Castellana de la Academia Española* ('Dictionary of the Castilian Language of the Spanish Academy'). The definition was 'science of the general of the army'.[33]

In Russian, the linkage with Greek ensured that the term had been present for a long time, but that it reflected Byzantine usage, as in *strategos* or stratagem. In addition, '*stratig*' (military leader) was longstanding. Alexander Suvorov, the impressive commander against the French in 1799, wrote a work, *The Science of Victory* (1796), that focused on combat rather than strategy. In contrast, the modern sense of 'strategy' was acquired at the end of the eighteenth century, and the Napoleonic Wars helped Russians to get a better sense of the term. By the 1820s, it was well established and was mentioned in the popular periodical press. The first dictionary to mention '*strategiia*' was the *Slovar' Akademii Rossiiskoi* ('Russian Academy Dictionary') of 1847.

Although the word 'strategy' was coming into use, many commanders did not employ it to describe the strategy that they certainly had. Thus, the Prussian general Gebhard Leberecht von Blücher (1742–1819) understood the concept of strategy, but without using the word. During earlier periods, generals had understood the concept of strategy but employed other terms. For example, when they formulated the strategy to follow during the seventeenth century, they used terms such as 'the policy to follow', 'the requirements of your Majesty', 'the needs of the

Monarchy' and 'to maintain the reputation'. As the language became more modern, the semantics changed.

The term 'strategy' was not employed in British official or private correspondence of the period when referring to strategic concepts, thinking and intentions. In 1808, Sir Arthur Wellesley, later 1st Duke of Wellington, used the word to refer to what is today understood as tactics or organisation. John Wilson Croker, a pro-government MP who handled for Wellesley the latter's business as Chief Secretary for Ireland, recorded of a discussion that the general said: 'Why to say the truth, I am thinking of the French that I am going to fight . . . They have besides, it seems, a new system of strategy, which has out-manoeuvred and overwhelmed all the armies of Europe.'[34] It is not certain that this memorandum was made at the time.[35] At any rate, it is unclear whether Wellington's reference is to the French corps system, or the use of infantry columns, or effective combined arms practices and structures. These would not be seen today as constituting strategy, although they capture the contemporary focus on specific tactical matters when assessing effectiveness.

In Britain, government policy or plans were often cited when referring to what we would term strategy. Prospects or plans with respect to Spain, Austria or other powers were other terms. 'Arrangements with nations' was another often-used phrase. It was chiefly the employment of the word 'government' that was used to signify a strategic concept. The 'art of war' was another commonplace term. Wellington's 1806 memorandum on British plans for South America and his 1809 memorandum on the defence of Portugal definitely articulated the concept of strategy. In 1806, Wellington scotched a plan to deploy forces simultaneously on the east and west coasts of South America, while in 1809 he clearly explained how the British army should be used to defend Lisbon, how this would facilitate the defence of Portugal, and how it might even enable the British to go onto the offensive in Spain. The means to accomplish this were 30,000–40,000 British troops, the retraining of the Portuguese army, and the construction of the defensive Lines of Torres Vedras to ensure that Lisbon was a secure base.[36] These lines saw off the subsequent French advance on Lisbon in 1811–12, and this defensive success was followed by an advance into Spain that led to a major victory over the French at Salamanca.

In 1819, Wellington presented a plan for the defence of Canada to Henry, 3rd Earl Bathurst, the Secretary for War and the Colonies. He identified the keys of Canada as Quebec, Montreal and Kingston, and, in an interesting guide to strategic assumptions and the idea of a centre of power, emphasised lines of communication from the fortified Atlantic access port at Halifax in Nova Scotia, rather than troops and fortifications. With reason, Wellington argued that the existing lines, the marine routes along the St Lawrence and the Great Lakes, were overly exposed to American attack, a view supported by American plans in the War of 1812. Instead, he proposed a new line of communications, one further back from America, a line that benefited from rivers and canals. As another important instance of what he regarded as significant in strategic terms, Wellington emphasised the importance of the local population remaining loyal, not least as this would provide militia to support the regulars.[37] The attitude of the population in Quebec, conquered by Britain from France in 1759, was particularly significant.

However, as with many other commanders, Wellington was somewhat less keen on strategy when it clashed with his interests. For example, he did not appreciate that his reiterated calls during the Peninsular War for resources, both military and naval, had to align with other governmental concerns. In particular, although he appreciated that he fundamentally received the naval support he required, Wellington's demands on it could be inappropriate. They were rejected by the Admiralty, which drew attention to its extensive other commitments, which had been increased by the outbreak of the War of 1812.[38] Although the navy could cover both contingencies, this situation underlined the problems posed by power projection and by independent army and navy structures; but also the existence of key questions of commitments and resources, irrespective of the nature of the organisational system. The implementation of one strategy could close down strategic options elsewhere.

The focus on military accounts can lead to an underplaying of the more widespread salience in the nineteenth and early twentieth centuries of public discussion of strategic issues, including capabilities and priorities. This discussion could be readily found in the press, and in Britain from its development after the lapsing of pre-publication censorship in 1695. Local newspapers discussed strategy. Thus, on 27 July 1912, an editorial on naval strength in *Trewman's Exeter Flying Post* explained: 'We cannot abandon the Mediterranean and we must maintain an adequate strength in home waters.' Newspapers readily referred to strategy, with the term employed loosely in the manner with which we are familiar today. During the Boer War in southern Africa, the *Western Times*, a local newspaper, in its issue of 4 January 1901 wrote of 'the strategical skill with which Lord Roberts led the British troops to Pretoria', the capital of Transvaal.

CONCLUSIONS

As a result of Clausewitz, the Prussian – later German – General Staff, and the Wars of German Unification of 1864–71, Germany dominates attention in the discussion of strategy in the period 1815–1914, but much of this is disproportionate. Russia and Britain were the key powers in 1813–60, a process demonstrated by Russia in 1849 crushing the Hungarian rising against Austrian rule. Military and strategic planning in this period have been criticised,[39] which in part is surprising given the repeated ability of the powers to deliver verdicts as with French success in Spain in 1823.

Moreover, as with the earlier focus on Napoleon, whose military career twice ended in total failure, in 1814 and 1815, so, with Germany, it is surprising that so much attention is devoted to a power that went down to failure, both in 1918 and in 1945. Ironically, in the major war that Germany began in 1914, its strategy proved poor, both in conception and in execution, and both that year and subsequently. Indeed, like Napoleon, the focus on Germany prior to 1914 establishes the significance of the period in leading to the dominance of operational command and its ultimate failure.

Instead of this emphasis, it is valuable to focus elsewhere, both for the long nineteenth century itself and concerning how it looks towards the succeeding one. In the case of China and Russia, there were revolutions in 1911 and 1917 that destroyed any such continuity. However, this was not the case for the United States, which was the world's largest manufacturer in 1914, and which played the key role in the power politics of the twentieth century. The United States in the nineteenth century is the subject of the following chapter. The one after considers Europe anew, but with the global scale receiving attention as well.

6

THE UNITED STATES IN THE NINETEENTH CENTURY

1812–98

Strategy in the American case is particularly instructive because, from the outset, the United States had public politics with a presidential leader greatly constrained by an electoral process and by representative politics in which control shifted. Moreover, aside from fighting state-to-state conflicts with Britain, Mexico and Spain, and wars of expansion and counter-insurrection against Native Americans, the United States, in 1861–5, confronted the great strategic challenge of a large-scale secessionist civil war. For these reasons, it is pertinent to focus on the United States.

AMERICAN STRATEGIES BEFORE THE CIVIL WAR

The range of Western imperial schemes in the long nineteenth century included American expansionism, not that the Americans saw themselves in this light. This is not a throwaway line, but a significant point given the focus on attitudes in providing the public strategic space for operations. Canada, which was unsuccessfully invaded in 1812, 1813 and 1814 during the War of 1812 with Britain, provided the Americans with a clear strategic goal to permit the pursuit of imperial schemes, notably against Native Americans allegedly helped by Britain. However, the Americans were unable to devise an effective means to obtain this goal. The size of Canada as then under British control, although far smaller than was to be the case by 1860, helped to make operational planning difficult for the Americans, as did the characteristics of the environment in the sphere of operations, the nature of contemporary communications, command and control, and also relationships between individual commanders. For these reasons, there was little prospect of co-ordinated campaigning, which would have been the best way to take advantage of the distribution of American resources. The alternative, their massing in a single concentration of power, was not possible for political reasons, in the shape of the authority of individual states over their militias, as well as not being feasible in logistical terms. A deficiency in planning, moreover, accompanied the organisational and political limitations affecting the American war effort.

The lack of an effective strategy and a developed strategic culture made it difficult to make use of tactical and operational successes: those comprised parts in a whole that was absent. More particularly, multi-pronged attacks during the War of 1812 were not co-ordinated, and did not exert simultaneous or sequential pressure on the British, which aided the possibilities for the latter to respond, and even to move forces to that end. This would have been difficult to achieve given the extent of operations, but functional problems alone were not responsible for the American failure of co-ordination.

There were also serious political divisions in America over strategy. There was much support for a focus on the Lake Champlain corridor in order to divide Montreal from Quebec. However, westerners were opposed to this emphasis and, instead, as part of their expansionist prospectus, wanted to prevent British help to the Native Americans. This led them to press for operations further west; operations, however, which were difficult to support militarily and to co-ordinate.

In turn, British naval strength permitted a dual economic–military strategy. It was possible to stop American trade, hitting both the economy and American state revenues, and to apply force against the American littoral. A political strategy was part of the equation as Federalist-dominated New England, much of which was against the war, could be spared the pressure.

The War of 1812 saw neither side victorious and still left unsettled the question of which power would dominate North America. In an instructive instance of the politicised process of presenting success, the United States described the conflict as a victory. Nevertheless, Britain had repelled successive invasions of Canada and easily remained the leading naval power with an unrivalled capacity for amphibious operations. This capacity, as well as the debate between the navalists and the anti-navalists, forced on the United States the strategy of littoral defence in the shape of constructing and manning coastal fortifications. Indeed, both the location of troops, a technique employed when considering the strategy of the Roman Empire and those of Imperial Russia, and that of fortifications provide valuable indications of strategic concerns and responses. Similarly, from the outbreak of the Opium War in 1839, littoral defence became a major theme in China, as it did in Japan from the mid-1850s. Steamships and shell guns on the part of attacking powers took forward the already significant threat to defenders posed by the combination of their coastal cities with the amphibious power projection of assailants. For the United States, China and Japan, moreover, civil war was to affect the equation, although in very different ways.

Rivalry between Britain and the United States was a key geopolitical theme until the Treaties of Washington in 1871. Yet, there was no war, and the peace option became the strategy of preference, as each side pursued its goals in a context given added unpredictability by uncertainty about the intentions of the other as well as by other issues. Given American expansionism, notably against Spain (in Florida) and Mexico, but also against Britain (in the Oregon Question) and more generally, it was the British response that was the crucial strategic element. In practice, the defence of specific British interests in North America repeatedly had to yield to the exigencies of a strategy of restrained goals and means within a context of global commitments. Specific interests were subordinated to the more general interest. That stance, in turn, made the American strategy work, providing it with a leverage that it did not enjoy in military terms. Similarly, there had been leverage until late 1812 due to Anglo-French animosity and then conflict, only for that leverage to go with Napoleon's failure in Russia in 1812.

British strategy towards the United States can be seen as that of accommodation and compromise.[1] That, however, underplays the impact of ideology. In particular, British ministers understood and presented national interests in terms of wider-ranging liberal causes.[2] At the same time, as a reminder of the wider parameters of strategy, the absence of conflict with America over Canada and Latin America greatly helped British imperialism at the global level by aiding concentration on the possibilities and problems posed in particular by south and east Asia. Moreover, Canada, through relatively benign imperial policies and being granted dominion status, became well grounded as a viable entity within the British Empire. This was so despite the absence of the large native forces, seen in India, that were able to provide assistance to the imperial power, and despite the presence of a threatening neighbour in the case of America. There are similarities between elements of British strategy in this period and that of the United States during the Cold War, notably the role of ideology and the extent to which restraint in one area was matched by the use of force elsewhere.

After the Napoleonic Wars, the British government's need to reduce expenditure was a major factor and one linked not only to concerns about fiscal stability, but also to the desire to assuage domestic discontent. Successive British governments were to be wary of North American entanglements, not only for the prudential reasons posed by likely American opposition, but also as a result of straightforward issues of cost and worth. The phrase 'nightwatchman state' has been coined to describe the limited role sought. Abroad, there was a drive to maintain Britain's status as the world's leading naval power, and a willingness to pursue international goals by conflict, if necessary. The central concern, however, was to avoid the recurrence of a major war. This was both because of anxiety about the cost and due to worry about the consequences for trade and industry. Britain was the world's leading trading power. In comparison, during the Cold War, the United States, with its different global posture and challenges, was readier for war, although also opposed to putting the burden upon taxation.

Avoiding the recurrence of a major war was also central to American strategy after 1815. This goal took precedence over the development of military capabilities. The army was established at 10,000 men, the largest American standing army so far, albeit a modest size that reflected the fear of a standing army and the hostility to an officer corps as the possible basis for an aristocracy. In contrast, the Naval Expansion Act of 1816 led to a marked increase in the size of the navy, and there was a systematic programme of coastal fortifications. Military education was set by this limited goal: that offered at West Point focused heavily on fortress engineering and ballistics, the latter necessary for officers who were to command fortifications designed to repel British naval attack. At the same time, economic factors encouraged restraint. Thus, the Panic of 1819 revealed economic weaknesses and hit government finances.

Indeed, rhetoric about goals was not matched by strategy. For example, Andrew Jackson's invasion of Florida in 1818 was not expanded to include American intervention in the Latin American Wars of Independence, as suggested by Henry Clay, a leading figure in Congress. President James Monroe's famous 1823 message to Congress, announcing that attempts by European powers to establish or re-establish colonies in the New World would be seen as 'dangerous to our peace and safety', was, in practice, simply a recommendation. Looked at differently, a bold geopolitical prospectus and a pledge to defend republican independence, the Monroe Declaration was not so much a strategy of rhetoric as a strategy without means, one to be followed when not resisted; although Clay, both as politician and as the Secretary of State, wanted America to act as leader of the Western Hemisphere. In practice, foreign affairs played a surprisingly small role in the presidential election of 1824, which was driven, ultimately, by popular concerns in the wake of a persisting depression. Moreover, America was unable to prevent, or even to try to prevent, French pressure on Haiti and Mexico in the decade after Monroe's message.

In part, the challenge from the United States in the nineteenth century was that of a different practice of politics, a difference that affected strategy. Alexis de Tocqueville, a French lawyer who visited America in 1831, described, in *De la démocratie en Amérique* (1835), a new type of society and political culture that was different from that of Europe. He discerned a mass society organised on the basis of an equality that ignored the aristocratic ethos of honour and threatened to create conformism, but that also helped ensure that America would, with Russia, be one of the great powers of the future. The populism that was a result was readily apparent, as with politicians speaking on the stump about their right to Canada, while domestic political opponents could be castigated as if British.[3] That this populism did not lead to war with Britain in the 1840s over the Oregon question, the future of the territory from British Columbia to Oregon, did not make it less of a factor in the formation of strategy.

THE MEXICAN-AMERICAN WAR, 1846-8

Instead, there was war with Mexico, the background and course of which very much reflected the primacy of politics in strategy. That was the case with the politics of the war, with the United States very divided on its desirability, and also with the course of the campaigning, and, more particularly, the decision to launch an amphibious invasion of central Mexico in 1847, rather than just invading across the northern border as in 1846. The reasons for this change were very different. The northern provinces were marginal as far as Mexico's centre of power was concerned, while the distances from the border to Mexico City were part of Mexico's natural defences. At the same time, troops were transferred from the army of Zachary Taylor, the commander in the north, a transfer which for President James K. Polk, a Democrat, had the beneficial consequences of weakening a Whig who was likely to be the presidential candidate in 1848: as a war leader, Polk was intensely political throughout. He also recalled Winfield Scott, the commander of the successful amphibious force, and another presidential hopeful.[4] Such a politics of command is frequently an element in strategic choices. It can clearly be seen for example in the allocation of provincial governorships, and therefore forces, during the Roman Empire, and was also an important element in Napoleon's rise to power.

In pursuit of a short war, American campaigning was what would subsequently be described as 'high tempo'. Its aggressive and fast-moving character was necessary for political as well as military reasons, as American domestic support for the war was seen to be fragile. Scott's amphibious invasion and advance to Mexico City displayed strategic insight, a skilful transfer of this insight into effective operational direction, and an ability to gain and retain the initiative. It was greatly praised by Wellington.

The situation became less favourable for the Americans after the initial stages of occupation. Opposition and guerrilla activity increased. Moreover, it proved difficult to negotiate a settlement because the Mexican élite did not wish to accept the loss of much of their country. As a result, it took longer to negotiate peace than the Americans wished, or had anticipated after the rapid fall of Mexico City in 1847. Instead, there was an anticipation of the problems facing Prussia when it invaded

France in 1870–1: it proved easier to defeat French armies than to force France to peace, or indeed to end resistance in conquered areas.

The social politics of the situation in Mexico were important to the outcome, as the war threatened the position of the Mexican élite and, in particular, their dominance of the indigenous population. In the end, concern about this factor took precedence over the failure bound up with accepting American demands by the Treaty of Guadalupe Hidalgo in 1848. So also in France with threats focused on the radicalism of the Paris Commune.

CONFLICT WITH NATIVE AMERICANS I

The emphasis on a short war seen with Mexico was very different to the strategy of attrition and the continual application of pressure that was followed in dealing with Native Americans due to the difficulty in 'fixing' the opponent, but also because of the preference for their annihilation, thus making political settlement unnecessary. Whether or not considered as an 'American way of war', this method was not possible in relation earlier to French colonists or in the nineteenth century to Mexicans. The potential cost in terms of uncertainty of the conflicts with Native Americans was less than that of the war with Mexico. Yet, partly although the Americans were far stronger, they had a capacity to fear the Native Americans, or at least to employ such fears in order to justify action.

The American response varied. Thus, in the 1830s, military strategy focused on the idea of an essentially stable frontier, rather than on supporting far-flung expansion, not least because it had become clear that the British from Canada were not, as had been feared, a challenge to American power in the Mississippi and Missouri valleys. Thus, a (prophylactic) strategy of expansion, as was to be seen in particular in Africa and south-east Asia from the 1880s, was unnecessary. The problems the army had encountered in the Upper Missouri Valley in the 1820s, as well as concern about funding and costs, encouraged caution and also suggested a more general limitation in military operations against Native Americans.

Subsequently, when the Americans resumed expansion, they benefited from Native disunion. Indeed, the latter encouraged some of the Native tribes to look to the Americans. This underlines the problems in assessing strategy. Military, political, economic, cultural and religious ties crossed American–Native divides, turning them into zones of inter-action in which symbiosis, synergy and exchange occurred alongside, and often instead of, conflict and war. Moreover, much of the violence also involved an important measure of collaboration between Americans and Natives.

AMERICAN CIVIL WAR, 1861–5

Strategic issues were (and are) particularly set by political factors during civil wars. This was seen with the American Civil War secession of the South. Only the Lower South seceded at first in 1861. In turn, President Lincoln's intention to resist secession with force, by invading the Lower South, played the major role in leading Arkansas, North Carolina, Tennessee and Virginia to join the Confederacy after 15 April 1861, as they did not intend to provide troops to put down what Lincoln termed an insurrection. This reshaped the geopolitics of the war: Virginia, Tennessee and North Carolina were each more important in economic and demographic terms than any state in the Lower South. In order, they were the leading states in white population in the Confederacy, while, together, they were to field close to 40 per cent of the Confederacy's forces, and provided half of its crops and more than half of its manufacturing capacity.

In military terms, the location of this productive capacity in frontier areas was a problem for the Confederacy, as they were vulnerable and thus rewarded Union attack, while also compromising the idea of a defence-in-depth, and notably so for Virginia. However, while the gain of the four states ensured that there was more territory to defend, it transformed the military potential of the Confederacy. The Union no longer had a common frontier with every seceding state bar Florida, and thus the Lower South became less vulnerable other than to amphibious attack. It also became easier to think of the Confederacy as a bloc of territory that could be defended in a coherent fashion, and that there-fore required a coherent strategy in order to bring it down. In particular, the secession of Virginia and North Carolina greatly altered the location of the likely field of operations in the east as, militarily, the front line of the secession was no longer on the northern border of South Carolina. Had that been the case, Charleston and Columbia in South Carolina would have been readily vulnerable to Union attack overland, just as Atlanta in Georgia would have been from the rail junction of Chattanooga in Tennessee.

Conversely, in the unpredictable division of what became the two sides, the Union was able to gain control of an important bloc of slave states: Delaware, Maryland, Kentucky, Missouri, and those parts of Virginia that, in 1863, became the state of West Virginia. Had these states joined the Confederacy, as Missouri and Kentucky sympathisers did, leading to their being seated in the Confederate Congress, then the situation would also have been very different. Instead, the Union consolidated its superiority in resources, blocked invasion routes into the North, and exposed the South to attack. These states in Union hands affected the offensive capability of the Confederacy. Given Robert E. Lee's willingness to march north across the Potomac in 1862 and 1863, it is instructive to consider what the military impact of having the frontier on the northern border of Maryland would have been. There was also a key demographic dimension in terms of the manpower available to both sides.

As Maryland stayed in the Union, the central battleground of the war lay between Washington, which remained the capital of the Union, and Richmond, Virginia, which became the capital of the Confederacy in May 1861. Their proximity helped give a geographical focus to the conflict, one that reflected the political importance of the two capitals, and also cut across the potential expansiveness of the conflict arising from the extent of the area in rebellion. Indeed, by suggesting that Richmond could readily be captured, this proximity offered the prospect of the rapid end to the war that Northerners sought. So also with the attempt by the Spanish Nationalists under Franco in 1936 to capture the capital, Madrid, although it did not succeed until the end of the Spanish Civil War in 1939.

The American Civil War, furthermore, was a civil conflict within the states that seceded. In the latter, the prevalence of slavery varied greatly, with, for example, few slaves in Appalachia, which was a reason why the Union was relatively popular in western North Carolina and eastern Tennessee. Conversely, fears of an abolitionist plot in Texas in late 1860, a major instance of the sequence of panics following John Brown's attempt on Harper's Ferry, helped lead to vigilante action and encouraged backing for secession.[5] The variation in the prevalence of slavery was linked to the degree of support for the war, though it was not the sole factor involved. About 104,000 white Southerners fought in the Union forces.[6] This was a major addition to the latter and cause of Confederate weakness. Moreover, the degree of opposition to secession underlined the degree to which chance factors played a considerable role in ensuring that it occurred.[7] There were many Northern 'dough faces' willing to accept slavery, but they did not provide a military support for the South equivalent to that of Southerners who fought against separation. Yet, alongside a commitment to slavery, many who fought for the South did not own slaves and were more motivated by a sense of the need to defend communities and culture, and the states' rights that were believed to protect both of those. These states' rights, however, were defined in part in terms of the defence of slavery.

The extent of different beliefs in the South serves as a reminder of the range of the issues at stake, and thus of the complexity of the geopolitics and strategy of the war. Initially unprepared for the difficulty of the struggle, both militarily and politically, Union forces, on the pattern of some other civil wars (as opposed to civil wars of conquest), had to try to shift the political balance within the South in order to lead to its surrender, and that indeed occurred in 1865. The military alternative of the conquest of the entire South was not viable given the size of the Confederacy, although it was followed in China in the contemporary suppression of the Taiping Rebellion, and again in 1946–9 during the civil war that led to the communist takeover.

The political option appeared clearer for the Confederacy. There was the hope that success in the conflict would lead the Union to change policy by abandoning the war and, secondly, that success would bring the British and French into the war, and thus ensure that the Union had to change its strategy. There was considerable weight in both strategies, notably in the latter in 1861–2; and if the playing out of the war revealed that neither was viable, that was not readily apparent to contemporaries in America and abroad until well into the conflict. The significance of intervention from the other side of the Atlantic was to be shown by the importance attached to American entry into the two world wars, a point that should be rephrased to note the importance from the outset of Canadian assistance.

The prospect of Confederate success helps provide a chronology. In 1861–2, there was a possibility of outcomes that left a distinct South as an option, but, from 1863, this possibility receded. Lincoln's victory in the 1864 presidential election both cemented the political coherence of the North and, as a consequence, created the basis for a political settlement that would entail not only victory over the Confederacy but also a postwar American order able to intimidate other powers in the New World, as indeed happened immediately after with the French in Mexico and, to a degree, the British in Canada. That the Civil War particularly invites counterfactuals testifies to the geopolitical volatility of this conjuncture and, with it, to the trends and developments that had led to it. The two most significant counterfactuals focus on the possibility of the Confederacy doing better in the conflict and on that of foreign intervention. As with other civil wars, for example, that century, the Carlist Wars in Spain and the civil war of the 1830s in Portugal, the two possibilities were linked, but separate. Each raises important questions about the relationship between agency and structure, as well as concerning the determinism about strategic capacity bound up with the argument from the availability of greater resources on one side. It is wrong to assume that one outcome was inevitable. There were foreign interventions that made a decisive impact, as of France in Spain in 1823 and Russia in Hungary in 1849, and others that did not, for example France in Mexico in the 1860s.

The impact of politics on strategy was shown at the outset of the American Civil War when political pressure in the North for a rapid advance on Richmond, to destroy the Confederacy by seizing the capital, in essence the policy followed in Mexico in 1847, led to a departure from the plan drawn up by Winfield Scott, the general-in-chief. He, instead, had called for an advance down the Mississippi, to bisect the Confederacy, combined with a blockade. Termed the 'Anaconda Plan' by the press, this strategy was intended to save lives and, by increasing support for a return to the Union, to encourage the Confederacy to peace or, failing that, to put the Union in the best situation for further operations. However, Scott's emphasis on planning, as well as on the indirect approach, training, and a delay in the offensive until the autumn of 1861, fell foul of the pressure for immediate and dramatic action.

In April 1865, in his farewell address to his soldiers, Robert E. Lee, the commander of the Army of Northern Virginia, the most significant

Confederate force, argued that they had been 'compelled to yield to overwhelming power', a theme that was to be taken up often. This argument, which was to contribute to the nostalgic 'Lost Cause' view of Southern war-making, had also been employed, to a different purpose, by Union representatives, seeking to explain to foreign powers why the North was bound to win and therefore should not receive support. Thus, reviewing the 1862 campaign, William Dayton, the Union envoy in Paris, told the French foreign minister that November that the Confederacy was running out of men and money and that the Union's superiority in both was linked to its success.[8]

Yet, resources do not explain conflict, firstly because a host of factors affect their use and effectiveness, and secondly because more than resources is involved in war. Thus, Lee's defeat, initially on the offensive in 1862 and 1863, and then on the defensive in 1864 and 1865, owed much to the effectiveness of his opponents, especially from 1863.[9] As in the First and Second World Wars, there is a tendency to explain why one side lost, when the emphasis should rather be on why the other side won. Linked to this difference, there are also the standard asymmetries in strategy found in conflicts. In this case, as in others, the asymmetry was that involved in resisting attack: in the Civil War, the Confederacy needed to keep fighting, while the Union had to achieve more, which created greater pressure on generalship as well as resources.

On both sides, but especially for the Union, generalship required the co-ordination and deployment of resources so that mass could be brought to bear, although this faced major problems. There were impressive aspects of planning and organisation. For example, in 1861, in response to reports that the Confederates were building an ironclad, the Union Navy created a board which called for ironclads and recommended the building of experimental vessels, so that effectiveness could be assessed. This, indeed, prompted a focus on ironclads, on the model of the *Monitor*.[10] More generally, such responsiveness drew on the resources of society, including patterns of associational behaviour, high rates of literacy, and the ability to comprehend, tap into and organise productive resources, not least the capital investment required for the large-scale manufacture of weapons. These factors were important to the Union's ability to overcome problems of military inexperience, logistics and the size of campaigning area, to take war to the Confederacy, and, eventually, to force it to surrender.[11]

Yet, it is necessary not to overestimate the sophistication of the organisation on either side. They cannot be described as war machines, if that is intended to suggest predictable and regular operating systems that could be readily controlled and adapted in the pursuit of strategy; while the possibilities and problems created by the changing nature of war led to additional issues.[12] Resource strength was applied through logistical systems that could not cope adequately, while it proved difficult to make an effective use of resources on the battlefield. Moreover, despite the role of West Point and other military institutions in the prewar training of many future commanders on both sides, much of the command culture and many of the techniques were amateurish. This was specifically so with the limited ability to co-ordinate widely spread operations and the absence of high-grade general staff work. Poor command and staff work, which accentuated the friction of war and led to a focus on individual skills and *ad hoc* co-operation, repeatedly helped throw away the chance of more striking victories,[13] which explains the importance of overcoming these problems.

As a result of this and other factors, the Union lacked an advantage equivalent to that which it had in overall resources. There was a gap between strategic capability and strategic potential. For example, superiority in manpower did not readily translate into trained troops on the battlefield, let alone the right battlefield. There was also an asymmetry of strategic aims, an asymmetry that helps explain international support for the idea of mediation: the Confederacy, ultimately, had only to fend off the Union, which did not require its conquest. In contrast, the Union had at least to crush Confederate military power and probably to occupy considerable swathes of the Confederacy in order to force it back into the Union. Thus, as in the American War of Independence, the weaker power was helped by having the more modest goal, while, for the Union, the failure of conciliation as a means to end the conflict was eventually linked to the definition of more radical war goals by Lincoln. In similar circumstances this was not a strategy followed by the British during the War of Independence. These goals put even greater premium on military victory, while, in turn, this premium made the issue of warlike ardour and political determination in the North of importance.[14]

In 1862, the Seven Days battles (25 June–1 July) both stopped the Union advance on Richmond and started a series of Southern advances and victories in the east that rapidly affected the political as well as the military development of the struggle. Lee was a figure around whom the Confederates could rally, and this factor was important in helping to create a Confederate 'nation' from people who stood for states' rights. He understood that Confederate public opinion had a preference for taking the initiative, not responding to Northern moves, that it sought offensive victories, and that, whatever the implications of the strategic depth offered by the size of the Confederacy, control of Virginia was politically crucial. Appreciating the implications of large-scale conflict between democratic societies, Lee fostered a strategy designed to hit Northern popular will,[15] at a time when Union strategy was still unfocused.

In particular, Lee's advance across the Potomac River into Maryland in September 1862 not only obliged the Union forces to follow, and thus reduced the threat to Richmond. It was also designed to shock Union opinion by carrying the war to the North and inflicting defeat there, as well as to convince foreign opinion of Confederate strength, and maybe to encourage Maryland to secede. Thus, the tide of the war was turned, but to a political as much as a military end. In the autumn of 1862, there was a possibility that Democrats might capture the House of Representatives in the North and press for peace, and, indeed, they were to make gains in the elections; although not sufficient to sway the struggle. As a reminder of the difficulty of looking for comparisons, there was no parallel in the general election of 1780 in Britain, nor, differently, in the political crisis of 1968 in the United States.

Lee's generalship had brought a reversal in the flow of the war in 1862, but, in the battle of Antietam on 17 September, he failed to sustain his success. Moreover, the heavy losses of his Army of Northern Virginia forced Lee to a cautious exploitation of the battle. He withdrew from Antietam two days later. Antietam, a serious blow to Confederate strategy and a qualification of its viability, both ruptured the run of Confederate success and suggested that the war would be longer and more costly than had been anticipated. It was clear, moreover, that success in an individual battle was not going to bring the destruction of the opponent's military strength. Antietam also greatly discouraged the British government from welcoming French calls for a joint mediation of the conflict, a measure that would probably have led to conflict with the Union.

There are some problems with applying modern notions of strategic clarity and planning to the Civil War, not least because the Union army lacked an equivalent to the navy's Blockade Board, which, newly established in 1861, laid down coherent strategic recommendations that remained valid for the rest of the war.[16] Contemporaries were uncertain as to how the geography of the war worked, in terms of the relationships between spheres of operations, and this uncertainty greatly affected the discussion of strategy, both its content and its viability. These relationships, in turn, subsequently became a matter of scholarly discussion and encouraged a concern with the role of geography in the planning and conduct of the war.[17]

As the international situation became more benign for the Union, so counterfactuals, instead, came to focus largely on operations and politics within America. The possibility that Confederate success would lead to a change of government in the North was voiced in 1862, 1863 and 1864, and, indeed, became more of an issue as Union goals became more radical. In November 1862, the Union's envoy in Paris told the French foreign minister that 'neither principle nor policy will induce the United States to encourage a "servile war" or prompt the slave to cut the throat of his master or his master's family',[18] a clear reference to deep-seated racial anxieties. Nevertheless, war goals and military methods altered in response to the difficulty of the conflict, changes that again underline the changing nature of strategy in the shape of its contextual and contingent character, notably the extent to which a difficult conflict could help radicalise the situation. Whereas George McClellan, a Democrat and the commander of the Army of the Potomac, the main Union field army, opposed attacks on private property, Ulysses S. Grant did so from the spring of 1862 in order to hit Confederate supplies and, thus, war-making ability. Similarly, Major-General John Pope, commander of the Union's Army of Virginia in 1862, agreed with the Republicans, and not with McClellan, and claimed that it was legitimate to confiscate rebel property and move civilians who refused to take the oath of allegiance. His army destroyed a large amount of property and thus made its presence unwelcome. Union forces responded harshly to opposition by becoming more destructive, and especially by living off the land.[19] Moreover, there were significant pressures on the home front, where frustration with the intractability of the struggle led to an abandonment of conciliation towards Southerners in late 1862.[20]

This change was a prime instance of political parameters being affected by military factors, which is the counterpart of the opposite process. McClellan had pursued a quick victory by means of a victorious advance in Virginia, alongside a conciliatory strategy to undermine Southern support for the rebellion; but this totally viable strategy was wrecked by failure. McClellan, who had advocated modest war goals as part of a general conciliatory Union approach, a policy that reflected his political engagement as a Democrat,[21] was dismissed by Lincoln after Antietam. Instead, as hopes of a quick war faded, the emphasis came to be on how best to win a long conflict. This emphasis led to a greater concern on securing control of the Mississippi Valley. This was a very indirect way to hit at the Confederate position in Virginia which in part arose from differential success in the two areas: again strategy, in rewarding operational success, was a reactive process. At the same time, conciliation ceased to be the political goal.[22] In addition, the conduct of the war became more brutal, although not in comparison with the contemporary conflict in Mexico nor with the hostilities involving Native Americans.[23] Moreover, the Union's insistence that Southerners were still American citizens affected their treatment.[24] It was an aspect of the strategic goal of national reunion.[25]

Initially, the Union had made no attempt to abolish slavery, both because Lincoln feared the impact of emancipation on sections of Northern opinion, especially in loyal border states such as his native Kentucky, and because, like many others,[26] he hoped that avoiding a pledge to support emancipation would weaken Southern backing for secession. After the battle of Antietam, in contrast, there was a major change in strategy. Lincoln heeded radical Republicans, many of whom were linked to the Congressional Joint Committee on the Conduct of the War;[27] and the Union became committed to the emancipation of the slaves in those parts of the South still in rebellion,[28] but not in the loyal border states. This commitment was seen as a way to weaken the Southern economy, and thus war effort, as well as providing a clear purpose to maintain Northern morale and a means to assuage the sin that was leading a wrathful God to punish America. The international audience was also in Lincoln's mind, and the international law on war influenced the Emancipation Proclamation.[29] Thus, there was a range of strategic purposes.

Emancipation, like conscription, another radical step, was also linked to the need for troops. In the second half of the Civil War, the recruitment of blacks for the Union army was a symbol to, and for, the Confederacy of what was a total war. Moreover, the recruitment of all-black regiments for the army, numbering more than 120,000 men, was also a major operational help to the Union. The symbolic power of black troops was shown in February 1865 when the forces that occupied Charleston, the site of the outbreak of the war, included black troops recruited by the Union from former Carolina slaves.[30] There was no comparable Southern use of slaves, which underlined the demographic problems posed by slavery for the Southern war effort.[31]

During the war, as another aspect of strategy, claims of necessity were employed to justify the extension of federal power, a process eased by the absence of Southern representatives in Congress and the weak position of the Northern Democrats. Moreover, radical Republicans claimed that, by their secession, the Southerners had forfeited their constitutional rights.[32] The power of the federal government was enhanced at the expense of the states, and a host of measures, including conscription and the establishment of a national banking system, were important in themselves and for what they signified in terms of strategic potential. This brought Alexander Hamilton's agenda to (temporary) fruition. To Democrats, the Lincoln administration seemed tyrannical, as with the suspension of *habeas corpus* in Maryland and action against critical newspapers; while, in the Congressional elections of 1862, the Democrats won the Indiana state legislature, only to find that the Republicans refused to attend the session and the governor, Oliver Morton, decided to govern without it.[33] Conscription, which was agreed by the Senate on 20 February 1863, greatly increased federal power[34] and led to anger, evasion and riots. The Democratic presidential platform, agreed on 29 August 1864, declared that 'under the pretence of a military necessity, or war power higher than the Constitution, the Constitution itself has been disregarded in every part'.

The difference between Democrats and Republicans led to reasonable predictions of change if Lincoln fell, predictions made by foreign diplomats as well as domestic counterparts. In the 1864 election, McClellan, now the Democratic candidate, wanted reunion as the price of peace, but his running mate, George Pendleton, was a Peace Democrat, and the platform pressed for an armistice. The Democrats were also against an Emancipation amendment for the Constitution, which was a policy supported by the Republican Convention.

Another aspect of division was provided by attitudes towards Latin America. When, in the House on 4 April 1864, a Democrat praised James Monroe, the Republican riposte was a call to a more ideological strategy: 'We wish to cultivate friendship with our republican brethren of Mexico and South America, to aid in consolidating republican principles, to retain popular government in all this continent from the fangs of monarchical aristocratic power, and to lead the sisterhood of American republicans in the path of peace, prosperity, and power.' Like much of the radical programme, this aspiration, which was primarily directed at the French-backed Royalists in Mexico, was only realised in small part.

Contemporaries were sure that the 1864 election would be decided by the campaigning,[35] and it was also seen as important to the success of conscription.[36] Lincoln had found a war-winning general with Grant, but this result was not apparent at first. Appointed general-in-chief of the Union army that March, Grant's decision to take field command, rather than act as military adviser to the government, can be queried in terms of the direction of the war effort, but he added strategic purpose and impetus to Union military policy. Moreover, in the Overland Campaign, Grant subordinated the individual battle to the repeated pressure of campaigning against the Confederates. Attacking their army became the key, and not capturing particular positions. Indeed, the near-continuous nature of the conflict from his advance that May, which led, initially, to the battle of the Wilderness on 5–7 May, combined with heavy casualties to give the war in the Virginian theatre an attritional character, which indeed was Grant's intention and strategy. In the long term, although repeated attacks failed to destroy the smaller Confederate army, Grant's attrition ground it down.

Yet, in the short term, the heavy casualties suffered by Grant's army hit civilian morale, as did William Tecumseh Sherman's initial failure to capture Atlanta, both reminders of the political parameters affected by military developments. Moreover, the Red River Expedition, which was intended to secure cotton for the textile industry in New England, failed. Faced by a range of bad news, Lincoln feared that he would not be re-elected. However, Sherman's defeat of Confederate forces defending

Atlanta on 22 July, and his capture of the city on 2 September, turned morale round.[37] Lincoln also benefited from Northern successes in the Petersburg campaign and the Shenandoah Valley,[38] while these campaigns exacerbated Confederate supply shortages, increasing the reliance on blockade-runners, which, in turn, the steadily more effective Union blockade thwarted.

The election, held on 8 November, saw Lincoln, who drew on Republican Party organisation and patronage, win by 212 electoral votes to 21, although the popular vote (55 per cent to 45 per cent) was far less unfavourable to McClellan than this figure suggests. The Republicans also won a substantial majority in Congress. Lincoln was helped by the backing of the War Democrats and by the army's support: 78 per cent of the Union soldiers who voted in the presidential election did so for him. This backing reflected the strong sense of religious mission that helped empower the Union soldiers and encourage them to prefer war for victory to negotiations. Having denied God's support by supporting sectional interests, America was to be made new, an affirmation of faith that reflected broad chords in American culture.[39] McClellan, the former general, did not attract this emotional commitment.

Lincoln's electoral triumph was followed five months later by the end of the war. Indeed, this point should be seen as central to the strategy of the war. This victory encourages a benign view of the continuance of the political process during the conflict. However, again, in part, this view is an instance of the broad-brush approach of hindsight, for, at the time, the politics of the war, both at the national and at the state level, and between and within the parties, had proved highly disruptive and threatened wartime strategy. Moreover, this divisiveness had absorbed much political effort, posing problems for the direction of the war.[40] Foreign diplomats seeking signs of opposition were able to find them in plenty. To suggest an alternative, however, is to prefer a functional approach to strategy rather than one that takes note of political contexts and purposes. Such a preference mistakes the significance of campaigning for the total character of a conflict.

Lincoln's re-election provided the continuing political background for the pursuit of a strategy designed to stop Southern support for the war by crippling morale and destroying infrastructure, a goal shared by his troops.[41] Although Sherman's devastation of the Confederate hinterland increased the resolve of some Southern soldiers, the ability to spread devastation unhindered across the Southern hinterland exacerbated the already serious tendency to desertion, helped destroy civilian faith in the war, and made the penalty for, and limitation of, guerrilla warfare apparent.[42] The slave basis of Southern society collapsed as Union forces advanced, with thousands of slaves using the opportunities of Sherman's advance to escape their masters. In making territory his objective, Sherman moved beyond the unproductive nature that that goal and method frequently entailed. Instead, he used the occupation of territory to fulfil his goal of focusing on the psychological mastery of Southern society. This mastery was a goal that proved more productive than that of seeking the chimera of victory in battle,[43] and one that matched the desire (on both sides) to achieve such mastery through humiliation and vengeance.[44]

Sherman's advance also threatened Lee's rear in Virginia, and was to be praised by Basil Liddell Hart accordingly as an instance of the indirect approach. Columbia, South Carolina, was occupied on 17 February 1865, North Carolina was entered the following month, Raleigh was occupied on 13 April, and this advance contributed to the situation in which Lee was defeated without his army being destroyed. The home front was literally collapsing, and this collapse was closely linked to the failure of the Confederate armies.[45]

In their different ways, Sherman and Grant ensured that the uncertainty of war undermined the Confederacy, for they managed risk and uncertainty while their opponents came, in 1864, to experience them. The tempo of Union operations exploited the uncertainty of conflict and directed it against the Confederacy's military as well as its sociopolitical underpinning. Sherman's advance was also the culmination of the long series of Union triumphs in the western theatre, the exploitation of which focused risk. In 1862 and 1863, these triumphs had not prevented Lee from advancing in, and from, Virginia, and, to a considerable extent, it had been possible for the Confederates to trade space in the west for time with which to attack in the east. This potentially war-winning Southern formula had failed, in the east, not across the Appalachians, and it was only after that the Union forces were able to exploit their success in the west in order to attack what could otherwise have been a defence-in-depth in the east.

This exploitation of Northern success was in part a matter of a psychological shift, a shift that was important to strategic capability. Grant brought a conviction that victory could be won, a confidence that reflected the repeated Union successes in the west. This conviction replaced the earlier hesitation of many Union commanders in the east, a hesitation born of a caution, if not a lack of confidence, that had been seen with McClellan's deliberative generalship and had been encouraged by Lee's attacks.[46] Conversely, Grant's reputation benefited from the usually poor Confederate generalship he faced in the west.[47]

A very different American strategy was advocated by Jefferson Davis, the Confederate president, who was determined to fight on after Lee's surrender to Grant at Appomattox Court House on 9 April 1865. The previous July, Davis had responded to the terms offered in Lincoln's amnesty proclamation of December 1863 by declaring: 'We are fighting for Independence – and that, or extermination, we will have . . . You may emancipate every Negro in the Confederacy, but we will be free. We will govern ourselves . . . if we have to see every Southern plantation sacked, and every Southern city in flames.'[48] Guerrilla war had been anticipated in 1862 by the French envoy after a trip to Richmond, and was proposed by Davis in 1865 in a proclamation after the fall of the city, a proclamation that very much suggested a new spatial under-standing of the South and of the war zone: 'Relieved from the necessity of guarding cities and particular points . . . with an army free to move from point to point . . . operating in the interior of our own country, where supplies are more accessible, and where the foe will be far removed from his own base . . . nothing is now needed to render our triumph certain but the exhibition of our own unquenchable resolve.'[49]

This was not an alien concept as guerrilla warfare had already been seen in areas, notably southern Appalachia, where terrain was difficult and the number of regulars limited. Moreover, the last stages of the Mexican–American War had shown the problems the American occu-pying forces confronted due to continued opposition,[50] and the same was even more true for the French in Mexico.[51]

Yet, despite the Partisan Ranger Act of 1861, the Confederate polit-ical and military leadership had proved largely unwilling to encourage guerrilla warfare that, while particularly important in Appalachia and in the Missouri–Kansas region, was not so in the crucial war zones.

Furthermore, some of what is now termed guerrilla warfare, with the misleading implication that it was not waged by regulars, can, looking back to earlier practices of 'small war', better be described as irregular warfare by regulars, particularly engaged in raiding activities, a process related to America's frontier war culture towards Native Americans. Prefiguring British policy during the Boer War (1899–1902), the Union forces were able to counter these methods, both by defensive tactical means, especially blockhouses and patrols, and by action designed to provide the exemplary operational threat of retribution and/or to find and engage those directly involved.[52]

Lee and his fellow generals ignored Davis's call. Such a strategy was antipathetical to their understanding of military and social order, and unacceptable under both heads. Greatly influenced by Lee's surrender, there had been no fighting on by the other armies. As a result, the bitterest conflict in American history came to a more abrupt end than might have been anticipated. However, to a degree, the conflict subsequently re-erupted in areas like Mississippi through Reconstruction with the actions of white militia in the Colfax massacre and the street fighting in New Orleans.

CONFLICT WITH NATIVE AMERICANS II

The pace of expansion at the expense of Native Americans resumed after the Civil War. Earlier practices of anti-societal conflict and winter campaigning were made more common. The policy was clear, that of dominance over the Native Americans and their land; but the strategy varied. Thus, the brutality of 1867–8 was followed by a major change after Ulysses Grant became president in 1869. Believing in 'conquest by kindness', in which Natives moved to reservations where Christian education and agriculture were intended to make them 'good' neighbours who were civilised and Christianised, Grant followed a peace policy.

Whatever the pace of conflict, Native American resistance had been largely broken, and a successful military methodology to that end had evolved. This was the product of a strategy that brought goals, means and methods into a potent congruence. The focus on wrecking Native civil society or, rather, on the notion that there was no civil sphere separate to the military, had been seen in the latter stages of the Civil War.

Against the Native Americans, where distance posed a more formidable context, the army had to adapt its military style and methods, and to enhance its mobility. The railway was used to move troops and supplies towards the area of hostilities, a good logistical system underpinned winter campaigns, the provision of breech-loaders enhanced firepower, and there was an underpinning of economic advance. The army's strategy became that of positioning the West into America not solely by enforcing the reservation policy and maintaining security, but also by playing a major role in supporting economic integration, notably by building roads, and encouraging the building of railways.[53]

CONCLUSIONS

Politics was to the fore in the aftermath of the Civil War. A mighty military was not used to intervene in Canada and/or Mexico, nor to begin a new period of overseas power projection. Instead, there was a demobilisation, albeit one compatible with continual expansion against the Native Americans. Unlike that in 1945, there was no shelter in the shape of the atomic bomb, and the demobilisation in 1865 was far more intense.

However, there was also the growing assumption that the United States was now clearly the great power in the Americas and the Pacific. This assumption helped create anxiety when other powers developed their strength, as Chile did in the early 1880s and, even more, Japan in the 1890s. This anxiety was made even more striking because of the role of a sense of racial superiority in American strategy. Correspondingly, racial uncertainty encouraged the development and deployment of strength.[54] Thus, strategic mastery in North America was followed by an uncertainty over America's position in the Pacific. Anxieties, in turn, led into a new navalism that became a means as well as a commitment of national power. Strategy was redefined accordingly.

7

EUROPE AND THE WORLD QUESTION
1816–1913

The international conflicts in Europe during this period were swifter than the American Civil War, which helped ensure that strategy was not as closely impacted in politics, although the situation was very different with rebellions, civil wars and related foreign intervention. For European states engaged in international conflict, it was not necessary to create a new military system, as had happened in the United States with civil war, and it was not so difficult to sustain domestic support. For example, that the German Wars of Unification (1864–71) did not require the conquests of Denmark, Austria and France made the campaigning less difficult for Prussia (Germany) than it would otherwise have been. Instead, the focus tended to be on operational goals, capabilities and processes. Yet, the decision to fight and the choice of opponent were both key strategic elements, the latter a longstanding aspect of the multipolar character of the European state system.

The focus in much contemporary and later consideration of war in this period was/is on Prussian/German victories over French armies in August 1870, culminating with the surrender of Napoleon III and the army he was with at Sedan on 2 September. The analysis of the Prussian/German campaign and battlefield victories attracted lots of attention. Campaigning skill was of course significant to operational success, but, in practice, the Franco-Prussian War (1870–1) indicated that much more was involved. A smaller population and a lower population growth rate than that of Germany reduced the pool for the French army, underlining the damage done to France by Prussia's success in overcoming its German opponents in 1866 as part of the Austro-Prussian War, and anticipating the problems that were to face France in both world wars.

At the same time, France did not use well the troops that it had, repeating, in a different way, the failure of Napoleon I in the Waterloo campaign of 1815.

Yet, the German strategy, with its focus on victory in battle as a means to secure a short war, also faced major problems. After their victories near the frontier, the Germans subsequently encountered difficulties as they advanced further, especially supply problems and opposition from a hostile population. More generally, the resources for the conquest of France were simply not present, because, among other factors, there was no real mobilisation of German economic and financial strength. German society and unification could not be pushed so far. Rather as the Union had done in the opening stages of the American Civil War, Germany thus sought a swift and popular conflict, with relatively low casualties, and without other powers intervening.

This strategy, however, fell foul of the French determination to fight on, rather as the Union one had done of the Confederate one. Napoleon III was replaced in September 1870 by a Government of National Defence that was resolved not to surrender territory and that discovered a justification and role through continued resistance. In turn, encouraging French persistence, the Germans were not prepared to concede generous terms. A key contrast to 1914 was that France (like the Confederacy in the American Civil War) fought alone and lacked the resources and strategic depth offered by an alliance. It was a difference for which the Germans were not adequately prepared in the First World War when Britain entered the conflict and supported France on the Western Front, while France was also allied with Russia and (from 1915) Italy. In 1871, faced by continued German success and by domestic instability that culminated in the Paris Commune, France was driven to surrender.

In contrast to German successes, Italian reunification owed much to the international politics of the period. In 1821, 1830 and 1848–9, anti-Austrian efforts in Italy were totally thwarted by the lack of foreign assistance, as also was the liberal cause in Spain in 1823, and Hungarian and Polish nationalist risings against Austria and Russia respectively. However, in 1859, French intervention under Napoleon III against Austria in northern Italy was crucial, both in defeating Austria and in providing the opportunity to overthrow Papal and Neapolitan forces in central and southern Italy, and thus bringing much of it under the control of the new Italian kingdom. In these areas, only the Papal States were left outside the new kingdom, and that due to French military intervention on behalf of their continued independence. In 1866, Prussia's defeat of Austria provided Prussia's ally Italy with the opportunity to gain Venetia from Austria, while the Franco-Prussian War gave Italy the chance to capture Rome in 1870. France could no longer protect the Papal position.

That account of the international dimension, while central to the course and consequences of the strategy of reunification, however, offers nothing on the difficulties facing Italian strategy as conventionally understood, in other words military operations. In 1866, these difficulties focused on the refusal of generals Alfonso La Marmora and Enrico Cialdini to co-operate and co-ordinate their offensives across the rivers Mincio and Po respectively as ordered to do by King Victor Emanuel. The generals hated each other for a variety of personal and professional reasons. Instead, La Marmora moved with part of his army without Cialdini's support, and was attacked and defeated by Archduke Albrecht at Custoza. The Crown did not exert sufficient authority over the generals. There was no powerful chief of staff or minister of war, and, in his choice of commanders, Victor Emanuel preferred loyalty to the ruling House of Savoy over ability. This is a longstanding pattern in many states and one that should be borne in mind when considering strategy. Looked at differently, this pattern of command serves as a reminder of the strategic significance of control over the army itself, and notably so for domestic politics.

As far as the military and campaigning were concerned, German strategy-making was the exception not the rule in this period; as earlier, to a degree, had been French strategy under Lazare Carnot in 1793–7 and Napoleon Bonaparte (Napoleon I). The prestige of German war-making as a result of the victories in 1864–71 subsequently led to an increase in interest in Clausewitz, an interest that was important to the development of a canon of 'classic' texts on military affairs that were not simply Classical. Such a canon was very much required in the late nineteenth century. A course of lectures on Clausewitz was given at the *École Supérieure de Guerre* (an institution modelled on Berlin's *Kriegsakademie*) in 1884, influencing French officers, although the majority of French strategists remained sceptical about the German sage.

By the turn of the century, cross-pollination from theorists into other languages was becoming more extensive than hitherto. Translation into Japanese led to claims that Clausewitz influenced Japan's victory over Russia in 1904–5. Similarly, Alfred T. Mahan's *The Influence of Sea Power upon History, 1660–1783* (1890) was translated into German and Japanese in 1896 and had some influence, although largely because it fed into already strong currents in both countries.[1]

It is no accident that strategy as a self-conscious and actively articulated practice was very much linked to the development of general staffs, which was particularly the case with Prussia in the nineteenth century. The Prussians established and improved a system of general staff work and of training at a General Staff Academy, a system which was to be given much of the credit for victory in 1866 and 1870–1 over Austria and France respectively. Training of staff officers provided the Prussian army with a valuable coherence, as these officers had an assured place in a co-ordinated command system: officers from the general staff were expected to advise commanders, and the latter were also required to heed their chiefs of staff. This led to a system of joint responsibility in which either the commander or his first general staff officer could issue orders. Such a system, which rested heavily on its reputation and that of the general staff, apparently made predictable planning possible, thus encouraging forward planning. Moreover, from 1857, there was an emphasis in the Prussian army on preparing for a whole campaign, rather than simply for battle, and thus on campaign plans. Preparing for battle did not require such prior planning. Sweeping Prussian successes in 1866 and 1870–1 gave the staff system prestige and greatly encouraged its adoption and emulation elsewhere.[2] Spenser Wilkinson, who became Oxford's first Chichele Professor of the History of War in 1909, wrote *The Brain of the Army: A Popular Account of the German General Staff* (1895).[3]

Clausewitz's influence certainly appeared appropriate in the aftermath of Prussian success in the Wars of German Unification. The place of formal education in the military was increasingly seen as significant to professionalisation, and links between armies grew, in part thanks to alliance planning and co-ordination, and due to drawing comparisons between armies.[4] German campaigns were studied in staff colleges, including in the United States, where they came to be of lasting significance. Moreover, German military missions and equipment became important.

In practice, Helmuth von Moltke was a more accessible and useful model than Clausewitz, while Germany's example was not accepted without question. National variations were significant. For example, in Denmark, the first real staff course started in the 1880s, the two main subjects taught being *krigskunst* (art of war) and *krigshistorie* (war history with battle focus), the latter being designed to support the former. The first time the word 'strategy' was found as a topic was for the 1911–14 course. Earlier, when used at all in Denmark, tactics and strategy were employed in a Jominian way, with applied tactics being seen as the employment of forces on the battlefield and strategy being planning for warfare on the map; what would now be described as the preparatory phase of operational art. Strategy did not acquire a link to the political intent until far later and this has affected the teaching of strategy to the present, both in Denmark and elsewhere.[5]

The Russians were divided over the extent to which they should look to German models. General Mikhail Dragomirov, who led the 'back to Suvorov' movement, emphasised the value of morale in his pressure for a Russian model focused on the example of earlier Russian commanders. In contrast, a supporter of reform, General Genrikh Leer, professor of strategy at the Military Academy in St Petersburg from 1865 to 1889 and the Academy's head from 1889 until 1898, saw Moltke as an exponent of the concept of the operational line, which, through manoeuvre, was to be translated into victory. To him, Moltke married the ideal and the practice of strategy. However, Leer also argued, with great perception, that manoeuvre itself only brought time and space, and could not in itself ensure victory.[6]

Leer's argument looked forward both to German failure in 1914 and to more general questions about the character of strategy. Alongside these questions, the German army had become too powerful in decision-making, and too focused on the operationalisation of strategy in the shape of the concept and pursuit of decisive victory through attack, as in Moltke's *Instruction for Large Unit Commands* (1869).[7] Moltke himself, however, had changed his views. While arguing that it was preferable to fight on the territory of one's opponent, he became increasingly sceptical after the Franco-Prussian War about the potential of the strategic offensive, because of increases in defensive firepower and in the size of armies. However, the pursuit of quick victory through taking the offensive and winning a decisive battle was something the Germans were repeatedly to attempt in 1914–44.[8] This Prussian/German system, moreover, both facilitated and reflected a reading of military affairs in which the views of the army came foremost, and with the navy neglected.

In practice, deficiencies in leadership, operational warfare, dispositions, weaponry and strategy on the part of Austria and France had played into Prussian hands in 1866 and 1870, enabling the Prussians to outmanoeuvre their opponents. However, the extent to which the role of these deficiencies could not be predicted for the future was underplayed by contemporaries, who were keen to argue that they had discovered the blueprint for success. In practice, such deficiencies were not to be sufficient in 1914 to give Germany victory. In the Second World War, they were readily apparent in 1939–41, but the situation was then redressed, and, in turn, the flaws of German strategy were fully revealed. These flaws were not simply operational, but also the belief that war was, essentially and rapidly, settled on the battlefield, and the understanding of strategy that came accordingly.[9] Wars elsewhere also encouraged change. The experience of weaknesses in the organisation of the American army in the 1898 war with Spain led to the reforms of 1903 introduced by Elihu Root, the Secretary of War. These included the creation of a general staff for the army.

The search for lessons was encouraged by the uncertainties and unease linked to the major role of technological change in weaponry and in related aspects of economic and social organisation, for example railways.[10] This role encouraged not only planning, but also the more specific issue of incorporating emerging technology into organisations. In the case of navies, this incorporation led to an emphasis on engineers, as well as a cultural shift that lent itself to strategic enquiry and operational consideration, as in the Naval War College founded in the United States in 1884.[11]

Like the discussion of land warfare in terms of the German model, Mahan's arguments about naval power, specifically the value of pursuing oceanic dominance by means of a large battleship fleet able to defeat the fleets of rivals, were similarly of only limited value. These arguments did not adequately address the consequences in terms of influence over land masses, although Mahan did use command of the sea to cover the conditions off an enemy's coast so that it could be blockaded. Nor, more specifically, did Mahan's arguments address the idea of pursuing a counter-weaponry and counter-doctrine in terms of limiting the effectiveness of battleships and/or challenging oceanic dominance by means of raiding cruisers, torpedo boats and submarines. All were to be attempted, although it was ultimately aircraft that were more significant in limiting the effectiveness of battleships, an effectiveness given greater force on 9 September 1943 when the Germans used the FX-1400 radio-guided bomb to sink the Italian battleship *Roma*. This bomb was a turning point as it could be fired from a cheap platform and with high accuracy and significant effect. In contrast, the sinking of the *Prince of Wales* by an attack from a large number of Japanese aircraft on 10 December 1941 showed that battleships could be sunk if they lacked fighter protection.

Mahan's notion of a decisive victory leading to a command of the sea that could be employed to strategic effect was an account of how to win wars that did not require the acquiescence of the defeated. This prospectus and potential for decisive victory corresponded with Mahan's strong belief in divine sovereignty and providentialism.[12] The will to believe in victory, notably decisive victory, was important to the analysis.

Combined with the creation of naval planning staffs, an emphasis on control of the sea – a more modern and nuanced notion than command of the sea – encouraged the development of strategic naval plans. Germany's first war plan against Britain, drafted in 1897, was followed in 1900 with an implausible German plan for an attack on the United States. After their entente in 1904, Britain and France were to plan jointly how to deploy their naval forces in the event of war with Germany.

The emphasis on the battleship did not mean identical doctrines and plans, for there were major differences in strategic culture and tasking. Moreover, an understanding of limitations was offered by Julian Corbett in *Some Principles of Maritime Strategy* (1911). This understanding was more nuanced than Mahan's approach to command of the sea.[13] In the event, the naval plans of the major powers were to be thwarted in the First World War, notably the commitment to a decisive victory in battle.

THE WORLD QUESTION

The strategies by which control over much of the world was contested were those of imperial expansion and naval power. Like those strategies that resulted in the strength and cohesion of the United States, they were more consequential on the world scale than the European-focused strategic agenda linked to Germany and the move towards the First World War, or, indeed, those related to the contesting of control within China from the 1850s to the 1910s. By 1914, the world was largely under the rule or control of European states, or of people of European descent. The world question therefore became that of the competition, eventually conflict, between the leading Western powers. This process was given a new technological context by the transformation offered by telegraphy, railways and steamships, and was given explicit theoretical focus from the late 1890s in the new vocabulary and subject of geopolitics.

This competition between the leading Western powers in part drew on longstanding tensions and particular strategic interests. Thus, although it is possible to depict the Crimean War of 1854–6 as an accident, the British, throughout the nineteenth century, appreciated both that their power depended in no small part on holding India and that the Ottoman (Turkish) Empire protected the lifeline of the British Empire to India. Napoleon's Egyptian expedition of 1798 remained strong in their memories; although Russia, the Black Sea expansion of which had already given rise to concern in Britain at the time of the Ochakov crisis in 1791, replaced France as the threat. To keep Russia away from the Bosphorus and the Dardanelles was a sound aim from that viewpoint, as were measures to resist Russian influence in Persia (Iran), measures that helped encourage British intervention in the Persian Gulf. So also with the protection of the North-West Frontier of India. To ensure that the frontier region was protected, and that Afghanistan was in friendly hands, were longstanding goals. Despite much recent emphasis on failure, Britain in the 'Great Game' secured its strategic goals following both the First (1839–42) and the Second (1878–80) Afghan wars. As a result, Russia felt thwarted in its Afghan strategy.[14]

The occupation of Egypt in 1882, although provoked by Egyptian bankruptcy and crowds attacking Europeans in Alexandria, was also strategically sound, ensuring British control of the Suez Canal and blocking a possible French takeover of Egypt, which had been a British concern from the 1780s and, even more, the late 1790s. When Robert, 3rd Marquess of Salisbury sent an army against the Mahdists in Sudan in 1895, and then sustained that effort, leading to the victory at Omdurman and the fall of Khartoum in 1898, he did it not to avenge the earlier killing of Major-General Charles George Gordon by the Mahdists in Khartoum in 1885, nor for British national pride, but to prevent French expansion threatening to lead to French control of the Upper Nile, and also a possible alliance between the Mahdists and the Ethiopians, who had just beaten the Italians at Adua in 1896. Concern about French expansionism led to the Fashoda confrontation on the Upper Nile in 1898, which nearly resulted in war between France and Britain. Similarly, strategic considerations were crucial in the Boer War (1899–1902). Aside from the significance of gold deposits, South Africa, with its naval base at Simonstown, controlled the other lifeline of empire to India, that round the Cape of Good Hope.

However, earlier it had been the struggle between Western and non-Western powers that was to the fore. Here again the prime strategic dimension was political, and, more particularly, one that linked peace and war. In both, Western powers, and notably where their soldiers and settlers were heavily outnumbered, depended on local allies. Thus, the key strategic element was that of winning such allies. This was not a new process, and had been seen from antiquity and, also with Western expansion, notably from the Iberian *Reconquista* in the eleventh century onwards. However, it is a dimension that is underplayed due to the emphasis on Western technological capabilities, which indeed expanded exponentially in the second half of the nineteenth century.

At the same time, so did Western ambitions both towards non-Western powers and in competing with other Western powers in the non-Western world. This expansion was seen, differently, in war with China, the intimidation of Japan, and the conquests of Africa and Oceania. Western powers benefited from the support of some non-Western élites, but even more from the recruitment of local troops. Partly as a result, emphasis had to be put on the processes by which control was negotiated.[15] As seen with the British in Malaya, this involved much beside force, but at the same time, the Indian army played a crucial role for Britain, both within India and more generally.[16] So also for native troops and France's takeover of much of west Africa.

159

In turn, the strategies adopted by non-Western powers were instructive. The pursuit of Western models was significant in some states, notably in Japan from the 1860s. The Japanese army was modelled on the French, and then the German, their navy on the British. This pursuit did not, however, achieve success for Egypt, despite being begun earlier: it was successfully invaded by Britain in 1882. Similarly, King Kalakaua of Hawaii built up the military on foreign models and using foreign arms,[17] but Hawaii did not remain independent from American control.

Westernisation as a strategy entailed political costs and was accompanied by domestic crises, as in Japan where it led to large-scale conflict, including the Satsuma Rebellion. As a result, issues of legitimacy relating to identity and status were as important to Westernisation as concerns about strategic competition.[18] Defeat at the hands of Russia in 1877–8 led Turkey to create a High Commission of Military Inspection and seek foreign assistance, especially the foundation in 1882 of a German military mission that actively pushed modernisation. Reform escalated, with the expansion of the War Academy, the creation of a staff system, the improvement of the conscription system, and the establishment, in 1900, of a Ministry of War.

China in the 'Self-Strengthening Movement' sought to adopt a Chinese version of modernisation in which the pressure of foreign powers was held at bay. At the same time, this could not involve the extensive use of advisers, weapons experts and weapons. Moreover, organisations similar to general staffs emerged in China in the era of military modernisation. Officials created *mufu*, which were essentially general staffs that consisted of experts in various areas.[19] Chinese modernisation was not without value, but encountered the problem in 1894–5 of war with a state, Japan, that had followed this strategy more effectively and that applied it in a limited war.[20] This operationalisation was more successful than when Japan launched a full-scale attack on China in 1937.

In conventional teleological terms, looking to religion, as both strategic goal and strategic means, in resisting Western power appears redundant and bound to fail, as with the *puputans* or final battles in Bali in 1906, in which the two raja families purified themselves for death and were all slaughtered as they advanced in the face of Dutch firepower, killing their own wounded as they did so. So also with other cases, including the failure of the Ghost Dance movement among American

Natives, the Mahdists in Sudan, the Boxers in China, and the Bambatha rebellion of Zulus against British rule and taxation in 1906. Yet, from the perspective of movements, including anti-Western ones, active in the 2010s, both Muslim and others, this depiction of earlier strategies seems less secure. In particular, a lack of short-term success is not itself a demonstration of redundancy in strategic terms. This is readily apparent for cultures that place an emphasis on martyrdom, but, even if a Western context is adopted, it can also be the case in terms of building up a narrative of exemplary, even sacred, resistance.

CONCLUSIONS

The nineteenth century appears more as history now that we are in a new millennium. Indeed, with the history of war focused on the two world wars, the late nineteenth century can seem the foolish precursor to the disastrous failure in 1914 to secure a rapid outcome. In practice, that is an inadequate reading of the 1914 campaign; of the First World War as a whole; of the relationship between the idea and practice of strategy in the nineteenth century, and both 1914 and the First World War as a whole; and lastly of the nineteenth century itself. In the last, the pursuit of ends through force, diplomacy, trade and finance had led to changes in control over much of the world and its population. Thus, the limitations of strategy were/are not readily apparent, and that essentially irrespective of the planning structures of the period.

Moreover, there is evidence of continuity between the nineteenth century and the First World War, and sophistication in the understanding of the issues posed by multiple commitments. To take the former, there were links between British policy in the 1830s and in 1914. Britain's role in the creation of Belgium in the 1830s, in order to keep the French out of ports on the North Sea, notably Antwerp, was a continuation of policy towards France and the Low Countries from the late 1670s (and one with earlier medieval and early modern anticipations), and anticipated the British reaction to the German invasion of Belgium en route for France in 1914. Indeed, in 1905–7, the Staff College focused on possible British responses if Germany launched such a move.[21]

To take the element of prioritisation, it is instructive to consider the memorandum on British strategy drafted in 1888 by Edward Stanhope,

Secretary of State for War, and published as a parliamentary paper in 1901. The priorities of the army were, in order, the support of the civil power in the British Isles; the provision of reinforcements for India; the provision of garrison units for fortresses, colonies and coaling stations; the provision of two corps for home defence; and the ability to deploy one of these for service in a European war.[22] Such documents, with their emphasis on priorities amid clashing commitments, were indications of sophisticated strategic thought. At the same time, there was little that was novel about the need to reconcile domestic and foreign commitments, and to distinguish among the latter. That was the key strategic quandary, one that was not greatly helped by essentially treating operational practice as military strategy. Moreover, the Committee on Imperial Defence was only established in 1902, a general staff was not created until the mid-1900s, and there were flaws in the strategic processes of the British military.[23] So also with other states that had to address these potential clashes over commitments.

There were in practice serious differences over military strategy and the related issues of prioritisation and procurement. Thus, in Britain in the 1880s, a group led by Field Marshal Frederick Roberts sought a continental strategy based on forces in India, while Field Marshal Sir Garnet Wolseley favoured a maritime one based on the Royal Navy carrying expeditionary forces from Britain. The Intelligence Department of the War Office was a key player in discussions. Wolseley greatly influenced the memorandum on strategy referred to above.

Ultimately, the collapse of a number of states in the 1910s, from China to Russia and Germany, reflected the failure to hold domestic and foreign commitments in creative tension and to appreciate that an appropriate prioritisation was crucial to a successful strategy, and in both its domestic and its military aspects. The 'strategic calculus' was poor due to the extent to which nationalist dynamics took precedence over 'realist strategic considerations', a point that is pertinent to Chinese assertiveness at present.[24] Contingent circumstances, whether or not referred to in terms of friction, were also highly important to the unravelling both of military operations and of domestic power systems.

In the case of both Austria and Germany, the empires that launched the First World War, the army was unduly dominant, and notably so in the planning for international crisis. Army views focused on a drive for autonomy, if not independence, from both political oversight and civilian society, and on a demand for resources. In part, these elements responded to the growing pressure on established roles and traditional assumptions that was perceived in societies that were changing rapidly, both in terms of industrialisation and urbanisation, and also with a decline of deference as new social assumptions came into play. In turn, the technological character of warfare was transformed more rapidly and comprehensively than before. Moreover, industrialisation produced the resources for a total change in scale. In many countries, there were also new sociopolitical practices and structures that were linked to the new economics. These changed the parameters for governmental control, political consent and, therefore, policy. The process and consequences varied by state, but they were significant not least in increasing the scale of government. In general, it became less a case of one individual in control of the state, and, instead, more one of rulership in practice by a group.

As a result, the group dynamics and psychological factors involved in war changed. This was not simply a new iteration of older patterns of the relationship between Crown and aristocracy, although that was involved. In the new governmental systems, the military was a structured and coherent formal organisation with a greater role in policy. The collective psychology of the élite in many, but not all, states was affected by this role, which often extended to the wider politics of the state in question. In this context, there was a tendency to envisage military outcomes to international alignments, let alone disputes. This tendency drew on influential ideas of the inherent competitiveness of human societies and of survival and growth through strength and conflict. There was also a drive for role fulfilment in the shape of action, a drive that was to be crucial to the international crisis that led to the outbreak of the First World War in 1914. None of this was new, but the developments in particular in the previous half-century mentioned above led to a novelty in scale and institutional structures.

Increasingly in the nineteenth century, alongside the challenges to established (and new) élites and practices from liberal politicians and movements, came those from socialists and other radicals. Moreover, there were the changes stemming from new technologies and from the prospect that this process would continue, if not escalate.[25] The challenges this dynamic situation posed to the military varied by context, notably national context, but also with reference to the professional speciality of the officers involved and to their political assumptions. Throughout the period, the military was used to suppress rebellions and opposition movements, or failed to do so. Thus, in the 1810s, British troops were deployed against the Luddites. Some of the movements in question were radical, as in Paris in 1871, but others were conservative in the sense of opposition to real or feared change, as in the United States and Japan in the 1860s. The biggest challenge in China was rebellion, notably that of the Taiping in 1851–66.

Alongside brute force, a range of responses to potential opposition existed and were discussed, often explicitly in terms of their political consequences. These included conscription, as a way to discipline and contain at least some of the new masses (and also to raise troop numbers, a key instance of the domestic–military overlap), as well as the military use of new technologies, and also, a point often related to the other, enhanced professionalism.

Although focused on international rivalry, the concept and practice of strategy was another response to the challenges of a changing situation. This was notably so in the intensively competitive nature of international relations in the late nineteenth century and at the start of the twentieth. This focus on strategy served to entrench military professionalism and politics, and to lessen civilian intervention, which was frequently presented as 'less strategic'. This argument scarcely defines and places strategy as a whole, but it helps explain its greater salience from the late nineteenth century. In essence, a term developed as an aspect of Enlightenment thought, notably of the classification of knowledge, became more prominent in a specific sociopolitical context and with reference to a particular stage and type of military professionalism. In short, as from the outset, the term was scarcely value-free; and repeated attempts to treat it as such are mistaken.

8

STRATEGIES FOR WORLD WAR
1900–18

An emphasis on the offensive, the general stance in the years leading up to the First World War (1914–18), ensured that strategy, in the widest sense, focused on access to manpower, because, to sustain the offensive, commentators called for ever-larger armies. In doing so, they emphasised the value not only of conscripts, but also of the reserve forces of former conscripts. Their effectiveness was maintained by annual manoeuvres which familiarised them anew to unit behaviour, command and weaponry. Strength was seen in terms of numbers, and in such related issues as public health, education and motivation. As such, strength was a social and cultural issue and concept, and one that underlined the growing centrality of concepts of war and society to understandings of strategic potential and capability, and to pressure to improve society accordingly. This led in Britain, after concern about the health of volunteers during the Boer War (1899–1902), to pressure for government action in order to improve the health of the public, as well as to discussion of the value of conscription.

Moreover, strategy was also inherent in the attempt to benefit from the process of change that now appeared inevitable in military affairs, and that therefore needed to be predicted, planned and prepared for. A degree of built-in responsiveness to the possibility of change within the military system became a technocratic ideal for the military, and encouraged both the institutionalisation of military attachés from the 1860s and a more conscious process of military planning. Attachés served to report on signs of change and means of improvement. They provided a better understanding of the strategic target.

At the same time, although there was preparation for a large-scale war from 1871, it was difficult to anticipate what would occur. A belief that the destructiveness of warfare would cause social collapse was advanced by Friedrich Engels and Jan Bloch, and this belief can be seen as anticipating the First World War. However, the Russo-Japanese War of 1904–5, while indicating the lethal character of new weaponry in defended positions, including rapid-firing artillery and machine guns, also suggested that the attacking power, in this case Japan, would win, and would do so relatively speedily, albeit with heavy casualties.

In practice, the situation, both as far as that war was concerned and also in terms of lessons with regard to future conflicts, was far more complex, a point also true of other wars of the period. For 1904–5, this was particularly the case, as the Russians came closer to success in 1904–5 than is sometimes appreciated. Focusing on operational and tactical issues, and failing to think strategically, commentators also neglected the pressure placed on Japan, which was such that the latter could not afford, economically or militarily, to pursue the Russians deeper into Manchuria. Indeed, the Russian retreat into Manchuria, and their army's escape from Japanese encirclement at Mukden, challenged the Japanese supply system and helped to force Japan to the peace table. There were echoes of the problems created for Germany, another short-war state, by the continuation of its war with France in 1870, as its forces advanced from victories near the frontier. Furthermore, Japanese victory owed much to political weakness in St Petersburg: notably the impact of the 1905 revolution, which was in part fostered by Japanese military intelligence, rather as the Germans were to move Lenin to exploit the developing crisis in Russia in 1917. Military commentators preferred to focus on the campaigning, not on the politics, a pattern that continues to the present.

More generally, while permanent general staffs were a source of strategic continuity that was in a way separate from public discussion, or, at least, of such would-be continuity, political objectives defined strategy and affected the response to intelligence information. In the broadest political sense, cultural factors, notably ideas of national honour, were crucial in the preference for the offensive, a longstanding theme, and, linked to this preference, in the desire for a quick war. This preference and desire were related to the political role of the military in many states, not least the extent to which the reconceptualisation of conservatism in a more active direction provided a new and expanded political space for the military. Within it, there was the pursuit of the technocratic search for military excellence and success, but also a failure adequately to address broader social and political questions in strategy.

Total war foregrounded the notion of national mobilisation, and very much linked the production of resources (including conscripts) on the home front to success in the conflict. Total war, moreover, became necessary and was understood as necessary, because the campaigning in 1914 neither delivered the victory that was planned for and anticipated, notably by Germany, nor provided the basis for a peace settlement. Nor did the campaigning and alliance-strengthening in 1915 alter this situation. In contrast to the Second World War, in which a verdict had apparently been delivered by the end of June 1940, after less than a year of campaigning, with Germany conquering Poland, Denmark, Norway, the Netherlands, Belgium and France, and allied with the Soviet Union and Italy, there was no 'closure' in 1915 on either of the major fronts. Indeed, in 1914, a German plan that unfolded at walking pace and on exterior lines was thwarted by a French redeployment by rail (and motor vehicle) on interior lines. This was the key element to the military aspects of the strategy on the Western Front in 1914, and it wrecked the short-war plan. In 1915, in turn, the Germans hit the Russians hard, but to operational, rather than strategic, effect. There was no comparison to the knocking out of Serbia in late 1915 by Austrian, Bulgarian and German forces. That was success on a lesser front and where the opponent, like Poland in 1939 and Yugoslavia in 1941, could be attacked from several directions.

Alongside excellent scholarly work, notably recently, on the strategy of the First World War, there has been singularly little impact of that dimension of the war on a modern popular perception of the conflict that, instead, very much remains fixed on the 'face of battle' itself. This is unfortunate as it leaves unclear why the combatants fought specific campaigns and, indeed, why they fought in the attacking mode that they did. In practice, war aims set the strategy and the counter-strategy. Having launched a war in order to take advantage of a particular international situation and in part because its ally, Austria, was taking the initiative in the Balkans, Germany subsequently determined its war aims: on 9 September 1914, the German Chancellor, Theobald von Bethmann-Hollweg, drew up a memorandum in which these included territorial gains, notably the Longwy-Briey iron ore basin from France, dominance of Belgium, and colonial gains in Africa. At the same time, particular German lobbies had their own goals. Thus, naval commanders, wanting bases against Britain on the coast of Belgium and, if possible, France, pressed for a focus on the Western Front, and a *status quo ante bellum* peace with Russia. There was no dynamic behind such a proposal, however, because of German interest in territorial gains in eastern Europe.

In contrast, Britain sought to secure the independence of Belgium and France, and to destroy what it termed the military might of Prussia, in other words Germany. The significance of the German violation of Belgian neutrality, a strategy-level decision taken essentially for operational reasons of ease of campaigning, to Britain's entry into the war was such that French eventual victory owed much to a political decision. This was the one made in January 1912 when the French government rejected the military advice that it was best to attack Germany via Belgium. Austria sought Russia's share of Poland and a stronger position in the Balkans at the expense of Serbia; and Russia control over both the German and Austrian portions of Poland and, from Turkey, the Straits (the Bosphorus and the Dardanelles).

The essential strategic fact of the war in 1915 was that Germany had seized much of Belgium and part of France and, without any offensive plan for the Western Front to supersede that employed in 1914, its short-war strategy, had dug in to protect its gains. This situation led in Britain to an 'Easterners' strategy aimed against Germany's ally Turkey, but, on the whole, obliged Britain and, even more, France to mount offensives on the Western Front in order to regain the lost territory, which was also seen as the best way to avoid further losses. There was a conviction that only through mounting an offensive would it be possible for the Allies to gain the initiative and, conversely, deny it to the Germans. Linked to this was the view, vindicated by events, that both gaining the initiative and mounting an offensive were prerequisites for victory.

Another necessity for the attack on the Western Front was provided by the wish to reduce German pressure on Russia and to prevent it from being knocked out of the war. This strategy of indirect assistance was more common. Similarly, the German offensive in Poland in 1915 was aimed at helping Austria and giving it time to recover from its defeats at the hands of Russia in southern Poland. Moreover, German pressure for the conquest of Serbia, for which most of the troops were supplied by

Austria and Bulgaria, was designed to open up a direct rail link to Turkey so that supplies could be sent to help an ally which had suffered defeats in early 1915.

It was widely believed that the stalemate of the winter of 1914–15 was due to the exhaustion of men and supplies in the previous autumn's campaigning with its unexpected demands; and, less plausibly, that it would be possible, with fresh men and munitions, to restart a war of manoeuvre. Trying to do so, however, required a difficult, and perhaps impossible, reconciliation of the bold operational planning by general staffs with the supply management of war ministries trying to adapt to unprecedented demands. Seeking to restart a war of manoeuvre by breaking through opponents' front lines was the strategic tool of choice.

There were other more specific problems with the strategic planning. For example, in Britain, the government lost control of the military strategy because there was no defence staff to question the plans; and, related to this, the relationships between ways and means were unprobed, as were the consequences of the military commitments to France and Belgium. In numbers, Britain lacked the army to match its commitments, and, once the numbers were gained, the army lacked the necessary training and sufficient appropriate equipment until 1917. In large part, this was a realistic assessment of the practical situation, but, in the event, British strategy was 'captured' by France in the sense of the political and military requirements of alliance with France.

The situation in 1915 underlined the political failure of the German 1914 offensive by obliging the Allies to try to regain the lost territories. Indeed, David Lloyd George, a leading Liberal minister, who had at first been unsure about Britain going to war, now pressed, in a speech in February 1915, for a 'holy war' against German militarism. He went on to become the prime minister in December 1916. The gains made in the 1914 offensive had encouraged German expansionism, and therefore lessened, if not removed, the strategic option for the Germans of a good compromise peace, in the sense of a peace-making, and then peace, that might work. As a result, the German efforts were devoted to a goal that was not worth the costs and risks it entailed. This goal, indeed, ultimately proved fatal for German stability and territorial integrity, and for those of their allies. Thus, risk had been miscalculated, or, rather, misunderstood, and strategy failed totally.

More immediately, the strategic problem for Erich von Falkenhayn, who became chief of the German General Staff in September 1914, replacing Helmuth von Moltke the Younger, was how to force Germany's opponents to accept its peace terms. Appreciating that Germany did not have the resources to defeat its enemies in the rapid, decisive campaign required by prewar planning, he sought to change strategy. Falkenhayn aimed for a negotiated peace, albeit on terms favourable to Germany. This goal built on earlier discussion, by Moltke the Elder and the academic commentator Hans Delbrück, of the limitations of the concept of decisive victory and of the doctrine of a war of annihilation cherished by the General Staff. For Falkenhayn, to develop a matching new operational method, however, proved difficult, not least because of opposition within the officer corps.

Despite the unsuccessful German attack at Ypres in April–May 1915, the second battle of Ypres, an attack begun on 22 April with the first mass use of poison gas on the Western Front, Falkenhayn focused on remaining on the defensive in the west, while trying to force Russia into a separate peace. This strategy was an admission of Allied strength on the Western Front, as well as of the difficulties of mounting a successful offensive there given the concentration of forces. As so often, for example with Britain's Mediterranean emphasis in the Second World War, legacy factors were also significant in encouraging strategic preferences: German failure, in the 'Race to the Channel' in late 1914, to outflank the Allies contrasted with the promising situation for Germany in Poland.

Anticipation, and therefore strategy, focused on prospects for gains, but also on hazards. Indeed, a deterioration for the German alliance system occurred in May 1915 when Italy came into the war on the Allied side, and was further threatened by Allied pressure on Turkey. Italy's entry into the war put pressure on Austria, which, in turn, underlined the need to strengthen the German position in eastern Europe. Thus, there was an interrelationship of real and potential fronts, and of the anxieties bound up in each. The role of personalities in strategic decisions also emerged clearly, with Falkenhayn pressed by Paul von Hindenburg, the commander in the east, and his chief of staff, Erich Ludendorff, both assertive figures, to send troops to the Eastern Front where they were in command.

The Germans made substantial gains conquering Russian Poland and Lithuania in 1915, capturing the cities of Warsaw, Kovno (Kaunas) and

Grodno in August, and Vilna (Vilnius) in September. However, break-throughs at the front did not produce strategic results, either in terms of the collapse of the Russian army or politically. The distance of Russian territorial losses from the centres of power in St Petersburg and Moscow ensured that they did not have the strategic effect that comparable losses of territory in France would have had. German forces advanced to near Riga, where the front stabilised, and not to near St Petersburg.

German successes against Russia, nevertheless, increased the pressure on the Allies to react by taking steps. The French General Staff concluded that the war was without direction on the Allies' part and required a co-ordinated strategic planning that France must provide. This planning would also tie Britain into French priorities. The Western Allies, however, found in 1915, and again in 1916 and 1917, that attacking in order to break the stalemate did not work as their armies had not mastered the problems posed by the numbers involved on the constricted Western Front and by the tactical defensive strength of trench warfare.

The alternative strategy, that pushed in Britain by the 'Easterners', was to combine alliance politics with military capability in the shape of winning allies by using amphibious operations. In 1915, naval power apparently offered a chance to attack the centre of Turkish power, which was then at Constantinople. Ankara did not become the capital until 1923. This was a strategy that geography made inapplicable for attacking Germany and Austria, and that appeared to its proponents to be a viable alternative to the effort required in any confrontation with the Germans on the Western Front.

This search for the indirect approach appeared to conform to British strategic traditions, notably the focus on secondary theatres, especially, eventually, Portugal and Spain, in the conflict with Napoleon. Such a focus would permit Britain to use its naval power and to achieve success with its relatively modest army without weakening the latter by attacking the main opposing force. This strategy would also enable Britain to direct a campaign without relying excessively on France as an ally.

The resulting Gallipoli campaign was an instance, however, of how, repeatedly, strategic conception was not matched by tactical and opera-tional success. The extent to which that outcome, however, invalidates the conception is open to debate. So also with British hopes in 1943 that Italy would prove the 'soft underbelly' of Axis Europe. Failure usually attracts a host of explanations including that of strategic mistakes. While generally well grounded, these explanations can underplay the close margin between success and failure.

Conversely, the Germans were also disabused of their hopes regarding the Turks. They had hoped to use them to further a strategy of *Insurgierung*, and thus to damage, if not overthrow, much of the empires of their competitors. The German leadership planned, through war, rebellion or revolution, to extend hostilities, especially to Egypt, the Caucasus and India, in order to put pressure on Russia and to threaten the strategic links and economic resources of the British Empire. They failed totally, in large part due to a misreading of the situation across the Islamic world, not least of Arab hostility to the Turks.

Political factors, notably the equations of alliances, were crucial to strategic choices. Thus, in November 1915, when the Allies landed an expeditionary force at Salonica in Greece, Herbert, Earl Kitchener, the Secretary for War, wrote of the French leadership: 'They simply sweep all military dangers and difficulties aside and go on political lines such as saving a remnant of Serbs, bringing Greece in and inducing Romania to join.'[1] In practice, the Serbs were not saved by this intervention. Instead, the Allied units that had advanced north from Salonica were forced to retreat in the face of larger Bulgarian forces. Indeed, the entire history of Balkan operations in the war indicated the strategic limitations at that juncture of amphibious forces acting against continental land masses. Conversely, such an offensive capability could oblige defenders to maintain large forces that were otherwise pointless, as with the Germans in Norway in 1940–5.

The failures of both sides led to planning in late 1915 for different strategies in 1916. This planning encompassed the intensification of war economies, as well as military schemes.[2] Aristide Briand replaced René Viviani as French prime minister in October 1915 on the platform of improving relations with France's allies so as to ensure a more co-operative war effort. For 1916, the Allies agreed in December 1915, in a conference at Chantilly, to follow a more coherent and ambitious grand plan than the more limited attacks mounted in 1915, notably the third battle of Artois (battle of Loos), which was launched in September to complement the second battle of Champagne. This represented an attack in two areas that had already seen attacks the previous winter.

Instead, for 1916, there was to be a series of concerted assaults by the British, Italians and Russians, mounted on all major fronts, and designed to make it impossible for the Central Powers to move reserves from one front to another, as well as to inflict sufficient all-round damage to permit follow-up attacks by the French, with the goal of delivering the long-awaited breakthrough. This strategy, however, was to be derailed by the earlier launch of its German counterpart.[3]

German strategy remained that of putting so much pressure on their opponents that they would be persuaded to accept peace terms that yielded Germany an effective hegemony in Europe. While the strategy remained constant, the plan changed. In 1916, the point of pressure was shifted from east to west, with the Germans concentrating on France, still a nearby target, instead of Russia, which had a year without pressure comparable to that in 1915.

Falkenhayn accepted that a breakthrough in the west was impossible given the nature of warfare on the Western Front, specifically the defensive strength of modern weapons and the possibilities of reinforcement. Instead, he sought in the Verdun offensive to break the French will by inflicting heavy casualties and forcing an attritional outcome. Falkenhayn regarded France as weaker than Britain, and hoped the offensive would knock it out of the war, and thus force Britain to abandon the Western Front. He failed, in part due to implementation, including in attacking on too narrow a front, but also because the strategic insight was flawed. France proved willing to take heavy casualties, while the British succeeded, with the Somme offensive, in taking pressure off the French. Falkenhayn was replaced by Hindenburg and Ludendorff in August 1916 and they did more as they sought with considerable success to displace Wilhelm II from the direction of overall strategy.

At the same time, the German navy maintained its focus on Britain and, knowing that it could not defeat it as a whole, planned to wear down the British Grand Fleet in the North Sea, to a point where victory might be possible. Intended as an engagement only with an outnumbered part of the Grand Fleet, Jutland, a clash between both fleets, was an accidental battle that the Germans escaped after inflicting their disproportionate attrition on the British in the fighting. The battle was no real success at all for the British, defensive or otherwise: the German High Seas Fleet got away when it might have been destroyed. The High

Seas Fleet came out again in August 1916, but the result was mutual containment. This in a sense was strategically decisive, not least as it drove the Germans to resume unconditional submarine warfare.

In contrast to the defensive success at Verdun, the Allies in 1916 did not do better on the offensive on the Western Front, the front on which it was easiest to apply force, than they had done in 1915. Ironically, the concept of strategy was used by British journalists trying to explain the Somme offensive. William Beach Thomas, the war correspondent of the *Daily Mail*, in the issue of 3 July 1916, provided a totally misleading account of the opening of the offensive two days earlier. The very heavy losses the British suffered were minimised and the fighting for relatively small amounts of territory explained:

> The toll of blood-taking has been fairly heavy, but I am glad to be able to state from reports received that it is by no means excessive, having regard to the magnitude of the day's operations – it is and for many days will continue to be siege warfare, in which a small territo-rial gain may be a great strategical gain and the price we must pay is to be judged by another measure than miles or furlongs of booty. We are laying siege not to a place but to the German army.

While in theory cogent, this did not capture the reality of the campaigning, and he later regretted his wartime reports.[4]

At the conference held in Chantilly in November 1916, the French called for a larger offensive on the Western Front than had been seen that year, and there was pressure for British, French and Russian attacks on Bulgaria. These proved impossible. Indeed, Allied failures in 1917 on the Western Front, notably for the French in the *Chemin des Dames* offensive and for the British at Passchendaele (Third Ypres), left the Germans in control of their 1914 gains. When combined with ever-greater German territorial success in eastern Europe, at the expense of Serbia, Romania and Russia, it was scarcely surprising that the situation did not lead the military who dominated Germany to seek a change of policy. Indeed, their position was both demonstrated and strengthened when Chancellor Bethman-Hollweg was removed in July 1917. The army sought a 'German Peace', and wanted to block pressure in the Reichstag for peace without territorial gains. On the part of the military, there was no intention of restoring Belgium. Its coal and iron were regarded as key industrial reserves, while, in German hands, it was seen as a threat to France and as a challenge to Britain's naval position.

In 1917, the Germans imposed heavy pressure on the Alliance in Russia, which was knocked out of the war; in Italy, which was nearly knocked out; and at sea. There was no attack on the Western Front. There was a revival of the 1915 strategy of unrestricted submarine warfare. This strategy, however, failed, and brought the United States into the war; a version of the strategically counter-productive invasion of Belgium leading to British entry in 1914. As in 1942, German submarines did not have the strategic impact that had been anticipated. The bulk of Allied shipping got through as did, crucially, the American troops destined for the Western Front.[5]

Political pressures and an apparently deteriorating military position helped explain why it was necessary for the British and French to renew their attacks on the Western Front in 1917. The psychology of their commanders contributed greatly to this. The new French commander, the vainglorious Robert Nivelle, had been convinced that he could break through the German lines, and he won the confidence of the French and British civilian leaders. Nivelle's total and costly failure in April 1917, in the *Chemin des Dames* offensive, led to a change in French strategy. For the remainder of 1917 and in early 1918, in part due to concerns about morale, there were no large-scale French offensives. Nivelle's replacement, Philippe Pétain, went for small-scale, competently mounted, attacks designed to achieve specific objectives. Well prepared and successful, these operations helped restore the morale and reputation of the French army. However, such an improvement was not the means to victory, and notably so in a strategic environment in which the prospect of the arrival of large numbers of American troops, in part thanks to the failure of the German submarines, a strategic-level failure, was overshadowed by the likelihood that German troops would be transferred from the Eastern Front.

Tactical, operational and strategic factors had seemed to coincide in late 1917 in encouraging a fresh offensive, this time mounted by the British. The best form of defence appeared to be attack on terrain of Allied choosing and where they could accumulate troops, guns and materiel. Moreover, as in 1916 with Verdun, it seemed necessary, after the *Chemin des Dames*, for the British to lessen pressure on the French, while an attack on the Western Front might well bolster Russia and thus make it harder for the Germans to transfer troops. The long term seemed increasingly precarious as Russia slipped away in 1917. The front chosen was that in Flanders, and for a number of reasons, such a number reflecting the generally accumulative nature of strategy (in contrast, single explanations and expositions are often flawed): the costly vulnerability of the Allied position in the Ypres salient required improvement; the Germans lacked many commanding defensive, surveillance and artillery positions in the low terrain, which lessened their defensive strength; and the German submarine facilities at Bruges, Ostend and Zeebrugge provided a worthwhile objective, one that had strategic point given the significance of the submarine war on British trade. The equivalent in the Second World War was the costly and difficult British bombing of German submarine bases, such as Brest.

Launched on 31 July 1917, the resulting Passchendaele offensive proved extremely costly, not least because Germany's residual strength was not adequately appreciated.[6] Moreover, the attempt to argue that the strategy adopted in the event provided the opportunities for attritional damage to the Germans, while not without a rationale, proved politically as well as military highly questionable. Field Marshal Sir Douglas Haig, the British commander, benefited from military wariness about civilian oversight and from his own links to George V and to the Conservatives who were in the coalition government.

In turn, failures in the field increased doubts within the military about Haig, lessened political support for him, and made it possible for Lloyd George to take more control of strategy and to insist on greater Allied co-operation and oversight. The Supreme War Council, established in November 1917, provided a forum for co-ordination for Britain, France and Italy, and increased civilian control: each power sent its prime minister, another minister and a permanent military representative.

More generally, 'the strategical reasons are vastly dependent on the political reasons':[7] this reflection of Lieutenant-Colonel Percy Worrall, a British officer, in February 1918 on the need to cross the river Piave reflected an understanding of the war that was well established by its close. In this case, Britain's ally Italy wished to regain territory recently lost to Austria, and needed British assistance to do so. Effort, in other words, had to be contextualised. Worrall, an experienced and able commander at the tactical level, understood that.

As a reminder of the range of elements understood as involved in strategy, and of definitions of the term, that could be offered, Colonel J.F.C. Fuller, then serving at Tank Corps Headquarters, observed in May 1918, in an item on 'The Effect of the Medium D Tank on Strategy': 'Strategy or the science of making the most of time for warlike ends, that is of opportunity, will practically cease for the side which pits muscular endurance against mechanical energy.'[8] This was an aspect of his pressure to understand and support the new capability brought by tanks, and, more particularly, his argument that it had strategic consequences, rather than simply operational and tactical ones. There was a comparable argument about aircraft.

Peace moves in 1917 had failed. In Germany, the opposition Social Democrats had called for a 'peace without annexations or indemnities', and the Reichstag passed a Peace Resolution on 19 July. This pressure, however, had no effect on a government, then in occupation of most of Belgium and part of France, expecting to benefit greatly from the collapse of Russia, and supported by the newly launched German Fatherland Party. The government was not interested in a peace that did not bring territorial gains that could justify both the war and the position of the military. German nationalists pressed strongly for gains and reparations, and their unrealistic claims played a disproportionately large role in public debate.

The strategic context could appear to be going their way. Indeed, in January 1918, Arthur Balfour, the British Foreign Secretary, suggested that the Allies help anti-Bolshevik movements in Russia that 'might do something to prevent Russia from falling immediately and completely under the control of Germany . . . while the war continues, a Germanized Russia would provide a source of supply which would go far to neutralise the effects of the Allied blockade. When the war is over, a Germanized Russia would be a peril to the world.'[9] Lenin wanted the spread of communism, not the Germanisation of Russia, but, in Allied eyes, his desire for peace amounted to, and led towards, the latter. Lenin had hoped that the spread of revolution would affect Germany and make negotiations unnecessary, but, instead, the Germans drove the pace of negotiation. When the Bolsheviks refused to accept the terms offered, the Germans rejected their strategy of 'neither peace nor war', resumed the offensive, and forced Russia to accept German terms in the Treaty of Brest-Litovsk. The Germans then continued the offensive in order to obtain further gains in Russia. This proved a seriously mistaken choice given the need to transfer troops to the Western Front. The equations of time, space and troops were neglected, as co-ordination between the fronts was trumped by a failure of effective prioritisation. More seriously than in 1918, the Germans in 1941 were to destroy the possibility of Russo-German co-operation created in 1939.

Attack, moreover, proved a deeply flawed strategy for Germany on the Western Front in 1918, as it brought neither the military outcomes envisaged nor the political goals that were hoped for. The Allies remained united, while the Germans lost many troops. Not under attack from Russia, the Germans in 1918 were in a far better situation, both militarily and politically, than that which was to face Hitler when he launched the battle of the Bulge in December 1944, and they were able to apply more military pressure. However, this pressure was applied poorly and its use rested on misjudged assumptions about the vulnerability of the Allies' political will to events at the front and concerning the fighting determination of the Allies. There was a failure to create 'the bridge' between on the one hand tactics and operations and on the other the 'political wish-list', and a lack of 'strategic realism'. In part, this failure rested on an understanding that Germany's comparative advantage lay at the tactical, not the strategic, level.[10] Strategic plans are built on the assumption of tactical success, but the latter itself cannot create a winning strategy. So also with the relationship once the operational dimension is introduced. Operational victory is important to strategic success but itself cannot create it.

Instead, Allied strategy in 1918 proved more appropriate and successful, not least because a full-scale and sustained offensive on the Western Front was combined both with anti-societal commercial warfare in the shape of the blockade, which had become more effective in 1917–18 as a result of American entry into the war, and with the destruction of Germany's alliance system. That proved a political cost too much for Germany, which, in response to Bulgaria leaving the war under the pressure of Allied attack, sought and accepted an armistice. At that juncture, the German army was clearly outfought, and its morale was low. Moreover, Bulgaria leaving the war increased the pressure on Germany's remaining allies, Austria and Turkey, each of which was in grave difficulties, both military and political, and looking for an end to the war.

Alongside significant differences, there are many parallels between the discussion of the American Civil War and the First World War. For both, there was, and is, an emphasis on the failure of the home front of the defeated power, particularly as a consequence of the pressures and priva-tions of the war (including, in each case, the results of blockade), but also with reference to the eventual weakness of the political coherence of the society that therefore surrendered. In each case, however, this approach underplays the strength of the victors, both in terms of their own home fronts and in terms of their ability to create an effective, confident and triumphant military system that eventually outfought its opponent. As the latter account is unwelcome in many quarters, it tends to be underplayed, and, in this, there is a comparison between Confederate arguments of the 'lost cause' and the German presentation of the 'stab in the back' in 1918. Instead, alongside the role of social and political contexts and contingen-cies, it is important to focus on a military theme that pulls together the eventually superior war-fighting of the victors, the motivation of their soldiers, which continued strong throughout the conflict,[11] the availability of their resources, and improvements in their command skills.

In the First World War, the Germans, whose strategic skill and insti-tutions had attracted much praise and emulation, were found seriously wanting in both; and not only in 1914 but throughout the conflict. There was a lack of the cross-governmental organisations necessary to provide the broader strategic formulation that was required and a failure to push through the necessary improvements. Wilhelm II failed to pull together military and civilian advice, while, under all of its leaders, the army's general staff treated naval power and diplomacy as superfluous and was contemptuous of civilian advice. Co-ordination with all of Germany's allies was deficient. The same flaws were to be seen in the Second World War, and, again, were linked to a structural problem in learning lessons.

Moreover, although tactically adept, and often also so in operational terms, German commanders lacked the knowledge and training appro-priate to engage with the range of necessary strategic tasks. Had Germany faced a comparable challenge earlier, then its strategic arrangements might also have been found wanting. That offers a perspective on the high reputation the Germans enjoyed in the late nineteenth century.

The First World War demonstrated the strategic role of alliances, and in diplomatic, economic and military terms, which is an important corrective to seeing strategy purely in a military context. Strategic capability was shown in the ability of the Allies to attract more countries to their side from 1915 and in the ability to integrate and deploy greater resources than their opponents. Linked to this, the failure on the strategic level of the 'lessons' of operational command was shown in Germany's lack of victory in 1914 and defeat in 1918.

9

STRATEGIES FOR TOTAL WAR
1919 – 45

INTERWAR YEARS

In July 1929, Basil Liddell Hart, the would-be leading British military commentator of the interwar years, addressed the relationship between policy and strategy in the political context of the time. This was a situation in which, as part of a less ordered and stable world, democratisation, notably accountability, and unpredictability were far more pronounced across Western society as a whole than prior to the First World War. In the *Quarterly Review*, a periodical published in London, he wrote:

> Perhaps only an absolute ruler, firmly in the saddle, can hope to maintain unswervingly the military ideal of the 'armed forces' objective, although even he will be wise to adjust it to the realities of the situation and to weigh well the prospects of fulfilling it. But the strategist who is the servant of a democratic government has less rein. Dependent on the support and confidence of his employers, he has to work within a narrower margin of time and cost than the 'absolute' strategist, and is more pressed for quick profits. Whatever the ultimate prospects he cannot afford to postpone dividends too long. Hence it may be necessary for him to swerve aside temporarily from his objective or at least to give it a new guise by changing his line of operations. Faced with these inevitable handicaps it is apt for us to ask whether military theory should not be more ready to reconcile its ideals with the inconvenient reality that its military effort rests on a popular foundation – that for the supply of men and munitions, and even for the chance of continuing the fight at all, it depends on the

consent of the 'man in the street'. He who pays the piper calls the tune, and strategists might be better paid in kind if they attuned their strategy, so far as is rightly possible, to the popular ear.[1]

Politics, indeed, was a matter of urgent concern for strategists. In particular, there was anxiety about the extent to which popular support for a war could be sustained. This in turn led to interest, by Liddell Hart and others, in strategy as a means to avoid too much bloodshed and to keep war short, an approach that was associated with Clausewitz.[2] The range of resulting strategic ideas was considerable, including bombing for strategic effect, in order to undermine such popular support in opposing countries, and thus overcome or supersede the heavy casualties of frontal conflict.

A key strategist in this sphere was the Italian Giulio Douhet. Just as commentators after 1815 wrote in the shadow of the French Revolutionary and Napoleonic Wars (1792–1815), so his work reflected the experience of the First World War. In this, Douhet, after much lobbying for air power, had ended up as head of the Central Aeronautic Bureau. Looking ahead to the next world war, Douhet, in 1921, published *Il dominio dell'aria* ('The Command of the Air'), in which he pressed for the use of air power based on the understanding that the sole defence was an effective offence. The purpose of the latter was not only to achieve aerial dominance but also to be able to target the opposing economy and popular will.

Bombing, Douhet argued, would lead to a popular revolution in order to achieve peace. In practice, its use, in the Second World War and subsequently, revealed that this was completely incorrect. Ironically, civilian pressure for peace arising from bombing was strongest in Italy in 1943; but that pressure also reflected other factors. Douhet was not interested in using aircraft to support operations on land.

Douhet went on to argue his case in a second edition (1927), and in *The War of 19–* (1930), in which Germany won a war with France and Belgium by rapidly mounting major bombing attacks, and also in articles. *Il dominio dell'aria* was speedily translated in the United States in 1923 and an English translation of the second edition was published in the United States in 1942, as the new world war led to renewed interest. Douhet's work contributed to the debate elsewhere about air power, a debate dominated by air power enthusiasts, although one in which in practice, as a crucial constraint, established investment in armies and navies proved more significant.[3]

Immediately, the sequel to the First World War had brought a whole sequence of civil wars that took the relevant political dimensions of strategy to the fore. As in other civil wars, seizing the capital and terrorising opponents became both ends and means, and there was a greater emphasis on controlling arms supplies than in international conflicts. The ideological dimension was pushed forward as a result of communist revolutions. Indeed, this prospect had affected Allied leaders prior to the end of the First World War. On 2 November 1918, General Sir Henry Horne, the commander of the British First Army, wrote to his wife: 'I think we must not be *too* severe with Germany, in case of there being a break up there, and we shall find no government to enforce terms upon! Bolshevism is the danger. If it breaks out in Germany it might spread to France and England.'[4] In the aftermath of the collapse of Russia, this factor in preserving Germany from too serious losses was of greater concern than the idea, which looked to the same conclusion, that a traditional strategic objective was that of Britain acting as a balancing power. In the latter view, Germany should not be destroyed in order to be replaced by another hegemon, which, to a degree, was to happen in 1944–5, greatly changing the geopolitics of the struggle with the Soviet Union and communism.

The communist revolutions led to the articulation of strategies of people's warfare, and to the total war this represented and forwarded. Leon Trotsky referred in 1918 to a threatening situation of 'neither peace nor war', one calculated to destabilise opponents. The ideas and practices were not particularly new, having generally been seen in earlier insurgencies, and notably so if linked to ideological strife, as with the European Wars of Religion of the early modern period. So also with the idea of a galvanising and dictatorial élite movement, in the shape now of the Communist Party. However, as part of their cult of modernity, it was necessary for the Communists to lay claim to novelty.

In China, in a very different context, the Communists took far longer to seize power than had been the case with Russia. Moreover, in China, they needed to rationalise their strategy, in part as an aspect of the struggle for primacy within their ranks, a process also seen in the Soviet

Union in the 1920s and 1930s. The three stages of strategy outlined by Mao in his *On Guerrilla Warfare* (1937)[5] were somewhat banal, but they served their ideological purpose, not least by relating moves to apparent historical laws. Guerrilla warfare was presented as drawing on the mass of the entire population and as a precursor to a move towards local, and then general, conventional warfare. This was a strategy that drew its force from apparently being both an appropriate response to circumstances and a means to progress from one stage to another, and thus to forward an inevitable trajectory.

The dependence on circumstances not only of strategy, but also of the understanding of strategy, was readily apparent on the international scale. For example, in the Middle East, the modernisation of armed forces in the 1920s and 1930s, notably in Egypt and Iraq, and the opening to foreign influences, led to the use of the word '*al-stratijiah*', a term derived from the Western world. There was not a word drawn from classical Arabic that could be used, and the idea would therefore have been previously conveyed as a phrase, notably 'planning and military leadership'. In the modern Middle East, '*al-stratijiah*' has become a very common term, one applied to economic programmes as well as military ones.

The key element in the understanding of strategy, however, came from assessing the likely course of future warfare in light of the experience of the First World War or, rather, the experience as it was shaped by commentators. It is instructive, for example, to note the definition of strategy in *The Compact Encyclopedia*, a British work of 1927 based on *The New Gresham Encyclopedia* (1921–4). This definition drew on Jomini, as reflected by General Sir Edward Hamley's *Operations of War Explained and Illustrated* (3rd edition, 1872) and Lieutenant-Colonel Walter James's *Modern Strategy: An Outline of the Principles which Guide the Conduct of Campaigns* (2nd edition, 1904). Such a process of reflection was, and remains, normal:

> Strategy is the art of war which deals with the movement of troops within the theatre of war, or, alternatively, the art by which a commander or other responsible authority is enabled to formulate his plan of campaign. Tactics, on the other hand, is the art of moving troops in the presence of the enemy, or of carrying out the move-

ments and operations necessary to bring the strategical plan to a successful conclusion. The two words are therefore complementary, and strategy depends more or less for its success on the tactical handling of troops by subordinate commanders. The aim of military strategy is the ultimate destruction of the enemy forces.[6]

This account assumed a form of decisive victory that drew on the First World War, a form that was frequently, in practice, neither viable nor sought, and one that underplayed the political dimension in conflict. The latter underplaying in particular arose when a definition of strategy in terms of what would later, notably from the 1980s, be called operational art was advanced, as in this encyclopedia entry. This operational definition reflected a militarisation of strategy that had helped to lead Germany to total failure in the First World War.[7]

The earlier pattern of military control, which focused on the ruler, had been superseded in the nineteenth century by one far more focused on the military high command. Ironically, but possibly not surprisingly,[8] this development, and indeed the general staff, the body entrusted with strategic planning, were not capable of the strategic acuity that was required. In part, this failure reflected a difficulty in moving from a linear pattern of strategy consideration, in which outcomes were planned and secured, to one in which strategy was relative as well as contextual. In the latter, the enemy gets their say, and it was necessary to adapt plans accordingly and in a perceptive fashion. This Germany failed to do in either world war.

Yet the definitions of strategy advanced in the interwar years of the 1920s and 1930s scarcely encouraged mature reflection focused on the political dimension. Instead, the task-based nature of strategy remained central. For Britain, speculations about the next war centred on the problems created by uncertainty over which power would be its leading opponent. Much of the recent discussion on the British military in this period focuses on the question of whether the correct responses were made to the possibilities of new technology, notably in the shape of aircraft and tanks. This question looks towards the issue of the British responses to the German and Japanese offensives in 1940–2, and, notably, the problem of the ability to adapt to the challenges of *Blitzkrieg*. These questions are indeed valuable.

However, they should be regarded as linked to, indeed subordinate to, the tasking of the military, and notably the question of likely opponents, a facet that is always significant. In short, technology and politics need to be reconciled, with strategy as the active response to the geopolitical challenges faced, and strategic planning a key context for procurement, training and deployment. At the same time, the planning and doctrinal aspects of strategy have to take note of contextual realities. For example, plans for Hungarian air power in the 1930s were constrained by the lack of domestic aircraft production.[9]

An indicative, and far from exhaustive, list of specific concerns and tasks is useful. Tasks for Britain in 1919–21 included occupation responsibilities, notably in Germany but also in Turkey and the Balkans, and, in addition, wide-ranging participation in the Russian Civil War, conflict with Afghanistan, instability in the Punjab, rebellion in Ireland, Iraq and Egypt, and challenges to British interests in Iran; and that is not a complete list. Although major war with a great power was not anticipated, 1922–30 again saw a range of issues for Britain, including concern about the possibility of war with Turkey over, first, Constantinople and the Dardanelles and, subsequently, its border with Iraq, as well as instability in the Arabian peninsula challenging Britain's role, including in Iraq, and attacks on British interests in China. In 1931–8, Japanese, Italian and German expansionism were all serious problems for British interests and views on international relations. There were also rebellions, or at least serious disturbances, in the British Empire, notably on the North-West Frontier of India and in Palestine, but also in Jamaica, Malta and Burma (Myanmar).

This incomplete list leaves out the possibility that tensions or disputes with other major powers, notably France and the United States, but also Russia, might lead to conflict. With hindsight, and notably in light of the developing challenges in the 1930s, these scenarios might appear implausible, but they led not only to speculation but also to planning, notably, as part of the colour-coded or rainbow plans, to American plans for war with Britain, including the invasion of Canada. For France, there was also a range, from commitment in the Russian Civil War to rebellion in Syria and confrontation with Italy and Germany.

The variety of these challenges, for Britain, France, the United States and other powers, helps explain why it was so difficult to determine strategy. So, even more, if the perspective is that of the lesser powers. Their number was less than is the case today, due to much of the world being under colonial control, but they were still important. The role of warlords in China in the 1920s is a corrective against any assumption that the bases of politics and warfare were necessarily defined in terms of modern states. So also with Arabia where, after the collapse of Turkish control and influence during the First World War, tribal leaders operated rather like Chinese warlords. Ibn Saud of Nejd proved the most successful, creating Saudi Arabia. This was a conflict of raids and loose sieges, a counterpart to earlier forms of 'small war'.

Military historians considering this period are apt to underplay the challenge of rebellion and the extent of 'small war', both within the West and more generally. Instead, there is a focus on the prospect of symmetrical conflict between the conventional forces of independent states, which, indeed, eventually became the future and then the present. However, that trajectory was not a certainty as far as British planners were concerned. Instead, with no clear symmetrical threat in the 1920s, they had to consider the hypotheticals of future conflict in such circumstances against the more pressing immediate issues of security within the empire. These latter issues were enhanced because of the extent to which the army was responsible there for what in effect was civil policing.

Moreover, the reliance of the British imperial system on native troops, notably in south Asia, underlined the need to emphasise the security of relevant areas, while also ensuring that certain tasks were best suited to a large part of the army and, conversely, others to only a small part of it. The same was not the case for the navy or the air force, and this point underlines the very different strategic dimensions, perspectives and planning of the particular branches of the military. British concern with empire reflected the experience of the First World War, when the British and French empires had provided Britain and France with crucial support, in men, money and supplies, in Europe, prefiguring the help from the United States. Thus, the empire was a source both of weakness through overextension, and of strength. This paradox was highly important to British strategy.

The concerns of imperial defence when faced by 'native' opposition helped explain the reluctance of some British generals to engage with what they saw as the hypotheticals of developing tank forces for conflict in Europe. An appreciation of the operational possibilities of the tank was seen within the army by practical modernisers, but they had to be more aware of financial restrictions than the publicists criticising from outside, notably Basil Liddell Hart.[10]

Imperial defence, instead, encouraged an emphasis on air power, not only for imperial policing, as in the Arabian peninsula and Iraq, but also as the best means to deter or fight Germany in Europe, and thus lessen the pressures on the allocation of army units. This emphasis on air power was also a reflection of the most worrying aspect of German power, the potential strength of its air force. Moreover, German air attack could not be deterred by France's landward defences, notably the Maginot Line.

Hitler came to power in 1933 having pledged to overthrow the 1919 Versailles settlement. Given the later situation, this might appear clearly to have been the foremost threat to the international order and British interests; but Germany only turned to war in 1939, whereas Japan did so in 1931 and Italy in 1935. Each of these moves challenged British interests and Britain's ideas of international order and relations, and threatened to lead to further problems. Indeed, Japan launched a full-scale invasion of China in 1937, while Italy encouraged Arab opposition to British control.

Strategic uncertainty therefore surrounded the prioritisation by Britain of the challenges posed by these three powers. This uncertainty was enhanced by a lack of clarity as to how these powers would respond to negotiations and/or pressure, by a corresponding lack of clarity as to whether they would co-operate with each other, and by the presence of other threats, notably Russia, which was a threat both in Europe and to the empire. Thus, rearmament, for Britain, as for France, was affected not only by limitations in industrial capacity and capability, and by financial problems, but also by a lack of certainty over tasking and, as a result, over appropriate force structure. Clarity over allies and enemies was necessary, or at least preferable, in order to produce effective strategic plans.

Hitler's rhetoric was far from encouraging but, to some, he appeared a possible element in any co-operation against the Soviet Union, while there was also the question of how best to reintegrate Germany into the international order. It was unclear whether Hitler would be another Napoleon III, or, indeed, another Benito Mussolini, the Fascist dictator of Italy. In 1933, the British were unwilling to make common cause with France towards Germany, and this remained their policy. More robust policies focused on alliance with France were rejected. Moreover, the Anglo-German naval agreement of 1935 was regarded by the French as a betrayal. In 1936, when Germany, in defiance of the Peace of Versailles, unilaterally remilitarised the Rhineland, providing a spring-board for military action against France, the British sought to discourage the French from acting. Western passivity in 1936 marked a major step in Nazi expansionism and was part of a reluctance to act in order to enforce the peace settlement that had been seen from Britain and, to a degree, France as soon as it was negotiated. In 1936, differences between Britain and France in their views of European development, the very limited nature of Anglo-French military co-operation over the previous decade, and their lack of preparedness, were understood by contemporaries as a poor basis for joint action.

There were already instances of Versailles revisionism having worked. The 1920 Sèvres peace settlement with Turkey had been overthrown as a result of Kemal Atatürk's military successes against Greece in 1922 and his intimidation of Britain in the Chanak crisis. Atatürk benefited from his skill in exploiting the divisions between the wartime allies, with Italy, France and the Soviet Union unwilling to support Greece or to back Britain. A very different peace settlement with Turkey was then negotiated at Lausanne in 1923. This then had served as the basis for a workable international relationship. Whether the same would be true with Japan prior to 1937, Germany prior to 1939, and Italy prior to 1940, was unclear.

If Japan was the leading challenger to Britain, then the principal response would be naval, specifically the development of a powerful naval base in Singapore such that it could be used to defend the British Empire in south-east Asia, Australasia and India from Japanese attack, while also serving for British force projection to east Asian waters. This naval strategy had many aspects and variants, including a network of bases to support the movement of warships and aircraft, co-operation with Australia, New Zealand and Canada against Japan, and alliance with the United States. There were also obvious military priorities, notably a lack in this case of any need to focus on the army other than to supplement naval capabilities.

Italy posed a similar, but different, set of priorities. The much-expanded Italian navy represented a major threat to the British, as to the French, in the Mediterranean and, with that, to the British route to the Indian Ocean via the Suez Canal and the French route to French North Africa.[11] At the same time, war over the Abyssinian crisis in 1935–6 would also have involved both army and air force, as, indeed, war with Italy was to do from 1940. The British army would need to defend Egypt, Sudan, British Somaliland and Kenya from invasion from the neighbouring Italian colonies of Libya, Eritrea and Sudan, while the air force would help protect the colonies, including Malta, and would also be used to bomb Italy.

Germany also posed a naval challenge, but the German navy appeared weaker as a strategic challenge than those of Japan and Italy, because, until the successive conquests of Denmark, Norway and France in April–June 1940, Germany lacked significant naval room for manoeuvre or ready access to the North Atlantic. Nevertheless, despite its strength as the world's foremost naval power, Britain did not have a navy capable of fighting Germany, Italy and Japan simultaneously. That was the product of the stop on capital ship construction under the Washington Naval Treaty, as well as the lack of sufficient British industrial capability and fiscal strength; but also of the build-up of the strength of these three powers.

However, to expect the arithmetic of naval power to provide for conflict at once with all three states was to anticipate a margin of superiority that was unreasonable given the state of the country and the fact that the potential enemies were well apart, but also one the need for which diplomacy sought to avoid. Allowing for the significance and consequences of serious rivalries between the views of the key ministries, the Treasury, Foreign Office and Admiralty, British naval strategy planned that, if necessary, operations against threats arising simultaneously would be conducted sequentially in separate theatres. This strategy assumed that operational flexibility could help lessen the constraints posed by tough fiscal limits and overcome the strategic challenge posed by simultaneous threats. In addition, war, it was hoped, was likely to bring Britain the support of allies, notably France against Germany and Italy, and the United States against Japan.

From Germany, it was the *Luftwaffe* that was a major threat, and in a way that the Italian, Japanese and, indeed, Soviet air forces could not be to Britain itself, although Germany failed to develop a strategic capacity in air power.[12] The threat from the air was an interwar obsession, in other words a misguided assessment of capability, at least in so far as the air forces of the 1920s and 1930s were concerned, although this capability was to be greatly enhanced in the case of Britain and the United States during the Second World War. For Britain, the strategic need for air defence appeared primarily dependent on the prospect of war with Germany.[13] Moreover, this became so as part of an integrated system: whereas aircraft could be moved, radar stations were fixed facilities. Thus, the defence of Britain, as opposed to that of particular imperial interests, however crucial, involved very different means as well as ends.

The challenge from Germany was also linked to views about the European order and Britain's relationship to it. Italy alone might be a threat to Abyssinia/Ethiopia (1935–6) and Albania (1939), and try (unsuccessfully) to be one to Greece (1940), but was not likely to prevail against France and, indeed, did not seek to do so. Instead, it was Germany that posed the major threat to other states in western Europe, while Germany and the Soviet Union did so in eastern Europe. The question of whether Britain should send troops to the Continent to counter such a threat was a difficult one, and not least because there was no peacetime conscription, while the Indian army was not to be deployed in western Europe. With Belgium, the Netherlands, Denmark and Norway resolved to remain neutral, the sole room for manoeuvre would be France, and the strategic option of the build-up of a large army in Britain to send to France was not an encouraging one in light of the range of British commitments as well as a reading of the lessons of the previous world war.

Thus, speculations about the next war related practically not only to the issue of what weapons systems could achieve, in absolute and relative terms, but what they would be expected to achieve in light of specific tasks. The direction of aggressive expansionism by Germany, Italy and Japan was unclear, as was the chronology and the sequencing. This was understandable due to the degree of opportunism involved in the devising of their strategies as well as their implementation. For example, on 5 November 1937, in the 'Hossbach' meeting in Berlin, Hitler argued that, in order to remove a threat to Germany's rear in the event of war with the West, it was necessary to overthrow Czechoslovakia and Austria. Hypotheticals interacted in an extraordinarily dynamic situation.

With the benefit of hindsight, it is possible to point to serious flaws in the decisions taken by British policy-makers, but it is also worth underlining the difficulties of assessing links between challenges and commitments, as well as the problems of prioritisation. This is instructive because it prepared the way for the position today, and the multiple uncertainties confronting Western powers. Appeasement, the favourite term of abuse, one derived from criticism of Anglo-French policies in the late 1930s, that is thrown at caution and prudence today, is not in fact a helpful analogy for the present.

The continuing role of politics was apparent in the use of force. For example, Francisco Franco, a dictator from a military background of considerable experience, proved weak as a formal strategist in the Spanish Civil War (1936–9), indeed had 'deficiencies as a stylish strategist', and made a series of mistakes. Nevertheless, Franco based his ultimately successful strategy on the primacy of political concerns, including a slow conquest that enabled him through terror to consolidate his political supremacy within Spain. To the angry contempt of his ally, Mussolini, who had not had to fight a civil war in order to gain power in 1922, Franco, after 1936, rejected the Italian concept of *guerra celere* (lightning war) and the ambitious plans involved. Breaking opponents through terror was the key strategy he pursued, and it worked. Indeed, the killings continued at a high level after the formal end of hostilities.[14]

As a separate point, relevant for peacetime preparation and planning, and wartime conflict, the always significant role of resources had come into a new iteration, notably with the production and operational requirements of machines, particularly the use of oil for land, sea and air warfare. This affected not only the major powers, but all states.[15] Thus, for Germany, which intervened from the outset on Franco's side in the Spanish Civil War, there were ideological and geopolitical goals, but also an economic strategy. Hitler sought a new European economic order in which Germany would become the leader of a European space free of Anglo-American influence and with the goals and terms of centrally planned rationalisation and specialisation set in Berlin. By early 1939, Germany was taking three quarters of Spain's exports, so that Spain was brought into an informal *Reichsmark* sphere. The sectors targeted were iron ore, pyrites, copper, tungsten and foodstuffs.

THE SECOND WORLD WAR

Strategy in the Second World War was similar to that in the First, but with the addition of more participants and with a more explicitly ideological dimension. The latter suggested a different set of criteria, but the contrast was less than total.

Prewar strategic goals, capabilities and tones continued into the Second World War, notably in the cases of Japanese policy in China and of German aggression and expansionism in Europe. In turn, war planning prior to the conflict responded to shifts in doctrine, force structures and weaponry, but was primarily set in the strategic transformations resulting from changes in political goals and alliances.[16] Each factor was to be of major importance in 1939–41 and underlined the unpredictability of developments. In 1939, Germany initially fought Poland alone. Its eventual ally against Poland that September, but not in the war with Britain and France which broke out as a result of the German invasion of Poland earlier that month, was the Soviet Union; and not, in 1939, its allies under the Pact of Steel, Italy and Japan. In turn, Anglo-French concern about Soviet policy was to lead, in the winter of 1939–40, to plans for military action, including the bombing of Soviet oilfields, although this strategic planning was not pursued. Thus, strategy had to cope with unexpected and rapidly changing contingencies. These included a military environment in which opposing capability, let alone intentions, was far from clear or fixed.

In China, Japanese strategy from 1937 had failed to address the difficulties of translating success into outcomes. Military leaders were surprised, and frustrated, by their failure to impose victory. Ishiwara Kanji, chief of the operations division of the general staff, had warned that an invasion of China would lead to an intractable commitment, with victory unobtainable and withdrawal impossible; but more aggressive plans had prevailed. Alongside the latter, there was, furthermore, a lack of clarity about Japanese goals which thwarted peace possibilities.[17]

In Europe, Hitler also failed to make any real effort to translate his initial victory over Poland in 1939 into a widely accepted peace. This was an aspect of what was under the Third Reich a more general failure of diplomacy, which is an important arm of strategy. German failures were not the sole issue as Britain and France were determined to fight on in order to prevent German hegemony. The British government was sceptical about Germany's capability to sustain a long war and confident that, as in the First World War, the Allied forces in France would be able to resist attack. Hoping to intimidate Hitler by a limited war essentially pursued through blockade, British strategy relied on forcing him to negotiate or on exerting pressure that led to his overthrow.[18]

In response, Hitler determined on an attack on France. Arguing that Germany enjoyed a window of opportunity thanks to being more prepared for war than France or Britain, the view also taken in 1914, he feared that the latter would be able to build up its strength, while also being concerned that the Allies would launch air attacks on the Ruhr, Germany's leading industrial zone. Hitler was also eager to profit from the ability Poland's defeat offered for Germany to fight on only one front. Moreover, his victory had enhanced his confidence in himself as a great strategist. The German requirement for a quick victory drove out other strategic requirements.

In the event, attacking in May 1940, the Germans benefited from a calculated risk by the Allies, one, very much directed by political considerations and related strategic priorities, that did not pay off. The Allies moved their mobile reserve into Belgium before they were aware of the main direction of the German attack, and were therefore unable to respond to where it unexpectedly came from: through the Ardennes, which was not tank country, and across the mid-Meuse, a high-risk approach. However, rather than treating the Allied response simply as a strategic blunder, it is important to emphasise both the contingencies of the 1940 campaign and also the degree to which for the Allies to have abandoned Belgium would have been unacceptable politically, as well as risking the loss of part of the Allied order of battle.[19]

This underlines the significance for the military of political factors, a consideration that also led to British intervention in Greece in April 1941 in an unsuccessful attempt to provide help against German invasion. The operational failures of this intervention can be related to a strategic mistake of spreading effort and underrating German strength. Nevertheless, there was also the strategic need not to abandon allies, the need that had encouraged intervention in favour of Norway and Belgium in 1940. The reinforcement of exposed positions, for example Hong

Kong in the face of Japanese attack in 1941, was an aspect of the same situation.

German victory over France and the surrender in June 1940 of the latter and, therefore, of the French Empire, meant that any successful challenge to Germany would now have to overcome German dominance of western Europe. That was an objective strategic consideration that Winston Churchill, the new British prime minister, did not really address other than with the hope that something would turn up. The use by Britain of blockade and air attack, and the support for resistance, the means envisaged, were unlikely to have the anticipated military consequences, or certainly those of strategic effect. So also with the consequences for Germany of Britain's successful attacks on the Italian overseas empire in 1940–1.[20]

War with Britain involved tri-service strategic planning and operational collaboration, and Germany was bad at both. Moreover, the dysfunctional nature of the Nazi system emerged in combination, such as the *Luftwaffe*'s determination to put itself centre stage in the attack on Britain in 1940, rather than operating as a preparatory adjunct to the role of the navy and army in Operation Sealion. The *Luftwaffe*'s focus on its own role, moreover, reflected a lack of clarity in the hastily improvised German strategy as to the relationship between air attack and invasion. There was also a serious failure to prepare for a strategic air offensive because the Germans, with their emphasis on tactical and operational imperatives, had not sufficiently anticipated its necessity. The *Luftwaffe* was primarily intended to act in concert with German ground forces, something that was not possible in the self-contained aerial battle with Britain. In moving to bombing London, the German high command set out to destroy civilian morale. In practice, there was an emphasis, in London and elsewhere, on 'taking it', forbearance and making do, notably at the docks, which continued operating successfully. The German hope that the British people would realise their plight, overthrow Churchill and make peace, proved a serious misreading of British politics and public opinion. Instead, British intelligence reports suggested that the bombing led to signs of 'increasing hatred of Germany', as well as to demands for 'numerous reprisals'.[21] The idea that Hitler had to be defeated and removed was strengthened. The German strategy in the Blitz totally failed. The attack on Britain was the last time in which a tri-service strategy was to the fore for Germany. The Soviet Union as a target, in contrast, was very much an army show, with the air force and navy given subordinate roles.

Hitler's attack on the Soviet Union in June 1941 indicated that he refused to accept what others might consider objective strategic considerations. This course reflected the success of 1940 when war with France had been won without the need for any particular strategic insight or planning, which was in accordance with Germany's quick-war tradition. Indeed, had the war ended in 1941 without a German assault on the Soviet Union, then the successive German victories in 1939–41, even 1936–41, could have been seen as comparable to Prussia's sequential successes in the German Wars of Unification in 1864–71.

Hitler's strategy, however, was much grander. He sought not to defeat, although that was important, not least to Germany's incessant domestic and international propaganda, but to conquer and hold. This achievement was important to his goal of remoulding Europe to the service and impact of a new ideology. To that end, Hitler jeopardised the strategic situation he had won, a process also seen with Napoleon in 1812 when he attacked Russia. However, to Hitler, earlier successes (like alliances) were of scant value unless they were means to his goals. This point also relates to the problematic notion of a strategic optimum in the sense of an objective measure of what was most desirable. Aside from the questionable nature of that thesis in functional terms, it suffers from lacking a political basis and from omitting the significance of ideological considerations.

The German strategy for the defeat of the Soviet Union, launched on 22 June 1941 with Operation Barbarossa, was optimistic and drew on the quick-war ideas for which they were prepared. Aiming to seize all objectives simultaneously, a major strategic failure stemming from a lack of prioritisation, the Germans argued that the defeat of the Soviet forces near the frontier would lead to the Soviet collapse. Linked to this, it was believed important to prevent Soviet forces retreating into the interior, which was another reason for seeking to envelop them. Hitler did not assume that the Soviet Union could be conquered, but rather that the destruction of most of its army, and a German advance to a defensive line from Archangel to the Volga, would achieve his goals. Such an advance, however, was implausible both for logistical reasons and with reference to the weather. In effect, the Germans mistakenly transposed the deep penetration they had achieved in France in 1940 onto the enormous distances of the Soviet Union, and in a time sequence in which the weather was far more challenging than in the earlier instance. The combined arms attack (or *Blitzkrieg*) that had worked in a confined geographic space could not work over the far greater spaces of the Soviet Union. At the same time, a range of factors played a role, notably the nature of the response by opponents.

In the case of Poland (1939) and Yugoslavia (1941), Hitler had also benefited from being part of an alliance system that attacked his opponents from a number of directions. The situation was different with the Soviet Union. Alliance with Finland and Romania greatly extended the length of the attacking front, but that was already long enough, and Japan, which would greatly have altered the military situation, was not included in German planning and, instead, had negotiated a non-aggression pact with the Soviet Union.

German strategy was geared to the future. Having destroyed the Soviet state, Hitler then intended to overrun North Africa and the Near East, with the advance of Army Group South to the Caucasus preparing the way for the latter. Soviet defeat would lead, it was hoped, to British surrender. Thus, victory on land would not only compensate for British strength at sea (Napoleon's intention in 1812) and in the air, but would also counteract the problems caused by the German lack of a unified command structure and joint staff.

The Soviets assumed that German strategy would be dominated by a grasp for resources for the German war machine, with any attack focusing on the grain and coal of Ukraine. By seeing struggle, however, primarily as a means of national purification and race war, Hitler ensured that the largely successful earlier stage of the Second World War was merely instrumental in moving towards what became a prolonged, indeed attritional, war in which the German military, war economy and policy-making were all found wanting, and repeatedly so. The nature of German strategic goals, including a new demographic order, meant that peace was not really an option. Military discussion at the time, however, focused more on operational than on strategic questions.

In contrast, Italian strategy was more limited in its goals and means. Territorial acquisition, not race war, interested Mussolini, and there was greater caution than in the case of Germany. For example, in response to the successful British air raid on the Italian naval base at Taranto in November 1940, the Italians withdrew units from Taranto northward and thus lessened the vulnerability of British maritime routes and naval forces in the Mediterranean, notably by increasing the problems of concentrating Italian naval forces and maintaining secrecy. In addition to the senior commanders understanding the limitations of their ships and industrial base, Italian admirals were also averse to taking risks because they believed the war would be won or lost by Germany and that, in a postwar world, the navy would be Italy's most important military asset. The likely postwar consequences of such steps appeared more significant due to a lack of knowledge of when and how the war would end, and notably with what alignments. Powers were differently affected by the determination to consider postwar consequences, but these consequences underlined the extent to which wartime strategy could not be seen as a separate category. Indeed, peace and war were in a continuum, and notably so for the Soviet Union under Stalin.

Part of the debate about Barbarossa focuses on whether, and how, the Germans could have captured Moscow. Nevertheless, this is an incomplete account, because, as with Tsar Alexander I against Napoleon in 1812, who continued resistance after the loss of Moscow, and successfully so, the Soviets intended to fight on. In 1941, they planned to hold the line of the river Volga east of Moscow, but, in the event, held Moscow. Had they not done so, the war would still have continued.

Moreover, a central aspect of Soviet strategy was provided by the change in Soviet space created by the ability to move large quantities of industrial plant and many millions of workers to the east, far beyond the range of likely German advance or air attack. About 16.5 million people were evacuated between the summer of 1941 and the autumn of 1942. Once relocated, these industries turned out vast quantities of military materiel, outproducing the Germans, for example in numbers of tanks.

Like that of Germany, Japanese strategy was also confused. There were parts that made sense. Taking control of French Indo-China in 1941 was of strategic importance as an axis of advance to the 'southern resources area' of Malaya and the Dutch East Indies. The latter (modern Indonesia) posed a problem for Japan as, despite the German conquest of the Netherlands in May 1940, the Dutch colonial officials rejected Japanese efforts to acquire oil and, instead, sought to align policy with Britain and the United States. Lacking naval power able to act in a strategic fashion on the global scale, Germany was in no position to prevent that. In addition, seizing Burma (Myanmar) in early 1942 from the British gave the Japanese a buffer against attack from India, as well as cutting the Burma Road, through which Nationalist China was supplied. Burma also provided a source of oil. More generally, seizing and keeping the initiative in 1941–2 enabled Japan repeatedly to translate numerical inferiority into a more favourable position at the point of engagement. This was in line with the short-war, 'grab and hold on' strategy of the conflicts of 1894–5 and 1904–5: the Sino-Japanese and Russo-Japanese wars.

However, in 1941–2, the Japanese suffered from the lack of a viable war plan, and not simply because the opponent was now the United States. This lack, in part, arose from the confusion in Japanese policy-making, with differences between military and civilian politicians, and between army and navy, interacting with rifts over strategy, and notably so over areas of prime geographical interest. As with Hitler and his attitude to Britain, the Soviet Union and, eventually, the United States, a conviction of the weakness of the opposing system led to a failure by Japan to judge resolve. The initial Japanese ability to mount successful attacks, to gain great swathes of territory, and to establish an apparent stranglehold on the Far East and the western Pacific did not deter the Americans from the long-term effort of driving back and destroying their opponents. The American government and public were not interested in the idea of a compromise peace with the power that had attacked Pearl Harbor. Japan, the weaker power, had gone to war with the one power that could beat it, and in a way calculated to ensure that it did so. As a result, helped greatly by the superior command skill that made possible the effective use of resources at a stage when they were in short supply, the Americans were able to exercise strategic leverage and to take the strategic initiative successfully by the end of 1942.[22]

Arguing that there was already in effect an undeclared war between the two powers in the Atlantic, and that the United States was part of an alleged global Jewish conspiracy, Hitler followed up the Japanese attack on Pearl Harbor by declaring war on the United States on 11 December 1941, the key event in making the war global. This declaration undercut ideas of a 'Japan First' strategy[23] and, instead, helped lead to a 'Germany

First' strategy on the part of the United States. Under this strategy, the bulk of American land and air assets were allocated to preparing for an invasion of Europe.

This strategy had already been outlined in a memorandum drawn up in November 1940 by Admiral Harold Stark, the Chief of Naval Operations,[24] in prewar plans by the American and British military staffs, in the Rainbow 5 war plan, and in the Anglo-American-Canadian ABC-1 Plan talks in early 1941. These had envisaged a defensive strategy in the Pacific in the event of war with the three Axis powers.[25] In a clear instance of prioritisation and of its centrality to strategic planning, President Franklin Delano Roosevelt had supported this because of concern that Britain might collapse, although this preference was controversial in some circles at the time, and has remained so. The logic was clear: Germany had a greater potential than Japan to overthrow its opponents, as well as to intervene in South America, whereas Japan, instead, was best placed only to defeat them. Thus, although colonies might be conquered, Britain was less vulnerable to Japanese power. Moreover, it was argued that only a land attack, which would require American participation, could defeat Germany.[26]

This strategy led the American army manoeuvres in 1941 to focus on preparing for European-theatre conflict, and, once the war had widened, was confirmed by the Washington Conference that began on 22 December 1941. The conference resulted in the creation of an Anglo-American planning mechanism based on the Combined Chiefs of Staff. It was also agreed both that American forces should be moved to Northern Ireland, to prepare for operations in Europe, and that the Americans should plan an invasion of Vichy-held Morocco, which would deny Germany the possibility of taking over. The preparation for the fight-back had begun.

'Germany First' had consequences throughout the war. An emphasis on fighting Germany helped the Soviet Union by diverting German resources to resist American attacks, as with the ending of the Kursk offensive in 1943, while an American focus on Japan would not have weakened the pressure on the Soviet Union, as Japan and the Soviet Union had agreed a neutrality pact on 13 April 1941. Conversely, an emphasis on the United States fighting Japan might have assisted China, with consequences for the results of the postwar Chinese Civil War, and have also ensured that the Japanese were not able to mount offensives there and against India in 1944.

Yet, as is often forgotten, military assets are not transferable and usable in the simple fashion that such remarks might suggest. There were major problems, particularly, but not solely, logistical, associated with the allocation and sustaining of units and resources. Linked to this, the capacity of the Pacific theatre to take more American troops in 1942 and 1943, and to employ them effectively, was limited.

Roosevelt's strategy looked back to the navalism of A.T. Mahan, and drew heavily on the naval power projection of President Theodore Roosevelt (r. 1901–9), on his own experience as Assistant Secretary of the Navy from 1913 to 1920 and on his interest in geopolitics. He was very committed to the invasion of Vichy North Africa in 1942. Many of his civilian advisers were also influential in strategic planning. Like Churchill, Roosevelt was very interested in maps, indeed creating a map room in the White House. For Christmas 1942, he was given a huge 50-inch, 750-pound globe, manufactured by the Weber Costello Company under the supervision of the Map Division of the Office of Strategic Services and the War Department, and presented to him by the Army Chief of Staff, General George Marshall. This photographed occasion was designed to show Roosevelt's interest in maps. Roosevelt, however, never got the futuristic briefing room planned in 1942 by William Donovan, head of the new Office of Strategic Services (OSS), a room with a large illuminated globe on which information could be projected. The plan was cancelled by the chiefs of staff and, instead, there was an emphasis on producing intelligence reports and maps.

An important element of the strategic nature of map-making was provided by Anglo-American co-operation. Under the Loper–Hotine Agreement of May 1942, the US Army Map Service was given full responsibility for mapping the Americas, Australasia, the Pacific, Japan, the West Indies and the North Atlantic, and the British for the rest. This allocation accorded with the systems the British had already in place for overseas production, most significantly centres in Egypt and India. As during the First World War, the Survey of India extended its activities beyond the British Empire: it was given the task of mapping Iraq, Iran, Afghanistan, Burma, Thailand, French Indo-China, China, Malaysia and Sumatra,[27] with most sections under direct military command, and air surveying, a means to map hostile territory and to map at speed, increased. As part of a broader pattern of co-operation, the Geographical Section of the British General Staff and the US Army Map Service exchanged map and geodetic material. The Western Allies initiated the World Aeronautical Chart 1:1,000,000-scale map series.

As the war became global, so it became more important to understand it accordingly. Aside from the interest in globes, aerial views and orthographic projections, there were also concerns to improve cylindrical maps. Samuel Whittemore Boggs, the chief cartographer at the State Department, commissioned Osborn Miller, the head of the Department of Technical Training of the American Geographical Society, to do so. Miller repositioned the poles in the Mercator projection. This provided a worldview similar to the latter, but with a reduced areal distortion in polar regions.

Map-making initiatives were of particular importance for air power operations, while air power was a key driver of requirements for mapping. The acquisition and protection of airbases reflected strategies carefully plotted in spatial terms, with reference to maps and with particular interest in the range of aircraft; and the bases helped determine strategic options and operational means.

The range of war led to the movement of air, sea and land units into areas with which they were unfamiliar, for example the Germans into Egypt in 1941, and to demands for the (improved) mapping of these areas and for a degree of consistency in mapping. There were readily apparent contrasts in cartographic requirements and availability from region to region. Aircraft flying from US bases in North America and US islands in the Caribbean, and from carriers, were operating in a very different context from those flying from new bases in Cuba, the Dominican Republic, Haiti, Panama and Brazil, which initially faced the problems posed by inadequate maps.

Strategy involved an effective use of information. The Allies eventually proved to be better than the Axis at understanding the areas in which they were fighting and the resources that could be deployed, and in planning accordingly. In contrast, improvisation strongly characterised Axis planning and response. Hitler's emphasis was on the socio-economic and political conditions he wished to see, and not on those that existed. In planning and campaigning, the Axis stress was often on the value of superior will, rather than on the realities of climate, terrain and logistics. The constraints posed by the last three were ignored, for example, in the totally unsuccessful Japanese offensive against the British on the India–Burma border in 1944. Such poverty of strategic understanding is difficult to capture in maps, both those produced at the time and subsequently, since Axis assumptions about willpower were not really subject to cartographic depiction. At the same time, there were clear contrasts between availability and use of information due to countries' differing cartographic capabilities – for example, the much greater American one as opposed to that of Japan.

Strategy is about timing as well as prioritisation. Major, and apparently inexorable, Japanese successes in early 1942, combined with those of the Germans against the Soviets that summer, led to American pressure for swifter action than the British had envisaged and were prepared for. The mid-term Congressional elections due in November were also a factor. The Americans pressed for an invasion of France in 1942. This also offered a way to counter Stalin's totally misplaced anxiety that Churchill wanted a separate peace with Germany so as to leave the latter free to oppose the Soviet Union.[28]

The success of Operation Torch, the largely American invasion of French North Africa that November, cannot, however, conceal the risks of an invasion of France that year, not least in terms of Atlantic and Channel weather, lack of shipping, and German opposition, including U-boats (submarines) in the Atlantic. There was still a need to win the battle of the Atlantic with German U-boats and to gain air dominance, as well as to plan operations and train, equip and move forces. The need for training had been made readily apparent by the deficiencies revealed in operations earlier in the war. The British were concerned about the risks of a premature invasion of France, in large part because they were aware that resources alone could not counteract German fighting quality. Nevertheless, in April 1942, it was agreed that France would be invaded in 1943, and the pace of the movement of American forces to Britain stepped up so as to prepare for that invasion. This movement was dependent on the battle of the Atlantic.

In June 1942, having stopped initially successful Soviet attacks earlier in the year, the Germans launched a fresh offensive against Soviet forces. To Hitler, gaining Soviet resources, in particular oil, was the best preparation for conflict with the United States, specifically for opposing a second front in western Europe. The initial plan called for the destruction of Soviet forces west of the river Don, followed by an advance into the Caucasus Mountains in order to capture the Soviet oilfields in the region, and then put pressure on Allied interests in the Near and Middle East. Cutting Allied supply links to the Soviet Union through Iran, links created when Britain and the Soviet Union jointly occupied the country in 1941, was seen as important, and there were hopes of winning the support of neutral Turkey, a potentially pivotal power in the eastern Mediterranean and the Middle East, as it remains. The seizure of the oilfields was regarded as a preparation for the lengthy struggle that American entry into the war appeared to make inevitable. Indeed, Hitler expanded the original objective in order to seize all the oilfields in the region, including those round Baku on the Caspian Sea. Resources were a key factor in strategic planning, in terms of goals as well as means.

However, in 1942, as in 1941, German strategy was both misguided and poorly implemented. Not envisaged in 1941, the 1942 offensive was not an adequate stage two. Hitler's conviction that the city of Stalingrad had to be captured foolishly substituted a pointless symbolic goal for the necessary operational flexibility, a situation already seen at Verdun in 1916 and one that captured the more general role of symbolical factors in strategic planning and implementation. In Stalingrad, the German force was fixed, the dynamism of strategy and operational warfare rapidly swallowed by the tactical dimension, and the Germans subsequently defeated with heavy losses by a Soviet counter-attack that was, as it should not have been, a surprise.

By 1943, the war had taken on an attritional character for Germany and Japan, and their opponents. The high tempo of campaigning used up troops and materiel, but the availability of massive resources enabled the Allies to attack on a number of fronts at once, and to return to the attack despite high casualty levels and serious wear and tear. The greatly superior nature of Allied air power was of strategic significance in terms of ground and sea power.

The Allies adopted a strategy of forcing unconditional surrender on their opponents, a decision announced by Roosevelt at the press conference after the Casablanca conference of January 1943. This underlined the flawed strategic insight of the German military leadership, as well as of Hitler. Their willingness to accept Hitler not only morally corrupted them, as the military came to collaborate in Hitler's genocidal policies, but also led them into a conflict in which, from 1941, limited war and political compromise ceased to be options.

The Germans could not translate their central position into lasting success because peace was not an option. As a consequence, the operational ability of the German military was linked to a task that risked, and in the end caused, not only their defeat but also their dissolution, along with the total conquest of Germany. In narrower terms, the Germans had not planned for the lengthy conflict into which they had blundered. Neither the military-industrial complex, nor the armed forces, were prepared for it.

In 1943, the Germans launched their last major offensive of the war on a principal theatre of the Eastern Front. This was an attempt to break through the flanks of the Soviet Kursk salient and to achieve an encirclement triumph to match the Soviet success at Stalingrad the previous winter. Still engaging in strategic wishful thinking, or rather in wishful thinking as strategy, Hitler saw this offensive as a battle of annihilation in which superior will would prevail and ensure the destruction of Soviet offensive forces. More mundanely, the elimination of this salient would rob the Soviets of a position from which they could attack two neighbouring German salients. Had Operation Citadel succeeded, the Germans were considering a further advance to the north-east, thus avoiding the direct approach eastward from Army Group Centre against strong Soviet defences on the route to Moscow and more generally.

Hitler was not temperamentally ready to accept the idea of staying on the defensive and conserving resources, while trying to make success cost his attacking opponents dear. Such a strategy, anyway, appeared politically unacceptable. It would test the morale of the German population, undermine the cohesion of the Axis coalition, and, at best, produce defensive successes and buy time, rather than winning victory. Instead, Hitler hoped that victory in the Kursk offensive would undermine the Allied coalition, by lessening Western confidence in the likelihood of Soviet victory and increasing Soviet demands for a second front in France. Matters of temperament on the part of the ruler were/are often crucial to strategy. Hitler was scarcely alone. Field Marshal Erich von Manstein was the principal architect of the plan, and his general agreed with Hitler that Germany could not afford to relinquish the initiative, an argument about strategy that, in itself, was not without point.

In the event, however, the Germans, although doing well on the southern side of the Kursk salient, were defeated by a strong Soviet defence-in-depth. This had more than simply a tactical strength and operational capacity. Moreover, the fate of the campaign, launched on 5 July 1943, also reflected wider German commitments as, on 10 July, Anglo-American forces invaded Sicily and Hitler then wished to move troops there. He called off Operation Citadel as a result of the invasion, which suggests that Churchill's instincts were correct about the value of an attack on Italy.

The 1943 campaigning on the Eastern Front showed the Germans to be beatable, both on the offensive and on the defensive, and led to major Soviet territorial gains as well as the prospect of more gains. The strategic advantage had passed to the Red Army as its strength, confidence and operational capability all increased. This shift was important to the dynamics of the Allied coalition. The Soviet Union was now clearly going to play a major role in the future of, at least, eastern Europe. Soviet confidence, a key strategic resource, improved.

Furthermore, the Germans now were less able to spare troops for the Italian campaign, while the mobile armoured reserve necessary to oppose successfully a second front in France was being destroyed in the Soviet Union. German tank and other losses on the Eastern Front in late 1943 and early 1944 were heavy and, although these campaigns after Kursk commonly receive relatively little attention in general histories of the war (as opposed to Operation Bagration, a major success, later in 1944), they were important in the degradation of the German army and even more so because the bulk of the German army was deployed there.

The course of campaigning would have been less serious for Germany had the political situation been different. The strategic context was clear: the failure to obtain peace with any one of their opponents (as had happened with Russia in early 1918) put the Germans in a difficult position to secure victory, or, at least, avoid defeat, on any of its fronts. The German strategic quandary was exacerbated as it was increasingly likely that an intractable conflict on the Eastern Front would be joined by fresh commitments in France in the shape of the Second Front. This quandary helped explain the Allies' adoption of the strategy of unconditional surrender: it was designed to fix the alliance and thus the pressure on Germany, as well as to avoid the problem of agreeing on terms both for the Allies and with the Axis powers. Thus, the policy fulfilled both military and diplomatic goals.

At the same time, this situation still left questions of emphasis for the Allies. In the case of Japan, the Americans were able to combine both the options: the southern drive on the Philippines favoured by the army, and the central Pacific drive that was backed by the navy and the marines. The situation proved very different in the assessment of strategy towards Germany, which was better placed than Japan to move forces to respond to factors. In particular, there were major disagreements over the timing of an invasion of France and concerning the extent to which there should be an Allied offensive strategy in the Mediterranean and, if so, what it should concentrate on. The Americans did not understand Hitler's paranoia about the south, including the Balkan approaches to the Romanian oilfields and refining facilities at Ploesti, and the Italian airbases from which they could be bombed. The interdependence of land and air warfare was also shown by Hitler's concern to retain control of as much of Italy as possible in order to keep Allied bombers as far from German targets as possible. This interdependence had been seen at a tactical level during the First World War, but now it was operational and strategic. The Americans were reluctant to support an invasion of Sicily and, even more, mainland Italy because they feared that it would distract resources from both the invasion of France and the war with Japan, and also be a strategic irrelevance.

More generally, American policy-makers were opposed to what they saw as the Mediterranean obsession of British policy.[29] An emphasis on focusing on key targets reflected persistent concerns, notably on the part of George Marshall, about limits to the American people's support for the war, in the shape of anxiety about how long the public would be prepared to tolerate a protracted struggle.[30] These concerns did not have to wait for the Cold War.

What in practice was a commitment to the Mediterranean, and not an obsession, however, reflected British strategic concerns in the region. These were the product of longstanding imperial geopolitical interests, but also of the legacy of conflict in the Mediterranean with the Axis since June 1940. There was war there with Italy as well as, from early

1941, Germany, war on land, at sea and in the air; and resources had been and were allocated accordingly. The British preference for an indirect approach, weakening the Axis by incremental steps, as the preparation for an invasion of France, was also important. As a reminder of the varied causes of strategic choice, this preference was a longstanding aspect of British strategic culture, one seen indeed from the seventeenth century, and notably with the Peninsular War of 1808–13, and linked to the emphasis on maritime power and themes. This preference was also a response to the specific military circumstances of 1942–3.[31] Both strategic culture and specific circumstances, or reactive strategy, have to be considered together. Each provided a context, and it is mistaken to see one as necessarily more significant. At the same time, the legacy of experience was an aspect of the 'effective strategic decision-making and direction'[32] discerned in the British case.

The British were concerned that a direct attack across the English Channel would expose untested forces to the battle-hardened Germans. Their experience in 1940–2 had made them wary of such a step until the Germans had been defeated, and this lesson was underlined by the costly failure of the cross-Channel raid on Dieppe on 19 August 1942, a failure that also showed the problems of focusing on a defended port. Instead, in the summer of 1944, beaches away from ports were the targets, both in Normandy (6 June) and in Provence (15 August).

In contrast, the Americans argued that Italy was a strategic irrelevance that would dissipate Allied military strength. Instead, they sought a direct approach, especially an engagement with the major German forces in western Europe and an advance into Germany. German weaknesses in 1943 suggest that this might have been an option that year. Many key units were allocated to the Kursk offensive, the Germans lacked the build-up in munitions production that 1943 was to bring, and their defensive positions in France were still incomplete.

Moreover, the Soviets mentioned their suspicion of their allies' failure to open a second front to the Germans when probing the possibility of a separate peace. Hitler was not interested in pursuing this option. However, the possibility of such a development indicated the potential impact of strategic decisions on geopolitical alignments.

Nevertheless, the British were correct to draw attention to deficiencies in Allied preparedness. As yet, there was only limited experience in (and equipment for) amphibious operations. There was not the capacity for the undersea pipeline that was to be used in Normandy in 1944. Moreover, it was unclear, at the beginning of 1943, how far it would be possible to vanquish the U-boat threat, while American aircraft production (and supply to Britain) took a while to reach full capacity.[33]

Aside from the need to build up forces for an invasion, there was also the requirement of assured, rather than transient or partial, air and sea superiority. The most important Anglo-American decision, made in January 1943, was to focus on winning the battle of the Atlantic. They had already reached the point where they were not going to lose it, certainly by mid-1942. However, only once the U-boat threat had been eliminated could Britain and the United States begin to plan properly, because major maritime invasions are not practical unless most (in this case nearly all) shipping is getting through. From that, everything else flowed for Britain and the United States, and indeed ship-building, particularly by the latter, was crucial to Allied strategic capability.[34] Winning the battle of the Atlantic required this ship-building as well as the more specific success against the U-boats.

This was the background to the second front sought by the Allies, and it underlined the strategic quandary faced by the Germans, with an intractable conflict on the Eastern Front likely to be joined by fresh commitments in France. Despite the hopes placed by their advocates, the U-boats were proven to have had only an operational capability.

Destroying the *Luftwaffe* was also a very sensible strategic decision as it made Allied strategic bombing more effective and eased operations on all the fronts. It would have been premature to invade Normandy without total air cover and the possibility of interdicting the battlefield, or, at least, of limiting the movement forward of German reinforcements.

Since, by early 1943, the Japanese threat had been much reduced, notably in the Pacific, although not yet from Burma or in China, the decision to continue to focus strategy on defeating Germany remained valid. Thus, the invasion of southern Italy was not a bad idea at the time it was made.

Amphibious operations in the Mediterranean in 1943 provided valuable experience in planning and execution, but also, notably at Salerno in 1943 and still more with the Anzio landing in January 1944, offered warnings about the difficulties posed by the exploitation of such operations and by the rapid German response. In 1943, that would have been a more serious problem in France than it was to be in practice in Normandy in 1944, as the Allies did not yet have sufficient air dominance to seek to isolate the area in conflict. Furthermore, operations in North Africa and Italy in 1943 were also important in improving military effectiveness on land. Both the American and the British armies benefited from this experience. It was important to strategic capability.

As it was not feasible to invade France in 1943, the Americans finally agreed to the attack on Sicily. From the outset, there was criticism of the decision to fight in Italy. In *Newsweek* on 13 March 1944, J.F.C. Fuller, a retired British general, wrote: 'The strategy is execrable. We should never have embarked on this Italian adventure because it was unstrategic from the start.' Claiming, correctly, that the topography helped the defence, Fuller stated that forces should have been conserved for the second front in France. He frequently used 'strategy' as a term in his writing and sometimes in an inventive fashion, as in a piece he wrote for the *Sunday Pictorial* of 27 April 1941 in which he commented on the Germans driving back the British forces in North Africa: 'Like a ladder in a girl's stocking, our splendid desert campaign is running backwards up our strategical leg from its ankle to its knee.'[35]

Churchill, in contrast, was anxious to use the Mediterranean as a staging post for amphibious operations into the Balkans. To the Americans, although the Mediterranean was certainly an opportunity,[36] operations into the Balkans were a distraction from defeating the Germans in France, and also a logistical nightmare. To Churchill, however, the Balkans presented an opportunity not only to harry the Germans, but also to pre-empt Soviet advances. This reflected his suspicion of the Soviet Union, and his linked strategic insight that the war was only a stage in the history of the twentieth century, a formative stage, but one that would be succeeded by challenges and rivalries that had only been partly suspended during the conflict. This insight was a reminder of the variety of chronological scales on which strategy is conceived, pursued and analysed. Churchill, like Stalin, but not Roosevelt, understood that the Second World War was in part a stage in the longstanding struggle over the position of the Soviet Union.

Hypotheticals or counterfactuals, the 'what-ifs' of history, come into play, as the results of amphibious invasions lead to the question of whether air and sea operations are inadequate unless supported by an invasion. As far as the Second World War itself is concerned, this is a question that arises with the German threat to Britain, with Axis pressure on Malta in 1941–2, with American 'island-hopping' in the Pacific in 1943–5, and with the 'endgame' for Japan. Similar questions can be raised about areas that were not islands, but were nevertheless vulnerable to amphibious attack, notably mainland Italy and Yugoslavia in 1943–5. In short, had a combination of naval pressure and air attack made the actual presence of invading troops less necessary or even redundant? These hypotheticals are of value because many of them played a role in strategic debate at the time.

The Second Front, launched on 6 June 1944 with the invasion of Normandy, was part of an assemblage of pressure that ended the war in Europe within a year. The success of the invasion, indeed, encouraged looking ahead to the strategic situation in the postwar world. However, for understandable reasons, strategic commentators did not always get it correct, not least because they could misunderstand the politics of the campaign. Fuller informed the readers of *Newsweek* on 10 July 1944:

> Though the German High Command is faced with forces beyond its means to check, it doesn't necessarily follow that it is checkmated because utilization of these forces depends upon the circumstances in which they are placed . . . the Russians, being more war-worn than their Allies, are more likely to welcome speedy termination of the war . . . the Americans and the British also seek its speedy termination so that they may still be fresh when they in turn fall on Japan . . . if the war can be prolonged throughout next winter, by spring or summer of next year political circumstances may have so changed that the Allied powers will be willing to bring the war in the west to an end on terms more favourable to Germany than those of unconditional surrender . . . Time is the crucial factor not only strategically but also tactically; tactically for the Russians in order rapidly to beat their enemy; strategically for the Germans in order slowly to sell ground at high cost.

This view seriously underrated the resolve of the Allies to defeat Germany, but helps remind us of the uncertainties of contemporaries and of the continued need to relate military developments to political objectives. That point throws further light on the long-running discussion over whether the Allies followed the best strategy in the West in 1944.

This discussion is often somewhat unhelpfully reduced to a debate over the virtues of the broad-front approach advocated by General Dwight Eisenhower, the overall Allied commander in France, and the very different narrow-front attempt for a rapid advance beyond the Rhine advocated by General Bernard Montgomery, the senior British field commander, a difficult character. This clash was linked to Montgomery's unsuccessful pressure for his appointment, under Eisenhower, as a deputy entrusted with command over ground forces. The idea of a narrow-front advance presupposed a war of manoeuvre in which the initiative and tempo were dictated by the Allies. However, the German 'Bulge' offensive of December 1944 indicated the riskiness of this approach. An Allied advance across the Rhine in 1944, the basis for the rash and unsuccessful Arnhem offensive, would have been vulnerable to counter-attack, as the Germans had been building up a significant armoured force in northern Germany from September. An Allied advance would also have been dependent on a precarious supply route. At the same time, the preference for a broad front helped the Germans withdraw without heavy casualties after defeat at Falaise, while Eisenhower's caution greatly lessened the chance of cutting off German forces and contrasted with the operational means of the 'deep battle' advances the Soviets employed to sustain their strategy of advance across eastern Europe.

Given the resilience of the German military, Allied hopes of victory in 1944 were misplaced. From that perspective, both Eisenhower's broad-front approach and Montgomery's usually methodical war-making (which was not in evidence in the Arnhem offensive) were sensible options. Each weakened the German army. Meanwhile, a combination of the Allied goal of unconditional surrender with the resolve of their opponents' leaderships, and their grip over their populations, ensured that the war would go on in Europe and Asia.

The focus for 1944 is generally on Allied strategy. This involved coalition dynamics which encompassed realism in the need for allies, not least in providing numbers, and responsibility in the bearing of burdens. So also with the overthrow of Napoleon in 1813–15.

It is also pertinent to look at the strategy of the Axis. In 1944, co-operation with allies continued to be non-existent, but, given the pace of the Allied advance, the options for such co-operation collapsed. Hitler's diminished grasp on reality exacerbated the difficulties of German command, but was also matched within much of the military, for example the *Luftwaffe*.[37] Having survived the July Bomb Plot and, in response, further radicalised the German state and military, Hitler was able to continue with his fantasy that willpower would prevail and that his opponents could be divided. That lay behind the German offensive that led that December to the battle of the Bulge. The strategy then was that of weakening the Anglo-American forces so as to lead them to abandon the struggle. This, however, was a total misreading of the situation, both militarily and politically; indeed an attempt to repeat the strategy of 1940 but in a totally different context. The offensive failed, but, had it been more successful militarily, it would still not have worked politically.

So also with Japan in 1944. As with the Germans, there was a conviction that a decisive victory could be obtained on one front that would overcome the more general role and impact of Allied resources. There was a certainty that victory would sap the inherently weaker will of opponents, and thus give the Axis the success to which they were entitled. In practice, success for Japan would only have delayed eventual defeat.

The Japanese planned a series of major clashes in 1944. An offensive from Burma was designed to forestall a British invasion, the prime objective, by overrunning the Imphal base area and destroying IV Corps. More ambitiously, it was also hoped that the offensive would knock India out of the war by causing a rising. This was a strategy similar to that attempted by the Germans, via the Turks, in the First World War. For this reason, (anti-British) Indian Nationalist forces played a major role in the Japanese advance. This operation was also designed to force China out of the war by cutting its supply lines from India. It failed in all its objectives.

In contrast, a Japanese offensive in China made significant territorial gains and overran important American airbases from which Japan could be bombed. The Japanese failed, as in earlier offensives, to knock China out of the war. However, controlling, for the first time, a continuous ground route from Manchuria to Vietnam gave Japan a land axis that was independent of American maritime intervention. This provided Japan with valuable strategic depth. The loss of airbases obliged the Americans to focus on seizing Pacific islands that could provide them, such as Saipan, and the Japanese campaign also gravely weakened the idea of a China-based American invasion of Japan.

In the Pacific, the Japanese aimed to destroy the spearhead of the advancing American fleet by concentrating their air power against it. The Japanese plan was for the American fleet to be lured into the range of Japanese island airbases, while the naval air force was to be concentrated in order further to minimise the American lead in carriers. There was the hope that the total success of the Japanese fleet over the Russians at the battle of Tsushima in 1905 could be repeated. This reflected a more general conviction, also seen in the Midway operation in 1942, that a decisive victory could be obtained on one front, which could overcome the more general role and impact of Allied resources. As seen from the outset of the attack on the United States in 1941 (as indeed also that on China in 1937), Japanese assumptions arose from the sway of historical examples that supposedly represented national greatness and, even more, from the role of factors of will in Axis thinking. Aside from the lack of political understanding underlying this policy, it was anachronistic militarily. Defeat in 1944 on one front would have delayed the Americans, but nothing more; and, by concentrating a target for the Americans, Japanese strategy made it more likely that the American attack would succeed in causing heavy casualties. The Americans had a better and more mobile fleet, a far greater ability to replace losses, and far more capable leadership than the Japanese. In the event, the Japanese failed totally in the battles of the Philippine Sea and of Leyte Gulf. In the former, the Japanese carrier air force was destroyed; in the latter the surface fleet.[38]

By the end of 1944, there was a breakdown of strategic thought on the part of the Japanese, an inability, in the face of Allied power, to think through any option once the decisive naval battle, Leyte Gulf, had been lost. Successes in China could not be translated into a broader strategic achievement, or even into knocking China out of the war. The destruction of naval assets, moreover, made it difficult to think of any further large-scale action, and reduced the Japanese to a defensive-offensive predicated on tenacious defence coupled with destructive suicide missions, both of which were designed to sap their opponents' will. Neither did so. The weak government had no real strategy left other than for the military to die heroically.

Similarly, Hitler was reduced to vain hopes that the alliance against him would dissolve because of its inherent divisions or, more specifically, due to the death of Roosevelt, which he saw as proof of a providential salvation that would lead to a change comparable to the death of Tsarina Elizabeth of Russia in 1762. That had unravelled the alliance against Prussia during the Seven Years' War. With its focus on the life of the opposing leader, this approach was a very traditional way to look at strategy. It did not work.

CONCLUSIONS

The Axis powers were overcome in 1945, but, by then, the campaigning in part looked towards the revival of the Cold War. The Soviet advance in Manchuria and Korea that August, a major defeat for the Japanese army, in practice also weakened the American position in east Asia and affected the future struggle between the Communists and the Guomindang in China. Already, in mid-1944, planners for the British chiefs of staff had suggested a postwar reform of Germany and Japan, so that they could play a role against a Soviet Union whose ambitions in eastern Europe were arousing growing concern. In turn, these ambitions were designed to provide the Soviet Union with yet more territory that would lessen the risk of any attack comparable to 1941.[39] The strategic overhang of recent years was to be important to strategies during the Cold War.

The failure of the powers that launched each world war to translate their initial victories into lasting political or military success helped to give an attritional character to each war, and at the strategic level as well as in the nature of fighting. In the Second World War, Allied attacks simultaneously on Germany from a number of directions proved more successful than they had done in the First World War. The cumulative pressure was intense. Ironically, this owed most to the total failure of Hitler's strategy, bound up in the attack on his onetime Soviet ally in 1941. Having sought to impose sequential warfare and prioritisation on other powers, Hitler had simultaneous warfare and total commitment imposed on Germany.

The parallel with Napoleon in 1812 was instructive, even if the ideological context of the two struggles was very different. That Napoleon was the key field commander, a role Hitler never fulfilled, does not negate this comparison nor alter this verdict of total strategic failure in both cases. Whereas Germany in the First World War had eventually, in 1918, succeeded in its goal of turning a two-front war begun in 1914 into a one-front one, Hitler, in 1941, went from a one-front to a two-front one. Like Napoleon in 1812 (but not 1805 or 1808), this proved disastrous; although Napoleon in 1812 at least had the advantage of the outbreak of a war between Britain and the United States that he had helped to cause.

For both Napoleon and Hitler, the broadening out of the war was not so much military adventurism, although that doubtless played a role, but, instead, a totally flawed reading of the international situation and, in particular, of the political situation within Russia/the Soviet Union, namely the ability and, crucially, willingness to continue fighting. Depending on the definition of strategy, Napoleon and Hitler lost the war because they should have chosen the strategy of continued peace with Russia/the Soviet Union, a conclusion amplified by Hitler's declaration of war on the United States later in 1941. However, such a choice would not have been in accordance with their ideologies, natures or regimes.

10

STRATEGIES FOR COLD WAR
1945–89

The Cold War is generally regarded, and notably so in the United States, as the sequel to the Second World War. Instead, it really began with the Russian Civil War (1918–21), which followed the Bolshevik (Soviet Communist) coup in Russia in 1917. The Bolshevik Revolution was crucial, as longstanding geopolitical concerns, particularly in Britain, about Russian expansion were given added point by the ideological ambition of communism. Its goal and strategy of world revolution were frightening, as was the related sense that there was no geographical boundary to communist territorial pretensions and military success.

This situation led to a counter-strategy, of the containment of the Soviet Union, notably by Western support for Poland, the Baltic republics and Finland, and the suppression of subversion linked to the Soviets and their supporters. The overthrow of the only Communist government established further west, that in Hungary under Béla Kun in 1919, was an important part of the equation. This overthrow was achieved, with French aid, by Czech and Romanian forces.

This repertoire provided the strategic ideas and practices for the confrontation that followed the Second World War. However, thanks in particular to Soviet advances in 1944–5 and the greater effectiveness of long-range air power, both ideas and practices had to face a very different geopolitical and technological situation to that in the interwar years. This situation was a matter of needs, opportunities and options. Thus, for example, alongside confronting communism, the German question was a significant issue, as it had earlier been after the First World War. The role that West Germany would take was a matter for speculation and planning. In the event, accession to NATO and the presence of

217

American troops after the postwar occupation ceased in 1955 solved this problem[1] without other western European powers having to accept German ideas, such as an atomic capability. In 1963, West Germany agreed to remain without nuclear forces in return for an American security guarantee. At the same time, Soviet forces in East Germany, as well as its membership of the communist bloc, solved the German question for the Soviet Union. For Germany as a whole, however, there was no equivalent to the military co-operation with the Soviet Union seen in the 1920s.

The discussion at this point habitually focuses on Western, notably American, strategy, but it is also necessary to look at that of the Soviet Union. The strategies of the two sides were separate, and, in large part, arose independently, but were also related, not least because each encouraged the other and affected the likely effectiveness of the other. American strategy in the Cold War arose from the perception of a Soviet threat, just as Soviet strategy in part arose from the perception of an American threat.[2] From the perspective of Bucharest or Prague, where the Communists seized power in coups, it was the Soviet threat that was more obvious.

There were three arenas of Soviet strategy, all of which overlapped but, nevertheless, stood out separately in various degrees. First was a philosophical strategy that emanated from the basic ideological worldview (*ideologicheskoe mirovozzrenie* – the last word mirroring to some extent the German *Weltanschauung*, although the two do not entirely capture the sense of the other) of the Soviet Communist Party that undergirded it. Soviet *mirovozzrenie* ardently postulated an elemental struggle between the third stage of history (capitalism) and the fourth (socialism), and argued that the Soviet Union, and its guiding Communist Party, were destined to lead this struggle, and to see it through, and with necessary success. The sequencing of the stages was regarded as inevitable.

This view was consistent, regardless of Stalin's belief in the inevitability of war between the Soviet Union and the Western countries, and the later shift under Khrushchev in the mid-1950s to the doctrine of 'peaceful co-existence'. This ideology manifested itself politically in the domestic, foreign, and military policies of the Soviet Union. In 1946, the Central Committee of the Communist Party decided to free Soviet culture from what it termed 'servility before the West'. Cosmopolitanism and Westernism were attacked in a campaign that continued until Stalin's death in 1953, one linked to a murderous anti-Semitism that also affected communist states in Eastern Europe.[3]

Second was diplomatic strategy. This advanced the basic ideological worldview, however bold or attenuated both support and success might be, depending upon temporal and geographical circumstances. This strategy also had to reckon with the non-ideological criteria (pre-Marxist or un-Marxist) of states and non-state actors. These criteria would include cultural and socio-economic developments, political structures and military strength. This face of Soviet strategy, combining as it did ideology and pragmatism, was the one to which Westerners were most exposed. They tended to equate the postures and actions of Soviet diplomacy with Soviet ideological direction as a whole, but, more than once, this was a fallacy.

Third was military strategy. The strong engagement with counter-insurgency was largely handled by security agencies, not the military, but was an important aspect of strategy.[4] The numerous stages in Soviet military development from the Russian Civil War to the 1980s responded firstly to variable inputs of ideology and external conditions (the latter focusing on the location of Soviet borders, and on the military capacity and friendliness of countries on the other side of the Soviet border, and of main adversaries further afield); secondly to the legacy of the world wars; thirdly to atomic weaponry; fourthly to trans-oceanic possibilities; and lastly to interservice co-operation and rivalries.

Soviet military strategy gave strong emphasis to sudden, offensive military operations in overwhelming strength, and did not preclude surprise attacks, such as the successful June 1940 assault against the three totally vulnerable Baltic states, the December 1979 invasion of Afghanistan, which was initially highly successful, and the plans for attacks on NATO forces in Europe, which were nearly launched as late as 1983.[5] However, such attacks did not necessarily succeed, as the North Vietnamese found in 1968 and 1972, and the Egyptians (eventually) and Syrians when attacking Israel in 1973.

Soviet strategy assumed that any non-theatre war was going to be a long war. That assumption went to the heart of how the Soviet people and economy must be mobilised in peacetime for that possibility. The related Soviet concept of the rear (*tyl*) was another significant component of Soviet military strategy. Destroying the rear of an opponent, in other words the population base and its industrial and transport capacities, was the same as destroying its front-line forces. The Soviets made less distinction between the two than did Western military theory, a point that is, or rather should be, relevant to the modern understanding of strategy. Post-1945 Soviet military publications – newspapers, journal articles and books – believed in the implacable hostility of the Western countries towards the Soviet Union, and incorporated this belief into Soviet military training and planning. Thus, Soviet strategy was long-term; incorporated a variety of domestic and foreign inputs, which were refracted through Marxism-Leninism; and exhibited, in its pronouncements and actions, both earnestness and deception.[6]

Soviet strategy had to be assessed by the West alongside the potent Soviet operational capability that had to be thwarted. In May 1945, considering the possibility of war between the Soviet Union and an Anglo-American alliance, the British Joint Planning Staff anticipated that Soviet resilience would prevent a speedy end, and that the conflict could only be waged as a total war, entailing, for the Allies, a fully mobilised American war economy, as well as German support.[7] Stalin would have agreed, which was a reason why he was determined to neutralise Germany as a whole and/or establish a Soviet-occupied client state in East Germany. A powerful Red Army in position in eastern Europe was very different to the situation after the First World War. Moreover, the very fast demobilisation of American forces strengthened the relative position of the Soviet military.

Unwilling to risk a return to interwar isolationism, the Americans, struggling to define and implement a relevant conception of national security,[8] instead turned to containment. This strategy was outlined in 1946–7 by George Kennan, the acting head of the American diplomatic mission in Moscow. He offered, like most commentators, much that was a statement of the obvious, as well as of ideas that were already circulating. Nevertheless, the articulation and publication of his assessment was still pertinent, and the popularisation of views in this fashion is important to debates within and outside government. Containment was to be expressed through American engagement, the establishment of regional security pacts, and the rebuilding of Western Europe through the Marshall Plan aid offered in 1947.[9] Military assistance was provided to Greece and Turkey from 1947, the first helping to defeat the Communists in the Greek Civil War, which ended in 1949.[10] However, aside from the key element of conflict on the ground between Greeks, that was also a war determined by the failure of communist strategy and the consequences of division between the communist powers as Yugoslavia came to oppose the Soviet-backed Communists.

The American strategic repertoire (like counterparts among allies and opponents) included the development and operations of espionage organisations, particularly the CIA, as well as measures against what were termed subversives, as in the McCarren Internal Security Act (1950) and the McCarren–Walter Act (1952) in the United States. The passage of civil rights legislation in the 1950s was regarded as part of a strategy of countering the risk of disaffection and Soviet subversion, an element that tends to be underplayed due to the stress on African-American agency in the shape of the civil rights movement.

So also in Britain, with the Labour governments of 1945–51 and their Conservative successors of 1951–64 trying to keep the working class away from communism by providing social welfare and, eventually, consumerism. This also became the basic domestic strategy in western Europe. For all powers, propaganda was an important aspect of the strategy of anti-subversion and of cementing the domestic base.[11]

At the same time, external strategy was being defined in terms of a limited war. The development of nuclear weaponry by the Soviet Union, a coup achieved by the combination of espionage and a massive expend-iture of resources on creating production facilities, ended the American monopoly in 1949. This change made deterrence readily necessary, and, indeed, necessary as a protective step. This nuclear duality, one that was to be speedily replicated by thermonuclear weapons (hydrogen bombs), also ensured that strategies had to take central notice of the value of a limited war, in other words a non-nuclear one. In consequence, but also as a response to Soviet superiority in conventional forces, the United States adopted a strategy of 'no roll-back', despite the Republicans, who won these elections, having rejected 'containment' in the 1952 elections as too passive and calling for 'roll-back'. This strategy helped ensure that the United States did not act in support of the Hungarian rebellion against Soviet domination in 1956, or, indeed, intervene in Cuba against the rise of Fidel Castro in the late 1950s.

Such caution, however, was scarcely new. It had been seen in American caution about support for the Guomindang in the late 1940s, even though the United States then alone had the atomic bomb. Moreover, in late 1950, the Truman administration had responded cautiously in the Korean War (1950–3) towards developing military possibilities in North Korea, and had not sought to escalate the war by attacking China, notably the Manchurian airbases from which Soviet aircraft operated on behalf of the North Koreans. The guiding principle for the American government was to contain the spread of communism where it existed, to be patient, and to assume that communism would wither away due to its inherent flaws.

Yet, alongside a desire for a limited, non-nuclear war, strategies for nuclear conflict were developed. In part, this was because of fears that such a conflict would break out, but Soviet conventional strength also encouraged that response. In 1953, the use of atomic weaponry was threatened by the Americans in order to secure an end to the Korean War. The success of this threat encouraged the view that nuclear weaponry had a major role to play in future strategy, as a capability, a deterrent and an option. This role also rested in fiscal and political contexts, including the heavy cost of conventional military capability and the manpower implications for the United States in a period of very low unemployment. The lower cost of nuclear weaponry appeared to offer more money for personal consumption and social welfare, and, thereby, in effect to provide another level of security, and thus a different strategic buffer.

The essential stages in American nuclear strategy were, firstly, an immediate nuclear response to a conventional Soviet assault; secondly, the massive nuclear retaliation outlined in 1954 by John Foster Dulles, the American Secretary of State; thirdly, the 'flexible response' theory, outlined in 1962 under the Kennedy administration, a theory which was capable of many interpretations; and, eventually, American stress on an enhanced conventional response, albeit with the potential backing of strategic and tactical nuclear weaponry.

A capability for deterrence was an important aspect of a strategy of containment. American air force thinking was dominated by strategic nuclear bombing. The ability to strike at Soviet centres was seen as an effective deterrent, and was given added force by the role of officers from

Strategic Air Command (SAC) in the senior ranks of the Air Staff, and by a fascination, on their part and that of commentators and some of the public, with aerial self-sufficiency. At the same time, the American focus on strategic air power, a focus that ensured that overall American military spending remained strong after the Korean War, encouraged concern about the Soviet counterpart, which, indeed, was being developed and swiftly threatened the United States itself with nuclear attack.[12]

Strategic air power and SAC were contrasted with tactical air power and Tactical Air Command (TAC), which were essentially a matter of ground support. There was no equivalent of operational air power. This reflected both the fact that the operational level of war had not been adequately conceptualised, and also the extent to which air force leaders were determined to argue that they could provide a war-winning capability and could do so without any joint or combined dimensions. This argument was attractive and convenient. It also inserted the technologies of atomic weaponry and long-range aircraft into a clear definition of strategic effectiveness. This definition was closely linked to the struggle for funding.

In the early 1950s, very differently, it was feared that the communist assault on South Korea in 1950 might be matched in western Europe. As a result, NATO developed as a defensive system, including with the preparation of resistance networks. This domestic dimension was an aspect of strategy and one that in some countries, notably Italy, overlapped with politics, as both narrowly and more widely defined. Part of the strategy was an attempt to develop opposition and division in the Soviet bloc. This was designed to lessen the military value of eastern Europe in the event of war. Aside from support for resistance groups, the development of émigré forces, and a major propaganda offensive, notably by radio,[13] there was a growing interest in trying to exploit divisions between the Soviet Union and its satellite regimes. This interest led to attempts to woo Tito's Yugoslavia from 1948, and to support for Romania when, from the 1960s, it took an independent stance in the communist bloc. The strategy became more successful in the 1970s when it finally exploited the Sino-Soviet split. Indeed, the attempts and often ability of second-rank and lesser powers to manoeuvre between the superpowers added greatly to the complexity of the strategic situation for both the superpowers and the lesser powers.[14]

Stalin, who died in 1953, was eventually replaced by Nikita Khrushchev, the party First Secretary from 1953 to 1964. A committed communist, who actively advanced Soviet interests in the Third World, notably through arms sales to Egypt, Khrushchev sought to achieve Soviet goals in Europe by demilitarising the Cold War and making communist rule more attractive to the subject people of eastern Europe. In 1955, he began articulating the doctrine of 'peaceful co-existence', an expression drawn from Lenin's canonical writings. This was a major change from the Stalinist doctrine of the inevitability of war between socialism and capitalism. Khrushchev tried to strengthen the communist bloc itself through de-Stalinisation. Economic growth that now emphasised consumer goods was intended to safeguard living conditions, and thus enhance popular support for communism.

The project of change, however, went out of control in Hungary, where a conflation of nationalism, popular pressure for change and élite liberalisation led to a hostility to communist rule. In an instructive instance of the role of strategic misunderstanding, one that, in this case, drew on an inaccurate paranoia, the KGB presented nationalist activism as ideological sabotage actively sponsored by Western intelligence agencies. The Soviet Union brutally reimposed control in 1956, as it did not do in Poland where the situation was less provocative. The situation was also easier to contain for a geopolitical or contextual reason as Poland was not a communist frontier territory.

Primarily military, Soviet strategy was also very much linked to a struggle to dominate the public space of opinion. In the late 1950s, this included Soviet claims that the United States and western Europe were being overtaken by the Soviets in military hardware, technological capability and standard of living. Indeed, the Cold War in part became a battle over technological modernity, both the reality of it and the perception. Competition over living standards reflected the increasing sense in the late 1950s that the Cold War was a battle for the hearts and minds of consumers on the home front, as much as of armed forces and military-technological development. A spirit of can-do optimism was propagated in the Soviet Union as Khrushchev saw 'a race to see who could do the best job at supplying the ordinary fellow on the beach with his cold drink'.[15] In the event, the Americans could deliver rockets and consumerism, while the Soviets found the latter an impossible goal, in large part because of the serious deficiencies of a Communist-controlled economy. This was apparent in the 1960s and far more so by the 1980s. These deficiencies also wrecked the optimistic claims about the provision of public services that were a key aspect of communist legitimation.

Meanwhile, the strategic debate was crowded out by the development of missile technology, notably long-range ballistic missiles. From 1957, there was a twofold Western response to the enhanced Soviet missile capability and to the crucial uncertainty about future developments. Notions of graduated nuclear retaliation, through the use of short-range ('tactical') nuclear weapons in association with conventional forces based in western Europe, were complemented by a policy of developing an effective intercontinental retaliatory second-strike capability, in order to make it dangerous to risk attack on the United States. This attempt to give force to the notion of massive nuclear retaliation[16] entailed replacing vulnerable manned bombers both with less vulnerable submarines equipped with Polaris missiles and with more potent land-based missiles located in reinforced concrete silos.

Weapons technology was discussed in terms of strategic implications. The American navy argued for conventional responses backed up by a nuclear threat to Soviet cities from its invulnerable submarines. From 1961, ballistic-missile submarines went on patrol. They could be deployed against China as well as the Soviet Union. However, the possibility of a sophisticated management of deterrence and retaliation by the United States was lessened by the extent to which the Polaris and Poseidon missiles were not very accurate and only suitable for their 'counter-value', in particular as a second-strike response if the land-based missiles had been knocked out in a surprise Soviet attack or used in response to one. It was only with the D5 Trident missiles that submarines became more accurate and could compete with land-based missiles.

The inhibiting effect of the destructive potential of intercontinental nuclear weaponry served as much to enhance the possibility of a nuclear war, by increasing interest in defining a sphere for tactical nuclear weapons and in planning an effective strategic nuclear first strike, as it did to lessen the chance of a great-power war, or to increase the probability that such a conflict would be essentially conventional. The risk of nuclear destructiveness, indeed, made it important to prevent escalation to full-scale war. This risk encouraged interest in defining forms of warfare that could exist short of such escalation, and in developing strategy accordingly, strategy in terms of planning, doctrine, procurement, deployment and training.

American critics of Eisenhower argued that his emphasis on massive nuclear retaliation both failed to match Soviet developments and closed the necessary option of limited wars. This argument influenced strategy under the following Kennedy administration (1961–3), by encouraging American interest then in limited nuclear war as well as in conventional conflict, each of which appeared necessary capabilities for a response to Soviet allies, including China. Moreover, Kennedy considerably increased defence spending as a key aspect of the pursuit of strategic superiority over the Soviet Union, a pursuit that included the race to put men on the moon, one won by the Americans in 1969.

At the same time, international tensions increased as a consequence of Soviet pressure. What became the core strategic symbol, the Berlin Wall, built from early 1961 between East and West Berlin, was a breach of the agreements between the occupying powers that permitted the citizens of Berlin to move freely through the whole city. This challenge to the Western powers, which was part of a Soviet plan for the signing of a peace treaty with East Germany designed to end Allied occupation rights in Berlin, indicated the extent to which Khrushchev's goal of the Eastern bloc 'stabilisation' of interests was, in practice, destabilising at the international level. While Western support protected West Berlin, it could not bring German reunification, which encouraged the West Germans to ease relations with the Soviet Union by means of what came to be called *Ostpolitik*.

In turn, Soviet pressure on Western interests became more frequent under Khrushchev in the early 1960s, reflecting in part his misplaced determination, while preserving peace, to gain, notably, prestige within the Soviet Union and the divided communist bloc, as well as success in, and by, pressing the West. This strategy of continual pressure, a strategy that drew on inherent Soviet assumptions about international relations and the asymmetry of communism and capitalism, led to a crisis over Cuba in 1962. In the face of American pressure, notably an effective naval blockade of Cuba and a maritime interdiction operation, Khrushchev, in the event, withdrew the missiles he had located there. These missiles very much posed a strategic threat to the United States, while other missiles were intended to deter any American invasion. This duality indicated the extent to which weapons systems could serve more than one strategic purpose.

Thereafter, American–Soviet relations were eased by the restraint Khrushchev learned. With the international system seen, after the crises over Berlin (1961) and Cuba (1962), in terms of risk, as much as opportunity, and with class conflict not at the forefront of Soviet thought, it became easier to think in terms of the co-existence of West and East. However, the increase in American defence spending in the early 1960s, the rise in the number of American nuclear warheads, the Soviet climbdown during the Cuban missile crisis, and the prospect of massive American nuclear retaliation, apparently lessened the Soviet threat in Europe. The Soviets, however, fearing attack, had responded to the Cuban missile crisis by expanding their intercontinental missile force. This was done so as to lessen their vulnerability to American attack, notably a nuclear first strike.

The rapid missile build-up in practice enhanced Soviet strategic capability. Moreover, the Americans proved mistaken in their conviction that they could use similar pressure to that in the Berlin and Cuba crises to force other communist powers to back down. Ho Chi Minh, the North Vietnamese leader, was not to back down. Thus, the Cuban crisis was followed by stability in Europe, but not elsewhere.

During the Berlin crisis, Kennedy had reaffirmed the willingness of America to use atomic weaponry, even if the Soviets did not. He, nevertheless, sought to move from the idea of 'massive retaliation' with nuclear weaponry to a policy that did not automatically assume escalation to nuclear war. This move was an aspect of a more general strategy of 'flexible response' adopted in 1962, in part as an answer to communist 'wars of national liberation', which, in the aftermath of the Soviets backing down over Cuba that year, were perceived as posing a greater threat than full-scale conventional conflict. Proposing a symmetrical posture and strategy, 'flexible response' postulated a spectrum of conflict, from nuclear deterrence and conventional warfare at one end, to guerrilla combat and non-military applications of national power at the other, with the possibility of the careful escalation of forces as an aspect of the response.

Whatever the language, the strategic options were greatly affected by the weaponry. Any conventional conflict between the two blocs would be unlikely to be anything less than devastating, and would rapidly become nuclear. Thus, alongside the possibility of a first-strike attack to pre-empt the arithmetic of missile deterrence, the nuclear deterrent helped prevent not only nuclear war but also, and more unexpectedly, the devastation of high-tech conventional warfare between well-resourced alliances. The nuclear deterrent created a new type and level of strategic uncertainty, one that related not only to the possible use of nuclear weaponry, but also to the consequences of the existence of such weaponry for the strategic character of non-nuclear conflict.

Partly as a result, space had to be found for a practice of limited warfare, in the shape of indirect conflict as far as the major powers were concerned. This practice reflected the issues of the period, at once opportunities and challenges, whether predictable or unpredictable. An emphasis on such limited war was readily apparent in American policy in the 1950s and 1960s, even though this was a period of enormous expenditure on the military and of a marked enhancement of military capability. The emphasis on limited war could be seen in the Korean and Vietnam wars, notably in the decision to restrict the geographical scope of each war. The United States did not intervene in the Chinese Civil War, did not attack China during the Korean War, and did not invade North Vietnam. In part, this strategy reflected concern during the Vietnam War about the prospect of attack by communist powers in Europe, the Mediterranean and Korea; or of Chinese intervention in North Vietnam. The North Vietnamese did not wage limited war, but both the Soviet Union and China did during the Vietnam War. So also for other powers. In duration and scale, the India–China War of 1962 was such a limited war, as was the India–Pakistan War of 1965. Israeli forces did not advance on Cairo, Damascus or Amman during the 1967 Six Days' War.

The resort to a strategy of limited war continues to be contentious in the United States today, and particularly with the Vietnam War. That serves as a reminder of the difficulties of defending strategy in a public sphere. The Vietnam War drives this process for Americans because of the experience of failure, indeed affront of failure for many, and the need to explain it. During that conflict, limited war was matched in the case of the communist great powers, but not of the local powers providing the bulk of the military opposition, both North Vietnam and the Viet Cong, as well as their counterparts in Cambodia and Laos. More generally, the asymmetries of strategy were readily apparent in the conflicts of the period, notably those of insurgency and counter-insurgency. These asymmetries were of goal, more than technology, however much the latter tended to attract attention. That looked towards the situation after the Cold War ended, and notably in the 2000s.

Another aspect of the emphasis on limited war was presented by 'hybrid warfare' in the shape of secret action, as by the CIA in Iran and Guatemala in the 1950s. The CIA became a key force not only in the implementation of American strategy, but also in its formulation. This led to total failure in Cuba in 1961 with the Bay of Pigs intervention, the apogee of the attempt to overthrow the Castro regime through subversion, an attempt that continued for several years thereafter, but again without any success. The Americans were to be more successful in the 1980s in exerting pressure on the Sandinista regime in Nicaragua, because the latter has land borders across which insurgent forces could operate. However, again, this strategy proved less effective than had been anticipated.

As a reminder that strategy drew on different currents, the emphasis on deterrence underlined the need for reliable intelligence, a key component of strategy,[17] and reflected need, practicality, and a stress in the culture of planning on restraint, caution and sobriety in judgement. The very idea of a Cold War presupposed restraint, with both sides avoiding direct and large-scale conflict that might have apocalyptic consequences. Such restraint generally characterised American policy, as the strategic vocabulary of the Cold War became that of mutual vulnerability, bipolar balance and stability, a normative vocabulary that led both to the quest for particular advantage and to the constraints of deterrence and, subsequently in addition, arms control.

In another instance of a key feature of strategy, that of the signalling of resolve, problems over Berlin, Cuba and relations with the Soviet Union encouraged Kennedy to turn to Vietnam to project strength. This also provided an opportunity to be seen to oppose the communist advance anywhere in the Third World. That had become a major area of volatility with the weakness and/or end of the western European empires. It also became a sphere of strategic engagement as the Soviet Union and China sought to challenge the United States indirectly, by encouraging supporters to attack and overthrow America's allies. As a reminder of the key element of strategic context, and its ability to draw on a number of strands, these attacks brought together notions of popular warfare, nationalism and revolutionary communism, in a programme of revolutionary struggle in which success was believed to be inevitable.

In turn, fear of anti-colonial movements and of communist exploitation encouraged a view in the United States that the West's front line ran round the world, and that communism had not only to be contained in Europe in order to prevent it spreading. In March 1955, in the aftermath of the end of the French–Vietnamese War in 1954, John Foster Dulles, the Secretary of State, told the Senate Foreign Relations Committee that, in south-east Asia, he regarded 'the subversive problem [as] . . . a greater menace than the open military menace of the activities of the Communists'.[18]

In practice, strategies of containment, with their assumption that world politics could be shaped in terms of a geopolitical and ideological competition directed by the great powers, were challenged by independent initiatives. Some were really or ostensibly linked to the ideological dynamic of the Cold War, but many were not, or not in the way sought by the great powers. Thus North Vietnam manoeuvred for independence by playing off China and the Soviet Union, and followed its own policy and timetable.

In turn, the Americans found it difficult to direct their allies in the 1960s: France withdrew from the military structure of NATO in 1966, Britain refused to help in the Vietnam War, and West Germany developed an independent *Ostpolitik*. In the Third World, the Americans saw the local military as a key support for containment, a policy that worked very well in Latin America, Pakistan, South Korea and Indonesia, but that failed in South Vietnam.

Concern that communist success in South Vietnam would be followed by advances elsewhere arose from a serious measure of confusion both about the ready export of revolution and concerning how best to prevent this export. Indeed, there was an incoherence in the pursuit of strategy in the United States, an incoherence that was more serious than the operational issues that tend to engage attention when explaining the problems confronting the Americans.

The Vietnam War, moreover, underlined the problems of American policy-making structures in a dynamic context. The Joint Chiefs of Staff disagreed among themselves and found, against a background of *ad hoc* decision-making, that successive presidents would not rely on them. Instead, Robert McNamara, the Secretary of Defense, a keen management guru, sought to direct through micromanagement, and ended up compromising both strategy and operational capability. Congress played a complicating role, but there was no ability to prevent a mission creep linked to a pressure to bring forward the means to further goals that were not adequately assessed.[19] There were different problems with reference to areas that did not engage this level of attention.

American strategy was intended to persuade an opponent to change direction, and an assessment of its viability requires a look at this opponent. North Vietnamese policy left no basis for the idea, backed by France in particular, that the future of South Vietnam could have been settled by negotiation. Indeed, meeting in December 1963, the ninth plenary session of the North Vietnamese Communist Party's Central Committee criticised the Soviet notion of 'peaceful co-existence', decided to step up the war in South Vietnam, and pushed forward more militant politicians.

This was not a stance that American strategy adequately confronted. President Lyndon B. Johnson (r. 1963–9) wanted to avoid an explicit choice between war and disengagement, as well as to apply more easily the strategic concept of graduated pressure. Committed to the need to show determination, Johnson was also convinced that the United States had a worthwhile mission in the world and must heed its calling. He did not see an automatic clash between the domestic and foreign spheres, because, to Johnson, this global mission was linked to his state-building at home.[20] The role of the communist great powers led American policy-makers to conclude that it was necessary to demonstrate that these powers could not succeed by means of such a proxy war. Thus, Vietnam became the place to show that the United States could, and would, act and, because it was this place, became the country where America must act. This took precedence over political and military practicalities, and was linked to a failure to admit the possibility of error and a related reluctance to develop new plans.[21]

This reluctance contributed to the shock caused by the surprise Tet Offensive of 1968. The role of perception and impression in strategic capability was amply seen as this offensive, however misleadingly, contributed greatly to a sense of crisis in the American world order. Winning the initiative was a key element in this perception, and led to a failure to note that there was no popular uprising or American defeat.

Yet, North Vietnamese strategy did not depend on continued success. Instead, it focused on denying their opponents control over territory while maintaining operational pressure on them. The details and success of the latter were less important than the former. By refusing to fight on American terms, the North Vietnamese retained the strategic initiative and, despite great strain, altered both the equations of success and its parameters.[22] A variety of remedies were sought by the Americans, including the use of more air power, pacification programmes, and trying to shift more of the burden of the fighting to South Vietnamese forces. The last was particularly popular with Richard Nixon, who became president in 1969, as it offered a way to end the draft and reduce the political cost of the war. Domestic goals set the strategy, with the domestic and international dimensions closely intertwined. The political dimension also came first in international terms. A *rapprochement* with China in 1972 helped lead North Vietnam in 1973 to terms under which American troops could withdraw.

This *rapprochement* and the Vietnam agreement accorded with the *Realpolitik* fostered by Henry Kissinger, National Security Advisor from 1969 to 1973 and Secretary of State from 1973 to 1977. In turn, his strategic ideas drew on his scholarly perceptions which looked back to his academic work on Klemens von Metternich, Austrian foreign minister from 1809 to 1848.

The reaction within the United States against the Vietnam War, or, more particularly, against its longevity and failure, led to a major rethinking of the political context of strategic decision-making. The War Powers Resolution (Kennedy–Cooper Act), passed by a Democratic-dominated Congress in November 1973, over Nixon's veto, stipulated consultation with Congress before American forces were sent into conflict, and a system of regular presidential report and congressional authorisation thereafter. This law, which was an attempt to scale back the accretions stemming from the 1947 National Security Resolution, was to be evaded by successive presidents and was not to be enforced by Congress. Nevertheless, the law symbolised a post-Vietnam restraint that set the strategic parameters, discouraging American military interventionism in the 1970s and 1980s. The contrast with the Soviet bloc's ambitious role in a series of conflicts in sub-Saharan Africa in the 1970s was striking. This, however, was not a contrast that attracted much attention in the United States.

However, the strategic consequences of defeat in Vietnam were tempered by the American *rapprochement* with China, by Vietnamese exhaustion, and by the strategic benefits derived from the replacement in 1965–6 of Sukarno, the left-wing nationalist leader in Indonesia, by a pro-American military dictatorship. Mao Zedong had come to regard better relations with the United States as a way to secure China's status as a great power, and these relations were a major strategic advantage for both powers as they were seen as a deterrent to the Soviet Union.

Similarly, the context changed in the Soviet Union. A growing conservatism owed much to the rejection of the adventurism associated with Khrushchev and his replacement in 1964 by the more complacent Leonid Brezhnev. In 1971, in his speech to the Twenty-Fourth Party Congress, Brezhnev called for international security and devoted scant space to the cause of 'national liberation'. Conflict in sub-Saharan Africa, notably in Angola and Ethiopia, saw opportunistic Soviet-bloc interventions, but these were *ad hoc* rather than game-changers. Indeed, the communist economies were hit by the economic downturn of the mid-1970s, and China, under Deng Xiaoping, its dominant leader from 1978 until 1989, cleaved to the American alignment. This set the context for the very different stages of the last decade of the Cold War in the 1980s. The alignment with China meant that the United States could focus on the Soviet Union and, as it turned out, win the Cold War far more rapidly and cheaply than would have been anticipated.

Developing technologies played a role. From the Second World War, air power provided strategic 'reach', but there were also significant innovations in capability at a variety of scales. These involved political strategies of securing basing. For example, in the 1980s, attempts to expand the repertoire of American strength included the deployment of tactical nuclear weapons carried on cruise and Pershing intermediate-range missiles. This deployment proved divisive in western Europe, with particular concern about it in West Germany. Both President Ronald Reagan (r. 1981–9) and British prime minister Margaret Thatcher (r. 1979–90) devoted considerable effort to winning support in western Europe. The zero option was offered of no deployment if all Soviet intermediate-range missiles were removed from Europe, with Reagan keen on it as a first step for getting rid of all nuclear weapons. In contrast, Thatcher supported the measure only because she believed the Soviets would not agree: she wanted the American missiles deployed in order to counter Soviet conventional superiority. This was a reprise of one aspect of the general strategy of nuclear deterrence, notably of the NATO strategy, although the Soviet strategy towards China had aspects of the same, as the Soviets were concerned about the size of the Chinese army and the vulnerability of the Soviet Far East.

Separately, and without the same strategic implications of deployment, there was an American commitment to the development of new space-mounted weaponry. The 'Star Wars' programme or Strategic Defense Initiative (SDI), outlined by Reagan in a speech on 23 March 1983, was designed to enable the United States to dominate space, using space-mounted weapons to destroy Soviet satellites and missiles. In 1986, albeit in a planned test, an American interceptor rocket fired from Guam hit a mock missile warhead dead on. This test encouraged the Soviets to negotiate. It was not clear that the technology would ever work; and this point looked ahead to debates in the 2010s over the effectiveness of new technologies. However, as a reminder of the problems of strategic miscommunication, American preparations encouraged the KGB to report, inaccurately, that the United States was planning a nuclear first strike.

On 2 September 1981, building on the Carter presidency's idea of a 'countervailing strategy', of greater destructiveness in the event of a Soviet first strike, such that the Soviet Union would end the attack or risk total annihilation, Reagan had warned (correctly) that the United States was prepared to pursue an accelerated nuclear arms race with the Soviet Union. Visiting Britain in June 1982, Reagan addressed British parliamentarians in Westminster, calling for a 'crusade for freedom' and for Marxism-Leninism to be discarded on the 'ash-heap of history'. Europe was the centre of his concern: 'From Stettin [Szczecin] on the Baltic to Varna on the Black Sea', there had been no free elections for three decades, while Poland, where the independent trade union movement, Solidarity, was under assault from the Communist state, was, he declared, 'at the centre of European civilisation'. This approach did not accept the idea that Poland should be securely located in the communist bloc. If it was not so, that would challenge the Soviet position in East Germany.

Reagan also provided encouragement and support for the Afghan resistance to the Soviet occupation that began in 1979, notably, from 1985–6, shoulder-fired ground-to-air missiles. This support strengthened the resistance, as well as providing the Soviets with a factor to blame when explaining continued opposition there, the latter an important aspect of the situation.

There has, however, been considerable controversy over whether Reagan had a grand strategy for confronting and weakening communism, as argued, for example, by John Lewis Gaddis.[23] Alternatively, it has been claimed that there was no such strategy, but, rather, a set of beliefs, notably the clashing aspirations of destroying communism and ending the risk of war: a 'crusade for freedom' alongside 'peace through strength'.[24] A 'grand strategy' and 'a set of beliefs' are not as incompatible as might be suggested. Bringing the two elements together, Reagan came to the conclusion, as argued by Caspar Weinberger, the Secretary for Defense, Richard Perle and others, that the arms race would be won by the United States, not least as the race would ruin the Soviet Union, and so end the Cold War. The eventual collapse of the Soviet bloc in 1989, and of the Soviet Union two years later, can be presented in terms of the success of American strategy, notably the economic burden on the Soviet Union of having to respond to a military build-up that the Americans could readily fund through the bond markets, a facility that the Soviet Union could not match. In practice, there is scant evidence of such strategic insights, let alone planning, and certainly not on a reliable timetable.

American military strategy in the Reagan years, meanwhile, increasingly focused on a confidence that a sub-nuclear war could be won. In particular, the Americans were emboldened by the Israeli success against the Syrian air force over Lebanon in 1982. This demonstrated, in the crucial test of combat, the superiority, in American eyes, of American avionics and air weaponry over their Soviet counterparts, and contributed to an AirLand Doctrine of victory through joint operations. The arguments arising from the competition for defence funding contributed to this belief, as did the need for a new military doctrine to deal with the reality that the Americans no longer had conscription and therefore could not maintain an army of the size that had met commitments in the 1960s, and certainly not one that matched Soviet strength. A group of defence politicians, intellectuals and opportunists, notably Weinberger, Perle and Paul Wolfowitz, all found the AirLand Doctrine useful as well as attractive. The doctrine fitted in with, indeed gave energy to, both the practice of strategic planning and the strategic rhetoric of the period.

As there was no war with the Soviet Union, the likely sustainability of the American strategy in prolonged combat was unclear, a situation that remains the case. The assumption that a sub-nuclear war could be fought without the feared escalation, and that containment in this fashion was possible, presumed a congruence in Soviet thinking that was unproven. Moreover, this assumption ignored all the RAND and other think tank studies of the 1960s and 1970s that concluded that escalation was unavoidable once fighting had broken out between the Soviet Union and the United States.

At the level of weaponry, in addition, there were questions of effectiveness, and notably if the weaponry had been used against a genuinely hard opponent, such as the Soviet Union, and not against soft opponents, such as Syria or, in 1991, Iraq. 'Star Wars' weaponry certainly failed to live up to its billing. It was hoped, with more reason, that stealth technology would permit the American penetration of Soviet air defences, obliging the Soviets to retain more aircraft at home. This was an instance of technology affecting the parameters of operational capability, rather than of vindicating or invalidating strategic choices. At the same time, hopes of enhanced capability due to technological developments addressed issues of doctrinal purpose and strategic role,[25] as part of the continuous struggle for priority and resources. Moreover, the emphasis on stealth technology for aircraft was linked to the more active strategic stance also seen with the 'forward offensive strategy' of the American navy, which increased the mobile missile pressure on the Soviet Union as well as challenging Soviet defensive buffers at sea. The Ocean Venture '81 exercise showed the capability to deploy a large force into the Norwegian and Barents seas. Already strong, the American navy was built up.[26]

Despite planning for a large-scale war with the West, the Soviet bloc fell without any conflict, other than localised fighting within Soviet-bloc states, notably in Romania. Moreover, this brought the Cold War to an end. There was an important military dimension, in that Mikhail Gorbachev was unwilling to use the Soviet Army to maintain client regimes, notably East Germany. Visiting Prague in April 1987, Gorbachev repudiated the Brezhnev strategy of intervention in order to uphold communism ('the defence of the Socialist Commonwealth' in Soviet terms), intervention which had been used in Czechoslovakia in 1968. Instead, Gorbachev claimed that 'fraternal parties determine their political line with a view to national conditions'. On 7 December 1988, he announced, significantly at the United Nations rather than at a communist gathering, that eastern European states should be free to choose their own political path. In the speech, he also declared that the Soviet armed forces would be cut, and thus, publicly, that attempts to match America's military build-up could not be sustained.

A contrary policy was attempted when nationalism threatened the Soviet Union itself, but these steps, notably the deployment of troops in Moscow in 1991, and earlier in the Baltic republics, did not intimidate the nationalists. Indeed, Russian nationalism, as organised by Boris Yeltsin, proved the key force in the collapse of both communism and the Soviet Union in 1991.

At the end, the Cold War remained as it had long been, a conflict of limited action and infinite potential. It was a struggle in which politics within, and between, the rival systems were particularly to the fore. There was a parallel with the earlier struggle between Christendom and Islam, in that protagonists with different civilisational values competed, with strategies focused on the interplay of long periods of limited conflict alternating with shorter ones of warfare, all the while laid over with constant doctrinal and military alertness.

The strategic culture of Soviet communism was a key element. Alongside an ideological commitment to an international mission, and to the inevitability of Marxist victory, came a strong sense of vulnerability. In part, this sense reflected real threats. These included serious challenges to territorial integrity and interests, notably from the late 1910s to the mid-1940s, from Japan in the Far East. There were also threats to the very existence of the Soviet regime, particularly in the Russian Civil War of 1918–21, and then again from Germany in 1941–2. Yet, there was also a paranoid concern about threats that were non-existent or greatly overplayed. This sense of vulnerability can be traced back certainly to the early seventeenth century. More recent events, and the perception of them, were also significant. These included foreign intervention in the Russian Civil War, the working of the Leninist-Stalinist political system predating the Second World War and its consistent belief in conspiracies linked to foreign powers, the experience of unexpected German attack in 1941, and the American development and deployment first of the atom bomb and then of the hydrogen bomb, and then of submarines armed with ballistic missiles.

Central to Soviet strategy, this sense of vulnerability encouraged a major stress on military expenditure. The Soviet Union sought an all-round capability to match that of the United States, developing for example the world's second largest navy even though that was marginal to the Soviet focus on land, air and rocket power. Thus, had there been a war, the Soviet navy's ballistic missiles would have been differently mobile versions of other types of nuclear missiles on which there was a greater emphasis. The Soviets would have used their land-based missiles as their major strike force while the ballistic-missile submarines acted as the strategic reserve. Moreover, the Soviet navy lacked the opportunities to be a strategic tool by means of naval combat or commerce interdiction.

The United States had similarities in its strategic position, but also major differences. It also had a tradition of concern and rational fear, as well as of irrational fear or paranoia. Like the Soviet Union, there was heavy military expenditure. However, America's stronger economy, more liberal fiscal system, and alliance with states that provided massive liquidity, notably the oil-producing states, made it easier to manage this expenditure and thus to sustain the Cold War. America's alignment with China also proved crucial in weakening the relative position of the Soviet Union and strengthening that of the United States. As a consequence of these factors, the Soviet Union was in a weak situation whatever its internal developments. Elements of this earlier contrast are still pertinent today, in favour of the United States, when confrontation between the United States and China is discussed.

A focus on the United States and the Soviet Union leads to an under-playing of other strategic actors during the Cold War. The insurgency struggles against Western rule in the Third World showed the pursuit of strategy along the lines advocated by Mao Zedong in the 1930s. However, there was a chronological overlap with insurgencies against independent states, for example Nigeria and Sudan. Success for the insurgents in these cases proved more problematic than those against Western rule, and notably so if there was not the foreign support that could bring success, as there was with Indian intervention in 1971 in East Pakistan, which became Bangladesh. The protection of minority peoples in separatist struggles provided conventional forces with a target for attack, including, as in Biafra in eastern Nigeria in 1967–70, by means of blockade. The latter was an aspect of the anti-societal strategies that proved so significant in many civil wars.

In contrast, state-to-state conflicts, for example between India and Pakistan, and between Israel and its Arab neighbours, involved swift moves, notably by air attack and tank forces, in which there was a gain of enough advantage to signal both to the opponent and to other powers that a settlement had to be reached on acceptable terms, which Egypt and Syria were both forced to concede in 1967 and 1973. In 1980, Saddam Hussein of Iraq pursued this strategy when he attacked Iran by air and land, only to find that the latter was unwilling to accept his strategic equation and, instead, fought on, successfully overturning initial losses in a war that lasted until 1988. Such strategic asymmetries, in terms both of goals and of the response to losses, were more common than those dependent on differing force structures and weapons. Indeed, the significance of differences in the character of competing goals offered a common factor across the strategic landscape.

11

STRATEGIES FOR THE CURRENT WORLD

1990 –

Writing about very recent history and the present world is always hazardous. Even for then, it can be difficult to establish precisely what has happened and why. There is also a lack of clarity about the relative significance of events, developments and causes. This lack of clarity is more apparent for very recent events. Strategy is no exception to this process, but that does not prevent most literature on strategy from focusing on the present day, and from assessing history largely as it relates to the present and, more particularly, in terms of supposed 'lessons'. This last is a driver, focus and, crucially, funder of much commentary.

As a consequence again of the search for lessons for the present, the emphasis generally is on recent history. This is deployed both as the explanation of the present, and, more specifically, in relevant controversies, notably over goals and force structures. Thus, strategic reviews are considered and discussed in terms of the previous review, of most recent wars, and of threat assessments looking from the present into the future. The public relevance of strategy relates to the last, as do the processes, policies, and politics of military planning and procurement. Historians address the past; but strategists plan for the future, albeit while trying to draw on the 'lessons' of the past and while seeking to counter the 'strategy' of their domestic opponents.[1]

Change of course is the basic narrative in the discussion of military affairs for past, present and future, and notably so in the assessment of capability. Change, therefore, provides the conceptual challenge that has

240

to be addressed. In assessing this challenge, past, present and future are organised as a predictive analysis explained in part by the supposed lessons of the past. That approach has its weaknesses, but they do not prevent it from dominating the discussion. This dominance indeed underlines the roles of rhetoric and politics in analysis, and also the paradoxical view that, whatever its supposed lasting characteristics, strategy is best understood, and most relevant, if considered in the here and now, and illuminated by the recent past.

In an instance of a paradigm shift, the recent past, indeed the past as a whole, appeared to be transformed in 1989–91 by the end of the Cold War, the demise of the Soviet Union, and the rise of the United States to be the 'unipower' or 'hyperpower', the very pressure on the vocabulary an indicator of apparent novelty. That transformation in the late 1980s and early 1990s most famously encouraged optimistic talk of the 'end of history',[2] and there appeared to be a parallel to this 'end of history' in terms of a 'revolution in military affairs' (RMA) that was allegedly in process, and that the United States could define, analyse, control and benefit from, not least in order to contest another of the substitute-for-thought phrases of the period, 'the Clash of Civilisations'.[3] The rapid defeat of Iraq in 1991 by an American-led coalition appeared to demonstrate a 'transformation' in military capability, one, focused on the application of information warfare capabilities, that the United States dominated and could direct. At the same time, there was a conflation of essentially distinct processes, those of the triumph of a single hyperpower and the technological RMA.

Comparable importance as far as the United States was concerned was attached to a strategic planning process in which it was difficult after the demise of the Soviet Union to envisage a significant clash between major powers. Indeed, this assumption, which echoed that of the 1920s after the defeat and collapse of imperial Germany, represented a major bridge from the very last stage of the Cold War when relations with the Soviet Union had greatly improved.

That situation, however, changed from the 2000s, as the alignment between China and the United States begun in the early 1970s collapsed in political and military terms, although not, at that stage, economic ones: the last was not really threatened until a tariff conflict began in 2018. Moreover, relations between Russia and the United States deteriorated. In turn, by the mid-2010s, the prospect of conflict between the United States and either, or both, China and Russia came to the fore, and that at a time when China had become a great power to a degree that had not been the case in the 1970s or, even, a decade earlier. Moreover, China and Russia, alongside continuing tensions, became closer.[4]

There were obvious military consequences. In November 2018, the National Defense Strategy Commission of former senior Democratic and Republican officials warned of the risk of American defeat in a future great-power war. While this warning was given as the rationale for a clear pitch for more funds, and thus was an aspect of the inherent politics and rhetoric of strategy, the risk was indeed increasingly apparent in military, economic and geopolitical terms. Contextual factors were also directly relevant, notably that for the United States an absence of victory that might lead to a longer struggle would itself amount to a defeat, while, as an alternative, there was no wish for an escalation to nuclear war, and certainly not to full-scale nuclear war.

This changing situation at great-power level led to new strategic possibilities and requirements for these powers and for others, and within a context in the 2000s of apparently growing international anarchy, or, at least, disorder. This impression was created both by an upsurge in terrorist attacks and by the difficulty in bringing the initially promising Western interventions in Afghanistan and Iraq to a successful, or any, close. Thus, issued in the aftermath of the terrorist attacks in New York and Washington, and the subsequent intervention in Afghanistan, all in 2001, and before the invasion of Iraq in 2003, the National Security Strategy (NSS) issued in September 2002 was both strategically and operationally ambitious. Pressing the need for pre-emptive strikes in response to what were seen as the dual threats of terrorist regimes and 'rogue states' possessing or developing weapons of mass destruction – 'America is now threatened less by conquering states than we are by failing ones' – the strategy sought to transform the global political order in order to lessen the chance of these threats developing. To that end, its first paragraph proposed a universalist message that linked the end of the Cold War to the new challenge:

The great struggles of the twentieth century between liberty and totalitarianism ended with a decisive victory for the forces of freedom . . .

These values of freedom are right and true for every person, in every society – and the duty of protecting these values against their enemies is the common calling of freedom-loving people across the globe and across the ages . . . We will extend the peace by encouraging free and open societies on every continent.

However, in turn, strategy and procurement changed in response to developments in global power politics. The strategic guidance document issued by the Pentagon in January 2012 promised anew to defeat al-Qaeda, the group responsible for the 2001 terrorist attacks, and to counter the threat from unconventional weapons. Nevertheless, the document also drew back from interventionism and warned about China:

In the aftermath of the wars in Iraq and Afghanistan, the United States will emphasise non-military means and military-to-military coopera-tion to address instability and reduce the demand for significant US force commitments to stability operations . . . US forces will no longer be sized to conduct large-scale, prolonged stability operations . . . We will of necessity rebalance toward the Asia-Pacific region.[5]

President Barack Obama had told the Australian Parliament on 17 November 2011: 'As a Pacific nation, the United States will play a larger and long-term role in shaping this region and its future.' This shift in priority was linked to a cautious, but also prudent, move from a two-war capability to a 'win-spoil' plan entailing an ability to obtain victory in one regional war while thwarting the military plans of another adversary.

Three years later came what the Department of Defense termed the 'third offset strategy'. This referred to developing technologies and doctrine in response to the military-technological rise of China, Russia, Iran and North Korea, in order to reinforce asymmetries to the benefit of the United States.[6] This approach to strategy readily ran together policy, strategy, capabilities and tasks, employing strategy as the unifying concept and term. That process was more generally seen.

The shift towards the Pacific occurred at the same time as stability in the Middle East declined, a process linked to growing instability within the region and indeed in North Africa as well.[7] So also with the continu-ation into the Trump administration of this instability, and the focus, at the same time, on China's strategic competition in the NSS issued in December 2017.[8] In 2018, the Trump administration secured a record $716 billion budget for defence. Moreover, this sum proved a matter of pride for the administration. Whether spending that sum is a sign of strategic strength, in terms of developing capabilities and showing public commitment, or a possible cause of weakness, in terms of lessening overall effectiveness as an economy, and thus a power, deserves attention.

In light of a pattern of international uncertainty, responding to events may appear the obvious course for strategy and strategic choice.[9] Looking back, this response appears certainly so as a 'lesson', given the challenges to the strategy of the long term presented by such totally unexpected events as the Cuban missile crisis (1962), the fall of the Shah (1979), the fall of the Berlin Wall (1989), the Iraqi invasion of Kuwait (1990), the terrorist attacks on New York and Washington (2001) and the disorder of the Arab Spring (2011), a list that can be readily lengthened. Yet, alongside unpredictability, and notably unpredictability in terms of the sequencing and/or simultaneity of problems, events can, at least in part, be anticipated in terms of historical experience[10] and, in addition or alternatively, are in part understood with respect to longer-term strategic concepts and policies.

Moreover, the unexpected can be 'normalised' by these processes, not that this necessarily makes it easier to cope with. Thus, the Sino-Soviet split, arguably the key structural novelty of the 1960s, was normalised by Western commentators in terms of the pre-existing strategy of the containment of communism. Moreover, China from the 1960s could draw on the legacy of rivalry with Russia in the late nineteenth century, while the Soviet Union could see China as a new instance of Josip Broz Tito's Yugoslavia in ideological terms, as well as the geopolitical successor in east Asia to Japan.

Conversely, the end of the Sino-Soviet split was a central strategic development of the 2000s, and a process, rather than an event such as those listed earlier. This process also drew on longstanding elements of strategic culture, for example the Russian concept of *derzhavnost* ('great-power-ness'), which amounts at present to a determination to display power in order to gain prestige. This was very much a process seen with President Putin's successive interventions in Chechnya, Georgia, Crimea, Ukraine and Syria, which enhanced his personal popularity as well as fulfilling his sense of role.[11] Better relations with China greatly eased this process by offsetting Western deterrence, which, separately, had to respond to Chinese assertiveness.

Although translating strategy into real-world effects is far from easy, American strategy worked for the Cold War in part because it was operationalised in terms of containment, and both militarily and diplomatically so. In contrast, 'roll-back', which, in practice, might readily have become the strategy of war, was restricted to more particular contexts. If 'roll-back' became more significant in the 1980s, at least in Central America in the aftermath of the Sino-Soviet split, that was a peripheral area.

After the Cold War, the emphasis for the United States has been in effect a mix of 'containment' in the shape of resisting revisionist forces, whether non-state actors, rogue states (Iraq in 1991) or major powers, and 'roll-back' in the extension of NATO. It has not always been easy to devise the means, both military and diplomatic, for containment, and co-operation with allies has been of mixed value. Moreover, the context has deteriorated markedly for the United States as the Sino-Russian *rapprochement* has become a central element in the strategic situation. Similarly, there have been major changes in the strategic context for other powers and for non-state actors, changes that in part reflect developing great-power rivalries.[12]

The stages of international change were (and will be) accompanied by contestation in analysis, as strategies were debated in terms of goals, capabilities and procurement. This process was focused on the occasions when formal strategic reviews were carried out, and by means of such mechanisms; but, in practice, strategic choices were reviewed throughout. The cost of weapon systems encouraged this process, as it involved difficult trade-offs as well as the influence and profitability of manufacturers, and the political and military interests linked to them. Costs were increased by the pressure to be at the cutting edge, and in the context of a particularly high rate of military inflation and for all sophisticated weapon systems, although, crucially, not for hand-held firearms and for related weapons used for insurgent struggles.

Focusing on events, and on the particular contingencies they create and the requirements they lead to, poses problems for procurement policies for the military, with their long timespans, and also for the pursuit of long-term alliance strategies. Indeed, the central strategic goal, and means, of prioritisation, in practice, is both events-driven and rests on longer-term assumptions. This is related to the extent to which procurement involves legacies as well as predictions and within a context of competition between alternatives.

Thus, the debate in the 1990s and 2000s about the role of air power in the present and future was greatly shaped by American success in the 1991 Gulf War and resulting predictions. The American air campaign drew on the strategic ideas of Colonel John Warden, who suggested a 'five-ring model' of the modern state, each ring linked to a level of activity and a category of target. By attacking the strategic centre, it was claimed, the regime could be defeated. The command-and-control system, at once political and military, was regarded as crucial. Warden saw this approach as leading to the paralysis of the Iraqi military system, what, indeed, was later to be termed 'strategic paralysis'.[13]

However, as mounted in 1991, the bombing campaign included a focus on all rings, apart from the population. The Americans were confident that one of the rings would decisively collapse. In the event, virtually all Iraqi communications were rendered unusable, and Saddam Hussein was forced to carry out his council meetings in a Winnebago caravan, although it is not clear that 'strategic paralysis' was, as a result, imposed on the Iraqi regime. As a targeting method, the systems approach proved adequate, but when raised to the level of strategic success, it was flawed, as virtually no amount of damage would persuade Saddam to evacuate Kuwait, which was the intention of the bombing campaign, thus avoiding the need for a land offensive. The political consequences of the air assault were limited. The Iraqi government did not fall, and, as anticipated, it proved necessary for the coalition to launch a ground offensive, which was, indeed, rapidly successful. Air power was highly significant to this success, but as a crucial tactical aid to an important operational capability, rather than as a strategic tool. The same can be anticipated for the future. Moreover, the capabilities of air power in a defensive war, notably a counter-insurgency one, were less apparent in the discussion of its offensive capabilities.

Instead of treating the nature of war, as Clausewitz had, as the complex interaction of policy, emotion and chance, systems warfare in the case of the bombing plans for 1991 focused on pieces of a readily comprehensible design that supposedly, if neutralised, would bring down the whole. This was a parallel to the German confidence in planning prior to the First World War. As with that example, the friction of events was important, but so, even more, was the lack of a grasp of wider strategic issues and the resulting limitations with an operationally driven account of strategy.

More generally, 'strategic narratives', about particular conflicts, war in general and the international situation, reflected both the challenge of discussing particular events and the longer-term assumptions at issue. Such narratives are simplest if they deal with generalities. Thus, addressing the General Assembly of the United Nations on 25 September 2018, it was easy for President Emanuel Macron of France to denounce nationalism as the cause of 'global war' and an inevitable cause of 'defeat', and to call for 'a new world order with a human face' to tackle inequality. This drew a standing ovation, but provided few answers. So also with Macron's critique of nationalism at the time of the anniversary of the end of the First World War in November 2018 and subsequently. President Trump's call in the General Assembly that September to 'reject the ideology of globalism' and to 'embrace the doctrine of patriotism' also provided few answers, and was met with criticism. It was possibly, however, a more apposite response to the location and nature of power around the world. States remain the key players. Macron's other call in late 2018, for a European army, one repeated in 2019, came up against the strength of the national perspective and did not gain traction to match the rhetorical support.

Moving from the broad-brush approach, including rhetoric, the presentation of precise accounts of strategy can create many problems in practice for formal governmental mechanisms. This is notably so in terms of taking forward prioritisation, as it is extremely difficult to conduct discussion about this goal and process in public. Thus, in India, successive governments have found it difficult to articulate a military strategy in public, not least because of a reluctance to talk of a reliance on American help against the Chinese challenge. Such difficulties, both in India and elsewhere, are often a cause, at least a contributory cause, of military anger about the nature of public policy, and, more specifically but also differently, are related to the focus in much military discussion on capabilities and not tasks. The latter, however, is the key element in strategy. This will remain the case in the future.

STRATEGIES FOR THE FUTURE

In looking to the future, there are the literatures of developing weaponries and, separately, potential flashpoints or, rather, flash occasions.[14] There are also key contexts, notably the major, continuing – and unprecedented – growth in the size of the world's population that is the basic context, although the rate of this growth varies greatly. This growth provides continual change through time, and also leads to ongoing, as well as contingent, crises in the shape of urgent resource pressures or rather the response to the perception of such pressures. The rate of population growth may slow, but there is considerable aggregate growth still to come in the system due to the large numbers of the young approaching fertility. Even if the overall size stops at nine billion at mid-century, this is still a major rise on current numbers.

This population growth relates to strategy in a number of direct ways, including climate change; the issues of resources and resource security, notably for water, food and energy;[15] the nature of politics; problems in subjugating peoples; and the specific questions caused by the difficulties of socialising larger and larger generations of young men, especially if unemployment is a major issue. This socialising is made worse by the choice of so many parents to abort female foetuses, which helps ensure a major imbalance between men and women, and especially so in India. In China, girls are given up for adoption far more readily than boys. Whether or not these choices are referred to as family strategies, a term that is frequently employed, they certainly are part of the context within which domestic and international security challenges are shaped.

Issues relating to population growth and resource pressure are not directly germane to all societies, and especially not for Japan, the population of which is falling rapidly; while in much of Europe, the native population is static or in decline. However, these problems are particularly pertinent in regions with a high risk of conflict, notably Africa, the Middle East and south Asia. Sub-Saharan Africa, the area with the highest growth rate, is predicted by the UN Population Division as likely to have four billion people in 2100, compared to 180 million in 1950 and 2.2 billion by 2050. Because many Africans marry young, population growth there is accelerated. It is not accompanied by the degree of economic growth seen in India (albeit very unequally there) and, even more, China. *Per capita* wealth is a particular problem across much of Africa. In contrast, *per capita* wealth is rising in China thanks to growing prosperity and a slowing rate of population growth.

Resource issues are also directly relevant in so far as the resulting emphasis in conflict is on civil warfare, rather than that between states. For example, in the Plateau State of Nigeria in 2018, Fulani cattle-herders clashed violently with farmers from the Berom tribe. In turn, as a reminder of the analyses that are possible, analyses that, in turn, affect the consideration of strategies, that conflict was also presented as a religious one, with the Christian Berom accusing the Fulani of seeking an Islamic takeover. This interaction of resource competition and religious animosity is found across the *sahel* belt of sub-Saharan Africa, as in the Darfur region of western Sudan. So also with South Sudan and Mali. The Boko Haram group, based in impoverished northern Nigeria, seeks to pursue a *jihad* across nearby parts of Africa in order to enforce their view of the rule of God.

Many of these conflicts reflect longstanding practices of total war in accordance with local realities. Politics, ethnicity and resources tend to be closely intertwined.[16] Syria provided a dramatic demonstration in the 2010s and Iraq a more longstanding one.

Less prominently, but on a longer timespan, these elements can be seen in the 'Four Cuts', the counter-insurgency strategy in Myanmar. This focuses on isolating rebels from civilian support by forcefully blocking access to food, money, intelligence and recruits. Ethnic cleansing is part of the process, as in the attack on the Shan in 2009.

The interaction of resources and religion may appear unhelpful in terms of the conventional discussion of strategy. However, it is highly pertinent, in both contextual and more immediate causes, and helps explain the decision by General James Jones, American National Security Advisor in 2009–10, to widen the role of the National Security Council to include overreliance on fossil fuels, poverty, disease, corruption and the global economic crisis. Comparable British interest in national stabilisation also drew, and draws, on these factors. This approach would not have surprised those arguing the value of reform as a means for stability, both in their own countries and more widely, whether they did so in the late nineteenth century, as with Japan and China, or in the 1950s and 1960s.

Religion can be an important part of the equations of instability and notably so since the Cold War ended. This is true not only of the *sahel* belt in Africa, but also of the strategic formulation of Asian peoples and polities from Israel and Saudi Arabia to Myanmar and Thailand. The Shi'a–Sunni dispute is fundamental in the Middle East and in south-west Asia more generally; while the Indo-Pakistani conflict is to a great extent modulated by the rivalry between Hinduism and Islam. So also with Sri Lanka and Hinduism versus Buddhism. Samuel Huntington overrated the religious issue, notably in so far as Christendom and Islam were concerned, but the issue cannot be totally neglected.[17]

Compared to the West, although it can be important there, the ethnic issue also remains an important marker in shaping strategic practices in Asia. Whether it is the Naga (Christian hill people) rebellion in Myanmar and India against the Buddhist and Hindu plainspeople, or the Muslim rebellion in Chinese Turkestan against the Buddhist but secular Han Chinese, ethnicity and religion interact to generate a continuing crisis. So also with the Kurds in Turkey, Syria, Iraq and Iran. Insurgency is more important in Africa and Asia, and more central to the nature of war, than most Western discussion of strategy allows.

The focus of the world's rise in population in south Asia and, increasingly, in Africa, suggests that the language and practice of strategy there may be of the greatest significance for the future; and this both for the powers in these regions and for outside powers that play a role, as China increasingly does in Africa and, to a degree, south Asia. It is unlikely that that situation will lead to a unitary view of strategy within the areas of rapid population growth, let alone more widely, any more than that which pertains at present, or was the case in the past. Nevertheless, it is pertinent to consider how far there will be common contextual or contingent elements in the strategies of states that have a major rise in population, or in the strategies of those that respond to them. For example, the states that are having a major rise in population, certainly those in Africa, will generally lack the force projection currently shown by major powers. Linked to this, but also due in part to political and governmental issues and weaknesses, the large populations of states such as Nigeria, South Africa, Zambia and Tanzania are unlikely to be of more than regional military significance.

In Africa and Latin America, civil conflict has taken precedence over international wars ever since independence in Africa, and certainly since the mid-1930s in Latin America. Civil conflict is therefore a key sphere for strategic practice. The largest and most deadly conflicts since the Second World War, those in China (1946–9) and in Zaire (Democratic Republic of Congo) in the late 1990s and early 2000s, were both civil wars. Moreover, some of the conflicts generally regarded as international wars deserve discussion as civil wars as well. This was the case with the Vietnam War, with the Iraq War after the overthrow of Saddam Hussein in 2003, and, to a lesser degree, with the Korean War of 1950–3. What can appear primarily as foreign interventions, for example by American-led coalitions in South Vietnam, Bosnia, Somalia, Afghanistan and Iraq, and by the Soviet Union in Afghanistan in 1979–88, were also to a degree civil wars. This dimension greatly compromised the possibilities for intervention and made the strategic assumptions of interventionism, let alone state-building, problematic.

At the same time, civil conflicts were, with reason, also seen as international struggles, and notably so with those linked to Islamic fundamentalism, as earlier with religious struggles within Christendom. This point is readily understandable in terms of the doctrine of al-Qaeda.[18] Non-state actors can operate most effectively in the context of international ideologies and support systems.[19] There is no reason why the overlap of civil and international struggles should not also be the case in the future.[20]

There can be instructive historical parallels in the discussion. For example, the argument that the 'ancient barbarian threat' is being mirrored today, and from both outside and within societies, encourages consideration of earlier counter-strategies. Indeed, the historical significance of raiding and of counter-raiding practices is certainly pertinent for today, although the contexts were very different, as is the nature of the resulting violence.[21]

The definition of strategy should reflect the roles of civil conflict and, as a closely related (although not always coterminous) matter, of non-state actors. Such an approach may appear even more plausible if attention focuses on states where the use of force, both by and against the government, is a crucial aspect of politics. If civil conflict potentially is the key element, then capabilities, deterrence, intervention and strategy focus as much on the police, full employment, social welfare and domestic policies, and the ideologies that affect domestic order and disorder, as on anything that is military or state-to-state war. Police numbers, deployments, methods and doctrine are not conventionally discussed in terms of strategy, but that indicates the deficiencies of the established treatment of the latter.

A very different agenda was offered by those who focused on apparently imminent conflict between China and the United States. Indeed, the revival of great-power confrontation was linked to the resurgence of interest in Clausewitz, just as the rise in popularity of Sun Tzu after 1990 was a response both to the situation after the Cold War and to the interest in non-Western concepts. Alongside the 'consistent set of geostrategic challenges that have shaped an American way of strategizing toward the region',[22] changing geopolitics played a role in understanding the Sino-American relationship. In part, they were a matter of technology. As a result of the latter, geographical space can be seen in very different lights. For example, with 'anti-access weaponry', which, to a degree, is a new term for contesting the dominance of the sea, the relationship between the maritime and the land has changed. This change poses issues for the United States, since 1943 the leading naval power. It now has to determine whether it can retain the maritime character (notably free access to and from the sea) of areas increasingly dominated by the nearby continental power, China, most particularly Taiwan.[23]

At the same time, Chinese investment in weapon systems that are similar to those of the United States, especially aircraft-carriers, ensures that, in the event of full-scale war, China, alongside an additional capability, is vulnerable at sea in conflict with the United States. This is similar to the build-up of German naval strength prior to the First World War in the form of battleships similar to those of Britain. Yet China will seek to use its surface warships alongside very sophisticated shore-based weaponry in a way that Germany could not.

The technological, political-cultural and strategic factors involved are also pertinent for other areas where continental and oceanic interests and capabilities clash. That clash puts the focus on littoral (coastal and near-coastal) areas, which are those in which the majority of the world's population lives, and where much industrial production and, even more, activities linked to service industries such as tourism and banking take place. Clashes in these regions do not occur in marginal areas where they might be overlooked or be more prone to compromise, and where the United States does not have a role, as between India and China in the Himalayas. The risk of international escalation is therefore greater.

At the same time as growing concern about relations between China and the United States, there was a discussion of the significance of the domestic dimension in the West, albeit from another direction to that of resources. Instead, the focus was on whether political divisions and social patterns of behaviour had left the United States, and indeed the West as a whole, unable to meet the requirements of conflict and confrontation, and certainly so if the conflict was sustained, let alone difficult. Questions were raised about the public ability to accept casualties. This issue became an aspect of the political debate, domestic and international, in the late 2010s, and notably of tensions within NATO. Thus, in 2018, President Trump repeatedly criticised Germany, much of NATO and, by extension, the American Democrats, whom he presented as pseudo-European, for failing to prepare for confrontation, and, instead, boasted of his increase in military expenditure.

'Culture wars' also play a part, especially, but not only, in the United States, notably with claims that a feminisation of culture is affecting the military capability of the West, claims that have become stronger since the late 1960s. That may indeed be an aspect of contextual change, and particularly if such a process is accompanied by a decline in bellicosity. While, somewhat differently, a retreat from American interventionism, and from what many commentators saw as the American Empire, appeared to match the wishes of many Americans, others saw this in a different way as they wanted no commitment, but, nevertheless, still reflexively sought the benefits of dominance and what they construed as related cultural images.[24]

The situation across the West, including in the United States, raises the question of whether Western democracies can readily have a strategy as conventionally understood, and certainly if they are not under the pressure and shock of a war that is more than a conflict at a distance that appears discretionary. In this perspective, leaving aside the important questions of popular determination, and a cultural alienation from bellicosity, the very multifaceted nature of strategy and the variety of influences at work make the public setting of goals difficult, and thus can leave strategy to be vacuous in public terms and secretive in reality. This is a combination that is difficult to manage, and definitely so in a context of adversarial domestic politics.

At the same time, against the background of contested readings on the relationship between economic change and military strength,[25] the United States no longer appeared the 'hyperpower' but, instead, a world power in a system of decentred globalism,[26] albeit, for at least a while, the leading world power. Its alliances were a key element in its strategic capability,[27] and thus also a possible source of vulnerability. Yet, it was also argued that, however much in debt, American social, economic, political and institutional capital provide a strength-in-depth that China lacks. Such points raise the question of how best to measure power and strength, and notably so for states like China and India with a large population but, arguably, weak or problematic fundamentals.[28] The best way for others to exploit these fundamentals becomes an aspect of strategy, as, conversely, do attempts to improve them.

Turning to a narrow and limited measure of power and strength, the variable nature of military expenditure is, in part, an aspect of altering contexts and changing contingencies, but one that is played out in terms of particular strategic requirements and responses. More generally, the lack of fixity of strategy as a practice will remain the case. Different explanations are offered. Thus, in 2009, Rupert Smith, a former British general who commented on current global developments, argued that it was necessary to distinguish between, on the one hand, politics and strategy, which, he claimed, were essentially activities, and, on the other hand, history and geography, which were bodies of information and theoretically based interpretations. Smith added: 'To run the two pairs together except in pursuit of a particular goal of one or both of the activities seems to me to be nonsense.'[29] Smith, indeed, captured how strategy was not inherent, but, instead, varied; which, looked at differently, is also an aspect of the extent to which 'varying assumptions about what comprises grand strategy determine the choice of evidence sought to study its actual practice'.[30] The two approaches are not as incompatible as they appear, but, instead, overlap.

The theme of variety and contingency has been extended to suggest that, with strategy understood as a multi-level decision-making continuum, with decisions being made on means and ends, these decisions, and the related behaviour, are not only contextualised and contingent, but are so at every level of an organisation and a sociopolitical structure. Thus, for strategy, decision-making can take place down the chain of command.[31] That approach, however, does not capture key differences in responsibility. An individual pilot may have crucial decisions to make, but the location, dispatch and tasking of aircraft cannot be seen in this light. So also with warship commanders.

The marked variation in strategic understanding and ambition, and, indeed, strategic culture across time, can be seen with China. The strategy of Deng Xiaoping, China's leading minister from 1978 to 1989, and still a major figure in the early 1990s, 'to observe carefully, secure our position, hide our capacities, bide our time, be good at maintaining a low profile, never claim leadership',[32] a maxim released in 1995, scarcely described Chinese strategy in the late 2010s. That was so even if the overall strategy remained that of developing an equation of international strength, military capability and domestic stability, as well as of taking the West's advanced technology. Now, despite cautious, even critical, talk among some Chinese scholars of 'strategic rash advance',[33] the emphasis for China under Xi Jinping, with his stress on strength, is on the very public display of military power and ambition, for example in the intimidation of Taiwan and in power projection into the South China Sea. This display clearly serves to maintain the legitimacy of the governing Communist Party in the face of a potentially critical domestic public opinion. At the same time, Chinese power projection is crucial to a strategy focused on securing resources, developing secure communication routes, and facilitating access to markets, notably in Asia but also further afield.

The strategy is one that, in part, challenges Western assumptions about the openness of the 'global commons' represented by the sea, or, at least does so in terms of threatening the security of passage, and notably so in the South China Sea. From the Chinese perspective, the same is true of American power.[34] These are two strategies that do not need to clash, but that require skill in their management. Moreover, it is far from clear how best to manage the issue, and not least in terms of other interests and priorities, for example those of Japan, in what is a complex range of 'strategic trade-offs'.[35] Japan is threatened not just by China, but also by an American settlement of issues and/or retrenchment of commitments that leaves it exposed. With China, there is also the sense of 'roll-back' in terms of repairing what were presented as historic wrongs, notably the 'loss' of Taiwan in so far as the democratic independence of the latter is understood. So also with Russia and its 'roll-back' which focused on the loss of territories and influence with the collapse of the Soviet Union in 1991, an issue very much felt and expressed by Vladimir Putin.

In outlining future possibilities, or even clear trends, there is still the uncertainty presented by the lack of understanding of how best to deal with a combination of crises, such as affected Britain in 1940–1. Confronted by China, Russia and Iran, and also, albeit less seriously, mindful of instability in the Caribbean basin, the United States is arguably faced with a similar situation at present, and again one in which a recalibration of status plays a major role.

As with Britain during its imperial period, so the far-flung nature of American commitments represents a form of deep strategic engagement that confronts questions of operational effectiveness in particular areas and of overall strategic viability as a whole. One apparent solution is that of a focus on a particular region, but, although attractive, that approach may only lead to modest resource savings and does not necessarily address wider questions of strategic posture and effectiveness.[36] There is no one measure of such effectiveness. Nevertheless, a valuable one is that of weapons sales as it captures the dynamic interaction of assumptions of capability with the strength and development of alliances. The United States continues to dominate the global market, as well as being the principal domestic market, one essentially served by national producers. In order, in 2013–17, American arms exports were purchased by Saudi Arabia, the United Arab Emirates, Australia, Taiwan, Iraq, India, Turkey, Britain, Egypt and South Korea, the first four taking 38 per cent of the total. The arms trade did not suggest a failure in American power comparable to that implied by several other economic indicators. At the same time, Chinese and Russian arms exports are rapidly growing.

Russian arms exports are in part a continuation of communist-era policies, but are very much so as a product of the power network that sustains the Putin system. Referred to as crony capitalism, this is a regime that exports instability in part as a way to cope with its own issues. Thus, in response to 'strategic vulnerabilities', there is a determination to undercut calls for reform, liberalisation and democratisation in Russia.[37] Russia's enhanced capability appears to include weaponry that the West lacks, including the hypersonic Avangard missile, the Poseidon undersea drone and a nuclear-powered cruise missile. They offer the prospect of applying decisive influence at a considerable distance, breaking the opponent without terrestrial invasion. The Avangard, first test-launched in 2012 and capable of travelling at 15,000 mph, is due to become operational in 2019. This has been achieved on a military budget about a tenth of the size of the United States, which is understandable as Russia is poorer, and less creditworthy. However, Russia has not committed a strategic blunder in the Islamic world comparable to that of the United States in Afghanistan and Iraq: Russia's Syrian commitment has been far less expensive. Furthermore, Russia has not tried to match the United States in surface warships and does not in military pay and conditions.

The meaning of this Russian capability in strategic terms is unclear. Faster delivery systems were also part of the Cold War. The analogy suggests that the equations of first strike and deterrence require revival and recalibration. This is 'business as usual', but with different tools and in a dynamic international situation. At the same time, there are multiple limitations in Russian capabilities, notably economic and demographic ones, and these contribute to Russian anxieties at what is presented as NATO expansionism.[38]

The international situation including the military counterweighting requires strategic acumen on the part of the United States, as well as resources and allies. President Trump appears better at providing the resources than at securing the allies, although Trump's emphasis on instrumental bilateralism works in some cases.

Strategy (like subsequent analysis) involves making choices, both structural and episodic; and, in doing so, also responding to the choices of others, all within the context of 'the awesome challenge of uncertainty'.[39] These choices include goals that pose specific questions of practicality, for example, in the 2000s, nation-building, a strategy now largely abandoned by the United States after failure in Iraq. In one light, the strategy described as nation-building represented an inefficient allocation of resources. More seriously, it reflected a marked failure in choices, one based on poor intelligence and on political ideology.

A totally different level of uncertainty is offered by the question of how artificial intelligence (AI) will change strategy, not least by speeding up decision-making. There is also the question of psychological characteristics, even contrasts with humans: 'How badly will those intelligences want their goals, and how tenaciously will they hold on to their gains?'[40] Another military dimension can be seen with war-gaming and other plans. However far this is dependent on computers, or even AI, the belief that war and international relations can be gamed using advanced game theory or an understanding of gambling[41] underplays the extent to which in war there are no 'rules'. Instead, the surprise elements that cannot be constrained always tend to dominate. This factor becomes more marked as change through time is considered, because, aside from contextual developments, the unpredictabilities of contingent factors become more apparent. So also, more specifically, with the multiple elements involved in more complex combined operations.

Possibly the appropriate conclusion is that strategies change, while strategy as an activity does not do so, or certainly not to the same extent. Instead, strategic thinking, as a process of defining and achieving goals, is a universal that overarches all societies, epochs and cultures. In contrast, strategy, as a self-conscious intellectual sphere, vocabulary and process (and also as a pretension), has developed since the mid-eighteenth century, or, more particularly, the mid-nineteenth, becoming more diverse as it does so.[42] Indeed, strength and strategy, military and otherwise, have symbolic, ideological and cultural elements, as much as they are based on 'realist' criteria of military, political and economic factors and power. Status, in particular, deserves attention as a key content and context of strategy. Status is very important in modern world politics.[43] It has been ever thus, but is becoming more so in an age of democratisation where ideas of national interest and identity are publicly presented accordingly across this range of factors, and notably for potentially critical domestic markets. Questions of status make both compromise and prioritisation between strategic choices more difficult. They link past practice both to the present and to the future.

CONCLUSIONS

In the aftermath of interventions in Iraq and Afghanistan, strategy became a centre of attention in the 2010s. In October 2010, the Sixth Report of the House of Commons Public Administration Select Committee in Britain unanimously concluded:

> Government has lost the capacity to think strategically. The burden of expert evidence we received was that short-termism and reaction to events predominate in recent Whitehall practice. The ability to articulate our enduring interests, values and identity has atrophied . . . We argued that the Government needs to reclaim the art of creating 'national strategy' which should encompass all areas of Government activity and not focus just on national security. Our Report advocated an overarching and ongoing strategy-making process.

The government's response was unsatisfactory as far as the committee was concerned, and the committee complained, in its Sixth Report, published on 25 January 2011, that the response confused 'interests with tactics'.[1] Similar doubts were repeatedly expressed.[2]

Attacks on the conduct of strategy by the British and American governments became frequent.[3] This approach had a long genesis in the military and from civilian supporters. There is less criticism of President Kennedy for choosing during the Cuban missile crisis of 1962 not to follow the advice of the Joint Chiefs of Staff for an air attack.[4]

The notion of a correct policy is itself problematic, conceptually, methodologically and with reference to specific states. For example, the

259

balance in Israel between internal security and external protection is unfixed and contentious. The commanders of the Israeli Defence Forces have long complained that the army is hampered in its preparations for a major war by being obliged to focus on internal security tasks. This tension, in practice, relates to different aspects of protection, each of which is crucial; but, in some countries, the military prefer to focus on external protection and to remain partly oblivious to the domestic dimension. This is not true of Israel, but can be seen in aspects of the discussion by American and, to a lesser extent, British military commentators. This point underlines the problem with the idea of a 'correct balance' as in commitments and capabilities.

Moreover, it can be too easy to mistake precision about terms for analysis, while such precision is not necessarily a prelude to successful analysis. In addition, the precise conceptualisation was not present in, or for, the past, and that despite the fact that many states had been militarily effective and across a great geographical range. Rather than thinking in terms of clearly defined systems, it is more pertinent to focus on complexes or bundles of institutional-practical ways of doing things,[5] and in a context of fitness for purpose. On 11 November 2018, Nancy Pelosi, the Democratic majority leader in the House of Representatives, said that the Democrats would be 'very strategic' in using powers of subpoena against President Trump, adding: 'We are not scattershot.' Strategy can also be used as a term meaning in effect leadership, a usage that goes back to Classical times.[6]

Separately, but contributing to a range from positive discussion to uncertainty and complaint, there has also been a lack of strategic autonomy, for Britain and many other states. In part, this is due to the move of authorisation and action from the national level to the international. Indeed, the interdependency of allies has a key consequence for the framework within which strategy is conceived, formulated and implemented. In turn, the transnationalism of strategic concepts, institutions and practices creates tensions within states as they clash with established methods of policy formulation and implementation, including military autonomy.

Alongside transnationalism, most of the world was left out, or at least underplayed, in much of the work on strategy in the past, other than as a sphere for Western operations;[7] and, despite valuable recent studies, this remains the case. Thus, in historical works, although not some present-day ones, there can be a failure to engage with China other than in the persons of Sun Tzu and Mao, neither of whom in practice was 'typical' of Chinese strategy. There can also be a failure to engage with India.[8]

Separately, there are problems with the general failure in works on the history of strategy to consider the past. This point is particularly apparent if the role of religion is addressed. The modern Western account of strategy is predominantly secular, indeed almost exclusively so. Alternatives are not really understood, other than in secular terms. That makes it difficult to appreciate alternative understandings of goals and means, and with all that this means for strategy. Thus, the Safavids, who seized power in Iran and Iraq in the 1500s, were a militant Shi'a religious order who collapsed tactical, operational and strategic goals into one in pursuing the seizure of Shi'a shrines, the desecration of Sunni shrines, and a form of martyrdom in the cause of violent proselytism. At the same time, the Safavids had to prioritise between goals, as in 1529–37, during which period there were the contrasting challenges of Uzbek invasion, Ottoman attack and rebellion in Baghdad.

There are other significant methodological issues. Thus, the attempt to argue, whether for the past or for the present, for a distinction between policy and strategy is not only questionable but also scarcely value-free. This is not least because this distinction is commonly employed to treat policy as inherently political and, to a degree, rhetorical, and strategy as, in some way, clearly different and separate, and, notably, more professional, military, grounded and precise.

In practice, domestic politics were, and are, an integral and sometimes integrated part of this strategy and strategic practice, and were understood in this light, rather than these politics being marginal to the military. In modern, institutional terms, this process was encouraged by the development of intelligence agencies as a significant (and costly) part of the state, and also by concerns about subversion. The latter was not new, but was revived as a central issue during the Cold War. Worry about subversion reflected both 'total war' ideas and related feelings of vulnerability. Post-Stalinist attempts in the Soviet Union to improve the living standards of workers, notably by encouraging expenditure on consumer industries, should be seen in this light. So also with social welfarism in western Europe, the corporatism of Christian democracy, the Thatcherite attempt to extend home and share ownership, and socialist policies, as ways to keep the working class away from communism as well as means to create a society where people could be free from worries about dearth, poverty and unemployment.

More specifically, in Britain and some other countries today, the challenge from Russia is as much linked to intervention in domestic politics as to external military threats. Indeed, as a consequence, the police are a key strategic capability. This is understood in many states, not least with paramilitary police forces and national guards. 'Hybrid warfare' does not simply happen to other countries.

In conceptual terms, there is also support for the integration of the domestic and international dimensions of strategy from those who endorse organic theories of country, nation and state. Moreover, strategies emerge, in part, as the product of coalitions of interest, both domestic and international; coalitions that were at once explicit and implicit, and at once well understood and less clear. The terms by which these coalitions are formed and re-formed become important to the process by which strategies are advanced, debated and reformulated. Indeed, the ability to keep such coalitions going is a key element of strategic activity, and a central link between war-making and domestic policies and politics. The changes in this relationship are an element, at once core and dynamic, in the strategic equation. This element is definitely not one that is secondary to military capabilities and developments, or to be isolated in terms of distinct and separate policy goals.

This situation has become more the case in the modern age as communications become more global, rapid and insistent, and as governments find it increasingly difficult to manage debate and also aware that foreign powers will seek to influence opinion across borders. This problem of managing debate and the resulting political pressures was readily apparent at the time of the Western public debate around policy towards the Middle East in the mid-2010s, notably in Britain where the Cameron government totally lost control of parliamentary opinion over the use of force in Syria.

Both in the public and by the military, the discussion of military affairs in terms of misplaced strategy tends to reflect a suspicion of politics and politicians. This suspicion is an aspect of more wide-ranging current views, indeed anti-politics, in at least part of the West, but not for example in China, or certainly not to any political effect there. These points, however, are longstanding. Complaint about politicians was found from Classical Greece, as in the Peloponnesian War. In the later Roman Republic, complaints about the political process were voiced by men who were at once politicians and generals, such as Caesar and Pompey. The Second World War saw British politicians get the blame for Appeasement, which was in fact in accordance with military factors and advice. Moreover, Neville Chamberlain, the prime minister, fell in 1940 due to military failures in the Norway campaign of that year. The military criticised civilians. Thus, in May 1940, the Chief of the Imperial General Staff referred to the usual 'useless talk' in the War Cabinet.[9] However, repeated failures in 1941 and early 1942, for example in Malaya and Singapore, that, in part, drew on command faults including misplaced central direction[10] did not have this effect for Churchill. Instead, he changed commanders, notably, but not only, in North Africa. Churchill, moreover, easily survived a parliamentary motion of no confidence in 1942.

President Lyndon B. Johnson's re-election prospects fell victim in 1968 to a sense of military failure that was linked to government direction. Political direction, separately, is frequently presented as incapacitating the American military in the Vietnam War. The charge, both for the Vietnam War and for later conflicts, relates not simply to the supposed failure of strategy due to political direction, but also to issues of resourcing, procurement, doctrine and goals, notably those of state formation and social engineering. Ironically, despite being complained about most in the United States, political direction was far stronger in the Vietnam War for the eventually victorious North Vietnam than for South Vietnam or the United States.

Moreover, there can be criticism of politicians not only for involving themselves in strategy, but also for devoting insufficient attention to it. Thus, in modern India, there is no formal process of strategy, and no 'national security strategy'. Basic concepts are not adequately discussed: the annual Ministry of Defence reports are helpful indicators but not the same as a real national strategy, and the sporadic forays into government strategic thinking do not address the situation. Many Indian defence writers comment bitterly on the absence of such a process and retired Indian military officers have routinely lamented that they received little or no guidance on defence matters from the civilian government.[11]

For the Vietnam War, the repeated claim that the prospects for victory were compromised by limits on American strategy set by politicians and domestic opinion, and as a result of essentially political considerations, is an instance of the longstanding 'stab in the back' approach, an approach seen back to antiquity. For Germany and Austria after the First World War, there were 'stab in the back' legends which took the blame from where it should have rested, the military leadership.[12] In the case of Germany, there was the prewar drive for war, the confidence in the military plan, and the subsequent opposition to serious compromise over peace terms. In Austria, the military's move to an aggressive emphasis on the offensive exposed its weaknesses and those of Austria as a whole. Instead, from 1918, the blame for failure was misleadingly placed on sectors of society, and in a strident fashion, as in criticism of socialists and Jews. There are elements of the same in the debate over failure in the Vietnam War.

Historical parallels scarcely prevent rhetoric. President Reagan set a widespread tone when on 11 November 1988, speaking at the Vietnam Veterans Memorial, he declared: 'Young Americans must never again be sent to fight unless we are prepared to let them win.' Leaving aside the fatal problem of neglecting the strategy of the other side, there is certainly a tendency to underplay the problems within the American army by the latter stage of the Vietnam War, as well as the degree to which a political role was inevitable.[13]

Setting up strategy as an area of rivalry between military and politicians helps blame military failure on politicians. This approach has a long provenance, for example in General Emory Upton's account of Union failings in the Civil War in *The Military Policy of the United States* (1904). The specifics of individual charges, however, repay examination, while, more generally, it is a misleading tendency to treat the military and civilians as inherently opposed abstractions, or the latter as necessarily wrong. For example, in 2003, the American State Department not only followed a different policy to that of the Department of Defense, but also one that was far more alive to circumstances within Iraq. In the case of Britain, the army, in both Afghanistan and Iraq, wanted to demonstrate its continued value and in the context of the challenge posed by major defence cuts. This was notably so in the 2000s as the army sought to vindicate its role in the aftermath of the expenditure cuts or 'peace dividend' of the 1990s. Yet, there was also a considerable degree of gesture strategy in the commitment by the British government of disproportionately small forces to Afghanistan, a process that was in part designed to demonstrate the continued value of NATO after the end of the Cold War. In practice, this goal entailed issuing blank cheques at the start of an operation with poorly defined goals and means. Both government and army were at fault, or, looked at differently, politicians whether out of or in uniform.

Arguing for contextualisation, political and otherwise, when considering strategy, and for variations and contention accordingly, does not address the issue of how best to discern any consistent elements, but it does explain why particular definitions and interpretations of strategy should be treated as emerging from specific circumstances. Somewhat differently, Clausewitz suggested: 'In strategy, the significance of an engagement is what really matters . . . All its essentials always derive from the ultimate intentions of both parties, from the conclusion of the whole sequence of ideas.'[14]

In part, the definition and discussion, in recent decades, and notably in the West from the 1980s, of an operational dimension to war, a dimension that is clearly military, provides, as a consequence, a key opportunity for reconceptualising strategy. To do so is to offer another approach in which it is appropriate to move strategy away from its usual military location, and, instead, towards an understanding of the concept that is more centrally political. That is a point that should not be thrown away in a sentence, for it reminds us of the extent to which modern conceptualisation affects earlier evaluations of previous situations, both current and historical. The use of the term 'strategy' offers a classic instance of this process. If the idea of an operational level of war, distinct from the tactical and strategic levels, is to be considered and applied widely, then the room for a definition of strategy in military terms is, at least in part, lessened and altered.

In any event, even at the operational and tactical levels, political considerations play a major role. Indeed, they can be seen as aspects of the political character of warfare, notably again the sense of limits in means and methods as well as goals, with this sense, moreover, well represented in modern military doctrine. This point is not a semantic play on the notion of limited war, instructive as that is in this context, nor, indeed, a reference to Clausewitz's discussion of politics. Instead, the emphasis here is on the extent to which war-making inherently involves limits or their absence, for example in the treatment of prisoners and civilians, or in the imposition and extent of scorched-earth policies, as well as in the attitude to casualties. Notions of victory, defeat and appropriate conduct vary greatly by context and occasion, and this is a significant aspect of the cultural approach to war and of the related concept of strategic culture. Moreover, as an aspect of a situation that can be related both to the politics of goals and to cultural elements in warfare, there are differences between conflict designed to retain and/or incorporate territory (or, at sea, to retain or gain access), and wars that are more focused on battle and the defeat of opposing forces.

The general tendency in work on strategy is teleological, a pattern also seen, again misleadingly, in the case of total war.[15] There is a strong assumption, whether explicit or implicit, that the understanding, pursuit and management of strategy became more professional with time. This professionalisation is commonly regarded as taking institutional form with the establishment and use of general staffs. Moreover, that process is understood as grounded in a wider assessment of the value of specific engagement with strategic thought and practice. The contrast is with an 'other' composed of chaos, the stygian past and untutored 'barbarian' practices. Phrased like that, there is clearly a simplification at play, but just such a set of assumptions is present in the focus and content of much of the discussion.

One aspect of this discussion is that of the superiority of the institution over the individual commander. The latter is taken to be inherently less consistent or even undisciplined, and there is frequently a tension at play in the consideration of strategic understanding focused on this apparent superiority. Douglas MacArthur was classified accordingly, as, in a very different context, was Adolf Hitler.

Again, there is a related teleology in the treatment of institutions, that of creation and improvement. Indeed, given the propensity of many to write about revolutions in military affairs, or rather of real or supposed improvements that are depicted as revolutionary, it is surprising that the rise of strategy-making structures does not more frequently enter the lists. Teleological approaches, misleading in themselves, have been encouraged by the use of quantitative methods and computational tools to stimulate strategic debates, model and measure outcomes, and suggest what were optimum means. Thus, cost–benefit analysis, critical path analysis and operations research were followed by big-data computer modelling.

And then we look at policy at present. Policy and strategy are collapsed into one and driven by a personal agenda in states that are regarded as maverick, such as North Korea, but also to a considerable degree in the (very different) United States under President Donald J. Trump and notably with his open embrace of *Realpolitik*.[16] Moreover, this process of personalised power and pursuit of *Realpolitik* can be seen not only in one-party states, such as China, but also in dictatorial democracies, for example Russia and Turkey. This process varies in its detailed manifestations, causes, course and consequences, and possibly in its future details; but it is relevant to note that the process calls into question the teleology of improvement and institutionalisation offered in the previous paragraph.

Modern circumstances suggest that it is pertinent to re-examine the monarchical systems of the pre-modern world, however defined. In particular, in place of structuring our understanding, and awarding praise in terms of change through time, namely improvability and improvement towards the present, it is appropriate to consider assessment in terms of fitness of purpose.

This assessment sits in a context that can appear very familiar. A sense of fluidity and unpredictability was scarcely kept at bay by conceptualisation in terms of systems of behaviour, such as the ideas of natural interests and the balance of power. These very systems were the compensatory response to the chaos of international relations, a desperate attempt to reduce the disorganised nature of volatile reality to form and order. The French envoy in Berlin was all too correct when he observed in 1732 of Frederick William I of Prussia (r. 1713–40): 'Neither he, nor his ministers, ever have a fixed plan.'[17] For the remainder of his reign, Frederick William acted in a maverick fashion that brought him no advantages.

Unpredictability was generally a characteristic applied to others and not to one's own state, and certainly so by most official figures. However, this unpredictability also had to be guarded against. It constituted the risk that both threatened and represented disorder, and that had a moral as well as a prudential consideration. As a consequence, strategy was primarily a device, both method and contents, ideology and implementation, designed against risk. The risk in question was, first, that posed by the other power(s) and, second, that of failure in the response.

There are, however, many problems today in judging the strategies of the past (and present) accordingly. Part rests on the lack of knowledge and on the difficulties of processing counterfactuals with any predictive accuracy. The mechanistic understanding of international relations in systemic terms poses major conceptual problems. For example, a fundamental issue arises from the thesis–antithesis assessment of international relations and military strength, namely the counterpointing, by the actions of others, of any success by an individual power, with the result that strategic dominance has a tendency to precariousness. This assessment suggests a self-righting 'hidden hand' that maintains a balance of power.

In contrast to this assessment, and very much adding confusion, there can, however, be a willingness, indeed eagerness, to accommodate to power and success, a process seen both with Napoleon up to 1812 and with Hitler up to 1941, and possibly with China today. It is unclear that the world, or parts of it, was, is, and will be, inevitably multipolar and therefore that dominance will fail. The absence, indeed, of some self-righting mechanism within a multipolar balance of power meant in practice that there was much more to play for in terms of strategy, but also greater risks. This was true at all levels, including the sub-continental and the global.

There were no obvious bounds to the ambition of powers; and strategic skill, happenstance and success in part rested on the relationship between activity at different levels and in particular spheres. The latter involved choice; and choice, including the decision not to choose, is central to strategy. As a result, the pressures and processes of choice, of making hard choices based on incomplete information, had to be considered. They have a far longer timespan than any formal institutionalisation of strategy. Choice in part involved the understanding and prioritisation of tasks, the selection of allies, and the establishment and maintenance of alliances.

The last was a prime issue in strategy, notably the pursuit of the compromises necessary to get alliances, and thus strategic choices, to work. Compromise existed within, as well as between, states. Indeed, not only domestic politics, but also the perception of such politics, by both the governments in question and by their allies and opponents, is often a key element in strategy. This brings to the fore the role of public opinion in strategy. It may be indirect, but that does not make it less important. Moreover, this importance exists for both sides in any confrontation or conflict, and efforts towards weakening the domestic support of opponents are the counterpart to attempting to strengthen one's own. Influencing the policy of neutrals by means of their publics is also important, as with the United States in 1917 and 1941.

Success is a crucial dimension in sustaining support and the appearance of support, but success is also open to a variety of definitions. This point undercuts the 'realist' approach to power politics that emphasises states as rational actors and defines the key actors as the states. Such an approach underplays the beliefs of leaders, domestic groups and changing political perceptions.

The public mood has long been significant in sustaining support for particular strategies, although the extent to which popular opinion is regarded as a source of political legitimacy has varied, and continues to do so. Nevertheless, from antiquity, propaganda has been deployed in an attempt to secure this backing and it is a major part of the strategic armoury. The effectiveness of propaganda is unclear as people tend to believe what they want to believe. At the same time, propaganda can affect the perception and discussion of strategy, both of one's own and of other states.

All these elements are true today, and will continue to be so into the future. The political dimension of strategy repeatedly emerges as multifaceted as well as highly significant. This was demonstrated in December 2018–19 when the French government felt it necessary to change certain aspects of the content or tone of domestic policy due to a dramatic breakdown of internal stability. This failure also affected France's international position. In early 2019, very differently, the interrelationships of Venezuela's international position and domestic politics were clearly seen.

Modern Western international strategic concerns have, since the 1990s, increasingly focused on non-Western areas and topics, notably in east Asia and the Islamic world, each of which provides very different cultural contexts, and with no sign of any convergence of practice with the West. Indeed the opposite has occurred, although this can be misunderstood due to the use of the same or similar weaponry. In comparison to these strategic concerns, however, some of the theoretical writing on strategy appears somewhat formulaic and stale, not least in deploying a familiar cast of subjects and themes. Instead, there is much to be said for starting afresh, not least because much that is presented as the fundamentals of strategy is, in practice, culturally located and conditioned, rather than the universals it is often suggested to be.

In contrast, in much work, there is the tendency to deploy past examples as if, far from them being problematic, indeed complex, there is no doubt about what they indicate.[18] This is mistaken, indeed ahistorical, although also seen with other subjects, for example geopolitics. If strategy is intended to meet the challenge of uncertainty about the future, and thus to face conditions that are inherently unpredictable,[19] then it is necessary to note the degree to which the nature of the context, within which both change is being experienced and the future considered, is far from constant. Furthermore, individual conflicts emerged, and will continue to emerge, from particular circumstances. These conflicts did/do not necessarily set unprecedented strategic tasks, not least because the political entities playing a role were/are often well established, while the relationships between external and domestic challenges were/are far from new. Yet, each conflict confronted or confronts different circumstances, whether the three Punic Wars between Rome and Carthage or the two world wars involving Germany.

Whether or not repeated strategic circumstances can be seen, with all that that might offer for those who wish to provide laws to analyse strategy, strategy, like war itself, has become a term that is widely defined. Indeed, strategy now appears to equate as much to deciding how to 'game' a dinner party as a conflict. Specifically, there are now many alternatives to a distinctive military character to strategy. It is readily apparent that the function of strategy, if understood as the relationships between ends, ways and means in power politics, is not necessarily military. Strategy has been taken to refer to the full range of human activity.

Definitions in terms of conflict may appear simple, as for the Western Allies in 1943, with attacking the 'soft underbelly' of Italy, rather than the German-constructed Western Wall in France. In contrast, tactics would be choice over formations, such as the Allies that year preferring the 'finger four' pattern for fighter aircraft over the 'vic', and also the response to specific environments. More broadly, in considering both definitions and their application, there are differences such as thinking about long-term structures and consequences, rather than the small-scale and short-term. In the context of migration, for example, there is the effect of migration on innovation, training, productivity, and the size and composition of the population; rather than the skills make-up allowed in through work permits. The former are strategic and the latter tactical, in so far as that distinction can be applied.

However, whatever the context, the definition of strategy is far from clear or easy to apply. The word has served as adjective, noun, verb and adverb. So also with different types of strategy, as in theatre strategy, or grand strategy, or 'sub-strategy'.[20] In addition, it is unclear why the national scale should be the key one in considering strategy, as opposed to an inclusion of the sub-national or, indeed, the supra-national. The ambiguities of the use of strategy in the more particular field of military history throw light on the issue of its usage in other fields. In practice, strategy, whether military or non-military, and, in the former case, whether or not focused on war, is a process of defining interests, understanding problems and determining goals. In the case of military affairs, strategy confronts the non-linear change represented by war, a process whose most significant outcome is generating violence and which therefore is inherently unpredictable. At the same time, much of life, both individual and collective, involves non-linear change and will continue to do so.

Strategy, an overarching vision of what an organisation or individual wants to achieve, coupled with a set of objectives designed to make that possible, is not the details of the plans by which goals are implemented by military means. The latter are the operational components of strategy, to employ another, later, term. The more the operational dimension is emphasised, as is the case with modern studies of war, the more strategy is 'pushed back' or reconceptualised towards goals rather than means. More particularly, since rulers ceased to command in the field, the heritage of military command is really operational and not strategic, while the military are only one part of any strategic framework, which is changing all the time. These, however, are not points that tend to be welcome to the military, in so far as the latter can be lumped together as an interest.

At the present moment, there is, certainly in Britain and the United States, an attempt to separate out strategy from politics, as part of a drive by the military to ensure autonomy, but also in order to achieve a precise set of analytical and operating concepts. In part, this is a working through of concerns about operational capability in response to the shocks of 2003–14. However, aside from this particular context and the 'ownership' bound up in its politics and legacy, it can be too easy to mistake precision about terms for analysis. Furthermore, such precision is not necessarily a prelude to successful analysis.

Indeed, as strategy is contextual, so are its definitions, and the process, as part of these definitions, of separating elements such as strategy itself, implementing strategy and factors influencing strategies. In practice, they are overlapping and interacting. The discussion of hows affects the definition of ends, and vice versa.

Rather than thinking in terms of clearly defined systems, it is more pertinent to focus on complexes, or burdens, of institutional-practical ways of doing things, and in a context of judgement in terms of fitness for purpose. In particular, for military purposes, the differentiation of strategy from policy is less valid and practical than is often suggested. A means-versus-ends distinction can be advanced when discussing strategy and policy, the relations between them, and the attempt to differentiate between them. However, ends are in large part set in relation with, and to, means; while means are conceived of, and planned, in terms of ends. Thus, distinguishing the two for analytical purposes, or even for planning ones, has its limitations.

Moreover, the presentation of strategy owes much to the propagandas of power, with governments seeking to offer acceptable accounts to both domestic and international audiences, and as part of a situation in which 'strategic narrative' is crucial in pursuing support.[21] Counter-insurgency struggles are an instance of this process, as with the American governmental and military accounts at the time of the Vietnam War. The public's response to the narratives can be/was significant, as, eventually, in this case. So also with predictions of the effectiveness of air power prior to the Second World War. In Britain, civilians influenced not only the politicians but even the military, as with panics about German air attack.[22]

Given the difficulties of assessing goals, whether past, present or future, it is often unclear how best to consider, and thus evaluate, strategy.

For example, to take French policy in the 1770s and 1780s, for which the sources are good, the focus can be on the failure to devise an effective response to the rise of Russian assertiveness. In that light, the war with Britain in 1778–83, and the related operational choices, can be presented as an appropriate response to the maritime situation, and the contingent opportunities presented by rebellion in North America, or as an ener-vating distraction from other tasks, notably confronting Russia. Linked to the latter, the belief of Charles, Count of Vergennes, French foreign minister from 1774 until his death in 1787, in a politics of honesty, restraint and legality, and his determination to act as the defender of the interests of the second- and third-rank powers, can be presented as naïve. Certainly, Vergennes found the situation in the 1770s disturbing. He was concerned about Russian expansion, personally so as most of his diplomatic career had been spent in Constantinople and Stockholm, and he was anxious to avoid a repetition of the Seven Years' War (1756–63). To Vergennes, France's defeat then demonstrated the danger of engaging simultaneously in maritime and European conflicts. It also led him to emphasise the value of the Family Compact with Spain, which he saw as a deterrent to British envy of French colonial development in the West Indies and to British aggression.

Moreover, to Vergennes, the First Partition of Poland by Austria, Prussia and Russia in 1772 was both the politics of thuggery and a chal-lenge to the pre-eminent position France should enjoy. The ambitions of Joseph II of Austria also worried Vergennes, although he did not want to let Austria abandon France and return to its former alliance with Britain. Vergennes saw better relations with Prussia as a way to block Joseph's expansionist schemes, but he did not want to let Frederick the Great dictate French policy.

In the event, Vergennes was fortunate that his death, on 13 February 1787, ensured that he did not preside over the collapse of French foreign policy in the Balkans and the Low Countries, nor over that of France's alliance system. For example, Vergennes undermined his strategy of persuading the Turks to avoid war by a trade treaty with Russia, the news of which was greeted in Constantinople with anger and dismay. The internal coherence of his diplomatic strategy, the desire to keep the Turks calm while at the same time improving relations with Russia (and perhaps also restraining it), was destroyed by the interaction of the strategy's own contradictions, and by events in eastern Europe. In a similar fashion, France's policy in the Dutch crisis was to collapse in 1787. There was, in short, a degree of unreality in Vergennes's reading of the international system and specifically of the assumptions and policies of other powers. Yet, if a more positive assessment of the goals is offered, then the analysis can alter.[23] Moreover, all strategies have contradictions, and commentators are particularly prone to find them.

From another perspective, strategy was, and is, conceptualised in terms of views on both world affairs and domestic political culture, with these views proving a key feature of the belief systems of policy-makers (and others), as well as their psychological drives. This approach is certainly useful when evaluating China. To separate out these factors is unhelpful as an account of the past. Such a separation puts an emphasis on a precision that is ahistorical as a description of the past, as well as being only essentially an aspiration for present and future, and a misleading one at that. A lack of coherence in strategy can be not a flaw, but, rather, an appropriate response both to complexity and to present and likely future contingencies. Moreover, an imprecision in the understanding and practice of strategy is, in part, a reflection of the variety of environments in which, and towards which, it is pursued.

There is, more generally, a problem with the idea of optimum grand strategies. It may be that a lack of institutional structures, historical or present-day, or of 'appropriate' structures, however 'appropriate' is defined, affects the efficiency of devising such strategies. Nevertheless, irrespective of this, the existence of such an optimum, itself a mechanistic concept, is very much open to debate. So also with the issue of the quality of decision-making that is suggested by such a comparison. Blundering to glory, a phrase applied to describe Napoleon,[24] is not much of a strategy; and it has many costs, and often scant glory. At the same time, offering apparent precision, in the search for an alleged optimum outcome, has its problems. While, doubtless, the pursuit of reason is a noble cause, it also has its fallacies and flaws. When two powers or forces go to war, generally both believe that they will win and gain benefits from their victory, and at least one is always wrong.

NOTES

ABBREVIATIONS

AE   Paris Archives du Ministère des Relations Extérieures
AST   Turin Archivio di Stato di Torino
BL   British Library
CP   Correspondance Politique
CRO County Record Office
LM   Lettere Ministri
SP   State Papers
TNA The National Archives Kew

PREFACE

1. House of Commons, Public Administration Select Committee: Evidence, 9 Sep. 2010, Ev 6, Q12; *The Times*, 5 Jan. 2019.
2. W. Murray and R.H. Sinnreich (eds), *The Past as Prologue: The Importance of History to the Military Profession* (Cambridge, 2006).
3. For the role of the Cold War on his work, see A. Lambert, *The Crimean War: British Grand Strategy against Russia, 1853–56*, 2nd edn (Farnham, 2011), Introduction. The first edition appeared in 1990.
4. For example by Liam Fox, British Secretary of State for International Trade, BBC Radio 4 interview, 23 Oct. 2018.
5. E.N. Luttwak, 'The Byzantine Empire: From Attila to the 4th Crusade', in J.A. Olsen and C.S. Gray (eds), *The Practice of Strategy: From Alexander the Great to the Present* (Oxford, 2011), p. 79.
6. T.G. Otte, ' "The Method in Which We Were Schooled by Experience": British Strategy and a Continental Commitment before 1914', in K. Neilson and G. Kennedy (eds), *The British Way in Warfare: Power and the International System, 1856–1956* (Farnham, 2010), p. 303.
7. N. Wouters and L. van Ypersele (eds), *Nations, Identities and the First World War: Shifting Loyalties to the Fatherland* (London, 2018).
8. F. Schumacher, 'The Philippine–American War and the Birth of US Colonialism in Asia', in A.S. Thompson and C.G. Frentzos (eds), *The Routledge Handbook of American Military and Diplomatic History, 1865 to the Present* (New York, 2013), p. 48; J.M. Carter, ' "Shaky as All Hell": The US and Nation Building in Southern Vietnam', ibid., p. 258.
9. P.C. Perdue, 'Culture, History, and Imperial Chinese Strategy: Legacies of the Qing Conquests', in H. van de Ven (ed.), *Warfare in Chinese History* (Leiden, 2000), pp. 252–87.
10. J. Lacey (ed.), *Great Strategic Rivalries: From the Classical World to the Cold War* (New York, 2016).

INTRODUCTION

1. See, for example, A.J. Echevarria, *Military Strategy: A Very Short Introduction* (Oxford, 2017).

2. G.J. Bryant, *The Emergence of British Power in India, 1600–1784: A Grand Strategic Interpretation* (Woodbridge, Suffolk, 2013), p. 321. For the question of a separate definition and role for 'grand strategy', see P.D. Miller, 'On Strategy, Grand and Mundane', *Orbis*, 60 (2016), pp. 237–47.

3. W.E. Lee, *Waging War: Conflict, Culture, and Innovation in World History* (Oxford, 2016), p. 407.

4. T. Kane and D. Lonsdale, *Understanding Contemporary Strategy* (Abingdon, 2012), p. 26.

5. Quoted in I. Popescu, *Emergent Strategy and Grand Strategy: How American Presidents Succeed in Foreign Policy* (Baltimore, MD, 2017), p. 1.

6. J.M. Dubik, *Just War Reconsidered: Strategy, Ethics, and Theory* (Lexington, KY, 2016).

7. P. Crimmin, 'The Channel's Strategic Significance: Invasion Threat, Line of Defence, Prison Wall, Escape Route', *Studies on Voltaire and the Eighteenth Century*, 292 (1991), pp. 67–79; L. White, 'Strategic Geography and the Spanish Habsburg Monarchy's Failure to Recover Portugal, 1640–1668', *Journal of Military History*, 71 (2007), pp. 373–410.

8. A.J. Stravers, 'Partisan Conflict over Grand Strategy in Eastern Europe, 2014–2017', *Orbis*, 62 (2018), pp. 541–56; N.D.F. Allen, 'Assessing a Decade of US Military Strategy in Africa', ibid., pp. 655–69, quote at p. 657.

9. Brian Collier to Black, 23 Jul. 2009, email.

10. *The Economist*, 30 Nov. 2018, p. 29.

11. *The Times*, 3 Dec. 2018.

12. J.A. Downie, 'Polemical Strategy and Swift's *The Conduct of the Allies*', *Prose Studies*, 4 (1981), pp. 134–45.

13. *Wall Street Journal*, 19 Oct. 2018.

14. M.T. Owens, 'Editor's Corner', *Orbis*, 58 (2014), p. 162.

15. L. Sondhaus, *Strategic Culture and Ways of War* (London, 2006); S. Poore, 'What is the Context? A Reply to the Gray-Johnston Debate on Strategic Culture', *Review of International Studies*, 29 (2003), pp. 279–84; D.P. Adamsky, *American Strategic Culture and the US Revolution in Military Affairs* (Oslo, 2008).

16. S.W. Khan, *Haunted by Chaos: China's Grand Strategy from Mao Zedong to Xi Jinping* (Cambridge, MA, 2018), p. 251; A.M. Tabatabai, *No Conquest, No Defeat: Iran's National Security Strategy* (London, 2019).

17. J. Snyder, *The Soviet Strategic Culture: Implications for Limited Nuclear Operations* (Santa Monica, CA, 1977).

18. T.H. Etzold and J.L. Gaddis (eds), *Containment: Documents on American Policy and Strategy, 1945–1950* (New York, 1978), pp. 84–90; J.L. Gaddis, *The United States and the Origins of the Cold War, 1941–1947* (New York, 1972); J.L. Gaddis, *George F. Kennan: An American Life* (New York, 2011).

19. A. Wendt, 'Anarchy Is What States Make of It: The Social Construction of Power Politics', *International Organization*, 46 (1992), pp. 391–425.

20. K. Booth, *Strategy and Ethnocentrism* (London, 1979); C.G. Reynolds, 'Reconsidering American Strategic History and Doctrines', in *History of the Sea: Essays on Maritime Strategies* (Columbia, SC, 1989); C.S. Gray, 'Strategic Culture as Context: The First Generation of Theory Strikes Back', *Review of International Studies*, 25 (1999), pp. 49–70; R.W. Barnett, *Navy Strategic Culture: Why the Navy Thinks Differently* (Annapolis, MD, 2009), p. 130.

21. H.A. Simon, *Models of Bounded Rationality* (Cambridge, MA, 1982); H. Crowther-Heyck, *Herbert A. Simon: The Bounds of Reason in America* (Baltimore, MD, 2005).

22. J.P. Clark, *Preparing for War: The Emergence of the Modern US Army, 1815–1917* (Cambridge, MA, 2017).

23. A. Forrest, *The Legacy of the French Revolutionary Wars: The Nation-in-Arms in French Republican Memory* (Cambridge, 2009).

24. R.I. Frost, review of J.P. LeDonne, *The Grand Strategy of the Russian Empire, 1650–1831* (Oxford, 2004), *English Historical Review*, 121 (2006), p. 850.

25. LeDonne, *The Grand Strategy of the Russian Empire*, pp. vii–viii.

26. A. Johnston, 'Thinking about Strategic Culture', *International Security*, 19 (1995), p. 35.

27. W. Martel, *Grand Strategy in Theory and Practice: The Need for an Effective American Foreign Policy* (New York, 2015).

28. P.H. Wilson, 'Strategy and the Conduct of War', in O. Asbach and P. Schröder (eds), *Ashgate Research Companion to the Thirty Years' War* (Farnham, 2013), p. 277.

29. E.A. Lund, *War for the Every Day: Generals, Knowledge, and Warfare in Early Modern Europe, 1680–1740* (Westport, CT, 1999). T.C.W. Blanning, *Frederick the Great: King of Prussia* (London, 2015), p. 226, more bluntly writes: 'A general staff was created.'

30. P.J. Speelman (ed.), *Henry Lloyd and the Military Enlightenment: The Works of General Lloyd* (Westport, CT, 2005), p. 13.

31. On the 'mimetic nature of war', see R. Girard, R.P. Harrison and C. Haven, 'Shakespeare: Mimesis and Desire', *Standpoint*, Dec. 2018–Jan. 2019, p. 63.

32. K.M. Swope, 'Manifesting Awe: Grand Strategy and Imperial Leadership in the Ming Dynasty', *Journal of Military History*, 79 (2015), p. 605.

33. D.A. Graff, 'Dou Jiande's Dilemma: Logistics, Strategy, and State Formation in Seventh-Century China', in H. van de Ven (ed.), *Warfare in Chinese History* (Leiden, 2000), pp. 77–105; D. Twitchett, 'Tibet in Tang Grand Strategy', ibid., pp. 106–79; P.C. Perdue, 'Culture, History, and Imperial Chinese Strategy: Legacies of the Qing conquests', ibid., pp. 252–87.

34. V.D. Hanson, *A War like No Other: How the Athenians and Spartans Fought the Peloponnesian War* (New York, 2005).

35. J.E. Lendon, *Song of Wrath: The Peloponnesian War Begins* (New York, 2010); P. Low, *Interstate Relations in Classical Greece: Morality and Power* (Cambridge, 2007); P. Hunt, *War, Peace, and Alliance in Demosthenes' Athens* (Cambridge, 2010).

36. The classic work, E.N. Luttwak's *The Grand Strategy of the Roman Empire: From the First Century AD to the Third* (Baltimore, MD, 1976), is criticised in B. Isaac, *The Limits of Empire: The Roman Army in the East*, 2nd edn (Oxford, 1992), pp. 372–418, and, conversely, taken forward by E.L. Wheeler, 'Methodological Limits and the Mirage of Roman Strategy', *Journal of Military History*, 57 (1993), pp. 7–41, 215–40; E.L. Wheeler, 'Rome's Dacian Wars: Domitian, Trajan, and Strategy on the Danube', *Journal of Military History*, 74 (2010), pp. 1185–1227, 75 (2011), pp. 191–219; M. Pavkovic, 'Roman Grand Strategy', *Military Chronicles*, 1 (2005), pp. 14–30; and K. Kagan, 'Redefining Roman Grand Strategy', *Journal of Military History*, 70 (2006), pp. 333–62. See, more recently, Y. Le Bohec, *La Guerre romaine: 58 avant J.-C.–235 après J.-C.* (Paris, 2014); G. Traina, 'La Tête et la main droite de Crassus: quelques remarques supplémentaires', in A. Allély (ed.), *Corps au supplice et violences de guerre dans l'Antiquité* (Bordeaux, 2014), pp. 95–8.

37. L. Loreto, *La grande strategia di Roma nell'età della prima guerra punica (ca.273–ca.229 a. C.): l'inizio di un paradosso* (Naples, 2007). For the earlier situation in the Greek world, see P.A. Brunt, 'The Aims of Alexander', *Greece and Rome*, 12 (1965), pp. 205–15; P.A. Brunt, 'Spartan Policy and Strategy in the Archidamian War', *Phoenix*, 19 (1965), pp. 255–80; J.K. Anderson, *Military Theory and Practices in the Age of Xenophon* (Berkeley, CA, 1970). For the emphasis on cultural factors, see J. Lendon, *Soldiers and Ghosts: A History of Battle in Classical Antiquity* (New Haven, 2005).

38. R.J. Brewer (ed.), *Roman Fortresses and Their Legions* (London, 2000); D. Graf, 'Rome and China: Some Frontier Comparisons', in Z. Visy (ed.), *Limes XIX: Proceedings of the XIXth International Congress of Roman Frontier Studies* (Pécs, 2005), pp. 157–66; E. Hammer, 'Highland Fortress-Polities and Their Settlement Systems in the Southern Caucasus', *Antiquity*, 88 (2014), pp. 757–74.

39. See also A. Eckstein, *Rome Enters the Greek East: From Anarchy to Hierarchy in the Hellenistic Mediterranean, 230–170 BC* (Malden, MA, 2008).

40. S.P. Mattern, *Rome and the Enemy: Imperial Strategy in the Principate* (Berkeley, CA, 1999).

41. N. Tackett, 'The Great Wall and Conceptualizations of the Border under the Northern Song', *Journal of Song-Yuan Studies*, 38 (2008), pp. 99–138.

42. J. Haldon, *Warfare, State and Society in the Byzantine World, 565–1204* (London, 1999); J. Shepard (ed.), *The Cambridge History of the Byzantine Empire* (Cambridge, 2008); E.N. Luttwak, *The Grand Strategy of the Byzantine Empire* (Cambridge, MA, 2009); D.A. Graff, *The Eurasian Way of War: Military Practice in Seventh-Century China and Byzantium* (Abingdon, 2016).

43. J.F. Verbruggen, *The Art of Warfare in Western Europe during the Middle Ages* (Oxford, 1977), pp. 249–300; P. Contamine, *La Guerre au Moyen âge*, 4th edn (Paris, 1994), pp. 365–79 (English version, *War in the Middle Ages* (Oxford, 1986), pp. 219–28); M. Prestwich, *Armies and Warfare in the Middle Ages: The English Experience* (New Haven, CT, 1996); F. Garcia Fitz, 'Hube estratégia en la adad media? A propósito de las relaciones castellano-musulmanas durante la segunda mitad del siglo XIII', *Revista da Faculdade de Letras: História*, series 2, vol. 15 (1998), pp. 837–54; B.S. Bachrach, *Early Carolingian Warfare: Prelude to Empire* (Philadelphia, PA, 2001), pp. 202–42; J.W. Honig, 'Reappraising Late Medieval Strategy: The Example of the 1415 Agincourt Campaign', *War in History*, 19 (2012), pp. 123–51; J.B. Gillingham, 'A Strategy of Total War? Henry of Livonia and the Conquest of Estonia, 1208–1227', *Journal of Medieval Military History*, 15 (2017). For a special issue of the *Journal of Medieval Military History* arguing for the importance of strategy, see this journal, volume 15 (2017). On Pere, see J. Black, *Geopolitics and the Quest for Dominance* (Bloomington, IN, 2016), pp. 38–9.
44. G.A. Loud, 'Some Reflections on the Failure of the Second Crusade', *Crusades*, 4 (2005), pp. 10–14.
45. C.J. Rogers, *War Cruel and Sharp: English Strategy under Edward III, 1327–1360* (Woodbridge, Suffolk, 2000); C.J. Rogers, *Essays on Medieval Military History: Strategy, Military Revolutions, and the Hundred Years War* (Farnham, 2010); C.J. Rogers, 'Medieval Strategy and the Economics of Conquest', *Journal of Military History*, 82 (2018), pp. 709–38.
46. J.J.L. Gommans, *The Rise of the Indo-Afghan Empire, c.1710–1780* (Leiden, 1995), pp. 136–42.
47. J. Waterson, *The Knights of Islam: The Wars of the Mamluks* (St Paul, MN, 2007).
48. J.E. Herman, *Amid the Clouds and Mist: China's Colonization of Guizhou, 1200–1700* (Cambridge, MA, 2005).
49. T. May, *The Mongol Art of War: Chinggis Khan and the Mongol Military System* (Yardley, PA, 2007).
50. B.F. Manz, *The Rise and Rule of Tamerlane* (Cambridge, 1989).
51. K. Chase, *Firearms: A Global History to 1700* (Cambridge, 2003), p. 51; E.L. Dreyer, *Zheng He: China and the Oceans in the Early Ming Dynasty, 1405–1433* (New York, 2007).
52. B. Heuser, *The Strategy Makers: Thoughts on War and Society from Machiavelli to Clausewitz* (Santa Barbara, CA, 2010); B. Heuser, *The Evolution of Strategy: Thinking War from Antiquity to the Present* (Cambridge, 2010).
53. G. Parker, *The Grand Strategy of Philip II* (New Haven, CT, 1998).
54. M. Rizzo, 'Sticks, Carrots, and All the Rest: Lombardy and the Spanish Strategy in Northern Italy between Europe and the Mediterranean (1550–1600)', *Cahiers de la Méditerranée*, 71 (2005), pp. 146–84.
55. E. Tenace, 'A Strategy of Reaction: The Armadas of 1596 and 1597 and the Spanish Struggle for European Hegemony', *English Historical Review*, 118 (2003), pp. 855–82. See also E. Ringmar, *Identity, Interest and Action: A Cultural Explanation of Sweden's Intervention in the Thirty Years War* (Cambridge, 1996).
56. G. Perjés, 'Army Provisioning, Logistics and Strategy in the Second Half of the 17th Century', *Acta Historica Academiae Scientiarum Hungaricae*, 16 (1970), pp. 1–52; D.A. Parrott, 'Strategy and Tactics in the Thirty Years' War: The "Military Revolution" ', in C.J. Rogers (ed.), *The Military Revolution Debate: Readings on the Military Transformation of Early Modern Europe* (Boulder, CO, 1995), pp. 242–6; J. Luh, ' "Strategie und Taktik" im Ancien Régime', *Militargeschichtliche Zeitschrift*, 64 (2005), pp. 101–31; J. Luh, *Ancien Régime Warfare and the Military Revolution: A Study* (Groningen, 2000), p. 178.
57. A. Lambert, *The Crimean War: British Grand Strategy against Russia, 1853–56*, 2nd edn (Farnham, 2011).
58. *The New Encyclopaedia Britannica*, XIX (Chicago, 1976), p. 558.
59. R.F. Weigley, 'The American Military and the Principle of Civilian Control from McClellan to Powell', *Journal of Military History*, 57 (1993); R.F. Weigley, 'The Soldier, the Statesman and the Military Historian', *Journal of Military History*, 63 (1999); R.H. Kohn, 'Out of Control: The Crisis in Civil–Military Relations', *National Interest*, 35 (1994), pp. 3–17.
60. On the problems of evaluation and implementation, see M.D. Cohen, J.G. March and J.P. Olsen, 'A Garbage Can Model of Organizational Choice', *Administrative Science Quarterly*, 17 (1972), pp. 1–25.

61. N. Houghton, 'Response to the Toast to the Guests', Livery Dinner of the Worshipful Company of Armourers and Brasiers, London, 19 Nov. 2015.

62. J. Fynn-Paul (ed.), *War, Entrepreneurs, and the State in Europe and the Mediterranean, 1300–1800* (Leiden, 2014); J. Black, *War in Europe: 1450 to the Present* (London, 2016), pp. 1–10.

63. H. Strachan, *The Direction of War: Contemporary Strategy in Historical Perspective* (Cambridge, 2013).

64. P. Cornish and A.M. Dorman, 'Smart Muddling Through: Rethinking UK National Security beyond Afghanistan', *International Affairs*, 88 (2012), pp. 213–22; P. Cornish and A.M. Dorman, 'Complex Security and Strategic Latency: The UK Strategic Defence and Security Review 2015', *International Affairs*, 91 (2015), pp. 351–70.

65. C. von Clausewitz, *On War*, edited by P. Paret and M. Howard (Princeton, NJ, 1976), pp. 88–9.

66. Strachan, *The Direction of War*, p. 50.

67. A. Monson and W. Schiedel (eds), *Fiscal Regimes and the Political Economy of Premodern States* (Cambridge, 2015).

68. Robert, 4th Earl of Holdernesse, Secretary of State for the Northern Department, to Robert Keith, envoy in Vienna, 21 Jun. 1756, TNA, SP 80/197, fol. 179.

69. J.C. Scott, *The Art of Not Being Governed: An Anarchist History of Upland Southeast Asia* (New Haven, CT, 2009); V. Lieberman, 'A Zone of Refuge in Southeast Asia? Reconceptualising Interior Spaces', *Journal of Global History*, 5 (2010), pp. 333–46.

70. G. Satterfield, *Princes, Posts and Partisans: The Army of Louis XIV and Partisan Warfare in the Netherlands, 1673–1678* (Leiden, 2003).

71. J. Black, *Plotting Power: Strategy in the Eighteenth Century* (Bloomington, IN, 2017).

1. STRATEGIC CONTEXTS IN THE EIGHTEENTH CENTURY

1. C. Noelle-Karimi, 'Afghan Polities and the Indo-Persian Literary Realm: The Durrani Rulers and Their Portrayal in Eighteenth-Century Historiography', in N. Green (ed.), *Afghan History through Afghan Eyes* (London, 2015), p. 77.

2. J. Shovlin, 'War and Peace: Trade, International Competition, and Political Economy', in P.J. Stern and C. Wennerlind (eds), *Mercantilism Reimagined: Political Economy in Early Modern Britain and Its Empire* (New York, 2014), p. 315.

3. George, 2nd Earl of Bristol, British envoy in Madrid, to William Pitt the Elder, 24 Sep. 1759, TNA, SP 94/160, fols 133–4.

4. Choiseul, French Foreign Minister, to Ossun, 24 Nov. 1759, AE, CP, Espagne 526, fol. 7406.

5. L. Silver, *Marketing Maximilian: The Visual Ideology of a Holy Roman Emperor* (Princeton, NJ, 2008).

6. J.Q. Whitman, *The Verdict of Battle: The Law of Victory and the Making of Modern War* (Cambridge, MA, 2012).

7. AE, CP, Espagne 419, fol. 67; Solaro, Sardinian envoy in Paris, to Charles Emmanuel III, 10, 20 Mar. 1734, AST, LM, Francia 170.

8. See illustrations in A. Husslein-Arco (ed.), *Prince Eugene's Winter Palace* (Vienna, 2013), esp. pp. 41, 59, 77–84.

9. *Owen's Weekly Chronicle*, 3 Jun. 1758.

10. W. Cobbett (ed.), *Parliamentary History of England* (36 vols, London, 1806–20), XI, 16.

11. Joseph Yorke, British envoy in Berlin, to Robert, 4th Earl of Holdernesse, Secretary of State for the Northern Department, 12 Apr. 1758, TNA, SP 90/71.

12. C. Pincemaille, 'La Guerre de Hollande dans le programme iconographique de la grande galerie de Versailles', *Histoire, Économie et Société*, 4 (1985), pp. 313–33; C. Mukerji, *Territorial Ambitions and the Gardens of Versailles* (Cambridge, 1997).

13. Delafaye to James, Earl Stanhope, Secretary of State for the Northern Department, 29 Sep. 1719, TNA, SP 43/63.

14. D. Chandler, 'Fluctuations in the Strength of Forces in English Pay Sent to Flanders during the Nine Years' War, 1688–1697', *War and Society*, 1:2 (1981), p. 11.

15. T.M. Barker, *Army, Aristocracy, Monarchy: Essays on War, Society, and Government in Austria, 1618–1780* (Boulder, CO, 1982); J.A. Lynn, *Giant of the Grand Siècle: The French Army, 1610–1715* (Cambridge, 1997).

16. Robert Keith, envoy in Vienna, to Robert, 4th Earl of Holdernesse, Secretary of State for the Northern Department, TNA, SP 80/197, fols 104–24.

17. N. Malcolm, *Agents of Empire: Knights, Corsairs, Jesuits and Spies in the Sixteenth-Century Mediterranean World* (New York, 2015), pp. 406–7.

18. A. Pettegree, *The Invention of News: How the World Came to Know about Itself* (New Haven, CT, 2014).

19. J. Black, *Insurgency and Counterinsurgency: A Global History* (Lanham, MD, 2016), pp. 57–86.

20. P.J. Speelman (ed.), *Henry Lloyd and the Military Enlightenment: The Works of General Lloyd* (Westport, CT, 2005).

2. THE STRATEGIES OF CONTINENTAL EMPIRES, 1400–1850

1. R. Law, *The Horse in West African History* (Oxford, 1980).

2. H. van de Ven (ed.), *Warfare in Chinese History* (Leiden, 2000).

3. A. Waldron, *The Great Wall of China: From History to Myth* (Cambridge, 1990), pp. 125–398.

4. F. Mote, 'The Tu-Mu Incident of 1449', in F. Kierman and J.K. Fairbank (eds), *Chinese Ways in Warfare* (Cambridge, MA, 1974), pp. 243–72.

5. K. Swope, 'Manifesting Awe: Grand Strategy and Imperial Leadership in the Ming Dynasty', *Journal of Military History*, 79 (2015), pp. 597–634; A.I. Johnston, *Cultural Realism: Strategic Culture and Grand Strategy in Chinese History* (Princeton, NJ, 1995), pp. 236–42.

6. M. Rossabi, 'The Tea and Horse Trade with Inner Asia during the Ming', *Journal of Asian History*, 4 (1970), pp. 136–68.

7. A. Chan, *The Glory and Fall of the Ming Dynasty* (Norman, OK, 1982), pp. 51–63; H. Serruys, 'Four Documents Relating to the Sino-Mongol Peace of 1570–1571', *Monumenta Serica*, 19 (1960), pp. 1–66.

8. J.D. Spence and J.E. Wills Jr (eds), *From Ming to Ch'ing: Conquest, Region, and Continuity in Seventeenth-Century China* (New Haven, CT, 1979); F. Wakeman, *The Great Enterprise: The Manchu Reconstruction of Imperial Order in Seventeenth-Century China* (Berkeley, CA, 1985).

9. P.C. Perdue, *China Marches West: The Qing Conquest of Central Eurasia* (Cambridge, MA, 2005).

10. Y. Dai, *The Sichuan Frontier and Tibet: Imperial Strategy in the Early Qing* (Seattle, 2009), p. 3.

11. J.P. LeDonne, *The Grand Strategy of the Russian Empire, 1650–1831* (Oxford, 2004). See also W.C. Fuller Jr, *Strategy and Power in Russia, 1600–1914* (New York, 1992).

12. T.B. Lam, 'Intervention versus Tribute in Sino-Vietnamese Relations, 1788–1790', in J.K. Fairbank (ed.), *The Chinese World Order: Traditional China's Foreign Relations* (Cambridge, MA, 1968), pp. 165–79.

13. B.S. Bartlett, *Monarchs and Ministers: The Grand Council in Mid-Ch'ing China, 1723–1820* (Berkeley, CA, 1991).

14. M. Elvin, *The Pattern of the Chinese Past* (London, 1973), pp. 95–7.

15. P.C. Perdue, 'Fate and Fortune in Central Eurasian Warfare: Three Qing Emperors and their Mongol Rivals', in N. Di Cosmo (ed.), *Warfare in Inner Asian History, 500–1800* (Leiden, 2002), pp. 390, 394.

16. G. Ágoston, 'Information, Ideology, and Limits of Imperial Policy: Ottoman Grand Strategy in the Context of Ottoman–Habsburg Rivalry', in V.H. Aksan and D. Goffman (eds), *The Early Modern Ottomans: Remapping the Empire* (Cambridge, 2007), pp. 77 (quote), 80–1; G. Ágoston, 'Where Environmental and Frontier Studies Meet: Rivers, Forests, Marshes, and Forts along the Ottoman–Hapsburg Frontier in Hungary', in A.C.S. Peacock (ed.), *The Frontiers of the Ottoman World* (Oxford, 2009), pp. 57, 78; A.T. Karamustafa, 'Military, Administrative, and Scholarly Maps and Plans', in J.B. Harley and D. Woodward (eds), *The History of Cartography, Vol. II/I, Cartography in the Traditional Islamic and South Asian Societies* (Chicago, 1992), pp. 209–27; R.A. Abou-El-Haj, *Formation of the Modern State: The Ottoman Empire, Sixteenth to Eighteenth Centuries* (Albany, NY, 1992).

17. M. van Bruinessen and H. Boeschoten, *Evliya Çelebi in Diyarbekir* (Leiden, 1988), pp. 13–15.

18. A.N. Kurat, 'The Turkish Expedition to Astrakhan in 1569 and the Problem of the Don–Volga Canal', *Slavonic and East European Review*, 40 (1961), pp. 7–23; W.E.D. Allen, *Problems of Turkish Power in the Sixteenth Century* (London, 1963), pp. 36–7.

19. R. Murphey, 'A Comparative Look at Ottoman and Habsburg Resources and Readiness for War *c* 1520 to *c* 1570', in E. García Hernán and D. Maffi (eds), *Guerra y Sociedad en la Monarquía Hispánica* (2 vols, Madrid, 2006), vol. I, pp. 76, 102.

20. D.N. Crecelius, *The Roots of Modern Egypt: A Study of the Regimes of 'Ali Bey Kabir and Muhammad Bey Abu al-Dhabab, 1760–1775* (Minneapolis, MN, 1981); V.H. Aksan, 'Manning a Black Sea Garrison in the 18th Century: Ochakov and Concepts of Mutiny and Rebellion in the Ottoman Context', *International Journal of Turkish Studies*, 8, 1–2 (2002), pp. 63–72.

21. Robert Olson, *The Siege of Mosul and Ottoman–Persian Relations, 1718–1743: A Study of Rebellion in the Capital and War in the Provinces of the Ottoman Empire* (Bloomington, IN, 1975).

22. LeDonne, *The Grand Strategy of the Russian Empire*, p. 221.

23. A. Smith, *An Inquiry into the Nature and Causes of the Wealth of Nations* (Oxford, [1776] 1976), p. 706.

24. G. Barratt, *Russia in Pacific Waters, 1715–1825: A Survey of the Origins of Russia's Naval Presence in the North and South Pacific* (Vancouver, 1981).

25. Walter Titley to Edward Weston, 23 May 1761, Farmington, CT, Lewis Walpole Library, Weston papers, vol. 21.

26. Joseph Yorke, British envoy in Berlin, to Robert, 4th Earl of Holdernesse, Secretary of State for the Northern Department, 12 Apr. 1758; Andrew Mitchell to Holdernesse, 8 Jul. 1758, TNA, SP 90/71, 72.

27. Amelot, French Foreign Minister, to Villeneuve, French envoy in Constantinople, 4 Nov. 1739, W. Holst, *Carl Gustaf Tessin* (Lund, 1931), p. 356.

28. C. Ingrao, 'Habsburg Strategy and Geopolitics in the Eighteenth Century', in B. Király, G.E. Rothenberg and P. Sugar (eds), *War and Society in East Central Europe, Vol II: East Central European Society and War in the Pre-Revolutionary Eighteenth Century* (Boulder, CO, 1982), pp. 53–4.

29. M. Hochedlinger, *Austria's Wars of Emergence, 1683–1797* (Harlow, 2003); A.W. Mitchell, *The Grand Strategy of the Habsburg Empire* (Princeton, NJ, 2018).

30. M. Braubach, *Die Geheimdiplomatie des Prinzen Eugen von Savoyen* (Cologne, 1962).

31. G. Mecenseffy, *Karls VI. spanische Bündnispolitik 1725–29* (Innsbruck, 1934); H. Hantsch, *Reichsvizekanzler Friedrich Graf von Schönborn* (Augsburg, 1929).

32. E. Lund, *War for the Every Day: Generals, Knowledge, and Warfare in Early Modern Europe, 1680–1740* (Westport, CT, 1999).

33. K. Benda, *Le Projet d'alliance hungaro-suédo-prussienne de 1704* (Budapest, 1960).

34. Ingrao, 'Habsburg Strategy and Geopolitics in the Eighteenth Century', pp. 49–66; C. Ingrao and Y. Yilmaz, 'Habsburg vs. Ottoman: Motives and Priorities', in P. Mitev, I. Parvev and M. Baramova (eds), *Empires and Peninsulas: Southeastern Europe between Carlowitz and the Peace of Adrianople, 1699–1829* (Sofia, 2010), pp. 5–18.

35. L. Frey and M. Frey, *A Question of Empire: Leopold I and the War of the Spanish Succession* (Boulder, CO, 1983); W. Troost, 'Leopold I, Louis XIV, William III and the Origins of the War of the Spanish Succession', *History*, 103 (2018), p. 570.

36. Ingrao, 'Habsburg Strategy and Geopolitics in the Eighteenth Century', p. 63.

37. J.R. Dull, *A Diplomatic History of the American Revolution* (New Haven, CT, 1985), pp. 107–8.

38. AE, CP, Bavière 102, fol. 78.

39. C.S. Gray, *The Leverage of Sea Power: The Strategic Advantage of Navies in War* (New York, 1992).

40. See also discussion of present-day Chinese expansionism.

41. Solaro di Breglio, Savoy-Piedmont envoy in Paris, to Charles Emmanuel III, 11 Sep. 1734, 21 Dec. 1734, 4 Jan. 1735, AST, LM Francia, 170, 172.

42. M. van Creveld, *Command in War* (Cambridge, MA, 1985), p. 18; L. Freedman, *Strategy: A History* (Oxford, 2013).

43. A.M. Eckstein, *Senate and General: Individual Decision-Making and Roman Foreign Relations, 264–194 BC* (Berkeley, CA, 1987).
44. Solaro di Breglio to Charles Emmanuel III, 3 May and 5 Jul. 1734, AST, LM Francia, 172.
45. R.D. Bourland, 'Maurepas and His Administration of the French Navy on the Eve of the War of the Austrian Succession' (PhD thesis, University of Notre Dame, 1978); memoire by Pelletier, 14 Feb. 1748, AE, CP Ang. 424, fols 156–62.
46. D. Pilgrim, 'The Colbert–Seignelay Naval Reforms and the Beginnings of the War of the League of Augsburg', *French Historical Studies*, 9 (1975–6), pp. 235–62.
47. Champeaux to Rouillé, French Foreign Minister, 16 Apr. 1755, AE, CP Ang. 438, fol. 413.
48. C. von Clausewitz, *On War*, edited by P. Paret and M. Howard (Princeton, NJ, 1976), p. 603.
49. C. Pichichero, *The Military Enlightenment: War and Culture in the French Empire from Louis XIV to Napoleon* (Ithaca, NY, 2017).
50. M.W. Mosca, *From Frontier Policy to Foreign Policy: The Question of India and the Transformation of Geopolitics in Qing China* (Stanford, CA, 2013), p. 11.
51. K. Yazdani, *India, Modernity and the Great Divergence: Mysore and Gujarat, 17th to 19th Century* (Leiden, 2017).
52. P. Macdougall, 'British Seapower and the Mysore Wars of the Eighteenth Century', *Mariner's Mirror*, 97 (2011), p. 306; P. MacDougall, *Naval Resistance to Britain's Growing Power in India 1660–1800: The Saffron Banner and the Tiger of Mysore* (Woodbridge, Suffolk, 2014).
53. T. Andrade, *The Gunpowder Age: China, Military Innovation, and the Rise of the West in World History* (Princeton, NJ, 2016).
54. S. Gordon, *Marathas, Marauders and State Formation in Eighteenth-Century India* (Delhi, 1994).
55. R.G.S. Cooper, *The Anglo-Maratha Campaigns and the Contest for India: The Struggle for Control of the South Asian Military Economy* (Cambridge, 2003).

3. THE REACH FOR WORLD EMPIRE: BRITAIN, 1689–1815

1. Boutel, French diplomat in London, to Antoine Louis Rouillé, French Foreign Minister, 12 Sep. 1754, AE, CP Ang. 437, fol. 300.
2. Robert, 4th Earl of Holdernesse, Secretary of State for the Northern Department, to Sir John Goodricke, envoy to Sweden, 14 Apr. 1758, Bodleian Library, Oxford, Ms. Eng. Hist. C. 62, fol. 4.
3. See also John, 4th Earl of Sandwich to Duke of Cumberland, 6 Feb. 1748, RA, Cumb. P. 31/198.
4. Bristol to William Pitt, 26 Jul. 1758, TNA, SP 92/66.
5. Mackenzie to Pitt, 9 and 23 Dec. 1758, TNA, SP 92/66.
6. B. Heuser, '*Regina Maris* and the Command of the Sea: The Sixteenth Century Origins of Modern Maritime Strategy', *Journal of Strategic Studies*, 40 (2017), pp. 225–62. For a more informed view, see T.J. Denman, 'The Debate over War Strategy, 1689–1712' (PhD thesis, University of Cambridge, 1985); J.B. Hattendorf, *England in the War of the Spanish Succession: A Study of the English View and Conduct of Grand Strategy, 1702–1712* (New York, 1987).
7. Richecourt to Austrian envoy in London, 14 Feb. 1748, Vienna, Haus-, Hof-, und Staatsarchiv, England, Varia, 10.
8. R. Harding, *The Emergence of Britain's Global Naval Supremacy: The War of 1739–1748* (Woodbridge, Suffolk, 2010), pp. 142–6.
9. Holdernesse to Joseph Yorke, envoy in The Hague, 22 Apr. 1755, BL, Egerton MS 3446, fol. 105.
10. H. Kleinschmidt, *The Nemesis of Power* (London, 2000), esp. pp. 114–70; H. Kleinschmidt, 'Systeme und Ordnungen in der Geschichte der internationalen Beziehungen', *Archiv für Kulturgeschichte*, 82 (2000), pp. 433–54; A. Osiander, *The States System of Europe, 1640–1990: Peacemaking and the Conditions of International Stability* (Oxford, 1994).
11. Ryder diary, 6 Oct. 1739, Sandon House, Ryder papers.
12. Villettes to Horace Mann, envoy in Florence, 7 Oct. 1739, TNA, SP 105/281, fol. 181.

13. Thomas Johnston to Sir Robert Walpole, 8 Jun. 1739, Cambridge University Library, CH Corresp. 2875.
14. N.A.M. Rodger, *The Insatiable Earl: A Life of John Montagu, Fourth Earl of Sandwich, 1718–1792* (London, 1993).
15. T.C. Imlay, *Facing the Second World War: Strategy, Politics, and Economics in Britain and France, 1938–1940* (Oxford, 2003).
16. For the latter, with reference to pressure in 1759 against returning conquests, see Bedfordshire County Record Office, Bedford, Lucas papers, L30/9/17/29.
17. Joseph to Philip Yorke, 17 Sep. 1754, BL, Add. MS 35364, fol. 12.
18. M. Schlenke, *England und das friderizianische Preussen, 1740–1763* (Munich, 1963), pp. 171–225.
19. Bristol to Pitt, 10 Mar. 1760, TNA, SP 90/161.
20. Denman, 'The Debate over War Strategy', p. 38.

4. THE RISE OF REPUBLICAN STRATEGIES, 1775–1800

1. Greene to Knox, 7 Dec. 1780, Greene to Lee, 31 Dec. 1780, Library of Congress, Department of Manuscripts, Greene Letterbook.
2. W.B. Wilcox (ed.), *The Papers of Benjamin Franklin, Vol. XXII: March 23, 1775 through October 27, 1776* (New Haven, CT, 1982), pp. 292–3.
3. Washington, DC, Papers of the Continental Congress, vol. 58.
4. P.D. Nelson, *Anthony Wayne, Soldier of the Early Republic* (Bloomington, IN, 1985), pp. 75–6.
5. D. Stoker and M.W. Jones, 'Colonial Military Strategy', in D. Stoker, K.J. Hagan and M.T. McMaster (eds), *Strategy in the American War of Independence: A Global Approach* (Abingdon, 2010), p. 30.
6. W.B. Willcox, 'Too Many Cooks: British Planning before Saratoga', *Journal of British Studies*, 2 (1962), pp. 56–90; P. Mackesy, 'British Strategy in the War of American Independence', *Yale Review*, 52 (1963), pp. 539–57.
7. J.R. Dull, *The French Navy and American Independence: A Study of Arms and Diplomacy, 1774–1787* (Princeton, NJ, 1975); J.R. Dull, *A Diplomatic History of the American Revolution* (New Haven, CT, 1985); O.T. Murphy, *Charles Gravier, Comte de Vergennes: French Diplomacy in the Age of Revolution, 1719–1787* (Albany, NY, 1982).
8. A. Stockley, *Britain and France at the Birth of America: The European Powers and the Peace Negotiations of 1782–1783* (Exeter, 2001).
9. Eden to Francis, Marquess of Carmarthen, Foreign Secretary, 6 Jun. 1786, TNA, FO 27/19, fol. 116.
10. P.P. Hill, *French Perceptions of the Early American Republic, 1783–1793* (Philadelphia, PA, 1988).
11. A.F.C. Wallace, *Jefferson and the Indians: The Tragic Fate of the First Americans* (Cambridge, MA, 1999); P.S. Onuf, *Jefferson's Empire: The Language of American Nationhood* (Charlottesville, VA, 2000), pp. 18–52.
12. P.S. Onuf and N. Onuf, *Federal Union, Modern World: The Law of Nations in an Age of Revolutions, 1776–1814* (Madison, WI, 1993).
13. J.B. Hattendorf, 'The Formation and the Roles of the Continental Navy, 1775–1785', in *Talking about Naval History: A Collection of Essays* (Newport, RI, 2011), p. 200.
14. J.M. Trautsch, *The Genesis of America: US Foreign Policy and the Formation of National Identity, 1793–1815* (Cambridge, 2018); L.D. Cress, *Citizens in Arms: the Army and Militia in American Society to the War of 1812* (Chapel Hill, NC, 1982).
15. A. DeConde, *The Quasi-War: The Politics and Diplomacy of the Undeclared War with France, 1797–1801* (New York, 1966); B. Perkins, *The Cambridge History of American Foreign Relations, Vol. I: The Creation of a Republican Empire, 1776–1865* (Cambridge, 1993), p. 84.
16. J. Israel, *A Revolution of the Mind: Radical Enlightenment and the Intellectual Origins of Modern Democracy* (Princeton, NJ, 2010), pp. 129, 150–3.
17. P. Paret, *The Cognitive Challenge of War: Prussia 1806* (Princeton, NJ, 2009).
18. Memorandum, Oct. 1796, BL, Add. MS 59280, fols 189–90.

5. NAPOLEON AND OTHERS, 1790–1914

1. Holdernesse to Joseph Yorke, British envoy in Berlin, 11 May 1758, TNA, SP 90/71.
2. Viry to Charles Emmanuel III, 27 Sep. 1758, AST, LM Ing. 63.
3. P.D. Hughes, *Small Wars, or Peace Enforcement According to Clausewitz* (Carlisle Barracks, PA, 1996); C. Daase, 'Clausewitz and Small Wars', in H. Strachan and A. Herberg-Rothe (eds), *Clausewitz in the Twenty-First Century* (Oxford, 2007), pp. 182–95; B. Heuser, 'Small Wars in the Age of Clausewitz: The Watershed between Partisan War and People's War', *Journal of Strategic Studies*, 33 (2010), pp. 147–59; C. Daase and J.W. Davis (eds), *Clausewitz on Small War* (Oxford, 2015).
4. J. Achenbach, 'War and the cult of Clausewitz: how a long-dead Prussian shaped US thinking on the Persian Gulf', *Washington Post*, 6 Dec. 1990, *Style*, D1, 4.
5. R. Muir, *Wellington: The Path to Victory 1769–1814* (New Haven, CT, 2013). It is also worth comparing Napoleon and Wellington in light of Clausewitz's reflections on command ability, indeed genius: see C.J. Rogers, 'Clausewitz, Genius, and the Rules', *Journal of Military History*, 66 (2002), pp. 1167–76.
6. Richmond to Francis, Marquess of Carmarthen, Foreign Secretary, 30 Dec. 1785, TNA, PRO 30/8/322, fol. 24.
7. H. Fasa'i, *History of Persia under Qajar Rule* (New York, 1972), pp. 52–4.
8. A-H. Jomini, *Summary of the Art of War* (Philadelphia, PA, 1862), p. 137.
9. O. Connelly, *Blundering to Glory: Napoleon's Military Campaigns*, 3rd edn (Lanham, MD, 2006); A. Zamoyski, *Napoleon: The Man behind the Myth* (London, 2018).
10. C.J. Esdaile, 'De-constructing the French Wars: Napoleon as Anti-Strategist', *Journal of Strategic Studies*, 31 (2008), pp. 515–52.
11. Napoleon, *De la guerre*, edited by B. Colson (Paris, 2012), pp. 147–9.
12. P. Firges, *French Revolutionaries in the Ottoman Empire: Diplomacy, Political Culture, and the Limiting of Universal Revolution, 1792–1798* (Oxford, 2017).
13. F.C. Schneid (ed.), *European Armies of the French Revolution 1789–1802* (Norman, OK, 2015).
14. E. Ingram, *Commitment to Empire: Prophecies of the Great Game in Asia, 1797–1800* (Oxford, 1981); E. Ingram, *The British Empire as a World Power* (London, 2001), pp. 178–83; R.W. Beachey, *A History of East Africa, 1592–1902* (London, 1996), pp. 14–15; P. Mackesy, *British Victory in Egypt, 1801: The End of Napoleon's Conquest* (London, 1995).
15. J. McAleer, *Britain's Maritime Empire: Southern Africa, the Southern Atlantic and the Indian Ocean, 1763–1820* (Cambridge, 2017).
16. For comparisons, M. Handel, *Masters of War: Sun Tzu, Clausewitz and Jomini* (London, 1992).
17. A-J. Rapin, *Jomini et la stratégie: une approche historique de l'oeuvre* (Lausanne, 2002); L.M. Crowell, 'The Illusion of the Decisive Napoleonic Victory', *Defense Analysis*, 4 (1988), pp. 329–46.
18. B. Heuser, 'Lessons Learnt? Cultural Transfer and Revolutionary Wars, 1775–1831', *Small Wars and Insurgencies*, 25 (2014), p. 864.
19. C. von Clausewitz, *Strategie: aus dem Jahr 1804, mit Zusätzen von 1808 und 1809*, edited by E. Kessel (Hamburg, 1937), pp. 37–82.
20. C. von Clausewitz, *The Campaign of 1812 in Russia* (London, 1992), p. 253.
21. D. Stoker, 'Clausewitz's Lost Battle: Sehestedt, 1813', *Military History Monthly*, 68 (2016), pp. 40–6.
22. C. Bassford, D. Moran and G.W. Pedlow, *On Waterloo: Clausewitz, Wellesley, and the Campaign of 1815* (Clausewitz.com, n.p., 2010).
23. A. Gat, *The Origins of Military Thought, from the Enlightenment to Clausewitz* (Oxford, 1989).
24. T.H. Ford, 'Narrative and Atmosphere: War by Other Media in Wilkie, Clausewitz and Turner', in N. Ramsey and G. Russell (eds), *Tracing War in British Enlightenment and Romantic Culture* (Basingstoke, 2015), pp. 182–4, quote, p. 184.
25. C. Bassford, 'John Keegan and the Grand Tradition of Trashing Clausewitz: a Polemic', *War in History*, 1 (1994), p. 325.

26. J.T. Sumida, 'The Relationship of History and Theory in *On War*: The Clausewitzian Ideal and its Implications', *Journal of Military History*, 65 (2001), pp. 333–54; J.T. Sumida, *Decoding Clausewitz: A New Approach to 'On War'* (Lawrence, KS, 2008); A. Herberg-Rothe, 'Primacy of "Politics" or "Culture" over War in a Modern World: Clausewitz Needs a Sophisticated Interpretation', *Defense Analysis*, 17 (2001), pp. 175–86.

27. P. Paret, '*On War* Then and Now', *Journal of Military History*, 80 (2016), pp. 481–2; P. Paret, 'The Function of History in Clausewitz's Understanding of War', *Journal of Military History*, 82 (2018), p. 1055.

28. P. Paret, 'Machiavelli, Fichte, and Clausewitz in the Labyrinth of German Idealism', *Ethics and Politics*, 17 (2015), pp. 78–95.

29. A. Gat, *The Development of Military Thought: The Nineteenth Century* (Oxford, 1993); H. Strachan, *The Direction of War: Contemporary Strategy in Historical Perspective* (Cambridge, 2013), pp. 46–63. Important recent works include B. Heuser, *Reading Clausewitz* (London, 2002); A.J. Echevarria, *Clausewitz and Contemporary War* (Oxford, 2007); A. Herberg-Rothe, *Clausewitz's Puzzle: The Political Theory of War* (Oxford, 2007); H. Strachan, *Clausewitz's On War: A Biography* (New York, 2007); P. Paret, *Clausewitz and the State: The Man, His Theories, and His Times*, 2nd edn (Princeton, NJ, 2007); D. Stoker, *Clausewitz: His Life and Work* (New York, 2014).

30. C. von Clausewitz, *On War*, edited by M. Howard and P. Paret (Princeton, NJ, 1976).

31. For the issues and problems of definition, see J. Black, *The Age of Total War, 1860–1945* (Westport, CT, 2006).

32. C.T. Allmand, *The 'De Re Militari' of Vegetius: The Reception, Transmission and Legacy of a Roman Text in the Middle Ages* (Cambridge, 2011).

33. *Diccionario de la Lengua Castellana*, 6th edn (Madrid, 1822), p. 368.

34. Croker's memorandum, 14 Jun. 1808, *The Croker Papers: The Correspondence and Diaries of the Late Right Hon. John Wilson Croker*, edited by Louis Jennings (3 vols, London, 1884), I, pp. 12–13.

35. See commentary at http://www.lifeofwellington.co.uk/commentary/chapter-fourteen-dublin-and-westminster-october-1807-july-1808#sthash.pylldowVD.dpuf (accessed 18 Mar. 2019); M. Robson, 'Sir Arthur Wellesley as a Special Advisor, 1806–1808', in C.M. Woolgar (ed.), *Wellington Studies V* (Southampton, 2012), pp. 38–60, esp. 39–54.

36. Arthur, 2nd Duke of Wellington (ed.), *Supplementary Despatches and Memoranda of Arthur, Duke of Wellington* (15 vols, London, 1858–72), VI, p. 35; Col. J. Gurwood (ed.), *The Dispatches of Field Marshal the Duke of Wellington* (8 vols, London, 1844–7), IV, pp. 261–3.

37. Arthur, 2nd Duke of Wellington (ed.), *Despatches, Correspondence, and Memoranda of Field Marshal Arthur, Duke of Wellington* (8 vols, London, 1867–80), I, pp. 36–44.

38. K.D. McCranie, 'Perception and Naval Dominance: The British Experience during the War of 1812', *Journal of Military History*, 82 (2018), pp. 1067–91.

39. L. Richardson, 'Strategic and Military Planning, 1815–56', in M.D. Toft and T.C Imlay (eds), *The Fog of Peace and War Planning: Military and Strategic Planning under Uncertainty* (Abingdon, 2006), pp. 15–25.

6. THE UNITED STATES IN THE NINETEENTH CENTURY, 1812–98

1. G.L. Bernstein, 'Special Relationship and Appeasement: Liberal Policy towards America in the Age of Palmerston', *Historical Journal*, 41 (1998), p. 727.

2. J. Parry, *The Politics of Patriotism: English Liberalism, National Identity and Europe, 1830–1886* (Cambridge, 2006).

3. R. Carwardine, 'Evangelicals, Whigs and the Election of William Henry Harrison', *Journal of American Studies*, 17 (1983), p. 66.

4. W.B. Skelton, 'Officers and Politicians: The Origins of Army Politics in the United States before the Civil War', *Armed Forces and Society*, 6 (1979), pp. 22–48.

5. D.E. Reynolds, *Texas Terror: The Slave Insurrection Panic of 1860 and the Secession of the Lower South* (Baton Rouge, LA, 2007).

6. R.N. Current, *Lincoln's Loyalists: Union Soldiers from the Confederacy* (Boston, MA, 1992); C.J. Einolf, *George Thomas: Virginian for the Union* (Norman, OK, 2007).

7. W.W. Freehling, *The Road to Disunion, Vol. II: Secessionists Triumphant* (New York, 2007).
8. TNA, FO 5/877, fol. 150.
9. E.S. Rafuse, *Robert E. Lee and the Fall of the Confederacy, 1863–1865* (Lanham, MD, 2008).
10. K. Hackemer, 'The Other Union Ironclad: The USS *Galena* and the Critical Summer of 1862', *Civil War History*, 40 (1994), p. 226.
11. M.R. Wilson, *The Business of Civil War: Military Mobilization and the State, 1861–1865* (Baltimore, MD, 2006).
12. W.H. Roberts, *Civil War Ironclads: The US Navy and Industrial Mobilization* (Baltimore, MD, 2002).
13. B.H. Reid, *America's Civil War: The Operational Battlefield, 1861–1863* (Amherst, NY, 2008).
14. Lord Lyons, British ambassador in Washington, to John, Earl Russell, British Foreign Secretary, 9 Jan. 1863, TNA, FO 5/874, fol. 81.
15. G.W. Gallagher, 'An Old-Fashioned Soldier in a Modern War? Robert E. Lee as Confederate General', *Civil War History*, 45 (1999), p. 321; G.W. Gallagher, *The Confederate War: How Popular Will, Nationalism, and Military Strategy Could Not Stave Off Defeat* (Cambridge, MA, 1997), pp. 58–9, 115; G.W. Gallagher, *Lee and His Army in Confederate History* (Chapel Hill, NC, 2001); J.L. Harsh, *Taken at the Flood: Robert E. Lee and Confederate Strategy in the Maryland Campaign of 1862* (Kent, OH, 1999).
16. K.J. Weddle, 'The Blockade Board of 1861 and Union naval strategy', *Civil War History*, 48 (2002), p. 142.
17. J.F.C. Fuller, *The Conduct of War, 1789–1961: A Study of the Impact of the French, Industrial, and Russian Revolutions on War and Its Conduct* (London, 1961), p. 102; J. Keegan, *The Military Geography of the American Civil War* (Gettysburg, PA, 1997); J. Keegan, *Fields of Battle: The Wars for North America* (New York, 1997); J. Keegan, *The American Civil War* (London, 2009).
18. TNA, FO 5/877, fol. 149.
19. D.E. Sutherland, 'Abraham Lincoln, John Pope, and the Origins of Total War', *Journal of Military History*, 56 (1992), pp. 581–2; B.F. Cooling, *Fort Donelson's Legacy: War and Society in Kentucky and Tennessee, 1862–1863* (Knoxville, TN, 1997).
20. M. Grimsley, 'Conciliation and Its Failure, 1861–1862', *Civil War History*, 39 (1993), p. 335; and *The Hard Hand of War: Union Military Policy toward Southern Civilians, 1861–1865* (New York, 1995).
21. S. Sears, *George B. McClellan: The Young Napoleon* (New York, 1988).
22. B.H. Reid, 'Rationality and Irrationality in Union Strategy, April 1861–March 1862', *War in History*, 1 (1994), p. 38; E.S. Rafuse, 'McClellan and Halleck at War: The Struggle for Control of the Union War Effort in the West, November 1861–March 1962', *Civil War History*, 49 (2003), p. 50.
23. Henry, 3rd Viscount Palmerston, Prime Minister, to Russell, 26 Sep. 1861, TNA, PRO 30/22/21, fols 567–8; M.E. Neely, *The Civil War and the Limits of Destruction* (Cambridge, MA, 2007).
24. D.W. Hamilton, *The Limits of Sovereignty: Property Confiscation in the Union and the Confederacy during the Civil War* (Chicago, IL, 2007).
25. L.E. Lehrman, *Lincoln and Churchill: Statesmen at War* (Guilford, CT, 2018).
26. Lyons to Russell, 21 Feb. 1862, TNA, FO 5/825, fols 247–8.
27. H.L. Trefousse, *Benjamin Franklin Wade: Radical Republican from Ohio* (New York, 1963).
28. A.C. Guelzo, *Lincoln's Emancipation Proclamation: The End of Slavery in America* (New York, 2004).
29. B.M. Carnahan, *Act of Justice: Lincoln's Emancipation Proclamation and the Law of War* (Lexington, KY, 2007).
30. J.T. Glatthaar, 'African-Americans and the Mobilization for the Civil War', in S. Förster and J. Nagler (eds), *On the Road to Total War: The American Civil War and the German Wars of Unification, 1861–1871* (New York, 1997), pp. 199–215; S.M. Grant, 'Fighting for Freedom: African-American Soldiers in the Civil War', in S-M. Grant and B.H. Reid (eds), *The American Civil War: Explorations and Reconsiderations* (Harlow, 2000), pp. 191–213; J.D. Smith (ed.), *Black Soldiers in Blue: African American Troops in the Civil War Era* (Chapel Hill, NC, 2002).

31. J. Ashworth, *Slavery, Capitalism, and Politics in the Antebellum Republic, Vol. II: The Coming of the Civil War, 1850–1861* (Cambridge, 2008).
32. Lyons to Russell, 11 Dec. 1863, TNA, FO 5/898, fol. 198.
33. M.E. Neely, *The Fate of Liberty: Abraham Lincoln and Civil Liberties* (New York, 1991); D. Farber, *Lincoln's Constitution* (Chicago, IL, 2004).
34. Lyons to Russell, 24 Feb. 1863, TNA, FO 5/878, fols 72–7.
35. Lyons to Russell, 4 & 22 Mar., 19 Apr., 18 & 26 Jul., 15 Aug. 1864, TNA, PRO 30/22/38, fols 19, 26, 37, 72, 79, 92.
36. Lyons to Russell, 26 Jul. 1864, TNA, PRO 30/22/38, fol. 79.
37. Lyons to Russell, 15 Aug. 1864, TNA, PRO 30/22/38, fol. 92; J.M. McPherson, *This Mighty Scourge: Perspectives on the Civil War* (Oxford, 2007), p. 178; R.M. McMurry, *Atlanta 1864: Last Chance for the Confederacy* (Lincoln, NE, 2000).
38. M.J. Forsyth, 'The Military Provides Lincoln a Mandate', *Army History*, 53 (2001), pp. 11–17.
39. O.V. Burton, *The Age of Lincoln* (New York, 2007).
40. M.E. Neely, *The Union Divided: Party Conflict in the Civil War North* (Cambridge, MA, 2002).
41. J. Glatthaar, *The March to the Sea and Beyond: Sherman's Troops in the Savannah and Carolinas Campaigns* (Baton Rouge, LA, 1995).
42. P.S. Carmichael, *The Last Generation: Young Virginians in Peace, War and Reunion* (Chapel Hill, NC, 2005); M.A. Weitz, *More Damning than Slaughter: Desertion in the Confederate Army* (Lincoln, NE, 2005).
43. A. Jones, 'Jomini and the Strategy of the American Civil War, a Reinterpretation', *Military Affairs*, 34 (1970), pp. 130–1.
44. C. Royster, *The Destructive War: William Tecumseh Sherman, Stonewall Jackson, and the Americans* (New York, 1991).
45. J. Glatthaar, *General Lee's Army: From Victory to Collapse* (New York, 2008).
46. M.C.C. Adams, *Our Masters the Rebels: A Speculation on Union Military Failure in the East, 1861–1865* (Cambridge, MA, 1978).
47. T.L. Connelly, *Autumn of Glory: The Army of Tennessee, 1862–1865* (Baton Rouge, LA, 1971).
48. J.M. McPherson, 'No Peace without Victory, 1861–1865', *American Historical Review*, 109 (2004), p. 10.
49. Lyons to Russell, 25 Apr. 1862, TNA, PRO 30/22/36, fols 74–5; N.A. Trudeau, *Out of the Storm: The End of the Civil War, April–June 1865* (Boston, MA, 1994).
50. Percy Doyle, British envoy in Mexico, to Palmerston, 13 Jan. 1848, TNA, FO 50/219, fol. 7.
51. Scarlett to Russell, 28 Apr., 9 Jun. 1865, TNA, FO 50/386, fols 146–7, 210.
52. M. Fellman, *Inside War: The Guerrilla Conflict in Missouri During the American Civil War* (New York, 1989); S.M. O'Brien, *Mountain Partisans: Guerrilla Warfare in the Southern Appalachians, 1861–1865* (Westport, CT, 1999); M. Crawford, *Ashe County's Civil War: Community and Society in the Appalachian South* (Charlottesville, VA, 2001); R.R. Mackey, *The Uncivil War: Irregular Warfare in the Upper South, 1861–1865* (Norman, OK, 2004); C. Mountcastle, *Punitive War: Confederate Guerrillas and Union Reprisals* (Lawrence, KS, 2009); D.E. Sutherland, *A Savage Conflict: The Decisive Role of Guerrillas in America's Civil War* (Chapel Hill, NC, 2009).
53. R.G. Angevine, *The Railroad and the State: War, Politics, and Technology in Nineteenth-Century America* (Stanford, CA, 2004).
54. M.H. Hunt, *Ideology and US Foreign Policy*, 2nd edn (New Haven, CT, 2009); T.M. Jamison, 'The War of the Pacific, Technology and US Naval Development: An International History of Regional War', *Journal of Military History*, 82 (2018), p. 1119.

7. EUROPE AND THE WORLD QUESTION, 1816–1913

1. J. Holmes, 'Mahan, a "Place in the Sun", and Germany's Quest for Sea Power', *Comparative Strategy*, 23 (2004), pp. 27–61; S. Asada, *From Mahan to Pearl Harbor: The Imperial Japanese Navy and the United States* (Annapolis, MD, 2006).

2. D.T. Zabecki, *Chief of Staff: The Principal Officers behind History's Great Commanders* (2 vols, Annapolis, MD, 2008).

3. See also B. Heuser, 'Clausewitz's Methodology and the Traditions of British Writing on War', Strategic and Combat Studies Institute Occasional Paper 52 (2007), pp. 46–58.

4. W.J. Philpott, 'The Making of the Military Entente, 1904–14: France, the British Army, and the Prospect of War', *English Historical Review*, 128 (2013), pp. 1155–85.

5. I have benefited from advice from Michael Clemmesen.

6. P. von Wahlde, 'A Pioneer of Russian Strategic Thought: G.A. Leer, 1829–1904', *Military Affairs*, 35 (1971), pp. 148–51.

7. D.J. Hughes (ed.), *Moltke on the Art of War* (Novato, CA, 1993).

8. C.J. Nolan, *The Allure of Battle: A History of How Wars Have Been Won and Lost* (New York, 2017).

9. D.J. Hughes and R.L. DiNardo, *Imperial Germany and War, 1871–1918* (Lawrence, KS, 2018).

10. C.J.J.J. Ardant du Picq, *Battle Studies*, edited by R.J. Spiller (Lawrence, KS, 2017).

11. S. Mobley, *Progressives in Navy Blue: Maritime Strategy, American Empire, and the Transformation of US Naval Identity, 1873–1898* (Annapolis, MD, 2018).

12. S. Geissler, *God and Sea Power: The Influence of Religion on Alfred Thayer Mahan* (Annapolis, MD, 2015).

13. G. Till, 'Corbett and the Emergence of a British School?', in G. Till (ed.), *The Development of British Naval Thinking* (Abingdon, 2006), pp. 65–88.

14. C. Tripodi, 'Grand Strategy and the Graveyard of Assumptions: Britain and Afghanistan, 1839–1919', *Journal of Strategic Studies*, 33 (2010), pp. 701–25.

15. M. Gershovich, *French Military Rule in Morocco: Colonialism and Its Consequences* (London, 2000); E.J. Mann, *Mikono ya damu: 'Hands of Blood' – African Mercenaries and the Politics of Conflict in German East Africa, 1888–1904* (New York, 2002).

16. T.T. Yong, *The Garrison State: The Military, Government, and Society in Colonial Punjab, 1849–1947* (New Delhi, 2005).

17. N.B. Dukas, *A Military History of Sovereign Hawai'i* (Honolulu, 2004), pp. 147–64.

18. E.O. Goldman, 'The Spread of Western Military Models to Ottoman Turkey and Meiji Japan', in T. Farrell and T. Terriff (eds), *The Sources of Military Change: Culture, Politics, Technology* (Boulder, CO, 2002), pp. 61–2.

19. J. Porter, *Tseng Kuo Tseng Kuo-fan's Private Bureaucracy* (Berkeley, CA, 1972); L.B. Fields, *Tso Tsung-Tang and the Muslims: Statecraft in Northwest China, 1808–1880* (Kingston, Canada, 1978).

20. A. Fung, 'Testing the Self-Strengthening: The Chinese Army in the Sino-Japanese War of 1894–95', *Modern Asian Studies*, 30 (1996), pp. 1007–31; S.C.M. Paine, *The Sino-Japanese War of 1894–1895: Perceptions, Power, and Primacy* (Cambridge, 2003).

21. R. Atwood, *General Lord Rawlinson: From Tragedy to Triumph* (London, 2018), p. 79.

22. I.F.W. Beckett, 'The Stanhope Memorandum of 1888: A Reinterpretation', *Historical Research*, 57 (1984), pp. 240–7. For an emphasis on the naval dimension, see B.M. Gough, '*Pax Britannica*: Peace, Force and World Power', *The Round Table*, 79 (1990), pp. 167–88.

23. H. Strachan, 'The British Army, Its General Staff and the Continental Commitment, 1904–1914', in D. French and B. Holden Reid (eds), *The British General Staff: Reform and Innovation, c.1890–1939* (London, 2002), pp. 75–94.

24. 'From the Editors', *Naval War College Review*, 71:4 (2018), p. 3; R.S.D. Ross, 'Nationalism, Geopolitics, and Naval Expansionism: From the Nineteenth Century to the Rise of China', ibid., p. 37.

25. J-J. Langendorf, *La Pensée militaire prussienne: études de Frédéric le Grand à Schlieffen* (Paris, 2012).

8. STRATEGIES FOR WORLD WAR, 1900–18

1. Kitchener to H.H. Asquith, Prime Minister, 5 Nov. 1915, TNA, PRO 30/57/66; D.J. Dutton, *The Politics of Diplomacy: Britain and France in the Balkans in the First World War*

(London, 1998); R.A. Prete, 'Imbroglio par excellence: mounting the Salonika campaign, September–October 1915', *War and Society*, 19:1 (2001), esp. pp. 68–70.

2. D. French, *British Strategy and War Aims, 1914–16* (London, 1986).

3. W.J. Philpott, *Anglo-French Relations and Strategy on the Western Front, 1914–18* (Basingstoke, 1996); W.J. Philpott, 'The Strategic Ideas of Sir John French', *Journal of Strategic Studies*, 12 (1989), pp. 458–78; E. Greenhalgh, *Victory through Coalition: Britain and France during the First World War* (Cambridge, 2005); R.A. Doughty, *Pyrrhic Victory: French Strategy and Operations in the Great War* (Cambridge, MA, 2008).

4. For his wartime stance, W. Beach Thomas, *With the British on the Somme* (London, 1917).

5. L. Sondhaus, *German Submarine Warfare in World War I: The Onset of Total War at Sea* (Lanham, MD, 2017).

6. N. Lloyd, *Passchendaele: The Lost Victory of World War I* (London, 2017).

7. Devon CRO, 5277M/F3/25.

8. A. Searle (ed.), *The Military Papers and Correspondence of Major-General J.F.C. Fuller, 1916–1933* (Stroud, 2017), p. 120.

9. BL, Add. MS 49699, fols 53–5.

10. J. Boff, *Haig's Enemy: Crown Prince Rupprecht and Germany's War on the Western Front* (Oxford, 2018), pp. 278–9; J. Boff, '1918: Year of Victory and Defeat', *History Today*, 68:11 (2018), pp. 28, 35.

11. E.J. Hess, *The Union Soldier in Battle: Enduring the Ordeal of Combat* (Lawrence, KS, 1997); J.M. McPherson, *For Cause and Comrades: Why Men Fought in the Civil War* (New York, 1997).

9. STRATEGIES FOR TOTAL WAR, 1919–45

1. *Quarterly Review* (Jul. 1929), p. 127; Liddell Hart papers, Liddell Hart Library, King's College London, 10.5/1929/1.

2. A. Danchev, *Alchemist of War: The Life of Basil Liddell Hart* (London, 1998), pp. 163–4. For a dissection of some of the myths Liddell Hart created about himself, see J.J. Mearsheimer, *Liddell Hart and the Weight of History* (Ithaca, NY, 1988).

3. T. Hippler, *Bombing the People: Giulio Douhet and the Foundations of Air-Power Strategy, 1884–1939* (Cambridge, 2013); S. Renner, *Broken Wings: The Hungarian Air Force, 1918–45* (Bloomington, IN, 2016).

4. S. Robbins (ed.), *The First World War Letters of General Lord Horne* (Stroud, 2009), p. 273.

5. T. Mao, *On Guerrilla Warfare*, introduced by S.B. Griffith (Champaign, IL, 1989).

6. *The Compact Encyclopedia* (6 vols, London, 1927), VI, pp. 158–89.

7. A. Mombauer, *Helmuth von Moltke and the Origins of the First World War* (Cambridge, 2001); D.E. Showalter, 'German Grand Strategy: A Contradiction in Terms?', *Militärgeschichtliche Zeitschrift* 48 (1990), pp. 65–102.

8. N. Dixon, *On the Psychology of Military Incompetence* (London, 1976).

9. Renner, *Broken Wings*, pp. 301–3.

10. Danchev, *Alchemist of War*.

11. R. Mallett, *The Italian Navy and Fascist Expansionism, 1935–1940* (London, 1998).

12. R.J. Overy, 'From "Uralbomber" to "Amerikabomber": the Luftwaffe and Strategic Bombing', *Journal of Strategic Studies*, 1 (1978), pp. 154–78.

13. U. Bialer, *The Shadow of the Bomber: The Fear of Air Attack and British Politics, 1932–1939* (London, 1980).

14. P. Preston, 'General Franco as Military Leader', *Transactions of the Royal Historical Society*, 6th series, 4 (1994), pp. 20–41.

15. P. Barbieri, *Hitler's Shadow Empire: Nazi Economics and the Spanish Civil War* (Cambridge, MA, 2017); B.M. Chesterton (ed.), *The Chaco War: Environment, Ethnicity and Nationalism* (London, 2016).

16. C.M. Bell, *The Royal Navy, Seapower, and Strategy between the Wars* (Stanford, CA, 2000).

17. M.R. Peattie, *Ishiwara Kanji and Japan's Confrontation with the West* (Princeton, NJ, 1975), pp. 304–5; M. Peattie, E. Drea and H. van de Ven (eds), *The Battle for China: Essays on the Military History of the Sino-Japanese War of 1937–1945* (Stanford, CA, 2010).

18. T.C. Imlay, *Facing the Second World War: Strategy, Politics, and Economics in Britain and France, 1938–1940* (Oxford, 2003); N. Smart, *British Strategy and Politics during the Phony War: Before the Balloon Went Up* (Westport, CT, 2003).

19. M.S. Alexander, 'The Fall of France, 1940', *Journal of Strategic Studies*, 13:1 (1990), pp. 10–44; N. Jordan, 'Strategy and Scapegoatism: Reflections on the French National Catastrophe, 1940', in J. Blatt (ed.), *The French Defeat of 1940: Reassessments* (Providence, RI, 1998), pp. 13–38.

20. B.P. Farrell, *The Basis and Making of British Grand Strategy, 1940–1943: Was There a Plan?* (Lewiston, NY, 1998).

21. War Cabinet, Chiefs of Staff Committee, Weekly, Résumé, no. 5b, Churchill Papers, Churchill College, Cambridge.

22. S.M. Judge, *The Turn of the Tide in the Pacific War: Strategic Initiative, Intelligence, and Command, 1941–1943* (Lawrence, KS, 2018).

23. M.A. Stoler, 'The "Pacific-First" Alternative in American World War II Strategy', *International History Review*, 2 (1980), pp. 432–52.

24. C.L. Symonds, *World War II At Sea: A Global History* (New York, 2018), pp. 180–1.

25. W.T. Johnsen, *The Origins of the Grand Alliance: Anglo-American Military Collaboration from the Panay Incident to Pearl Harbor* (Lexington, KY, 2016).

26. C.E. Kirkpatrick, *An Unknown Future and a Doubtful Present: Writing the Victory Plan of 1941* (Washington, 1992), p. 128.

27. T. Withington, 'Military Mapping by the United States', in M. Monmonier (ed.), *The History of Cartography, Vol. VI: Cartography in the Twentieth Century* (Chicago, IL, 2015), pp. 886–7.

28. J. Haslam, 'Stalin's Fears of a Separate Peace, 1942', *Intelligence and National Security*, 8:4 (1993), pp. 97–9.

29. M.A. Stoler, *Allies and Adversaries: The Joint Chiefs of Staff, the Grand Alliance, and US Strategy in World War II* (Chapel Hill, NC, 2000).

30. W. Heinrichs and M. Gallicchio, *Implacable Foes: War in the Pacific, 1944–1945* (New York, 2017), p. 430.

31. A. Danchev, 'Great Britain: The Indirect Strategy', in D. Reynolds, W.F. Kimball and A.O. Chubarian (eds), *Allies at War: The Soviet, American, and British Experience, 1939–1945* (New York, 1994), pp. 1–26.

32. A. Jackson, *Persian Gulf Command: A History of the Second World War in Iran and Iraq* (New Haven, CT, 2018), p. 345.

33. G.J. Bailey, *The Arsenal of Democracy: Aircraft Supply and the Anglo-American Alliance, 1938–1942* (Edinburgh, 2013).

34. C. Symonds, 'For Want of a Nail: The Impact of Shipping on Grand Strategy in World War II', *Journal of Military History*, 81 (2017), pp. 657–66.

35. Rutgers University Library, Fuller papers, Scrapbooks, vol. 6.

36. A. Buchanan, *American Grand Strategy in the Mediterranean during World War II* (Cambridge, 2014).

37. H. Boog, G. Krebs and D. Vogel, *Germany and the Second World War, Vol. VII: The Strategic Air War in Europe and the War in the West and East Asia 1943–1945* (Oxford, 2006).

38. H.P. Willmott, *The Battle of Leyte Gulf: The Last Fleet Action* (Bloomington, IN, 2005).

39. J. Lewis, *Changing Direction: British Military Planning for Post-War Strategic Defence, 1942–1947*, 2nd edn (London, 2003).

10. STRATEGIES FOR COLD WAR, 1945–89

1. F.J. Gavin, 'The Myth of Flexible Response: United States Strategy in Europe during the 1960s', *International History Review*, 23 (2001), p. 870.

2. V. Mastny, *The Cold War and Soviet Insecurity: The Stalin Years* (New York, 1996).

3. Y. Gorlizki and O. Khlevniuk, *Cold Peace: Stalin and the Soviet Ruling Circle, 1945–1953* (New York, 2004); J. Rubenstein and V.P. Naumov (eds), *Stalin's Secret Pogrom: The Postwar Inquisition of the Jewish Anti-Fascist Committee* (New Haven, CT, 2002).

4. A. Statiev, *The Soviet Counterinsurgency in the Western Borderlands* (Cambridge, 2010).

5. T. Downing, *1983: The World at the Brink* (London, 2018).

6. Marshal V.D. Sokolovsky (ed.), *Voennaia strategiia* ('Military Strategy') (Moscow, 1962; 2nd edn, 1963; 3rd edn, 1968), English translation, *Soviet Military Strategy* (Englewood Cliffs, NJ, 1963); D. Glantz, *The Bases of Future Soviet Military Strategy* (Fort Leavenworth, KS, 1990); R. Braithwaite, *Armageddon and Paranoia: The Nuclear Confrontation* (London, 2017).

7. J. Lewis, *Changing Direction: British Military Planning for Post-War Strategic Defence, 1942–47*, 2nd edn (London, 2003).

8. M.P. Leffler, 'The American Conception of National Security and the Beginnings of the Cold War, 1945–48', *American Historical Review*, 89 (1984), pp. 346–400.

9. T.H. Etzold and J.L. Gaddis (eds), *Containment: Documents on American Policy and Strategy, 1945–1950* (New York, 1978).

10. H. Jones, *'A New Kind of War': America's Global Strategy and the Truman Doctrine in Greece* (New York, 1989).

11. K. Osgood, *Total Cold War: Eisenhower's Secret Propaganda Battle at Home and Abroad* (Lawrence, KS, 2008); A. Webb, *London Calling: Britain, the BBC World Service and the Cold War* (London, 2014).

12. W.S. Borgiasz, *The Strategic Air Command: Evolution and Consolidation of Nuclear Forces 1945–55* (Westport, CT, 1996); C.H. Builder, *The Icarus Syndrome: The Role of Air Power Theory in the Evolution and Fate of the US Air Force* (New Brunswick, NJ, 1998); W.I. Hitchcock, *The Age of Eisenhower: America and the World in the 1950s* (New York, 2018).

13. P. Grose, *Operation Rollback: America's Secret War behind the Iron Curtain* (Boston, MA, 2000).

14. J. Heller, *The United States, the Soviet Union and the Arab–Israeli conflict, 1948–67: Superpower Rivalry* (Manchester, 2016).

15. W. Taubman, *Khrushchev: the Man and His Era* (New York, 2003).

16. C. Craig, *Destroying the Village: Eisenhower and Thermonuclear War* (New York, 1998).

17. C. Andrew, *The Secret World: A History of Intelligence* (New Haven, CT, 2018).

18. *Executive Sessions of the Senate Foreign Relations Committee, Vol. VII: 1955* (Washington, DC, 1978), p. 390.

19. N.J. Schlosser (ed.), *The Greene Papers: General Wallace M. Greene, Jr and the Escalation of the Vietnam War, January 1964–March 1965* (Quantico, VA, 2010).

20. J. Carter, *Inventing Vietnam: The United States and State Building, 1954–1968* (Cambridge, 2008).

21. A. Preston, *The War Council: McGeorge Bundy, the NSC, and Vietnam* (Cambridge, MA, 2010).

22. M. Elliott, *RAND in Southeast Asia: A History of the Vietnam War Era* (Arlington, VA, 2010).

23. J.L. Gaddis, *The Cold War: A New History* (London, 2005).

24. J.G. Wilson, 'How Grand Was Reagan's Strategy, 1976–1984?', *Diplomacy and Statecraft*, 18 (2007), pp. 773–803.

25. V. Fedorchak, *British Air Power: The Doctrinal Path to Jointery* (London, 2018).

26. J. Lehman, *Oceans Ventured: Winning the Cold War at Sea* (New York, 2018); W.M. Arkin and D. Chappell, 'Forward Offensive Strategy: Raising the Stakes in the Pacific', *World Policy Journal*, 2 (1985), pp. 481–500.

11. STRATEGIES FOR THE CURRENT WORLD, 1990–

1. Writing of 'the doves' strategy', E. Colby, 'If You Want Peace, Prepare for Nuclear War: A Strategy for the New Great-Power Rivalry', *Foreign Affairs* (November/December 2018), p. 29. Colby was US Deputy Assistant Secretary of Defense for Strategy and Force Development in 2017–18.

2. F. Fukuyama, 'The End of History?', *National Interest* (Spring 1989), pp. 2–18.

3. S.P. Huntington, 'The Clash of Civilisations?', *Foreign Affairs*, 72 (1993), pp. 21–49.

4. P.J. Bolt and S.N. Cross, *China, Russia, and Twenty-First Century Global Geopolitics* (Oxford, 2018).

5. 'Sustaining US Global Leadership: Priorities for 21st Century Defense', US Department of Defense, January 2012.

6. D. Fiott, 'Europe and the Pentagon's Third Offset Strategy', *RUSI Journal*, 161:1 (2016), pp. 26–31; D. Stokes and K. Waterman, 'Beyond Balancing? Intrastate Conflict and US Grand Strategy', *Journal of Strategic Studies*, 41 (2018), pp. 824–49.

7. A. Teti, P. Abbott and F. Cavatorta, *The Arab Uprisings in Egypt, Jordan and Tunisia: Social, Political and Economic Transformations* (Basingstoke, 2017); F. Wehrey, *The Burning Shores: Inside the Battle for the New Libya* (New York, 2018).

8. 'National Security Strategy of the United States of America', December 2017, https://www.whitehouse.gov/wp-content/uploads/2017/12/NSS-Final-12-18-2017-0905.pdf (accessed 22 March 2019).

9. As argued by I. Popescu, *Emergent Strategy and Grand Strategy: How American Presidents Succeed in Foreign Policy* (Baltimore, MD, 2017).

10. M. Rose, 'Iraq invasion would be error to rival Hitler's attack on Russia', *The Times*, 25 May 2002, p. 19.

11. M. Light, 'Russian Foreign Policy', in S. White, R. Sakwa and H.E. Hale (eds), *Developments in Russian Politics 7* (Basingstoke, 2010), pp. 225–44; M. Urnov, ' "Greatpowerness" as the Key Element of Russian Self-Consciousness under Erosion', *Communist and Post-Communist Studies*, 47 (2014), pp. 305–22.

12. S. Rynning (ed.), *South Asia and the Great Powers: International Relations and Regional Security* (London, 2017).

13. J.A. Warden III, *The Air Campaign: Planning for Combat* (Washington, DC, 1988); J.A. Warden, 'The Enemy as a System', *Airpower Journal*, 9 (1995), pp. 40–5; J.A. Olsen (ed.), *Airpower Reborn: The Strategic Concepts of John Warden and John Boyd* (Annapolis, MD, 2015).

14. P. Scharre, *Army of None: Autonomous Weapons and the Future of War* (New York, 2018); P. Cornish and K. Donaldson, *2020: World of War* (London, 2017).

15. N. Brown, *The Future Global Challenge: A Predictive Study of World Security, 1977–1990* (London, 1977); P. Cornish, *Strategy in Austerity: The Security and Defence of the United Kingdom* (London, 2010), pp. 12–13.

16. G. Kynoch, *Township Violence and the End of Apartheid: War on the Reef* (Woodbridge, Suffolk, 2018).

17. K. Roy, *Hinduism and the Ethics of Warfare in South Asia: From Antiquity to the Present* (Cambridge, 2012).

18. A.A. al-Muqrin, *Al-Qa'ida's Doctrine for Insurgency: 'Abd al-'Aziz al-Muqrin's 'A Practical Course for Guerrilla War'*, edited by N. Cigar (Dulles, VA, 2009).

19. A. Kruck and A. Schneiker (eds), *Researching Non-State Actors in International Security: Theory and Practice* (Abingdon, 2017).

20. D.J. Kilcullen, 'Countering Global Insurgency', *Journal of Strategic Studies*, 28 (2005), pp. 597–617.

21. J.J. Grygiel, *Return of the Barbarians: Confronting Non-State Actors from Ancient Rome to the Present* (Cambridge, 2018), quote, p. 217; E. Grigg, *Warfare, Raiding and Defence in Early Medieval Britain* (Ramsbury, Wiltshire, 2018).

22. M.J. Green, *By More than Providence: Grand Strategy and American Power in the Asia Pacific since 1783* (New York, 2017), p. 5.

23. S. Biddle and I. Oelrich, 'Future Warfare in the Western Pacific: Chinese Antiaccess/Area Denial, US AirSea Battle, and Command of the Commons in East Asia', *International Security*, 41 (2016), pp. 7–48.

24. V. Bulmer-Thomas, *Empire in Retreat: The Past, Present, and Future of the United States* (New Haven, CT, 2018).

25. M. Beckley, 'Economic Development and Military Effectiveness', *Journal of Strategic Studies*, 33 (2010), pp. 43–79.

26. B. Buzan, 'A World Order without Superpowers: Decentred Globalism', *International Relations*, 25 (2011), pp. 3–25.

27. 'China v. America', *The Economist*, 26 Oct. 2018, p. 13.

28. M. Beckley, *Unrivaled: Why America Will Remain the World's Sole Superpower* (Ithaca, NY, 2018).

29. Rupert Smith to Jeremy Black, 16 Feb. 2009, email.

30. L. Milevski, *The Evolution of Modern Grand Strategic Thought* (Oxford, 2016), p. 151.

31. J. Fennell, *Fighting the People's War: The British and Commonwealth Armies and the Second World War* (Cambridge, 2019), p. 6.

32. L.R. Sullivan, *Historical Dictionary of the Chinese Communist Party* (Lanham, MD, 2011), p. 85.

33. X. Pu and C. Wang, 'Rethinking China's Rise: Chinese Scholars Debate Strategic Overstretch', *International Affairs*, 94 (2018), p. 1035.

34. J. deLisle and A. Goldstein (eds), *China's Global Engagement: Cooperation, Competition, and Influence in the Twenty-First Century* (Washington, DC, 2017).

35. See S. Stashwick, ' "Getting Serious about Strategy in the South China Sea": What Analysis Is Required to Compel a New US Strategy in the South China Sea?' *Naval War College Review*, 71:4 (2018), pp. 131–6, criticising H. Brands and Z. Cooper, 'Getting Serious about Strategy in the South China Sea', ibid., 71:1 (2018), pp. 13–32.

36. D. Stokes and K. Waterman, 'Operational Change and American Grand Strategy in the Context of the China Challenge', *Chinese Journal of International Politics* (2019), https://doi.org/10.1093/cjip/poz002.

37. R. Sakwa, 'The Dual State in Russia', *Post-Soviet Affairs*, 26 (2010), pp. 185–6; quote, G.P. Herd, 'Russia's Hybrid State and President Putin's Fourth-Term Foreign Policy', *RUSI Journal*, 163:4 (2018), p. 25.

38. B. Renz, *Russia's Military Revival* (Cambridge, 2018).

39. C.S. Gray, *Strategy and Defence Planning: Meeting the Challenge of Uncertainty* (Oxford, 2014), p. 204.

40. K. Payne, *Strategy, Evolution, and War: From Apes to Artificial Intelligence* (Washington, DC, 2018), p. 221.

41. F.C. Zagare, *The Games of July: Explaining the Great War* (Ann Arbor, MI, 2011); J. Conrad, *Gambling and War: Risk, Reward, and Chance in International Conflict* (Annapolis, MD, 2017).

42. See, for example, P. Layton, *Grand Strategy* (Columbia, SC, 2018).

43. T.V. Paul, D.W. Larson and W.C. Wohlforth (eds), *Status in World Politics* (New York, 2014).

CONCLUSIONS

1. House of Commons Public Administration Select Committee, *Who Does UK National Strategy?, Further Report with Government Response to the Committee's First Report of Session 2010–11, Sixth Report of Session 2010–11*, HC 713, 25 Jan. 2011, p. 3.

2. H. Strachan, *The Direction of War: Contemporary Strategy in Historical Perspective* (Cambridge, 2013); M. Clarke, *The Challenge of Defending Britain* (Manchester, 2019), pp. 91, 101.

3. H. Sicherman, 'The Revival of Geopolitics', *Intercollegiate Review* (Spring 2002), pp. 16–23; L. Simón and J. Rogers, 'The Return of European Geopolitics: All Roads Lead through London', *RUSI Journal*, 155:3 (2010), pp. 58–64.

4. D. Martins, 'The Cuban Missile Crisis and the Joint Chiefs. Military Operations to Meet Political Ends', *Naval War College Review*, 71:4 (2018), pp. 91–110.

5. J. Haldon, review of M.C. Bartusis, *The Late Byzantine Army: Arms and Society, 1204–1453* (Philadelphia, PA, 1992), *War in History*, 1 (1994), p. 235.

6. Advice from Chris Gill, 9 Dec. 2018.

7. See, for example, J.L. Gaddis, *On Grand Strategy* (London, 2018).

8. L. Freedman, *Strategy: A History* (Oxford, 2013).

9. E. Ironside, *Ironside: The Authorised Biography of Field Marshal Lord Ironside* (Stroud, 2018), p. 350.

10. B.P. Farrell, *The Defence and Fall of Singapore, 1940–1942* (Stroud, 2005).

11. M. Wills, A.J. Tellis and A. Szalwinski (eds), *Strategic Asia 2015–16: Foundations of National Power in the Asia-Pacific* (Washington, DC, 2015); M. Wills, A.J. Tellis and A. Szalwinski (eds), *Strategic Asia 2016–17: Understanding Strategic Cultures in the Asia-Pacific* (Washington, DC, 2016); A.J. Tellis, A. Szalwinski and M. Wills (eds), *Strategic Asia 2017–18: Power, Ideas, and Military Strategy in the Asia-Pacific*, *Strategic Asia* (Washington, DC,

2017); Express News Service, 'Ajit Doval to head key panel set up to assist National Security Council', *Indian Express*, 10 Oct. 2018, https://indianexpress.com/article/india/ajit-doval-to-head-key-panel-set-up-to-assist-national-security-council-5394594/ (accessed 25 Mar. 2019). I have benefited from the advice of Jack Gill.

12. L. Sondhaus, 'The Strategic Culture of the Habsburg Army', *Austrian History Yearbook*, 32 (2001), pp. 232–4; L. Sondhaus, *Franz Conrad von Hötzendorf: Architect of the Apocalypse* (Boston, MA, 2000).

13. G.A. Daddis, *Withdrawal: Reassessing America's Final Years in Vietnam* (New York, 2017).

14. C. von Clausewitz, *On War*, edited by P. Paret and M. Howard (Princeton, NJ, 1976), pp. 509–10.

15. J. Black, *The Age of Total War, 1860–1945* (Westport, CT, 2006), pp. 1–11.

16. P. Dombrowski and S. Reich, 'Does Donald Trump Have a Grand Strategy?', *International Affairs*, 93 (2017), pp. 1013–37.

17. AE, CP Prusse 93, fol. 293.

18. See, for example, M. van Creveld, *More on War* (Oxford, 2017).

19. C.S. Gray, *Strategy and Defence Planning: Meeting the Challenge of Uncertainty* (Oxford, 2014).

20. J. Mooney and J. Crackett, 'A Certain Reserve: Strategic Thinking and Britain's Army Reserve', *RUSI Journal*, 163:4 (2018), p. 89.

21. C.F. Roennfeldt, 'Productive War: A Re-Conceptualisation of War', *Journal of Strategic Studies*, 34 (2011), pp. 39–62; G.R. Dimitriu, 'Winning the Story War: Strategic Communication and the Conflict in Afghanistan', *Public Relations Review*, 38 (2012), pp. 195–207; E. Simpson, *War from the Ground Up: Twenty-First-Century Combat as Politics* (London, 2012).

22. B. Holman, *The Next War in the Air: Britain's Fear of the Bomber, 1908–1941* (Farnham, 2014).

23. O.T. Murphy, *Charles Gravier, Comte de Vergennes: French Diplomacy in the Age of Revolution, 1719–1787* (Albany, NY, 1982); J.R. Dull, *A Diplomatic History of the American Revolution* (New Haven, CT, 1985).

24. O. Connelly, *Blundering to Glory: Napoleon's Military Campaigns*, 3rd edn (Lanham, MD, 2006).

SELECTED BIBLIOGRAPHY

Adamsky, D.P., *American Strategic Culture and the US Revolution in Military Affairs* (Oslo, 2008).

Aksan, V.H. and Goffman, D. (eds), *The Early Modern Ottomans: Remapping the Empire* (Cambridge, 2007).

Alexander, M., *The Republic in Danger: General Maurice Gamelin and the Politics of French Defence, 1933–1940* (Cambridge, 1992).

Anderson, J.K., *Military Theory and Practices in the Age of Xenophon* (Berkeley, CA, 1970).

Andrade, T., *The Gunpowder Age: China, Military Innovation, and the Rise of the West in World History* (Princeton, NJ, 2016).

Bachrach, B.S., *Early Carolingian Warfare: Prelude to Empire* (Philadelphia, PA, 2001).

Barfield, T.J., *The Perilous Frontier: Nomadic Empires and China, 221 BC to AD 1757* (Cambridge, MA, 1989).

Barker, T.M., *Army, Aristocracy, Monarchy: Essays on War, Society, and Government in Austria, 1618–1780* (Boulder, CO, 1982).

Barnett, R.W., *Navy Strategic Culture: Why the Navy Thinks Differently* (Annapolis, MD, 2009).

Barratt, G., *Russia in Pacific Waters, 1715–1825: A Survey of the Origins of Russia's Naval Presence in the North and South Pacific* (Vancouver, 1981).

Baugh, D.A., *The Global Seven Years War, 1754–1763* (Harlow, 2011).

Bell, C.M., *The Royal Navy, Seapower, and Strategy between the Wars* (Stanford, CA, 2000).

Biddle, S., *Military Power: Explaining Victory and Defeat in Modern Battle* (Princeton, NJ, 2004).

Black, J., *Parliament and Foreign Policy in the Eighteenth Century* (Cambridge, 2004).

Black, J., *The Age of Total War, 1860–1945* (Westport, CT, 2006).

Black, J., *Insurgency and Counterinsurgency: A Global History* (Lanham, MD, 2016).

Black, J., *Plotting Power: Strategy in the Eighteenth Century* (Bloomington, IN, 2017).

Black, J., *Combined Operations: A Global History of Amphibious and Airborne Warfare* (Lanham, MD, 2018).

Black, J., *Fortifications and Siegecraft: Defense and Attack through the Ages* (Lanham, MD, 2018).

Böhler, J., Borodziej, W. and Puttkamer, J. von (eds), *Legacies of Violence: Eastern Europe's First War* (Munich, 2014).

Booth, K., *Strategy and Ethnocentrism* (London, 1979).

Brand, H., *What Good Is Grand Strategy?* (Ithaca, NY, 2015).

Bryant, G.J., *The Emergence of British Power in India 1600–1784: A Grand Strategic Interpretation* (Woodbridge, Suffolk, 2013).

Buchanan, A., *American Grand Strategy in the Mediterranean during World War II* (Cambridge, 2014).

Buchholz, F., Robinson, J. and Robinson, J., *The Great War Dawning: Germany and its Army at the Start of World War I* (Vienna, 2013).

Butler, M., *Popular Piety and Political Identity in Mexico's Cristero Rebellion: Michoacán, 1927–1929* (Oxford, 2004).

Carpenter, S.D.M., *Southern Gambit: Cornwallis and the British March to Yorktown* (Norman, OK, 2018).

Chickering, R. and Förster, S. (eds), *War in an Age of Revolution, 1775–1815* (New York, 2010).

Chickering, R., Showalter, D. and van de Ven, H. (eds), *The Cambridge History of War, Vol. IV: War and the Modern World* (Cambridge, 2012).

Citino, R.M., *Quest for Decisive Victory: From Stalemate to Blitzkrieg in Europe, 1899–1940* (Lawrence, KS, 2002).

Clark, J.P., *Preparing for War: The Emergence of the Modern US Army, 1815–1917* (Cambridge, MA, 2017).

Contamine, P., *War in the Middle Ages* (Oxford, 1986).

Dai, Y., *The Sichuan Frontier and Tibet: Imperial Strategy in the Early Qing* (Seattle, 2009).

DiNardo, R., *Invasion: The Conquest of Serbia, 1915* (Santa Barbara, CA, 2015).

Doughty, R.A., *Pyrrhic Victory: French Strategy and Operations in the Great War* (Cambridge, MA, 2008).

Dreyer, J.T., *Middle Kingdom and Empire of the Rising Sun: Sino-Japanese Relations, Past and Present* (New York, 2016).

Dull, J.R., *The French Navy and American Independence: A Study of Arms and Diplomacy, 1774–1787* (Princeton, NJ, 1975).

Dull, J.R., *A Diplomatic History of the American Revolution* (New Haven, CT, 1985).

Echevarria, A.J., *Military Strategy: A Very Short Introduction* (Oxford, 2017).

Edgerton, D., *England and the Aeroplane: Militarism, Modernity and Machines* (London, 2013).

Ehlert, H., Epkenhans, M. and Gross, G.P. (eds), *The Schlieffen Plan: International Perspectives on the German Strategy for World War I* (Lexington, KY, 2014).

Engels, D.W., *Alexander the Great and the Logistics of the Macedonian Army* (Berkeley, CA, 1978).

Etzold, T.H. and Gaddis, J.L. (eds), *Containment: Documents on American Policy and Strategy, 1945–1950* (New York, 1978).

Fairbank, J.K. (ed.), *The Chinese World Order: Traditional China's Foreign Relations* (Cambridge, MA, 1968).

Faulkner, N., *Lawrence of Arabia's War: The Arabs, the British, and the Remaking of the Middle East in WWI* (New Haven, CT, 2010).

Foley, R.T., *German Strategy and the Path to Verdun: Erich von Falkenhayn and the Development of Attrition, 1870–1916* (Cambridge, 2005).

Freedman, L., *Strategy: A History* (Oxford, 2013).

French, D., *British Strategy and War Aims, 1914–16* (London, 1986).

Fuller, W.C. Jr, *Strategy and Power in Russia, 1600–1914* (New York, 1992).

Fynn-Paul, J. (ed.), *War, Entrepreneurs, and the State in Europe and the Mediterranean, 1300–1800* (Leiden, 2014).

Gaddis, J.L., *The United States and the Origins of the Cold War, 1941–1947* (New York, 1972).

Gaddis, J.L., *George F. Kennan: An American Life* (New York, 2011).

Gat, A., *The Development of Military Thought: The Nineteenth Century* (Oxford, 1993).

Gerwarth, R., *The Vanquished: Why the First World War Failed to End, 1917–1923* (London, 2016).

Glete, J., *Navies and Nations: Warships, Navies, and State-Building in Europe and America, 1500–1860* (2 vols, Stockholm, 1993).

Gommans, J.J.L., *The Rise of the Indo-Afghan Empire, c.1710–1780* (Leiden, 1995).

Gooch, J., *Mussolini and his Generals: The Italian Armed Forces and Fascist Foreign Policy, 1922–1940* (Cambridge, 2007).

Gray, C.S., *The Leverage of Sea Power: The Strategic Advantage of Navies in War* (New York, 1992).

Gray, C.S., *Strategy for Chaos: Revolutions in Military Affairs and the Evidence of History* (London, 2002).

Gray, C.S., *The Strategy Bridge: Theory for Practice* (Oxford, 2010).

Greenhalgh, E., *Victory through Coalition: Britain and France during the First World War* (Cambridge, 2005).

Greenhalgh, E., *The French Army and the First World War* (Cambridge, 2014).

Hall, C.D., *British Strategy in the Napoleonic War, 1803–15* (Manchester, 1992).

Handel, M., *Masters of War: Sun Tzu, Clausewitz and Jomini* (London, 1992).

Harding, R., *Seapower and Naval Warfare, 1650–1830* (London, 1999).

Hart, P., *The IRA and its Enemies: Violence and Community in Cork, 1916–1923* (Oxford, 1998).

Heuser, B., *The Evolution of Strategy: Thinking War from Antiquity to the Present* (Cambridge, 2010).

Heuser, B., *The Strategy Makers: Thoughts on War and Society from Machiavelli to Clausewitz* (Santa Barbara, CA, 2010).

Heuser, B. and Shamir, E. (eds), *Insurgencies and Counterinsurgencies: National Styles and Strategic Cultures* (Cambridge, 2016).

Hippler, T., *Bombing the People: Giulio Douhet and the Foundations of Air-Power Strategy, 1884–1939* (Cambridge, 2013).

House, J.M., *Controlling Paris: Armed Forces and Counter-Revolution, 1789–1848* (New York, 2014).

Hughes, D.J. (ed.), *Moltke on the Art of War* (Novato, CA, 1993).

Isaac, B., *The Limits of Empire: The Roman Army in the East*, 2nd edn (Oxford, 1992).

Jeffery, K., *1916: A Global History* (London, 2016).

Johnson, K.D., *China's Strategic Culture: A Perspective for the United States* (Carlisle, PA, 2009).

Jomini, A-H., *Summary of the Art of War* (Philadelphia, PA, 1862).

Jones, B., *The Marshall Plan and the Shaping of American Strategy* (New York, 2017).

Kane, T. and Lonsdale, D., *Understanding Contemporary Strategy* (Abingdon, 2012).

Kennedy, P. (ed.), *Grand Strategies in War and Peace* (New Haven, CN, 1991).

Khan, S.W., *Haunted by Chaos: China's Grand Strategy from Mao Zedong to Xi Jinping* (Cambridge, MA, 2018).

Kleinschmidt, H., *The Nemesis of Power* (London, 2000).

Knight, A., *The Mexican Revolution* (2 vols, Cambridge, 1986).

Knight, R., *Britain against Napoleon: The Organisation of Victory, 1793–1815* (London, 2013).

Knight, R. and Wilcox, M., *Sustaining the Fleet, 1793–1815: War, the British Navy and the Contractor State* (Woodbridge, Suffolk, 2010).

Laband, J., *Zulu Warriors: The Battle for the South African Frontier* (New Haven, CT, 2014).

Lambert, A., *The Crimean War: British Grand Strategy against Russia, 1853–56*, 2nd edn (Farnham, 2011).

Le Bohec, Y., *La Guerre romaine: 58 avant J.-C.–235 après J.-C.* (Paris, 2014).

LeDonne, J.P., *The Grand Strategy of the Russian Empire, 1650–1831* (Oxford, 2004).

Lee, W.E., *Waging War: Conflict, Culture, and Innovation in World History* (Oxford, 2016).

Lehrman, L.E., *Lincoln and Churchill: Statesmen at War* (Guilford, CT, 2018).

Lewis, J., *Changing Direction: British Military Planning for Post-War Strategic Defence, 1942–1947*, 2nd edn (London, 2003).

Lieven, D., *Towards the Flame: Empire, War and the End of Tsarist Russia* (London, 2015).

Lindström, P. and Norrhem, S., *Flattering Alliances: Scandinavia, Diplomacy, and the Austrian–French Balance of Power, 1648–1740* (Lund, 2013).

Lloyd, N., *Passchendaele: The Lost Victory of World War I* (London, 2017).

Loreto, L., *La grande strategia di Roma nell'età della prima guerra punica (ca.273–ca.229 a. C.): l'inizio di un paradosso* (Naples, 2007).

Lund, E.A., *War for the Every Day: Generals, Knowledge, and Warfare in Early Modern Europe, 1680–1740* (Westport, CT, 1999).

Luttwak, E.N., *The Grand Strategy of the Roman Empire: From the First Century AD to the Third* (Baltimore, MD, 1976).

Luttwak, E.N., *The Grand Strategy of the Byzantine Empire* (Cambridge, MA, 2009).

Lynn, J.A., *Giant of the Grand Siècle: The French Army, 1610–1715* (Cambridge, 1997).

Lyon, J., *Serbia and the Balkan Front, 1914: The Outbreak of the Great War* (London, 2015).

McPherson, A., *A Short History of US Interventions in Latin America and the Caribbean* (Chichester, 2016).

Maiolo, J., *Cry Havoc: The Arms Race and the Second World War, 1931–1941* (London, 2010).

Maley, W., *The Afghanistan Wars*, 2nd edn (Basingstoke, 2009).

Mansoor, P.R. and Murray, W. (eds), *Grand Strategy and Military Alliances* (Cambridge, 2016).

Martel, W., *Grand Strategy in Theory and Practice: The Need for an Effective American Foreign Policy* (New York, 2015).

Mattern, S.P., *Rome and the Enemy: Imperial Strategy in the Principate* (Berkeley, CA, 1999).

Mawdsley, E., *Thunder in the East: The Nazi-Soviet War, 1941–1945*, 2nd edn (London, 2016).

May, T., *The Mongol Art of War: Chinggis Khan and the Mongol Military System* (Yardley, PA, 2007).

Mitchell, A.W., *The Grand Strategy of the Habsburg Empire* (Princeton, NJ, 2018).

Mitter, R., *China's War with Japan, 1937–1945: The Struggle for Survival* (London, 2013).

Mitton, K., *Rebels in a Rotten State: Understanding Atrocity in Sierra Leone* (London, 2015).

Morewood, S., *The British Defence of Egypt, 1935–1940: Conflict and Crisis in the Eastern Mediterranean* (Abingdon, 2005).

Morgan-Owen, D.G., *The Fear of Invasion: Strategy, Politics, and British War Planning, 1880–1914* (Oxford, 2017).

Murray, W. and Hsieh, W.W., *A Savage War: A Military History of the Civil War* (Princeton, NJ, 2016).

Murray, W. and Mansoor, P.R. (eds), *Hybrid Warfare: Fighting Complex Opponents from the Ancient World to the Present* (New York, 2012).

Murray, W. and Sinnreich, R.H. (eds), *The Past as Prologue: The Importance of History to the Military Profession* (Cambridge, 2006).

Murray, W., Sinnreich, R.H. and Lacey, J. (eds), *The Shaping of Grand Strategy: Policy, Diplomacy, and War* (New York, 2011).

Naveh, S., *In Pursuit of Military Excellence: The Evolution of Operational Theory* (London, 1997).

Olsen, J.A. and Gray, C.S. (eds), *The Practice of Strategy: From Alexander the Great to the Present* (Oxford, 2011).

Ostwald, J., *Vauban under Siege: Engineering Efficiency and Martial Vigor in the War of the Spanish Succession* (Leiden, 2007).

Otte, T.G., *July Crisis: The World's Descent into War, Summer 1914* (Cambridge, 2014).

Parker, G., *The Grand Strategy of Philip II* (New Haven, CT, 1998).

Parry, J., *The Politics of Patriotism: English Liberalism, National Identity and Europe, 1830–1886* (Cambridge, 2006).

Peraino, K., *A Force So Swift: Mao, Truman, and the Birth of Modern China, 1949* (New York, 2017).

Perdue, P.C., *China Marches West: The Qing Conquest of Central Eurasia* (Cambridge, MA, 2005).

Philpott, W.J., *Anglo-French Relations and Strategy on the Western Front, 1914–18* (Basingstoke, 1996).

Popescu, I., *Emergent Strategy and Grand Strategy: How American Presidents Succeed in Foreign Policy* (Baltimore, MD, 2017).

Prestwich, M., *Armies and Warfare in the Middle Ages: The English Experience* (New Haven, CT, 1996).

Razoux, P., *The Iran-Iraq War* (Cambridge, MA, 2015).

Reardon, C., *With a Sword in One Hand and Jomini in the Other: The Problem of Military Thought in the Civil War* (Chapel Hill, NC, 2012).

Reynolds, C.G., *History and the Sea: Essays on Maritime Strategies* (Columbia, SC, 1989).

Rieber, A.J., *Stalin and the Struggle for Supremacy in Eurasia* (Cambridge, 2015).

Ringmar, E., *Identity, Interest and Action: A Cultural Explanation of Sweden's Intervention in the Thirty Years War* (Cambridge, 1996).

Robinson, D.M., *Martial Spectacles of the Ming Court* (Cambridge, MA, 2013).

Robson, B., *Crisis on the Frontier: The Third Afghan War and the Campaign in Waziristan, 1919–20* (Staplehurst, Kent, 2004).

Robson, M., *Britain, Portugal and South America in the Napoleonic Wars: Alliances and Diplomacy in Economic Maritime Conflict* (London, 2010).

Rockoff, H., *America's Economic Way of War: War and the US Economy from the Spanish–American War to the Persian Gulf War* (Cambridge, 2012).

Rogers, C.J., *War Cruel and Sharp: English Strategy under Edward III, 1327–1360* (Woodbridge, Suffolk, 2000).

Rogers, C.J., *Essays on Medieval Military History: Strategy, Military Revolutions, and the Hundred Years War* (Farnham, 2010).

Rothenberg, G.E., *Napoleon's Great Adversaries: The Archduke Charles and the Austrian Army, 1792–1814* (London, 1982).

Schneid, F.C. (ed.), *The Projection and Limitations of Imperial Powers, 1618–1850* (Leiden, 2012).

Showalter, D.E., *The Wars of German Unification*, 2nd edn (London, 2015).

Showalter, D.E. (ed.), *Forging the Shield: Eisenhower and National Security for the 21st Century* (Chicago, 2005).

Smele, J.D., *The 'Russian' Civil Wars, 1916–1926: Ten Years That Shook the World* (London, 2015).

Snyder, J., *The Soviet Strategic Culture: Implications for Limited Nuclear Operations* (Santa Monica, CA, 1977).

Sondhaus, L., *Franz Conrad von Hötzendorf: Architect of the Apocalypse* (Boston, MA, 2000).

Sondhaus, L., *Strategic Culture and Ways of War* (London, 2006).

Stahel, D., *Operation Barbarossa and Germany's Defeat in the East* (Cambridge, 2009).

Starkey, A., *European and Native American Warfare, 1675–1815* (London, 1998).

Stern, J. and Berger, J.M., *ISIS: The State of Terror* (London, 2015).

Stewart, A., *The First Victory: The Second World War and the East Africa Campaign* (New Haven, CT, 2016).

Stockings, C. and Hancock, E., *Swastika over the Acropolis: Re-interpreting the Nazi Invasion of Greece in World War II* (Leiden, 2013).

Stoker, D., *The Grand Design: Strategy and the US Civil War* (New York, 2010).

Storrs, C. (ed.), *The Fiscal-Military State in Eighteenth-Century Europe* (Farnham, 2009).

Strachan, H., *The Direction of War: Contemporary Strategy in Historical Perspective* (Cambridge, 2013).

Sutyagin, I. with Bronk, J., *Russia's New Ground Forces: Capabilities, Limitations and Implications for International Security* (Abingdon, 2017).

Swaine, M. and Tellis, A., *Interpreting Chinese Grand Strategy: Past, Present, and Future* (Santa Monica, CA, 2000).

Tanner, H.M., *The Battle for Manchuria and the Fate of China: Siping, 1946* (Bloomington, IN, 2013).

Tanner, H.M., *Where Chiang Kai-shek Lost China: The Liao–Shen Campaign, 1948* (Bloomington, IN, 2015).

Taylor, W.A., *Military Service and American Democracy: From World War II to the Iran and Afghanistan Wars* (Lawrence, KS, 2016).

Trautmann, F. (ed.), *A Prussian Observes the American Civil War: The Military Studies of Justus Scheibert* (Columbia, MO, 2001).

Ucko, D.H., *The New Counterinsurgency Era: Transforming the US Military for Modern Wars* (Washington, DC, 2009).

Vaisse, J., *Zbigniew Brzezinski: America's Grand Strategist* (Cambridge, MA, 2018).

van Creveld, M., *Command in War* (Cambridge, MA, 1985).

van de Ven, H.J., *War and Nationalism in China, 1925–1945* (London, 2003).

Varin, C. and Abubakar, D. (eds), *Violent Non-State Actors in Africa: Terrorists, Rebels, and Warlords* (Cham, Switzerland, 2017).

Verbruggen, J.F., *The Art of Warfare in Western Europe during the Middle Ages* (Oxford, 1977).

Waldron, A., *From War to Nationalism: China's Turning Point, 1924–1925* (Cambridge, 1995).

Waley-Cohen, J., *The Culture of War in China: Empire and the Military under the Qing Dynasty* (London, 2006).
Wawro, G., *A Mad Catastrophe: The Outbreak of World War I and the Collapse of the Habsburg Empire* (New York, 2014).
Whitman, J.Q., *The Verdict of Battle: The Law of Victory and the Making of Modern War* (Cambridge, MA, 2012).
Wilson, M.R., *The Business of Civil War: Military Mobilisation and the State, 1861–1865* (Baltimore, MD, 2006).
Wilson, M.R., *Destructive Creation: American Business and the Winning of World War II* (Philadelphia, PA, 2016).
Yong, T.T., *The Garrison State: The Military, Government, and Society in Colonial Punjab, 1849–1947* (New Delhi, 2005).
Zabecki, D.T., *Chief of Staff: The Principal Staff Officers behind History's Great Commands* (2 vols, Annapolis, MD, 2008).
Zamoyski, A., *Warsaw 1920: Lenin's Failed Conquest of Europe* (London, 2008).
Zhang, X., *Deng Xiaoping's Long War: The Military Conflict between China and Vietnam, 1979–1991* (Chapel Hill, NC, 2015).
Zook, D.H., *The Conduct of the Chaco War* (New York, 1960).

INDEX